TWO YEARS
BELOW
THE HORN

OPERATION TABARIN, FIELD SCIENCE,
AND ANTARCTIC SOVEREIGNTY, 1944–1946

TWO YEARS BELOW THE HORN

Andrew Taylor

EDITED BY DANIEL HEIDT AND P. WHITNEY LACKENBAUER

UNIVERSITY OF MANITOBA PRESS

University of Manitoba Press
Winnipeg, Manitoba, Canada
Treaty 1 Territory
uofmpress.ca

Cataloguing data available from Library and Archives Canada
ISBN 978-0-88755-791-0 (PAPER)
ISBN 978-0-88755-550-3 (PDF)
ISBN 978-0-88755-548-0 (EPUB)

Cover design by Frank Reimer
Interior design by Jess Koroscil
Cover image: Andrew Taylor capturing survey photographs
at Blyth Point (UMA, PC 110 Box 2 File 11).

Printed in Canada

This book has been published with the help of a grant from the
Federation for the Humanities and Social Sciences, through the Awards
to Scholarly Publications Program, using funds provided by the
Social Sciences and Humanities Research Council of Canada.

The University of Manitoba Press acknowledges the financial support for
its publication program provided by the Government of Canada through
the Canada Book Fund, the Canada Council for the Arts, the Manitoba
Department of Sport, Culture, and Heritage, the Manitoba Arts Council,
and the Manitoba Book Publishing Tax Credit.

Funded by the Government of Canada | Canadä

Contents

List of Illustrations

List of Maps

Acknowledgements

This book began with an email from John Gilbert, a former Joint Arctic Weather Station radio operator, who secured funding to do develop an exhibit featuring the Andrew Taylor collection at the University of Manitoba Archives and Special Collections. It was his suggestion that we examine the late engineer's papers and memoir that led us to take up this project.

While undertaking this research, the University of Manitoba Archives staff, and especially Shelley Sweeney, did everything they could to help our research along. This included alerting us to the T. Glendenning Hamilton Research Grant and the Dr. Andrew Taylor Northern Studies Award. Some of these funds were used to hire Mary Grace Golfo, who digitized over 100 images for this book and a website for the "archive".

We also enjoyed assistance from other Antarctic professionals. Ieuan Hopkins at the British Antarctic Survey Archive helped us locate additional maps, images, and records. Peter Kikkert shared background materials on Antarctic history and provided feedback on parts of the introduction. We also appreciate the two anonymous peer reviewers' detailed feedback on our original submission.

We would also be remiss if we overlooked the generous financial support of the St. Jerome's University Faculty Research Grant and the Awards to Scholarly Publications Program. Daniel Heidt is also grateful for the postdoctoral support of the Social Sciences and Humanities Research Council.

We also thank Arlene Brown and Jessica Heidt for their careful work transcribing the original volume, and to Armand Naik, who helped with the index.

Finally, we must thank the Taylor family for sharing their records, meeting with us, and helping us to bring Andrew Taylor's life to the attention of all Canadians.

— Daniel Heidt and P. Whitney Lackenbauer

Editors' Note

As we explain in the afterword, Taylor hurriedly composed *Two Years Below the Horn* while taking up a new job and travelling to the Arctic in 1947. He then submitted the original manuscript to publishers, admitting that it required "some expert revision" before it would be ready for publication.[1] Twenty-seven years later, he reiterated the same point when he returned to it and again contemplated its publication.[2]

When we came upon this manuscript, we could not help but agree. Simply transcribing the text would not be sufficient. To become a book, the narrative would require a deep edit: some narrative would have to be reduced, other sections expanded, and material re-arranged to reduce repetition and enhance coherence. Furthermore, Taylor's propensity for passive voice—which was both a stylistic quirk and a reflection of his leadership style, which downplayed taking credit for achievements as an individual—made many sentences difficult to follow. Many of the paragraphs in the original draft also lacked purpose or direction and required considerable restructuring to become clear. This, in addition to extensive copy editing, represented a daunting task.

Because Taylor is deceased, we faced the particular challenge of not being able to confer, as editors, with him to determine whether he agreed with the changes that we proposed to turn his manuscript into a book. We contacted the Taylor family, who concurred with our editorial plans and lent us their support and permission to proceed. We spent months going through Taylor's extensive correspondence and writings to develop an intimate knowledge of his diction and turns of phrase. Sometimes, we moved small and interesting points that were not pertinent to the paragraph into "author's notes." While editing the text itself, we regularly turned to the extensive archival holdings in the Andrew Taylor fonds at the University of Manitoba Archives, as well as alternative unpublished accounts held by the British Antarctic Survey Archives, to clarify parts of the account. Definitions of unusual words and notes on additional content added to paragraphs from this research, as well as citations for other materials that Taylor quoted but did not fully source, can be found in "editors' notes." In the end, we believe that the book that you have before you is a version of *Two Years Below the Horn* that, while heavily edited, is an accurate reflection of Taylor's voice and message.

To introduce readers to Taylor and his journey, we decided to add a new opening chapter. The original draft of the manuscript opened abruptly with

Taylor's recruitment into Operation Tabarin (which appears as Chapter 2 in this book) and provided readers with no information about his enlistment, early experiences in the Canadian Army, or his last-minute trip to Manitoba in 1943. To set this context, we compiled an additional chapter that draws mainly from his detailed private journal in both language and substance.[3] From this point onward, we have retained his original chapter organization but have moved material within chapters where appropriate to improve clarity and flow.

To help readers follow Taylor's sledging travels, we have also drawn twenty maps. The maps of Port Lockroy, the manhauling journey, and Hope Bay are derived from the website of the British Antarctic Survey (BAS) "Place-Names Committee" (http://apc.antarctica.ac.uk). In addition, we imposed the routes of the first and second dog-sledging journeys onto a scanned copy of a map produced by Andrew Taylor and Victor Russell that is held by the University of Manitoba Archives. Despite its occasional inaccuracies and vagaries, the sledgers' map is remarkably detailed and, most significantly, includes the places names that Tabarin personnel assigned to various locales. The BAS Place-Names Committee subsequently overturned many of the names that the sledgers assigned to various geographic formations, but we decided to maintain Taylor's use of the original names in the manuscript and map because they illustrate the sledgers' perceptions and moods.

Plotting the three sledging journeys onto these maps was a painstaking process. After spending days following Taylor's own descriptions of their routes, we filled in descriptive gaps by consulting several additional sources. First, we utilized the surveying route that Taylor and Russell plotted on a copy of the sledgers' map held by the BAS Archives. This map, however, did not describe the sledgers' daily meanderings or clearly distinguish campsites, so we filled in these remaining gaps by consulting the sledging journals of Taylor's companions that are also housed at the BAS Archives.

Finally, we found that many of the photographs that Taylor picked to accompany his text were not well selected either in quality, topic, or placement. Accordingly, we worked with the University of Manitoba Archives to digitize a large sample of the photographs in his fonds and have selected images for this volume that, we feel, better complement and amplify the text.

Introduction

"My place as the first Canadian to have commanded an Antarctic Expedition should be acknowledged—now!" — ANDREW TAYLOR, 1988[1]

ON 10 AUGUST 1946, THE *TORONTO STAR* WEEKLY printed an article about the Antarctic that included an interview with the commander of a British expedition to the region, a "quiet, sturdy and ruddy complexioned" Canadian Army major named Andrew Taylor. This soldier and his men had lived "dangerously" in the Antarctic for two years, "almost cut off from civilization." Several of the expedition's members survived an avalanche. The expedition crew persevered against 130-mile-per-hour blizzards that could disorient and kill men from exposure and throw heavy sledges "a hundred feet through the air." The mission even had to manage without two-thirds of its 1945 supplies after "two huge icebergs" collided with their resupply ship and forced it to limp back from the Falklands. "Despite the storms," reporter Douglas Liversidge extolled, Taylor led three other men on a month-long sledging journey to chart part of Graham Land's east coast. After making several important surveying discoveries and reaching Swedish explorer Otto Nordenskjold's famed 1902 winter encampment, the team endured "bitter privations" during their return to Hope Bay. Slush, covered by four feet of soft snow in –40°F conditions, weakened their dogs and slowed their progress to three or four miles per day, forcing the sledgers to resort to killing one of their dogs and feeding it to the remaining starving animals before reaching their food cache.[2]

Liversidge's brief and exciting account of "Operation Tabarin"—the secret British expedition to Antarctica in the last two years of the Second World War—highlighted Taylor's polar exploits, and the Canadian officer certainly believed that his leadership and achievements would attract public interest and recognition. Unfortunately, Taylor's wartime contributions to science and to British Antarctic sovereignty went largely unrecognized for several decades. This was a consequence of the remote theatre in which Taylor served, his Canadian background, the sheer scale of postwar Antarctic expeditions that overshadowed the wartime activities of which he was a part, as well as his failure to publish his memoir of the Antarctic operation, *Two Years Below the Horn*.

Taylor's recollections of his involvement in and subsequent command of Operation Tabarin between February 1945 and January 1946 are worthy of remembrance and study. As the first and only Canadian to command a British Antarctic expedition (or that of any other country to that point), he oversaw the establishment of Britain's permanent presence on the Antarctic mainland.[3] Taylor and his sledging teams travelled over 750 miles while combing the tip of the Graham Land peninsula on two separate journeys, correcting several major cartographic mistakes, and collecting tons of geological and botanical specimens. Only scant accounts of the expedition's second sledging trip have been published even though it accounted for approximately 500 miles of the total distance travelled by the participants in Tabarin, cemented the expedition's field science contributions, and, according to Sir Vivian Fuchs, "laid the foundations of the high efficient sledging for which Hope Bay was to become renowned during the next nineteen years."[4] Moreover, Taylor and his men accomplished all of these feats on the Antarctic mainland while making due with wartime shortages and without losing a single man.[5]

Taylor's accomplishments and perspectives have not been well-served in published accounts of Operation Tabarin. Previous books, such as those by David James, Sir Vivian Fuchs, and Dean Beeby, provide brief but positive assessments of Taylor's leadership. These publications, however, did not benefit from Taylor's perspective because he either withheld his records from the authors or only allowed them to access small portions of his papers. The resulting accounts consequently neglect various themes and events that Taylor considered most important.[6] British historian Stephen Haddelsey, whose recent history of Tabarin draws heavily from Taylor's papers, gives the original British commander of the operation, James W.S. Marr, the benefit of the doubt when assessing the expedition's early leadership. By comparison, Haddelsey misses few opportunities to question Taylor's decisions.[7] The Canadian narrative, published here for the first time, offers an important corrective.

Operation Tabarin occurred during a transitional period in Antarctic history, between the so-called heroic age of Robert Falcon Scott, Ernest Shackleton, and Roald Amundsen and the modern scientific age marked by the establishment of permanent scientific installations during the International Geophysical Year (IGY) in the mid-1950s. When Taylor wrote *Two Years Below the Horn* in the early postwar period, the genre of heroic polar exploration narratives was well established and entrenched, offering readers a pantheon of stories about courageous polar explorers struggling against harsh environmental conditions.[8] When the invention of the airplane made transiting polar space seem safe in the popular imagination, explorers such as Richard Byrd maintained a sense of danger and heroism by emphasizing the weather's unpredictability as well as the unreliability of aviation technology.[9] The importance of adventure also permeated scientific circles. During the late nineteenth century, Western scientific culture developed what Bruce Hevly describes as the "authority of adventurous observation."[10] Glaciologists, for example, buttressed their authority by leaving laboratories and models behind and risked their lives on glacial slopes to conduct in-situ observations. In the early twentieth century, scientists such as Lauge Koch of Denmark and Canadian anthropologist Vilhjalmur Stefansson continued to cite their time at the remote places that they studied to legitimize their professional authority.[11]

Taylor's writing, however, was complicated by a shift in field science culture that valued professionalism over heroism, and scientific analysis over surveying. By the end of the Second World War, the Allies' need to deploy across the globe led their geographers and engineers to take unprecedented steps to categorize regional environments and to develop and test new technologies.[12] Growing respect in the scientific community for the control afforded by immense laboratories that could replicate harsh environments threatened the reputations of field scientists whose outdoor research did not afford a similar degree of control. While polar environments often continued to frustrate these aspirations, scientific "adventures" were no longer celebrated or viewed as a source of professional authority. By using modern technologies such as airplanes, field scientists hoped to transcend polar weather and conduct more controlled and systematic observations and experiments to improve their stature and authority in scientific circles.[13] Nevertheless, state-sponsored field science became even more integral to postwar Antarctic geopolitics. Decolonization made overtly imperial exploration increasingly unfashionable on the international stage, so states with

Antarctic claims or interests gradually turned to scientific research as a means to justify the continuation of their authority and resist others' attempts to internationalize the continent. National pride still informed government funding, but Antarctic expeditioners increasingly focussed on the calm and systematic collection of scientific knowledge to legitimize their professional authority and geopolitical utility. This shift, which had its roots in the Second World War, was fully manifest in the IGY (1957–1958). The 1959 Antarctic Treaty enshrined this ideal when it made "substantial scientific research" a prerequisite for any state to become a contracting party.[14]

Taylor was aware of both of these traditions during and immediately after the war, and he attempted to straddle both heroic and modern scientific expectations in *Two Years Below the Horn*. Like many of his contemporaries, he consistently referenced preceding polar expeditions and described dogs as well as comrades affectionately, thus implicitly framing aspects of Operation Tabarin within the traditional genre of heroic exploration. He also carefully avoided the sensational aspects of the operation, did not cast himself in heroic terms, and only rarely applied such descriptions to other Tabarin personnel. Instead, he considered and treated his team as professionals and emphasized their substantive contributions to surveying, geology, and biology. Throughout his memoir, Taylor applied his systematic engineering mind to the challenges of polar science and exploration, recording in meticulous detail the experiences and achievements of a modern operation that did not lose a single man to extreme conditions. Taylor's background experience, broad interests, and strong sense of commitment to both his mission and his colleagues made him an appropriate leader for a wartime expedition that left an indelible imprint on Antarctic science and politics.

Canadians, however, have traditionally focused on the Arctic at the expense of Antarctica. Despite Taylor's exotic wartime service, few Canadians have heard of him or his Antarctic experiences. "One thing I have discovered," Taylor wrote to a fellow Tabarin veteran in October 1947, "is that the subject [of Antarctic exploration] is not nearly so popular on this side of the water as it is in England. There is little market here for the books that are being sold, and the Americans are only interested in the work of Americans."[15] Interest in polar history, however, has surged since Taylor's death in 1993. Taylor not only offers his unique perspective as a Canadian on Operation Tabarin, but he also adds substantively to our understanding of this landmark polar expedition.

Concerns about the effects of climate change, melting ice, and rising sea levels on historic sites, moreover, will stoke appreciation for Taylor's detailed descriptions of Tabarin sites as well as the material remains of heroic-era sites.[16]

ANDREW TAYLOR: BACKGROUND

Andrew Taylor was born in Edinburgh, Scotland, on 2 November 1907. "Since I began my life on a paralytic bed in Scotland," he wrote to Sir Vivian Fuchs, "a weak back and bad legs" would make some of his later field work difficult.[17] He persevered through these physical ailments. When Taylor was three, his father—lured by Canadian Pacific Railroad posters advertising it as the "coming Industrial Heart of Canada"—purchased passage for the family to Moose Jaw, Saskatchewan. Arriving in Halifax in April 1911 with his family onboard the ship *Saturnia*, they boarded the train to head west. "Five days later, Mother (having two very young children to tend) decided to forego the Industrial Heart of Canada," Taylor explained. "She put her foot down, saying she was getting off at the next stop, which happened to be a place called Winnipeg—another town I had not heard of previously." Here the family put down their Canadian roots, and Taylor would settle in the city for most of his life.[18]

"All my life I have enjoyed school," Taylor later recalled, "although I realise now I never studied assiduously enough to do myself justice." In Winnipeg, he attended Lord Selkirk School from 1913 to 1921 and then St. John's Technical High School from 1922 to 1924. At sixteen, he decided to attend the University of Manitoba and his parents who were "anything but wealthy . . . made the sacrifice to finance me for a year." As a child, he had built a practical knowledge of electronics, and his university studies allowed him to develop his interest in radios and electrical engineering. Unfortunately, financial pressures prevented him from continuing his studies at the end of his first year. "Jobs were not abundant in the summer of 1925 for a teenager with no practical experience in anything," he recalled. He managed to find temporary work on a threshing gang on a farm near Carman, Manitoba, that fall. That winter, Taylor began work with Eaton's department store, progressing from the ladies' shoe department, to mail orders, to the "fancy goods" stockroom. Recognizing that he would never "get very far at Eaton's," he returned to drive a stock team on the same Carman farm. "As the summer of 1927 began to wane," he lamented, "the prospect of resuming my engineering course at the University seemed more and more appealing."[19]

Figure 1. Andrew Taylor surveying, 1935.

Receiving a loan from family friends Alex and Kathleen Campbell, Taylor returned to the University of Manitoba in fall 1927. He completed the pre-engineering year, with its emphasis on arts courses supplemented by science and mathematics, "without difficulty" before moving into four years of dedicated study in engineering.[20] He made the pragmatic decision to pursue a civil rather than an electrical engineering stream after witnessing several unemployed electrical engineers hand digging a deep ditch for a sewer line in 1929. "On the surface," Taylor later commented, "stood their overseer—a civil engineer."[21] During the summers of 1929 and 1930, he assisted with federal land subdivision surveys in the Peace River district of northern Alberta and British Columbia, working first as a chainman and later as instrument man and assistant to the chief of the party.[22] He received his bachelor of science in civil engineering in 1931, graduating cum laude, third in his class of twenty-six students.

Upon graduation from university, Taylor landed a job as a provincial surveyor with the Manitoba Surveys Branch of the Department of Mines and Natural Resources. In that capacity, he observed first-hand much of northern and rural Manitoba before it was transformed by hydro-electric, agricultural, mineral, timber, and urban development. While in the office, he examined plans, computed and plotted surveys and map grids, drafted, and indexed. In the field, he inspected and conducted baseline surveys, retracement surveys, township outlines, and mining claim surveys, all the while preparing field maps and sketches.[23] They worked summer and winter, through all weather conditions and in extreme temperatures. One trip in 1933 involved tent camping near Oxford Lake at −72°F.[24] All of this field experience would prove instrumental in establishing Taylor's credentials for and in Antarctica a decade later.

After receiving his formal Dominion Land Surveyor's Commission in 1932 and his Manitoba Land Surveyor's Commission in 1933, Taylor moved to the newly established community of Flin Flon, Manitoba, where he became town engineer in 1936.[25] He was responsible for maintaining and operating "all [of the] municipal works (water, sewage, and construction) for an expanding mining town in the 'bush country,' having a population of about 10,000, situated on the southern margin of the permafrost," he recalled.[26] Although town folk might consider the roadways and the first extensive use of utilidors in a northern environment as his main legacy,[27] Taylor insisted that his most important achievement in Flin Flon was meeting Martha Jane Porter, a school principal whom he married on 12 September 1939—just two days after Canada declared war on the Axis Powers.[28]

Taylor had volunteered for military service with the Canadian Army prior to the outbreak of the Second World War and was called up on 13 September 1940 (two days before the birth of his first son). Commissioned as a lieutenant in the Royal Canadian Engineers, he was posted immediately to the Geographical Section, General Staff (GSGS) at Rockcliffe (a unit mainly concerned with surveys and mapping) because of his surveying experience. The following year, he was

Figure 2. Lieutenant Andrew Taylor, n.d.

posted to the United Kingdom, where he served as a field engineer with the Second Canadian Division along the Channel Coast, with the 1 Corps Field Survey Company in Surrey, and with the Canadian Army Headquarters at Leatherhead, where he was attached to the staff of the deputy director of surveys. His duties involved completing detailed water supply surveys, instructing other soldiers in topographical and photogrammetric surveys, and mapping classification work.[29] In late August 1943, he received his promotion to captain and within a month found himself "involved in Canadian Army negotiations which resolved themselves into my secondment to the Royal Navy for a period of more than two and a half years."[30]

In September 1943, the Royal Navy circulated a request for a surveyor accustomed to working in cold climates. Taylor's pre-war work in northern Canada made him an appropriate, even obvious, choice, but he later admitted that he "had barely heard" of the South Pole. Lieutenant Colonel Meuser, the deputy director of surveys, called Taylor into his office in Leatherhead "to advise me that he had recommended me for a special job, in which I was to report to Lt-Cmdr J.W.S. Marr, R.N.V.R. at 2 Park Street in London immediately."[31] Unlike previous Canadians in Antarctica, who sought polar adventure to advance their careers or to satisfy scientific curiosities,[32] Taylor was motivated by an overriding sense of duty. As he recalled later in life, the call to service in one of the remotest parts of the globe made him realize the veracity of the old adage "that once a man enlisted, the Army could make him do anything but have a baby."[33] When asked to embark on a special mission, his values dictated that he would acquiesce to military requirements for his skills. Accordingly, Canadian military correspondence noted, Taylor was "seconded to the Colonial Office as a member of a mission of a highly secret nature."[34]

In Chapter 1, Taylor describes his excitement at learning of his secondment to Britain's Naval Party 475. He recorded in his letterbook that his wife was less impressed:

> Her initial reaction to the new turn of events in my life was one of
> horror. If I had any choice, she wanted me to back out of it. Well, I
> had no choice. I am something of a fatalist. When leaving her in
> Ottawa on 4 April, 1941, I might have requested compassionate
> leave, and been sent on the next troop shipment. . . . We spoke of
> it and I didn't. The next troopship which went across the Atlantic
> was sunk off Ireland with a heavy loss of life. I felt the same about

this transfer—it was intended that I should take it, and I did.[35]

Whatever one's feelings on fate and purpose, Taylor's secret Antarctic mission implicated him in a project that, while ostensibly "military," was at its core about sovereignty and science, the culmination of centuries of waxing and waning British interest in the remotest outposts of its global empire.

THE BRITISH AND ANTARCTICA: SETTING THE STAGE

Canadians like Taylor were very familiar with sagas of polar exploration, but Arctic rather than Antarctic narratives framed their country's polar consciousness. The exploits of British explorers such as Martin Frobisher, Henry Hudson, and John Franklin, seeking a commercial route to the Orient via the fabled "Northwest Passage" above northern North America, had been assimilated into Canada's history and the dominion's broader "myth of the north." By the mid-twentieth century, the British naval officers who had opened these northern waters were celebrated as Canadian heroes for having established Canada's claim to Arctic sovereignty.[36] Geographical realities placed Antarctica as Canada's antipodes, however, and national interests relegated the southern continent far from Canadians' mental map of their world. Through an imperial lens, however, the region fell into a more applicable and relevant focus.

Operation Tabarin grew from Britain's longstanding but inconsistent attention in the Antarctic.[37] Over the centuries, Britain's interest in the region ebbed and flowed, a reflection of Antarctica's status as an unknown frontier, its perceived utility to Britain, and the interests and activities of other states in the region. Captain James Cook, the famed navigator, explorer, and cartographer, opened Britain's southern polar horizons in the eighteenth century. On his first voyage (1768–1771), he proved that there was no southern continent north of 40°S. Then, in 1772, he embarked on his second scientific expedition with orders to find and circumnavigate the "Great South Land"—the missing continent commonly held by geographers and scientists to dominate the southern hemisphere.[38] While French expeditions had already discovered several islands in the sub-Antarctic (including the Bouvet, Crozet, Prince Edward, and Kerguelen Islands),[39] they had not sailed beyond the Antarctic Circle—66°33'45.8" below the equator, the northernmost latitude in the Southern Hemisphere at which the sun can remain continuously above or below the horizon for twenty-four hours. On 17 January 1773, Cook, onboard HMS *Resolution*, achieved this pioneering feat, reaching a farthest south of 71°10'S, 106°54'W (120 km from the Antarctic coast) before turning back. On his northward journey, Cook landed at Possession Bay on the sub-Antarctic island of South Georgia, hoisted a flag, fired three volleys, and claimed it for King George III. Soon after, he discovered the South Sandwich Group[40]—but the Antarctic continent itself, which Cook insisted must exist but would yield "no use for man," remained undiscovered. For the next fifty years, the sub-Antarctic islands were the preserve of American and British sealers who, enticed by Cook's reports, slaughtered with reckless abandon the fur seals who inhabited the beaches and virtually exterminated them from many islands by mid-century.[41]

After the Napoleonic Wars, the British Admiralty's polar interests grew with vigour, propelled by the Royal Navy's ascendance to hegemony over the high seas and the search for new outlets to test officers and ships and to bring glory to the Empire.[42] In 1819 and 1820, explorers finally landed on the islands around the Antarctic Peninsula and sighted the continent itself. Edward Bransfield's expedition spotted the rocks and peaks of "Trinity Land" (likely the northernmost point on the Antarctic mainland, the coast of which he began to chart).[43] American sealers soon claimed to be the first men to set foot on the Antarctic continent, prompting unsuccessful appeals in Washington for a national expedition to claim the newly discovered lands for the United States.[44] But it was the British who dominated Antarctic exploration for the next decade and a half, with their sealers claiming the South Orkneys, reaching a new furthest south in the Weddell Sea.[45] Captains James Weddell, John Biscoe, Peter Kemp, and John Balleny established the existence of a large continent, prompting additional exploration backed by government funds. "There was an element of national prestige involved," historian Maria Pia Casarini observed, "but also a great deal of pure scientific interest, since influential scientific circles were at the time deeply concerned with phenomena which could be best studied in the polar regions, and the main scientific problem to be solved was terrestrial magnetism" after German mathematician Johann Gauss calculated the position of the South Magnetic Pole.[46]

The "magnetic crusade" of the mid-nineteenth century did not last long,[47] but it continued to generate greater awareness about the polar regions. James Clark Ross's discovery of the North Magnetic Pole in 1831 led the Admiralty to task him with searching for its southern counterpart from 1840 to 1843. After surmounting heavy pack ice, he reached the open water of what became known as the Ross Sea, where he discovered a mountainous coastline that he named after his Queen. Although he was unable to land on the continent, Ross rowed to a small islet just off the tip of Victoria Land and claimed the entire area he had explored for Britain.[48] He extended his farthest south to 78°10'S on 23 January 1842 but failed to locate the South Magnetic Pole, and the Antarctic entered into an "age of averted interest" for the next five decades.[49] Although whalers and sealers continued to visit the Southern Ocean, quickly exhausting the most accessible living resources, exploratory voyages ceased until the 1890s. With no Indigenous population or incentive to try to colonize the southern continent's frigid shores, Antarctica "defied the process of European imperial expansion that was going on in much the rest of the world."[50]

The "heroic age" of Antarctic exploration grew out of the Sixth International Geographical Congress in 1895, which declared that "the exploration of Antarctica is the greatest piece of geographical exploration still to be undertaken," and the coordinated program of geophysical investigations in Antarctica recommended by the Seventh International Geographical Congress held in Berlin in 1899.[51] The great powers did not repeat their actions in Africa by racing to carve up Antarctica, with the British government adopting a "low key and relatively disinterested approach" to the southern continent during the early years of the twentieth century.[52] Nevertheless, European countries launched nine major expeditions to Antarctica between 1898 and 1910.[53] The Belgian Geographical Society's Antarctic Expedition (1898–1900), led by Adrien de Gerlache de Gomery, attempted to locate the South Magnetic Pole, but was forced to overwinter in the ice west of the Antarctic Peninsula and made extensive explorations of the Graham Land coast and the string of islands to the west.[54] The British Southern Cross Expedition (1898–1900), a privately funded affair led by the Norwegian Carsten Borchgrevink, became the first to winter on the continent after setting up camp on Cape Adare in Victoria Land and was the first to use dogs for local exploration.[55] (Canadian Hugh Evans, who had previous experience as a whaler in Antarctic waters, participated in the adventure as assistant zoologist.[56]) Robert Falcon Scott and the British National Antarctic Expedition (1901–1904) established a base on Ross Island in McMurdo Sound and then set a new farthest south record in their attempt to reach the Pole, achieving 82°17'S and discovering the polar plateau.[57] Although Scott "paid little attention to claiming a territory that had no obvious value," his base on Ross Island and his explorations into the vast continental interior "all added weight to any claim that Britain might make."[58]

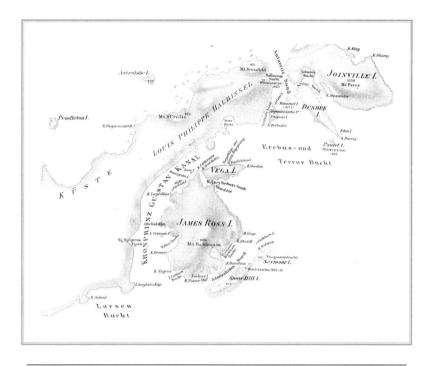

Map 1. Partially redrawn map of Nordenskjöld's expedition from *Wissenschaftliche Ergenbnisse der Schwedischen Südpolar-Expedition, 1901–1903: Georgraphie, Hygiene und Erdmagnetismus* (1920). Operation Tabarin would visit many of the same places and correct several of the Swedish expedition's charting errors.

Inspired by a similar sense of curiosity and desire for prestige, explorers of various nationalities set out to expose the secrets of the Antarctic Peninsula that extended northward toward the southern tip of the Americas. From 1901 to 1904, a privately financed Swedish expedition led by geologist Otto Nordenskjöld produced, in the words of distinguished polar explorer and historian Sir Vivian Fuchs, a "story of courage and endurance outstanding even in the polar context." Having resurveyed and redrawn the charts of the west coast and offshore islands of the Antarctic Peninsula onboard the *Antarctic* (commanded by Captain C.A. Larsen), the ship anchored off Snow Hill Island, just east of the Antarctic Peninsula at 64°21'S, where Nordenskjöld, five companions, and five dogs landed to set up winter quarters. From this point they surveyed 400 miles of the coastline by sledge, reaching almost as far as the Antarctic Circle. When heavy ice cover prevented the ship from evacuating them the following open season, a party of three landed with the intent of reaching Snow Hill Island and bringing the main party back to the ship overland. Instead, the three men were forced to winter unprepared in Hope Bay, on the tip of the Peninsula, apart from their colleagues. The *Antarctic*, trapped by the ice, sank in February 1903 and its crew had to winter in a stone hut on Paulet Island. Fortunately, Nordenskjöld came upon the three men at Vega Island during his northern exploratory trip in September 1903, while an Argentinian relief expedition in the gunboat *Uruguay*—completing that state's first voyage into Antarctic waters—rescued two other groups on the extreme northern end of the peninsula. Despite the near-disaster, the expedition yielded significant geographical and scientific insights, exploring the east coast of Graham Land and finding fossils that began to uncover the history of Antarctica.[59]

The French also engaged in scientific exploration during this era through expeditions led by Jean-Baptiste Charcot (1903–1905 and 1908–1910). When his initial plan to rescue Nordenskjöld's Swedish expedition became unnecessary, Charcot proceeded to the west coast of the Antarctic Peninsula to carry up on the *Belgica*'s research. After wintering on Wandel Island (now Booth Island), he explored the islands off the western coast of Graham Land (the Palmer Archipelago) and discovered Loubet Land (actually part of Adelaide Island) to the south. He returned to the same area in 1908 to 1910 on the ship *Pourquois-Pas,* which boasted eight scientists and cutting-edge scientific equipment, and conducted scientific observations on Deception Island, discovered Marguerite Bay, chartered the Fallières Coast on the western side of the Peninsula, and constructed buildings to overwinter on the shore of Petermann Island. In 1910, Charcot sighted Alexander I Land and discovered Charcot Land (later found to be an island), thus defining the basic geography of the western coast of the Antarctic Peninsula and the islands south of 65°S.[60]

The major turning point in Britain's imperial ambitious for Antarctica came in the aftermath of William Speirs Bruce's Scottish National Expedition of 1903 to 1904,[61] which established a meteorological station (Omond House) on Laurie Island in the South Orkneys. Bruce believed strongly in the scientific importance of the station, but a lack of British state funding, coupled with the island's perceived lack of strategic utility from an imperial perspective, prompted the resident British Minister in Buenos Aires to ask the Argentinian government to assume responsibility for the station's operation—without requesting any acknowledgement of British sovereignty to the island. The Argentinian government quickly accepted the offer, and sent a postmaster (a demonstration of effective administration) back to the island with Bruce even before the formal handover took place on 22 February 1904. The British thus "effectively gave the observatory away," handing the Argentinians the basis for a territorial claim on the grounds of continuous occupation of an Antarctic site. Consequently, historians John Dudeney and David Walton argue that "Tabarin had its roots directly in William Bruce's decision to hand over" the Laurie Island observatory to Argentina.[62]

Only a few months after this transfer, Colonial and Foreign Offices began to reassess the importance of these remote islands. The overexploitation of sea mammal resources in the North Atlantic during the late nineteenth century prompted a renewed focus on the South Atlantic in the early twentieth, and Norwegian whalers now requested British permission to hunt around South Georgia. The allure of revenues from regulating these activities through licences now made British officials worried about the "complex pattern of possible Argentine challenges to British sovereignty" over other South Atlantic and Antarctic territories. Prompted by media rumours of Argentina's intention to construct a permanent observatory in the South Orkneys, the British government officially "reminded" the Argentinian government in 1906 that the islands were British territory. The British government formalized its sovereignty when it announced the Falkland Islands Dependencies (FID) by Letters Patent in 1908, encompassing "the group of islands known as South Georgia, the South Orkneys, the South Shetlands, and the territory known as Graham's Land, situated in the South Atlantic Ocean to the south of the 50th parallel of south latitude, and lying between the 20th and 80th degrees of west longitude . . . as Dependencies of our Colony of the Falklands." This set the foundation for "more than a century of protest and counter-protest, and of claim and counterclaim."[63]

From this point onward, historian Adrian Howkins notes, "the history of Antarctica became increasingly caught up with the wider history of the British Empire."[64] The wind-blown islands of the South Atlantic and the Antarctic Peninsula now converged with British imperial aspirations, evoking images of the need to paint the ice pink to conform with the cartography of an Empire upon which the sun never set.[65] (When the midnight sun of the Antarctic summer fell below the horizon, it would be replaced by the midnight sun in Canada's Arctic territories.) Historian Peter Kikkert observes that, beginning in the early twentieth century, Britain—more than any other nation—viewed the Antarctic through the lens of its imperial ambitions. At first, British imperialists viewed Antarctic exploration as a potential cure to the pessimism that was an "all-pervasive" characteristic of Edwardian imperialism. During the Boer War, the poor health and performance of British soldiers shocked the country. Heightened international competition, especially from Germany, engendered national doubt, and Antarctic exploration and expansionism "resonated in a society beset with anxieties about national decline." The efforts of the polar explorers became part of a new drive for British efficiency, which included the Boy Scouts, conscription, rifle clubs, even imperial motherhood. British explorers such as Scott and Shackleton even marketed their expeditions as a race against other national competitors and rival empires, which Britain was winning. The Antarctic became more than a testing ground for British manhood, however, when the British government made its first formal territorial claim in the region.[66]

Establishing formal Antarctic claims resonated with the popular British imperial imagination that had been invigorated by the exploits of Robert Falcon Scott and Ernest Shackleton—two men who came to embody the heroic age of polar exploration.[67] Between 1907 and 1909, Shackleton's expedition reached the polar plateau, found the South Magnetic Pole, and made it to within 100 miles of the South Pole—a point at which he ceremoniously claimed the polar plateau for King Edward VII.[68] (Canadian Dr. William Michell served as ship surgeon on the *Nimrod*, which carried Shackleton's crew to and from Antarctica.)[69] But it was Norwegian explorer Roald Amundsen, the first man to traverse the Northwest Passage, who managed to reach the South Pole on 14 December 1911 (and claimed it for Norway). Captain Scott and his four companions arrived at the Pole on 17 January 1912, and their heroic trek ended with tragedy, overshadowing their achievements in the scientific fields of biology, geology, glaciology, meteorology, and geophysics. (Canadian Charles Wright navigated for the dog-team party that found the frozen bodies of Scott and two of his men at their final camp.)[70] Shackleton's Imperial Trans-Antarctic Expedition of 1914 to 1916, which attempted to cross the entire continent from the Weddell Sea to the Ross Sea, proceeded despite the onset of the Great War—and their epic hardships to reach the Norwegian whaling station on South Georgia and be rescued by a Chilean ship in the middle of the Antarctic winter became legendary.[71] Particularly in the lead up to the First World War, British commentators drew hope from the bravery and self-sacrifice that these men had demonstrated in the face of intense hardship and tragedy, imparting "a heroic quality to the process of Antarctic exploration and, in this instance, to Britain's role therein."[72]

Broader foreign relations led the British to maintain a cautious Antarctic policy before the First World War, seeking to avoid possible territorial claims by France and the United States in the region, but this changed soon after. The war had increased global demand for whale oil, a rich source of glycerine (a raw material for explosives), and thus enhanced the economic and strategic value of the region. In response, the Colonial Office formed an Inter-departmental Committee on Research and Development in the Falkland Islands Dependencies in 1917 to initiate biological studies in the Southern Ocean.[73] Concurrently, Britain attempted to substantiate its Antarctic claims in the early postwar period through a more coherent polar policy, largely at the behest of Leopold S. Amery, the under-secretary of state in the Colonial Office. By the end of 1920, he urged Britain to annex the entire Antarctic continent on the grounds of whaling and the need for a single conservation authority, potential mineral wealth, scientific benefits, and strategic concerns about enemy aircraft or submarines using bases in the South Atlantic to attack the Falkland Islands or Australasia. At the Imperial Conference of 1926, his plans to incorporate Antarctica piece-by-piece into the British Empire became official imperial policy.[74] "British officials implied that the superior capacity to understand the Antarctic environment that they possessed by virtue of their scientific institutions and administrative experience, gave them both a right and a duty to claim possession of the Falkland Islands Dependencies," Howkins notes. This logic extended more broadly, providing a moral justification for expansive imperial sovereignty claims such as New Zealand's claim to the Ross Dependency in 1923, while Australia's claim to East Antarctica in 1933 bolstered the cartographic image of a British Antarctica wrapping the southern part of the globe.[75]

As a demonstration of British scientific authority, the Colonial Office launched the Discovery Investigations (named after Captain Scott's ship the *Discovery*) between 1926 and 1938 to investigate the marine biology of the Antarctic ocean, conduct sea-ice studies, measure temperatures, chart ocean currents, survey harbours and anchorages, and survey various coastlines.[76] These scientific endeavours, coupled with the establishment of the Scott Polar Research Institute in Cambridge in 1920 and the Rymill Expedition to Graham Land between 1935 and 1938 (which confirmed by dog-sledge that the Antarctic Peninsula was connected to the continent), strengthened the connection between environmental science and British sovereign control in Antarctica. Nevertheless, "huge gaps [remained] in human understanding of Antarctica as speculation continued to substitute for scientific knowledge," Howkins observes. "In 1938 the Australian Department of the Interior published a map of Antarctica, which contained the most up to date information available. Many of the map's coastlines were drawn as dotted lines, indicating that the cartographer had no idea of their exact shape; most of the interior was simply left blank."[77]

Other countries, however, harboured different visions of Antarctic ownership and control. France laid claim to a sliver of Terre Adélie in 1924, thus challenging the sector marked out for Australia and "compelling the Australian and British governments to accept a French enclave therein." The rise of pelagic whaling, and the unwillingness of Norway's increasingly nationalistic whalers to respect Britain's weak historical claims to several sub-Antarctic islands, led the Norwegian government to reluctantly annex both Bouvetøya (1928) and Peter I (1931) islands by royal decree.[78] Argentina retained its permanent footprint (the Laurie Island Observatory) and refused to apply for licences or comply with British rules governing wireless stations in the British Empire. The United States' interest in the Antarctic also grew exponentially during the 1920s and 1930s, largely propelled by the prestige-seeking personal initiatives of Richard Byrd and Lincoln Ellsworth. Historian Peter Beck noted that the American expeditions not only yielded valuable information on Antarctica (such as Byrd's revelations that helped to prove that it was a single continent) and bolstered potential U.S. territorial claims, but also introduced new technologies to polar exploration, such as airplanes and other forms of mechanized transport. These advances "enabled explorers to achieve not only an overview of the whole continent but also more rapid and extensive coverage of a given area," Beck explained. "Byrd, Ellsworth and [Australian Hubert] Wilkins pioneered the use of the plane and brought the air age to Antarctica, such as evidenced by Byrd's flight over the South Pole in 1929 and by Ellsworth's trans-continental flight of 1935–6."[79] Canadian bush pilots played important supporting roles in these pioneering expeditions, with their experiences of braving Canadian winters in their youth serving as "a kind of calling card when they applied to join."[80] Although the United States had adopted an official policy in 1924 that it would not recognize any Antarctic claim that was not backed by "effective occupation," by the late 1930s it seemed poised to follow Britain, France, and other claimants in submitting its own claim (with speculation that the U.S. Antarctic

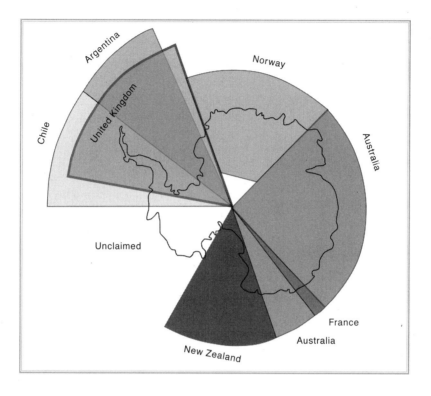

Map 2. Sector claims by Antarctic states, c. 1945.

Service was created in 1939 to serve this purpose).[81] When Admiral Byrd embarked on his third expedition in 1939 (the first officially sponsored by the U.S. Government), he held specific instructions from President Roosevelt to prepare the case for a U.S. sovereignty claim. He also took Argentine and Chilean observers who, in turn, shared his enthusiasm about the mineral potential of the southern continent with their South American brethren.[82]

Howkins has ably charted the Argentinian and Chilean governments' renewed interests in the question of Antarctic sovereignty immediately preceding and following the outbreak of the Second World War. A Norwegian invitation[83] to these South American nations in 1938 to attend a polar conference on the question of Antarctic sovereignty prompted officials in Buenos Aires and Santiago to think anew about their legal rights to Antarctica. Accordingly, both countries established Antarctic commissions to study the legal basis of putting forward their claims. In Argentina, the promotion of the country's interests offered President Roberto Ortiz with a means to appease growing popular nationalist sentiment and to cater to the traditional "territorial nationalism" of the Argentine elite who dominated his government. In Chile, some officials thought that Argentine sovereignty in Antarctica would pose a direct geopolitical challenge to national security and they pressed their government to take pre-emptive action.[84]

The outbreak of the Second World War on 3 September 1939 changed the context and opened a new chapter in the international politics and law of the region. With Britain's attention now fixated on Nazi advances on the European continent, Argentina and Chile—which decided to maintain a position of official neutrality until 1945—saw an opportunity "to pursue their reawakened territorial ambitions in Antarctica with relative impunity." In November 1940, Chile laid formal claim to the sector between 53°W and 90°W—a jurisdiction that clearly overlapped substantially with Britain's Falkland Islands Dependencies and with the potential Argentine claim. Shortly after this announcement, the Argentine and Chilean Antarctic Commission leaders met to discuss Antarctic sovereignty. While they did not agree on the boundaries between their countries on the southern continent, they concurred that the Antarctic Peninsula belonged to South America and not a distant colonizer. Although Argentina did not advance an official claim to Antarctica akin to Chile's, they established a post office at their Laurie Island meteorological station in late 1941 and sent the naval ship *Primero de Mayo* to visit islands and plant flags as ceremonies of possession the following year. If Britain lost the war, which seemed a distinct possibility, these acts could situate them in a strong position to assert sovereignty over the region.[85]

Britain found itself in a political quagmire. Its survival as an island nation demanded a secure food supply, and it depended heavily upon Argentina as its commercial ally and main supplier of beef. German surface ships and U-boats operating in the South Atlantic posed a threat to this supply chain, as well as to the free passage around Cape Horn that connected Britain to New Zealand. If control of the Falkland Islands and Antarctic Peninsula fell into German hands, they would have ready access to possible refuelling bases. The British erected coastal defence batteries in the Falklands and South Georgia, and implemented a "scorched earth" policy if a German cruiser attacked the latter island group. In March 1941, the armed merchant cruiser HMS *Queen of Bermuda* destroyed oil and coal stocks in the South Shetlands to ensure that they did not fall into German hands, and later that year HMS *Neptune* scoured the islands east of South Georgia for evidence of German activities. Given the connections between some Argentine nationalists and Nazi Germany, and British dependency on food imports from the South American nation, Argentine claims to the Falkland Islands and their Dependencies posed a double-edged sword that required very careful handling.[86]

British officials thus faced a difficult scenario wherein they wished to protect their sovereign interests and sea lanes of communication, but could not afford to alienate Argentina because this would jeopardize British food security. Prolonged interdepartmental debates ensued about the value of the Falkland Islands and Dependencies to Britain and appropriate responses to South American claims, even after Japanese advances in the Pacific in late 1941 and 1942 amplified fears about South Atlantic security. When the Americans declined to assume responsibilities for defence of the Falklands owing to the Argentine dimension,[87] the British chiefs of staff requested Canadian troops to garrison the islands. Prime Minister William Lyon Mackenzie King turned them down, however, choosing to focus Canada's resources on the war in Europe.[88] In response, Winston Churchill ordered that British troops be sent to the Falklands to deter the Japanese, given that the loss of the islands "would be a shock to the whole Empire." The arrival of 2,000 British soldiers in August 1942 left no doubt about Britain's commitment to the colony, and also meant that any Argentine invasion would now constitute an act of war and would precipitate armed conflict between the two countries. The British Foreign Office remained careful to avoid an armed confrontation, however. It expressed relief when the HMS *Carnarvon Castle* had no contact with Argentines during its "administrative tour" of the Dependencies in 1942 and 1943 (conducted on the pretext of countering Axis raider activity), when it obliterated sovereignty markers left by a second Argentine expedition. In any case, a military coup in June 1943 threw Argentine politics into a period of uncertainty that stymied that country's Antarctic activities for the next three years, and Chile lacked the shipping capacity to mount its own expedition to Antarctica.[89]

Although this changed context diminished the immediate sovereignty threat posed by Britain's South American rivals, the Colonial Office succeeded at convincing the Admiralty and the Foreign Office to take tangible steps to safeguard British sovereignty over the Falkland Island Dependencies in 1943. Accordingly, the War Cabinet decided to fund a top secret military expedition to establish bases of "effective occupation" in Antarctica. The utmost secrecy had to be maintained to prevent the Argentine and Chilean governments from confronting the British and to maintain commercial connections.[90] By winning the "race to install permanent bases at the relevant locations" (and simply avoiding the Argentine outpost on Laurie Island), officials believed that Britain could contain any official Argentine response. Although launched as a military operation, Tabarin "had little direct bearing on the conduct of the war against the axis powers," Dudeney and Walton note. "Rather, it was an integral part of a long term imperial strategy from the earliest years of the twentieth century to paint Antarctica pink, the colour of the British Empire in 20th century atlases."[91]

Throughout 1943, British officials in the Colonial Office, the Admiralty, and the Foreign Office Research Department prepared for the expedition, working through the night so frequently that the expedition was dubbed Operation Tabarin, after the famous Bal Tabarin nightclub in Paris. In July, the Admiralty recalled Lieutenant Commander James W.S. Marr from Ceylon (Sri Lanka) to lead the expedition, given his previous Antarctic experience with Shackleton's final *Quest* expedition and as a marine biologist with the Discovery Investigations. He joined the expedition committee in London and began assembling "Naval Party 475" immediately, recruiting a small team of men— most of whom boasted previous polar experience—to accompany him to the Antarctic Peninsula. As Dudeney and Walton summarize:

> The committee, which met regularly through the latter half of 1943, envisaged an over-wintering base on Deception Island and at Hope Bay, on the coast of Graham Land, and, if limited resources permitted, a summer occupation of Signy Island in the more re-mote South Orkneys. Such change of plan had been required to counter the Argentine and Chilean territorial claims to Graham Land. Marr's "Political Instructions" and "Regulations" made it plain that "the main political object of the expedition" was to establish "parties on the islands concerned rather than to deny access to them to Argentine and/or Chilean parties." They emphasised how "force, in a sense implying the possibility of bloodshed or similar violence, should at all costs be avoided." Marr was otherwise required "to establish bases at selected points in the FID and to conduct

scientific research and survey therefrom (sic)." A detailed scientific programme, which was to constitute "the principal occupation for the shore party," was prepared by [Neil Mackintosh from the Discovery Committee] covering the disciplines of sea-ice, geology and physiography, glaciers, surveying, meteorology, zoology, botany, and tidal observations.[92]

The comprehensive scientific program contemplated by the interdepartmental expedition committee actually fit with the geopolitical agenda that drove Britain's decision to mount a wartime operation to Antarctica. "The demonstration of superior scientific capabilities offered a convenient way to . . . prove their sovereignty rights without an outright display of physical force," Howkins argued, and most Antarctic experts to whom British officials turned for advice about Operation Tabarin were scientists. The involvement of pre-eminent polar explorer and scientist J.M. Wordie of Cambridge University, who had been seconded to naval intelligence, "and other scientists in the Antarctic problem ensured that British interest towards the region continued to have an important scientific component," Howkins explained. "Despite the pressures of the war, these scientists saw Operation Tabarin as offering a still rare opportunity to conduct scientific research. As a consequence, Operation Tabarin would have a much greater scientific component than most wartime naval expeditions, and this connection between Antarctic politics and Antarctic science would set the tone for much of the ensuing Antarctic sovereignty dispute."[93]

So it was that Captain Andrew Taylor, who did not have formal polar scientific training but had extensive surveying experience in the Canadian North, found himself drawn into Operation Tabarin. When he learned of his secondment to Naval Party 475, he was never told its purpose or its plans—only that it was "super-secret" and he was "admonished never to talk about it." After receiving assurances that a prolonged secondment would not prejudice his normal promotion to major,[94] Taylor agreed to the task. *Two Years Below the Horn*, his first-hand account of what transpired, offers a unique perspective on the landmark Antarctic mission that he eventually commanded.

Taylor divided his draft manuscript into chapters, which we have aggregated into sections for this published version. Part 1 concerns Taylor's preparations for departure with Naval Party 475. After being recruited as a surveyor with "cold weather" experience in September 1943, Taylor spent the following month on a brief sojourn home to Manitoba where he visited his family and met his two-and-a-half-year-old son. By the time Taylor returned to Britan, "Naval Party 475" was nearly packed. Marr had secured a wooden-hulled former sealer called the *Veslekari* (renamed the *Bransfield* after refitting) from Iceland to serve as the expedition ship,[95] but its small size forced Taylor and another expedition member to sail separately on another vessel. Unfortunately, both ships proved ill-prepared for the long, rough journey and were forced to return to England. Consequently, the expedition did not reach the Falkland Islands until late January 1944, aboard the ocean liner *Highland Monarch*. From there they transferred their supplies and personnel to the smaller and more rugged *William Scoresby* and RMS *Fitzroy* and sailed south. After re-occupying the former whaling base at Deception Island, the ships headed for Hope Bay at the tip of the Graham Land peninsula. Poor ice conditions, however, thwarted repeated attempts to enter the bay and establish a base on the Antarctic mainland. Instead, the expedition sailed for the northwest coast of Graham Land and eventually established a base at Port Lockroy in February.

Part 2 focuses on the activities at Port Lockroy and describes the successes and struggles that subsequently influenced the expedition's work on the Antarctic mainland. These included offloading supplies, constructing Bransfield House on Goudier Islet, creating amenities from leftover materials, eating indigenous animals, learning some of the dangers of travelling on the Antarctic mainland, and developing a diverse scientific research program. When discussing the ensuing months and winter, Taylor shares his observations about his fellow expeditioners, including their talents and personalities, as well as how the team endured the ups and downs of Antarctic isolation. Taylor also uses this section to introduce readers to his surveyor's perspective. He was intensely interested in his surroundings, and developed an extensive knowledge of Port Lockroy's landscape, wildlife, and seasonal changes. His powers of observation were put to good but limited use during the expedition's September-to-October manhauling trip to Wiencke Island. The trek was hard-going, suffered from adverse weather, and, compared to the "armchair" expectations of its participants, was not a great success. By this time Marr was not well. Determined to improve the expedition's performance, however, the commander returned to Port Lockroy in December to plan the next year's operations with the governor. During his absence, Marr left Taylor in charge of Port Lockroy. The following February, Marr, suffering from depression, announced his decision to permanently leave the operation. To Taylor's surprise, Marr recommended that he, the Canadian, take command of the British imperial expedition.

Taylor immediately assumed command of Operation Tabarin and oversaw the establishment of Britain's permanent presence on the Antarctic mainland. In Part 3, he describes this process, including base construction, exploring and comparing the new surroundings to Port Lockroy, and learning how to work with the dogs that arrived from Newfoundland in early 1945. Taylor also devotes considerable space to describing the expedition's heavy reliance on the sealifts, and on the SS *Eagle* in particular. His willingness to emphasize not only the crew's professionalism but also their courage in the face of extreme danger is noteworthy. With only rare exceptions, however, Taylor hesitated to describe himself or his colleagues at Deception Island, Port Lockroy, or Hope Bay as "heroes" in the explorer tradition.

This downplaying of polar heroism is most surprising in Part 4, detailing the first dog-sledging journey (8 August to 11 September 1945) which covered 271 miles. Their route around James Ross Island led the team past landmarks and buildings discovered or constructed by famous Antarctic explorers including Otto Nordenskjöld, and Taylor relied on these encounters to affiliate Operation Tabarin with the heroic age. He avoided, however, any explicit suggestion that his team mimicked their heroic predecessors. When the four-man sledging team nearly ran out of food while returning home, for example, Taylor downplayed the crisis and offers an account that is much less sensational than David James' version.[96] Instead, Taylor's narrative consistently emphasizes professionalism, knowledge, and logic over perseverance and luck.

Taylor most fully develops the professionalism theme in Part 5, which describes the second sledge journey. All other accounts of Operation Tabarin either ignore this trek or give it superficial attention. For Taylor, however, the second sledge journey was the culminating triumph of Tabarin. From 9 November to 29 December, Taylor and his team covered 500 miles and systematically surveyed James Ross Island and its surroundings. As they crisscrossed the region and circled islands, the team systematically surveyed the coastlines. They also followed up on observations from their first sledge journey and corrected several cartographic mistakes made by previous explorers. The team also collected an impressive set of geological and botanical specimens that the expedition brought back to England in 1946. Unlike previous trips, this second dog-sledging journey was notable in its lack of crises. By now, the sledgers knew the region and understood the snow conditions. They brought plenty of food, and had enough left over to leave a cache for future sledgers.

Taylor's final chapter, which recounts his team's preparations for departure as well as their journey back to England, introduces his frustration with imperial bureaucrats. Taylor faulted the Discovery Committee for not communicating its plans for their return, as well as failing to provide for them when they arrived in Chatham in March 1946. As our afterword describes in greater detail, this contempt would persist (in diluted form) for the rest of his life as he faced hurdles in securing recognition from both British and Canadian authorities for his leadership role during Tabarin. But such challenges lay far in the future for Andrew Taylor when he learned of his secret mission in September 1943, launching him on the greatest adventure of his life.

TWO YEARS
BELOW
THE HORN

PART ONE

Preparations and Departures

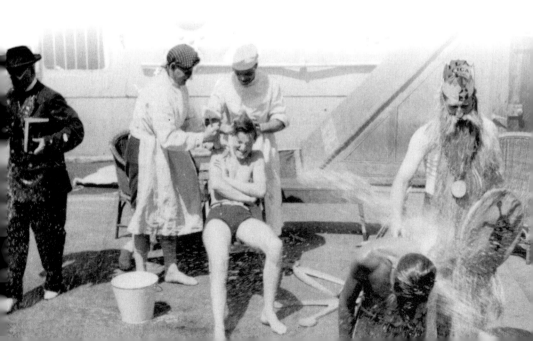

CHAPTER ONE

Recruitment and Goodbyes[1]

I WAS A CANADIAN ARMY CAPTAIN STATIONED NEAR LEATHERHEAD, Surrey, in the summer of 1943. The Canadians had been largely immobile for three years in England, and life had not been particularly exciting for many of us. For the past year and a half, I had served in the Survey Company of the Royal Canadian Engineers. I was well qualified for the work, and enjoyed the frequent opportunities to enlarge my technical horizons and gain experience in aerial surveying and interpreting aerial photographs. My unit was based in a two-storey red-brick house beside which, in pre-war days, people sat beneath the apple trees and enjoyed the magnificent view along the valley leading to Box Hill and Dorking. We messed at a large Army Headquarters mess at the Mansion House near the centre of the town. Three times a day we walked the 300 yards separating these two buildings. On sunny days, it was a pleasant trek, and even in the rain, the distance was not great enough for us to forget that the journey was the only daily exercise that we indulged in. Our billets were good, our food was good, the people were friendly, and several pubs were handy. Life was pleasantly dull.

My life became more interesting when, on 17 September, my commanding officer returned from a conference at the Geographic Section, General Staff in London and announced that I had been recommended for a "special job." I followed my CO to his office and asked for more information. He replied that the project was very secret, but hesitantly divulged that it involved "penguin country."

---

1. Editors' note: Nearly all of this chapter did not appear in Taylor's original draft. It is, however, largely derived from his private journal, which Taylor consulted extensively when writing the manuscript. The journal is preserved in Taylor fonds, UMA, MSS 108 Box 3 File 11.

"The Falkland Islands?" I instantly queried.

"How did you know?" he almost involuntarily snapped back. My reply stirred him to disclose some additional administrative details and inform me that I had until the following day to request the withdrawal of my name from the assignment.

Needless to say, my mind whirled with excitement that night as I thought over this sudden turn of events. It was exceedingly pleasant to contemplate relief from my boredom. The new work would still be technical in nature, so I would be able to continue developing my skills. On the other hand, I also knew enough about the distances, probable transportation delays, the lateness of the season, the possibility of being frozen in, and the indefinite nature of the plan to realize that it would require many months, if not years, to transpire. I had last seen my wife in 1941, and in the interim our only child had been born. Although I did not contemplate declining the appointment, I resolved to bend every effort toward getting home—no matter how short the period—to renew the friendship and love of wife and family.

A few days later, I received instruction to proceed to Park Street, Mayfair, in London as soon as possible for an interview with the leader of the expedition, James W.S. Marr of the Royal Navy Volunteer Reserve (R.N.V.R.). I left right away and learned more details about "Operation Tabarin."[2] The project, he explained, would last between 18 months and two years, all expenses would be met, and all hands would receive a bonus pay of £100 per annum. I would be seconded from the Canadian Army to the British Forces. Marr emphasized the necessity of maintaining the strictest secrecy, as well as the urgent need to complete the expedition's supply and organizing arrangements so that it could depart at the earliest possible moment. He was therefore eager to obtain my services immediately, but sympathized with my request to return home, and agreed to forgo my services provided that I returned to London before 31 October. If I obtained passage, which he could not help arrange, Marr requested that I provide him with a list of the stores I would require prior to my departure.

By 28 September, my appointment to the Colonial Office was in order, and I began to make tentative inquiries about transportation to Canada. I met with Major Fleury, an administrative officer at the Canadian Military Headquarters,

---

2. Editors' note: At the time, the operation was known as "Naval Party 475." It would not be known as Operation Tabarin until later that fall. See Haddelsey, *Operation Tabarin*, 30–1 and 235n28.

who insisted that there was absolutely nothing that he could do to help arrange my passage. While I was there, Major Coleman at the Canadian Military Headquarters also informed me that no prisoner-of-war transport would be available in time for my voyage. I next went to the Colonial Office and spoke with several individuals, including A.B. Acheson and his assistant Captain J.L. Hayward.[3] I inquired about several modes of transportation including aircraft. They did not object to my travel plans. In fact, given the lengthy absence that Tabarin would entail, they professed to be anxious that I visit my family. Yet, they were also powerless to help procure my transport to Canada. I did, however, secure a reluctant promise for assistance with my return passage because the two men probably believed that I would not be able to get to Canada and that they would never have to make good on their gesture.

By this time, I was less optimistic about getting home, but I was not ready to give up hope. I solicited the Canadian Postal Corps (whose two planes ran a transatlantic service bringing mail to and from the troops in England). I also tried to secure an interview with the Canadian High Commissioner, Mr. Massey, but he was not in. Instead I met with his secretary, Mr. George Ignatieff, and his satellite Mr. H.W. Kember. The latter gentleman informed me that I had to travel back to Canada as a civilian and that I would require a passport.

On 30 September, I therefore headed to the Canadian Immigration Office feeling somewhat like an Austrian immigrant attempting to travel to Canada. When I arrived, the official was surprised by my shopping about and suggested that I instead ask for Major Gill at Canadian Movement Control a few blocks away. If Movement Control arranged my trip, I would not require a passport, visa, or any other papers. When I met Gill, he claimed that he could arrange for me to travel by sea if I was willing to either obtain authority and an order for the passage, or if I was willing pay for my own passage (which I was). I ground my teeth when Gill told me that I was about one day too late to catch the *Queen Mary*. Had Major Fleury directed me to Movement Control three days earlier, I could have already been well out to sea. The next ship, according to Gill, did not depart for two weeks. Aerial transportation was impossible, he contended, because war priorities and Army orders prevented it.

After leaving Gill, I decided to try one more office: the American Air Priority Board. They informed me that they had plenty of space but required the

---

3.   Editors' note: Acheson and Hayward were both members of the Expedition Committee. Taylor did not provide first names in his manuscript.

authority of Lieutenant Colonel Wallace at Canadian Movement Control—the same office that I had visited earlier in the day. So, as a last resort, I returned to Movement Control and met with Wallace. He tried to obtain an official order for me to travel by air from Major Fleury, without result. The Major looked upon me as a nuisance by this stage, and I had indeed earned that sentiment. However, when I explained to Col. Wallace that I had secured the time, leave, and authority to make the journey, he phoned the Ministry of Sea Transport and then turned me back over to Gill. The latter called Liverpool and, after dropping the phone on its cradle asked, "How soon can you leave? Can you make it tonight? The train leaves Euston station at 11:30 p.m., and the passage will cost £38." So, at 5:30 p.m., I made out a cheque to cover the ticket, and called Captain Hayward at the Colonial Office to inform them of my travel arrangements.

"I just rang up to let you know that I'm leaving."

"Leaving! Where for? When?" came the response.

"Canada. Tonight."

"Have you time to pay us a visit? Can you be here by seven o'clock?"

Before departing, Gill introduced me to Captain D.M. Irwin of Inverlynn (near Whitby), Ontario, who was returning on the same ship. He was returning to Canada to serve as an instructor after having spent time in Italy. We received our tickets, warrants and instructions to report to the embarkation staff officer at Liverpool the next morning. Gill then provided us with a car to transport Irwin's luggage to the station and to visit the paymaster at the Canadian Records Office. After running these errands, suffering delays, and dropping Irwin off at Trafalgar Square, I took a train to the Colonial Office and bounded up the stairs two at a time to meet the two patient gentlemen awaiting me in Mr. Acheson's office.

They were as surprised as I was by my success at securing passage to Canada, and were anxious to know what arrangements I had made for the return journey.

"Actually," I said, "none at all."

"How then will you get back? Where will you begin to make the arrangements? Whom will you contact," asked Acheson. He had shrewd and penetrating eyes, but they were not unkind.

"I do not know," I replied. "I expect to have eight or ten days on the boat to figure that out."

"Aren't you taking a bit of a chance? You may not be able to return on time."

"Yes probably," I conceded, "but life is full of chances these days, isn't it?"

Acheson conceded, and after a good luck handshake and a friendly admonition to wire them immediately upon arriving in Winnipeg, I dashed from the office as the clock's hands crept relentlessly toward eight o'clock. I did not catch my breath until after I reached the railway carriage. My train reached Leatherhead at about nine o'clock, and I quickly returned to base, bathed, and packed a small bag and a haversack. My general officer commanding was, like many others, surprised that my departure had been arranged so suddenly. I left the base by car and arrived at Euston with plenty of time before my train departed at 11:40 p.m.

Liverpool's Lime Street Station did not impress during wartime, but at half past four in the morning it was dingily lit to comply with the blackout. I met Irwin on the platform—for we had missed each other among the crowds at Euston—and we made our way across to the officers' club where we joined a few other sleepy-looking individuals. We managed to procure some sandwiches and tea, and wearily spent the hours perusing the morning's papers. At ten o'clock we went down to the docks and boarded the grey-white vessel *Capetown Castle*. We warped out of the dock at half past eleven that morning, and were well out to sea by mid-afternoon. I could not help feeling amazed, for only twenty-four hours before, I had practically given up hope at being able to take advantage of this wonderful opportunity.

Although we travelled unescorted and alone, the voyage across the sea was uneventful. The huge ship, which probably carried 900 passengers in peacetime and 4,000 troops during the war, brought thirty-five people across the Atlantic to the United States. Two of us were Canadians, the balance were Americans. I got along well with Irwin, and he became my cabin mate. For the first three days, the weather was rough and dirty, and I suffered from my usual *mal de mer*. On the fourth day, however, the weather became quite warm and the voyage improved. One day, a racing school of dolphins provided an entertainment highlight. On another occasion, four Martlet fighters[4] suddenly appeared overhead. On still another day, an unannounced gun practice brought us all to the deck where we cast our anxious eyes at white plumes streaming toward a smoke float. Still, the journey contrasted with the convoy that took me to England in the spring of 1941. During that passage, we were crowded on-board like sardines in a tin while battleships and destroyers escorted our ship. There had been gun

---

4.   Editors' note: The British purchased F4F Hellcats from the United States during the war and called them Martlets.

drills twice a day, boat drills every day, and we were possessed by a sense of constant anticipatory tenseness. Perhaps the possibility of attack had considerably reduced, but I think that thoughts of war and danger crowded from our minds because we were sailing in the opposite direction toward our loved ones. Pleasant as the days were, I grudged every one of them, for each meant one less day at home. The voyage, in fact, felt unusually long.

We were all very happy to sight the warning beams of the lighthouse and lightships along the coast approaching New York, and were happier still the next morning to see the great city's skyline. The *Capetown Castle* pulled up to the pier on Sunday, 10 October. After some running around, I purchased a $43 train ticket to Winnipeg. I put in a long-distance call to my parents in Winnipeg, but received no reply after waiting for an hour. At 2:30 p.m., I boarded the train. Travelling on a tourist ticket in America is the same as travelling third class in England, but there is a much more social atmosphere. This is because the passengers are anxious to befriend one another for the journeys that are almost inevitably longer in America, and longer still in Canada. It would be difficult, even in England, to preserve an icy indifference to the person seated beside you if you shared that seat for twenty-four hours. The train rushed through the countryside, stopping only at the larger cities such as Newark, Philadelphia, and Pittsburgh. It was good to pass through towns and cities that were not seared with the jagged gashes of bombs, and yet things seemed Hollywoodian without them. More than anything else, however, one noticed the lights from the main streets and stations of the hundreds of towns that we passed. After transferring in Chicago and Minneapolis, I arrived in Winnipeg on the morning of 12 October.

After reuniting with my wife, parents, sister, and brother-in-law, I met our young son, Andy Jr., and my niece for the first time. They were both two-and-a-half years of age. We spent the next two days telling each other about our respective experiences since my departure, and romping around with the children. I transmitted a wire to Captain Hayward to oblige his request and, hoping to prolong my stay for as long as possible, asked him to "spare the horses, please." But both Martha and I knew that a wire instructing me to report somewhere on the east coast could arrive at any time. However, we tried to avoid letting this awareness interfere with the happiness of our unexpected meeting.

On the evening of 13 October, Martha, Andy Jr., and I caught a bus to Dauphin to visit my in-laws and a few friends. I watched Andy play with his grandfather, whom he called "Bampa," and it was patently obvious how well he had taken my place, for they were the very best of friends. Toward evening, I reserved a compartment on a night train back to Winnipeg that left at 1:30 the following morning, for I was anxious to secure Captain Hayward's reply when it arrived by wire and meet with several people. After reaching Winnipeg at eight o'clock in the morning, I chose to go off on my own that same afternoon to visit several business associates. I met with the director of surveys, H.E. Beresford, who promised me that work would be waiting for me when I returned, as well as the director of mines, George E. Cole, who had been kind enough to write to me several times while I was in England. I then hurried home to spend another precious evening there.

The visit took on a new character on Saturday, 16 October. We spent most of the day talking endlessly with my family, including my brother-in-law, Orval. While we were eating dinner with a friend at their club in the evening, Orval arrived unexpectedly with news that the telegraph office had tried to contact me by phone to notify me of a wire from Captain Hayward. We left the dinner, picked up the wire, and found instructions to contact the British Ambassador in Washington immediately. I wired him the next morning, and my movement instructions arrived on Monday the 18th. I was to report in Montreal by noon on Friday the 22nd to a Mr. Cooper at Dorval Airport. So, six days after my arrival home, we began to organize for my return.

In the morning, Orval drove Martha, Junior, and me uptown. After taking a walk around Upper Fort Garry Park, I went over to the Hudson's Bay Company's store and purchased a few articles of warm clothing. The journey to Montreal would take approximately two days by train, and Martha and I eventually decided that she and Junior would accompany me. We had a pleasant evening at home, knowing that it would be my last for some time.

The following day, we packed our bags and said goodbye to friends and family at the train station before departing at ten o'clock that evening. The goodbyes reminded me of the farewells we had exchanged in 1941 at the same station. This one, however, did not seem as sharp and final because Martha and our son accompanied me. When we arrived in Montreal on the 22nd, I phoned Mr. Cooper and he informed me that I did not need to be ready until eight o'clock the next morning, so Martha, Junior, and I spent a pleasant day in Montreal along the river and visiting our friends the Van Wyks.

At eight o'clock sharp the next morning, the hotel desk phoned to tell me that a station wagon was waiting. Martha came down with me and I said goodbye to them at the door with a large lump in my throat. Martha was dry-eyed, as she had been just two days before Junior was born in 1941. As the RCAF car pulled away, I looked back at them, and they both gave me a smiling wave just before the car turned the corner and cut them from my view. The image of their smiling faces remained engraved in my memory.

The car stopped at the Windsor Hotel and Mount Royal until we sped around the wet and slippery road with seven passengers. It did not look like the best day for flying, for it was dull and the clouds hung low. Within half an hour, we arrived at Dorval Airport and stopped in front of the RAF Ferry Command Office. A large four-engine plane idled its engines and we all presumed that it would shortly take us aloft. We did not have time to read a piece of paper that we signed in about three places, but I understood that it released the RAF from responsibility for an accident and forestalled any legal claims for damages. We were then led out in the rain to another building about 100 yards away, and herded into a little room where an RAF squadron leader explained how to use the various apparatuses that sat around him. He held up, for example, an oxygen mask, explaining that we would fly above 10,000 feet and would need to plug the mask's hose into wall sockets along the fuselage. He also warned that we would become drowsy if we did not get sufficient oxygen, and did not guarantee that we would wake in very useful condition. We were all instructed to keep an eye on each other for signs of insufficient oxygen and watch for folded supply hoses. It all seemed rather portentous to me. He delivered similar lectures concerning parachutes and life jackets.

The lecturer then thanked us for our attention and directed us back to the original office we had entered. When we got back, much to my joy, we learned that we would not leave that day. Instead we were to hold in readiness for the following morning. I climbed back into the station wagon with the others and returned to my hotel. I secured our room for another night and then surprised Martha, who was at the Van Wyks' home. It was one of the most exquisite moments I have ever experienced. Martha, who had bravely stemmed her tears that morning, now cried happily. Martha and I left Junior with the Van Wyks for the night and went out with another couple to the Normandy Roof where we had a few drinks, dances, supper, and enjoyed the odd cabaret turn. It was the only nightlife we experienced during my entire visit, and we arrived back at our hotel around 2:30 in the morning, dog-tired.

We were up again the next morning, and I prepared to leave again at eight o'clock. But the airport called to inform me that my flight was cancelled once again. We were in a delirium of happiness. After visiting with the Van Wyks again, we returned to our hotel to take a nap and recover from the furious pace of the past ten days. We overslept, however, and were two hours late for our dinner engagement.

On the morning of the 25th, the sky was clear and blue, and we knew that there would be no further delays. This time, Martha stood at the door to our hotel room with our little boy beside her, and gave me another happy wave as the elevator doors closed. I climbed back into the station wagon and rode the same route to Dorval with the same seven passengers. After arriving, we sat in the same waiting room, but this time the place was bustling with activity. All of our baggage littered the counters, and we had to use bits of paper to indicate which bags we wanted to take with us into the fuselage, and which could be stowed in the nose of the plane. We each signed for RAF-insulated clothing, helmets, sheepskin-lined boots, oxygen masks, and lunches. Our parachutes, harnesses, and life vests were on the plane. We were also instructed to empty our fountain pens, since they were more likely to leak and ruin clothing at high altitude. A bus then took us to the passenger terminus and, after waiting a few minutes, we climbed up a little ladder into the belly of a big four-engine Liberator. The door slammed behind us, and the engines took up their deep roar. Amidst what seemed at the moment to be a terrific vibration, we swept across the field into the wind and lifted gently and easily into the air. As we climbed over the sprawling city, the St. Lawrence gradually lost its width and I whispered a goodbye prayer to my wife and son.

Once we were airborne, I began to notice my fellow passengers. I sat on the starboard side just below the trailing edge of the big wing. We were positioned in the bomb bay. There were no seats in our part of the plane. Instead, we lay upon a layer of mattresses. We sat, or rather lay, facing each other. A wall of freight lined the bulkhead of the crew's compartment, with only a small aperture at the bottom that a member of the flight crew climbed through every few hours to ensure that we were all right.

· After 6:00 p.m. GMT, we began to descend and tilted in a broad sweeping curve until we saw a huge airport. It was Goose Bay, Labrador, one of two large airfields carved out of the wilderness by the Americans[5] to accommodate transatlantic traffic. Our plane settled lightly on one of its huge white concrete runways. We disgorged ourselves from the plane's belly and enjoyed resuming an erect posture. It was good to stretch one's legs and feel the ground under one's feet again. A bus took us over to the RAF mess, where we ate a late "hottened up" meal.

We expected to resume our journey in about an hour, so I hurried over to the administration building to inquire for leading aircraftman Jim Porter. He was Martha's brother, and had been stationed at Goose Bay for about a year. I had not seen him for about three years, and after considerable delay, was informed that he had been transferred to Bagotville and had in fact departed that same day. It seemed unfortunate that I should miss him by a fraction of day when my one-in-a-million chance to see him came through. While we had been over the St. Lawrence that morning, another plane flew in the opposite direction well below us, and I could not help but wonder if Jim had been in it.

Returning to the mess, I scribbled off a few letters, including one to Martha informing her that I had missed Jim. The evening passed very slowly, for I gained no further benefit from delays. We were all called together for a snack at 11:30 that evening, donned our warm clothing, and prepared to depart at midnight. The bus took us back to the plane and we crept up the ladder and into the fuselage. Number one port engine started. Number one starboard engine roared to life. Number two port engine spat a few sheets of flame, coughed, and was away. Number two starboard motor only groaned, and we listened to it groan until 2:45 a.m. while the other three motors purred. Finally, the plane was wheeled into a nearby hangar and mechanics climbed all over the recalcitrant engine. We were fortunate that the engine balked on the airfield rather than mid-ocean, for I was told that three engines only carried a Liberator for about an hour before seizing up.

We were unexpected guests at the bunkhouse that night. I found myself invading a double room where the other occupant was fast asleep. Fortunately, I managed not to wake him as I crawled into bed at 4:15. Most of my fellow passengers chose to sleep in the next morning. Although I did not get up early, I rose in time to eat breakfast with two of my travel companions. One of these

---

5.   Editors' note: On the origins of the Goose Bay airbase, see William G. Carr, *Checkmate in the North* (Toronto: Macmillan, 1944); John Cardoulis, *A Friendly Invasion*, vol. 1 (St. John's, NL: Breakwater, 1990); and Herman Jensen, "Building Goose Bay: A Firsthand Account," *Them Days* 16, no.4 (1991): 14–33.

men was an elderly Englishman named Commander Stephen King-Hall. He was an MP for a constituency in North Liverpool and was en route from an official trip to Washington. King-Hall had arranged to inspect the airport and invited us to join him. We both jumped at the chance and spent the morning touring facilities including the control tower. There were four men on duty, and one of them immediately replied to an incoming Mitchell bomber that circled the field once before making a beautiful landing. While we watched this unfold, another plane reported its arrival, and came in a few moments later. All told, we saw three aircraft follow the nonchalant instructions of the American controller during our brief visit to the control tower. It was fascinating to watch.

After eating lunch, I ventured on my own to the hangar where Jim had worked, and spoke with his peers for about an hour. The rest of the day passed uneventfully, until we received word from the captain to prepare to leave at 11:00 p.m. We put on our warm clothes, boarded the aircraft, retook our respective positions in the bomb bay, and took off at 12:45 in the morning.

Our part of the plane was well illuminated, with no blackouts at the portholes, but even if there had been anything of interest below it was all but impossible to see anything outside when it was dark. The journey was not particularly exhilarating. The deafening roar from the engines combined with the myriad of vibrations to preclude protracted conversations. The best one could do was shout an occasional remark, point, gesture, or make weird facial expressions and grimaces. Nor could we fall asleep, for if the supply of oxygen cut off, or if condensation froze and plugged our masks, one worried that awakening might be difficult. Now and then someone got up to stretch, rub the frost from the porthole, press his face against the glass, and peer into the gloom for signs of dawn. Two things occupied a large part of our attention. We watched the altimeter's needle climb steadily upward, and observed a corresponding drop on the thermometer. At 8,000 feet, the thermometer approached 0°F and I began to feel a bit drowsy. A nudge from my neighbour roused me at 10,000 feet and I wearily reached up for my oxygen mask. I barely possessed the energy to plug it into its socket on the wall, but almost instantaneously felt its reviving effect. We continued to climb to 18,000 feet and the temperature steadily dropped until about 5 in the morning when it stood at −30°F. We spread the supply of six eiderdown sleeping bags over us, but still felt cold.

Dead astern, in the tail gunner's "glasshouse," was our "convenience." One perceived considerable lateral sway there, as well as quite a draft. Yet it was a pleasant enough place to visit on a sunny day at 5,000 feet. At the altitude that we now flew, however, the journey became something of an adventure. First, one filled one's lungs with oxygen until they seemed ready to burst. Then, withdrawing the oxygen plug, one stumbled over the sprawled bodies of the other occupants and proceeded tailward. Except for the light that filtered from the bomb bay, there was no illumination in the compartment. Upon arrival, it was essential to first locate the tiny oxygen socket somewhere in the darkness. A few drafts of oxygen overcame the weakened condition that even this slight exertion incurred, and allowed one to consider the business of the moment. The many clothes that we wore, however, spawned a certain reluctance and trepidation, for no two pieces of clothing seemed to have fastenings or apertures in corresponding positions. Moreover, the thought of exposing any of one's more tender spots to the two inches of hoarfrost that seemed to cover everything, as well as the −30°F temperatures, must have caused stouter heats than mine to decide that they had only been imagining their previous discomfiture.

Dawn arrived finally arrived at about quarter to six, and we soon spotted Iceland. Our pilot lined the aircraft up to land at the Americans' Meek Field at 7:45 a.m. As we touched down, a beam wind caught the plane and moved it laterally to one side of the runway. The pilot side slipped to port, but did not quite succeed in re-levelling the 150-mile-an-hour monster before the port wheel touched the runway and depressed the shock absorber beyond its limit. There was a terrific bump and the plane bounded 10 or fifteen feet back into the air before ungainly impacting the runway a second time. After an additional two or three lesser bounces, we stopped and taxied over to the hangars. Even the crew agreed that it had been a rather extraordinary landing.

We walked to the little neighbouring town of Keplavik [Keflavík] in southwestern Iceland. In some respects, the sprawling little town looked like many in the Canadian west. Its streets were almost always in worse condition than the roads that adjoined them. The buildings were spaciously scattered to advertise that space was not at a premium, and that land was cheap. A store or restaurant was almost always present at each intersection on the main street. The buildings were mainly constructed from wood, but corrugated iron structures also appeared here and there. Perhaps we arrived at the wrong time of year, or perhaps the day's drizzly weather created the wrong impression, but Keplavik was a decidedly ugly place to me. There was no sign or attempt to beautify the place, no flowers, gardens, or even a concerted effort to paint the buildings. Much of this may have been due to the area's mushroom development, for it was a boomtown that catered to the American presence. Certainly the storekeepers made hay while the sun shone. Their prices were sky-high. I bought a little souvenir diary and a few other items for several times the price I would have paid at home. I also found the shopkeepers to be unfriendly. We returned to the base, ate dinner, and turned in early expecting to still depart that night.

We were not aroused, however, until eight o'clock the following morning and by noon learned that we would not depart until late that night. We again spent the day in Keplavik and on the base. Our group ate dinner together and turned in around 11:00 p.m. By this time, some of the passengers became impatient at the duration of our passage, for it had been about ten days since our orders had brought us to Montreal. One of our number had a phrase that he habitually used when such impatience was expressed: "If you've time to spare, go by air." Yet, the weather was improving, and with it, the prospects of our departure.

Three hours later, early in the morning on 29 October, we were roused from our beds. We spent the next two hours in our flying suits impatiently waiting for the order to board the plane before finally flying into the darkness at 4:45 in the morning. The plane climbed steadily to 12,000 feet, and its powerful motors carried us forward more steadily than many a train I travelled in. As a matter of fact, after several hours of flying, one imagined that the plane was careening along a smooth track of steel rails. We did not notice air pockets as one does on smaller and slower planes. At about 9:00 a.m. someone shouted "land below!" and we all looked down at the Outer Hebrides. Our plane levelled off at 5,000 feet and gave us a view of Scotland before landing at Prestwick in Ayreshire.

We left our flying clothing on the plane, for we became insufferably hot on the lovely autumn day. We then claimed our baggage and entered the main building. Customs, immigration, and security people then went to work on us. I had no trouble, but one or two of the others encountered slight delays. I can still recollect one of our number recounting his difficulties convincing the customs officer of his need for three dozen pairs of women's silk stockings. At the last of a series of offices, we received our railway tickets and I caught my train from Prestwick at 8:00 p.m. After spending the night in a sleeper, I said goodbye to my companions at Euston at 8:30 in the morning, got a fresh shave and some breakfast, and then proceeded to pay my respects at the Colonial Office.

CHAPTER TWO

Beyond
the Tropics

CAPTAIN HAYWARD WAS IN A GENIAL MOOD WHEN I ARRIVED at his office. After joking that they had not expected me to return, he said that I had arrived with plenty of time to spare. The operation had encountered several delays during my absence, and would not be ready to depart for another week. In the end, it was two weeks before we departed, and these weeks amounted to a short leave for me.

While I had been in Canada, preparations for the expedition's departure from London had steadily proceeded. Marr flew to Iceland and located a wooden Norwegian sealer called the *Veslekari*, which sailed to London for a refit by her Norwegian crew before being requisitioned for his purpose. She had spent many of her days sealing in the icy waters around Spitsbergen, for she was one of the two largest Norwegian sealers afloat in 1937. She had also been used for exploratory work. Her name was connected with many deeds of assistance to distressed vessels in northern waters, and she had carried Miss Louise A. Boyd's expedition to Greenland in 1938.

Built in 1918, the *Veslekari*'s bow was reinforced to withstand the strains and impacts of a voyage through ice-strewn waters. Her black-tarred hull was 125 feet long and had a beam of 27 feet; she had a gross registered tonnage of 296 tons at the time Marr inspected her at Iceland. Two-masted, she was what sailors call "ketch rigged," in that her foremast was the taller of the two with a gaff topsail, all sails being fore-and-aft. A jib on the bow and a sizeable spanker on her mizzen mast completed the sails, which were supposed to be auxiliary to her engines. The latter was located well aft, which probably accounted for the much greater draft she had toward the stern at the time of this inspection. I knew little about her engines at that time, but the expedition would learn more about them as its voyage proceeded. Our expedition's cargo was carried forr'ard, with only the fore-castle beyond the hold. The crew's bunks were located along the side. To some of the old salts aboard, the bunks were considered a "bit fancy" because features such as shutters and lockers were not usually found on such vessels. They dismissed the matter, however, by attributing their presence to the tenure of Miss Boyd, and walked away mumbling something about "lace curtains." The ship's superstructure was well aft. She had a stubby look about her that suggested great strength, but any impression of squatness which these lines may have given her were at once dispelled by the tall wooden masts reaching for the sky. The bridge lay about amidships, with the chartroom and radio cabin alongside. Below, on the main deck, the entrance to a small saloon above the ship's stern held a narrow companionway that led below decks to the wardroom and passenger cabins that the expedition's personnel would occupy. She lay for refit in the Royal Albert Docks during the months of September and October in 1943, and when she emerged toward the end of that month, though not much altered in appearance, she was re-christened the HMS *Bransfield*.

Since the *Bransfield* had to transport two years of supplies, the expedition was, of necessity, not a large one. Our numbers were divided into three groups: a ship's party, and two shore parties. The *Bransfield* would be commanded by Lieut. Victor A.J.D. Marchesi, R.N., and had a complement of three officers and fifteen men. The shore parties numbered ten and four men. After she transported the expedition members and supplies south, the intention was to have the *Bransfield* remain (probably with the larger party aboard) and freeze in at the base during the winter of 1944. This measure would give the shore party great mobility up until the last possible moment during the ensuing summer and extend the scope of some of the planned scientific work.

The expedition's operational theatre lay due south of that wild southerly tip of South America—Cape Horn—and extended over two of the five dependencies of the Falkland Islands. A small party of five men would go ashore at Deception Island, one of the South Shetlands Group. The larger party of ten men, together with the ship, would winter at the eastern tip of Graham Land, at a point well known in the annals of Antarctic history: Hope Bay. The general latitude of the area including these two localities lay between 63° and 64°S, while the longitude varied between 57° and 61°W.

The above outline was the approximate extent of our knowledge of the intended project by September of 1943. Of course, each of us learned further details that were pertinent of his own particular job. Toward this end, we compiled
stores, equipment, and supplies that suited the conditions we would experience.
Being a surveyor, for example, I had to prepare an order for all the instruments
and supplies that I expected to use under winter conditions. The expedition's
steward, A. Tom Berry, had charge of the procurement of all the food and clothing requirements. And so each of us helped to arrange for all the multifarious
articles required for a dozen men to live and work for two years without further
assistance or supplies, just in case a resupply ship could not reach us after our
first year. All supplies and equipment had to be packed and assembled at the
Royal Albert Docks by about 25 October at the latest to allow the ship to sail
on 1 November as planned.

During these preparations, the expedition's members slowly became acquainted. As I already mentioned, my first meeting was with Marr. An Aberdonian, and
a graduate of Aberdeen Grammar School in 1910, Marr first encountered the Antarctic after being selected from among a group of volunteer Boy Scouts as one of
the crew of the *Quest* on Sir Ernest Shackleton's third and last 1921-to-1922 voyage. Later, Marr served as zoologist with the *Discovery II*, and out of this service
grew his memoir on the South Orkney Islands.[1] During the Second World War, he
served with the navy on shore stations in Iceland, South Africa, and Ceylon, before
being recalled to take command of Operation Tabarin. Prior to our departure from
England, he received a promotion to lieutenant commander, RNVR [Royal Naval
Volunteer Reserve]. Marr was forty years of age at the time.

Tom Berry, the other member of the party whom I met at this time, was
one of the older men, and subsequently proved to be the oldest one of us to winter in the south. Born in London in 1890, he had tried his hand as a writer in
the offices of various solicitors before the sea claimed him first as a baker, later
as a cook, and finally as a steward. He served with the Merchant Navy through
both wars, and spent about ten years as steward aboard the *Discovery II*; he
knew his job well, and was an excellent cook. He had a build that goes with
middle age—one might almost call it "stylish stout"—for he was very light on
his feet. Berry was also a most fastidious dresser. When I first met him seated at
a table deep in long lists and statements in Marr's office, and after our return to

---

1.   Editors' note: J.W.S. Marr, "The South Orkney Islands," *Discovery Reports* no. 10 (1935):
283–382.

England, I was always impressed by his nattiness. It appeared that there might be other things in life to which he could devote himself more wholeheartedly on a pleasant sunny afternoon.

Meanwhile at the docks, the pile of supplies began to accumulate as the ship's refitting proceeded. I went down there twice to see Marchesi, who had left much of the preparatory and organizational work to his number one, an RNVR sub-lieutenant named Fleck, whose rich brogue told of his recent departure from Ireland. I heard that he had previously served with coasters. Fleck had little time for visitors because he was too preoccupied handling and re-handling the cargo. The other officer aboard the HMS *Bransfield* was Sub-lieutenant Ian Graham, a very friendly though dignified young chap with a charming smile that the ladies found most captivating. Graham had been stationed for some time on the coast of West Africa earlier in the war.

30 October of that year fell on a Saturday, and in the afternoon the government arranged a gathering at the Goring Hotel in London to, apparently, meet some of the people it was shipping off for two years. At this festivity, I met quite a number of the other members of our crew including William Flett, Ivan Mackenzie Lamb, and Norman Layther. We were also introduced to part of the *Bransfield*'s complement, including the cook Charles Smith, who later became part of a shore party. At the end of the function, we each received bills for about £2, which caused someone to remark that this must have been the first occasion that an Antarctic expedition encountered a "rookery" before it left London.

By this time, work on the *Bransfield* was finished and loading was well under way. The vessel, however, was too small for the expedition's cargo and passenger requirements. Arrangements had to be made to ship some of the cargo aboard another vessel consigning it to Montevideo, Uruguay, where a local steamer servicing the Falkland Islands would take over. This solved the cargo difficulty, but other arrangements had to be made to take care of the passenger accommodation. About 1 November, Marr informed me that I would travel to Port Stanley separately on a vessel leaving Liverpool on 15 November with a meteorologist named Gordon Howkins.

The *Bransfield* had been due to sail on 6 November, but the day before this, when the loading was all but complete, we discovered that the fresh water tanks leaked so badly that they required immediate replacement. The installation entailed removing most of the cargo and delayed the vessel's departure until 12 November when, aided by an ebb tide at 2:45 p.m., HMS *Bransfield* slipped out of her berth at the Royal Albert Docks. Her stained and blackened timbers creaked as the auxiliary engines vibrated and racked her hull. Swinging compasses the next morning, the ship moved a little farther down the river, anchoring that night off Southend Pier. At 1:40 p.m. on Sunday, 14 November, the *Bransfield* joined a small coastal convoy headed for Falmouth in a northwesterly gale. By next morning, she had rounded North Foreland, slipped through the Straits of Dover, and rolled in a northerly gale out of sight of land.

The *Bransfield* soon encountered problems. Our medical officer, Surgeon Lieutenant E.H. Back, RNVR, who was aboard the vessel at the time, later wrote that "during the night, the vibration of the two-bladed screw had become more pronounced than ever, and the whole ship seemed to shake with each 'chug-chug' of the screw, so that one of the convoy, a tug, offered us a tow, which was refused." She put into Portsmouth for repairs, where she remained until 25 November. When the *Bransfield* departed again at 4:00 a.m. for Falmouth, she was unable to keep up with the convoy and put into Portland that afternoon. Two days later, she ran into a squall and lacked the power to pump and steam simultaneously. The *Bransfield* anchored that night in Falmouth Roads and went alongside a jetty in Falmouth dockyards the next day. The vessel was clearly unfit for the expedition's purposes.

In the meantime, I took the train to Liverpool in time to make the appointment for Howkins and me on 15 November. He was a newly fledged sub-lieutenant in the RNVR of probably twenty-three years of age. After receiving some training in the West Indies as a pilot in the Fleet Air Arm, he had worked at the naval station at Port Stanley in the Falkland Islands doing meteorological duties.

We learned that our ship was the *Marquesa*, an 8,000 tonner on the meat run to South America with accommodations for eight passengers. We moved gently out of the wharf shortly after 1:00 p.m. and lay at anchor in the roads by late afternoon. By morning, the tide dropped us neatly on a submerged wreck, and we were stuck fast. Half a dozen tugs came alongside and tried to pull us clear, but by the time they managed it, the *Marquesa* lost some of the plates from her bottom and began to settle slowly by the head. With about twenty-five feet of water in the forward holds, the tugs successfully towed us back to our berth, and the ship subsided. The naval-officer-in-charge at Liverpool ordered us to proceed with all dispatch to Falmouth, and as we rolled southward in the cold unheated train, we assumed that our companions on the *Bransfield* were probably approaching the heat of the tropics.

We are all given at times to ruminating on what the future may hold for us individually, but not many people conjectured as actively as Howkins, and fewer still think as loudly as he did. He first concluded that we must rendezvous with another meat or cargo vessel at Falmouth, but later decided that the port was not a usual point of departure for such ships, so we would have to take a smaller vessel to an intermediate port, such as Gibraltar, and board some southbound ship. Or, perhaps, we would take part of our passage on a destroyer or some other naval vessel, for our orders were to report with all speed. He even suggested we could go to some West African port and then fly to South America. I must confess, it was difficult for me not to be interested in each of these proposals even though I was aware that some of Howkins's anxiety was spurred by Cupid's bow. In the back of both of our minds, however, we had each reserved a very small recess for the thought that in some inexplicable manner, we were going back aboard the *Bransfield* to further strain her already overcrowded appointments.

On the morning of our arrival at Falmouth on 16 November, we reported to the naval-officer-in-charge for orders. From the time of our departure from Liverpool the previous night, Howkins's potful of surmises had been in imminent danger of boiling over; but at this interview, the naval-officer-in-charge took the pot off the fire for him. Though he could not tell us when she might arrive, he did inform us that the *Bransfield* would put into Falmouth to pick us up. We remained puzzled as to why she was not clear of England, and our perplexity increased as another ten days crept by without news of where she was.

It was not until a miserable rainy morning of the eleventh day following our arrival at Falmouth that she arrived at the docks. Since the tide was out, she lay twenty feet below the level of the dock, so we boarded her by climbing down a long, rickety ladder. We found most of the chaps aboard, dressed in white submarine jerseys, hatless in the rain, and looking none too warm. One of the geologists, named Buck, had endured a particularly uncomfortable passage to date, having felt the cold most severely. A cheery-looking rotund man of about fifty-five, Buck's features never appeared quite complete without a pipe stuck in his mouth. Having a round, contented-looking face, he regaled the boys with stories of the strange places his profession took him. Though I did not have the opportunity of getting to know him well, he seemed a most modest and obliging person, and we were all genuinely sorry when he announced his intention to withdraw from the expedition.

For a few days, the expedition's plans were vague and unsettled, for no one knew exactly what would happen. The *Bransfield* could go no further without extensive repairs. Such work, however, meant indefinite delay during a shipping season that was already late enough. Most of us felt almost certain that we would sail no further in the *Bransfield* and that, as the galley wireless had it, she would be abandoned here in Falmouth, as far as the expedition was concerned.

This new delay afforded me a chance to become better acquainted with a number of the companions whom I would live with during the many months ahead. The studious-looking bespectacled young naval lieutenant with the crimson band of the medics between his two gold stripes was our medical officer Eric Back, or "Doc," as he became better known to us. A recent graduate of Cambridge, and a native of Emsworth, Hampshire, he was twenty-three years of age at this time. Something over a hundred years ago, an illustrious ancestor of his travelled by land and sea over large tracts of Canada's then unexplored north land, discovering on one journey what he called the Great Fish River, which subsequently bore the name of its discoverer.[2] During the Blitz of 1940 and 1941, Doc was stationed at various hospitals in the east end of London, and this appointment with our expedition was the first time that he had any serious intentions of emulating his great-grandfather. Though he was still a boy and his frame had not yet fully developed, Back quickly made himself a popular member of the expedition. The responsibilities that came his way lay lightly upon his shoulders and his bright and cheery disposition made friends readily for him. While officially the operation's medical officer, he also had an active interest in meteorological work.

Dr. I. Mackenzie Lamb, though of English birth, received most of his early education in Edinburgh, and was well inculcated with many of the more admirable of the Scottish national characteristics. Professionally, Lamb was known as a cryptogrammic botanist who had been drawn from his work at the British Museum of Natural History to accompany the expedition and, in my opinion, possessed the best scientific mind of any of us. Subsequent events probably threw me into closer contact with Lamb than any other individual in our party. A diligent worker as well as a modest and courteous gentleman, he was one of the most unselfish characters I have ever met. It was a privilege to know him so well. Possessing a humour that at times approached elfishness, he was a most

---

2.   Editors' note: Taylor is referring to the Back River, named after explorer George Back, that runs through the Northwest Territories and Nunavut.

sincere and earnest person. Both logical and imaginative, he possessed a realism that did not allow any histrionics or dramatics to warp his steady judgment. Even at this early date, his fine manners and powerful build gave promise of the character he lived up to in our life with him in the south.

The other geologist on the party besides Buck was William R. Flett, an Orcadian on leave of absence from Glasgow University, where he had been a lecturer in the Department of Geology. Flett had that dry wittiness which comes readily to the tongue of dour northern Scotsmen. Older than most of us, and of a rather serious scholarly mien, the hands of time had laid themselves lightly upon him for all his forty-three years. He was but newly married, and leaving the homeland for him was a bit more of a tug than it was for most of us. The silver grey thatch on his head and his ruddy complexion made him look like a good sailor, as indeed he proved to be.

Uncertain as the plans for the future were, the unsuitability of the *Bransfield* was sufficiently obvious and she was emptied of all her stores within a few days. On 3 December, Marr returned from a trip to London, confirmed the abandonment of the *Bransfield*, and announced new arrangements for us to sail from Avonmouth on a troop ship. A special train moved our personnel and equipment to that port by 8 December, and our gear and supplies were immediately placed aboard the RMS *Highland Monarch*.

The *Bransfield* was left tied up to the docks at Falmouth; what became of her after that I do not know. While we all felt some measure of relief at not putting to sea for so long a voyage aboard a vessel in unseaworthy condition, her loss to us was much more serious than it seemed. No vessel was available to replace her, though an arrangement was made to have her officers relieve those aboard a vessel then in naval service at Port Stanley in the Falklands, and to have this vessel serve us as well as possible, consistent with her naval duties. This did not seem an ideal arrangement then, nor did it prove to be so in the field. The crew of the *Bransfield* were most disappointed at this sudden termination of their services to us. Smith did not accept lightly such a severance of his connection with the projected expedition, and doggedly pressed to be taken along. At the very last moment, special arrangements were made to allow his inclusion. Smith proved to be a happy, joyous character, and was a real asset to the lonely company he later kept.

With thousands of troops and a sprinkling of Gibraltarians aboard, the *Monarch* sailed from Avonmouth on 11 December. Joining a convoy, we must

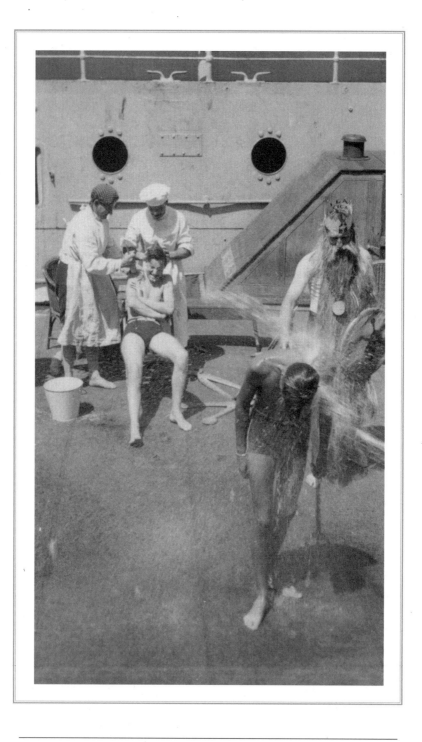

Figure 3. The equatorial line-crossing ceremony, 3 January 1945.

have taken a rather tortuous route to arrive at Gibraltar on Christmas Eve of 1943, where most of the troops disembarked. While in port, we spread ourselves into more commodious quarters than the six to a cabin that we suffered up to this point in our passage.

Christmas Day at "The Rock" was a beautiful one, almost perfectly calm, and with a clear blue sky overhead. We sat on the side of the hill a few hundred feet above the water, with a quart of beer and a bunch of grapes, and soaked in the scenery. The wharves and jetties were crammed with ships, our own vessel lying almost immediately below us, and alongside a cruiser in drydock lay the squat black shapes of a couple of submarines. Near the end of a jetty, the bow and stern of a ship were afloat, waiting for a midships section to marry them into a useful unit. Beyond the docks, the water of the bay was of a placid blue, sparkling in the sun, as a zephyrish breeze freshened the air, while in the distance, the brown hills of Spain rose up. It seemed one of the finest sights I had ever enjoyed, as we sat beneath the craggy heights of the Rock itself and watched more ambitious people toil up the hill in the midday heat.

At ten o'clock the next morning, we passed through the defense boom, and sailed in a much smaller convoy toward the coast of West Africa under escort. The ships were blacked out at night and a first view of phosphorescent waves alongside barely made up for the hot stuffiness of the cabins. Calling for a few hours at Dakar, we broke from the escort vessels and headed for the South American coast. These were pleasant days, as we sailed along through the gentle tropical swell, watching the flying fish skittering away from our bow as we lay in the shade swotting up early lessons in Spanish in anticipation of Montevideo. We passed a cargo ship one day—a Spaniard—looking strangely naked with her docks clear of the guns and life-saving rafts that cluttered up most merchant vessels in those days. Another day the highlight was a Flying Fortress streaking at 5,000 feet for the African coast. The food was good and the days slipped by peacefully.

Several hundred troops destined to replace the garrison at the Falkland Islands were still aboard the vessel. Though organized largely for their benefit, Neptune's ceremony on crossing the equator on 3 January caught a number of us in its web, viz. Flett, Smith, Buck, Lamb, myself, and Norman F. Layther, one of our radio operators from Auckland, New Zealand. The latter inadvertently dropped the remark at some time that he had made the trip northward from "down under" without paying this homage to His Oceanic Majesty. As bumptious and carefree a character as could be found, even among nineteen-year-olds, he had the time of his young life on our voyage out from England. Full of the joys of the spring we were approaching, good-natured and utterly irrepressible, Layther was a happy and joyful lad, with an intelligent interest in most subjects that confronted him. He was a handsome chap of very neat appearance, and as spontaneous in his reactions as the weather itself. Several other members of our party took an active part in executing the ceremony, and we found King Neptune to be Fleck (one of the *Bransfield*'s officers), while his spouse was Gwion "Taff" Davies, with two bulbous lumps appended to his chest. The two shavemasters were John "Jock" Matheson and Lewis "Chippie" Ashton (our carpenter), while Tom Berry made a wonderfully self-righteous parson. Proceedings became a little rough when some of the troops gained possession of the hoses being used in the initiation, though none suffered more than an angry cook who stuck his head out of a porthole on the poop deck and in the midst of delivering his own harangue on Neptune's Court, received a direct hit from four streams of sea water as he became the "target for tonight."

We became better acquainted with each other on those days aboard ship, and I met a number of the chaps whom I had not known well before, including Davies, Ashton, and Matheson. Davies was twenty-six, and had the sea in his blood. He was born in North Wales, went to Denmark at the age of eighteen, picked up the language, and went away to sea within three months in a motor ketch. Since then he served aboard a three-masted topsail schooner, in whaling factory ships below the Cape and out of South Georgia, in the Home Guard, and in the Merchant Marine during the war. A frank and open likeable Welshman, Davies was better known as "Taff" to us all, and though not a big man, he was extremely powerful and ever ready to give help to any of us who could use his strength. Not many knew that he was university-trained to become a zoologist, for he seldom spoke of it. He preferred to work with his hands and was one of the most sincere socialists I have ever met. He was almost ashamed to possess anything better than his "mate," including a better education. Honest and hardworking, he improved with acquaintance, and became one of the most popular members of our entire party.

For a long time, I did not know that Ashton's Christian name was Lewis, so familiarly had we all known him as "Chips," or "Chippie." He was another Londoner and perhaps forty-five when we first met. Where he learned his trade, I do not know, but he was one of the most accomplished and resourceful men at fine manual work that one would ever expect to meet. His latent qualities and abilities did not become fully apparent until long after we had started on the work toward which we were bent, but before that work was completed, few of us had not become indebted to him for his skillful assistance. His pleasant and courteous personality, in addition to his modesty, made him a popular figure among us. Chippie had been a ship's carpenter for many years, and had visited most parts of the world while plying his trade, but it was seldom that his casual references betrayed where they were. I once heard him remark that he had been on a ship that was torpedoed earlier in the war, but I could not now tell her name, nor where the sinking occurred. Ashton was a man who believed in doing his work without ostentation, and yet he was never too busy to show another the "tricks of the trade."

A stoutly built, clean-shaven man of fifty with a serious but serene expression on his face, John "Jock" Matheson was a sailor descended from sailors, and hailed from the west of Scotland's Isle of Islay. Matheson had sailed through Antarctic waters many times before, so that the immediate prospect did not hold the novelty for him that it possessed for most of his companions. There is a tale that Matheson mothered four or five youngsters who became stormbound with him on King George Island in the South Shetlands. Jock never spoke of it himself, but a lengthy account of the incident is recorded in F.D. Ommaney's *South Latitudes*.[3] A practical and experienced salt-water sailor to his fingertips, Matheson gained his expert knowledge of small boats with Scottish fishermen. His speech had a Highland inflection that was pleasant, and which he used purposefully but with typical thrift. Among our party, Davies had an admiration for Matheson which approached idolatry.

Another young member of the party was K.C. Blair, who was drawn from the navy. He was a West Indian, from Barbados I was told, and was dark with a fine physique. Blair had quite a talent for sketching, and also possessed a strong baritone voice, which he exercised with some gusto.

Our senior radio operator was a Belfast Irishman from Manchester named J.E.B.F. Farrington of about my own age (thirty-six). After gaining his Post Office certificate in 1929, he had spent six years in the Merchant Service prior to the war, and also made three voyages in the RRS *William Scoresby* into Antarctic waters between 1935 and 1938. In 1939, he became Air Ministry inspector

---

3.   Editors' note: Taylor is referring to F.D. Ommaney's *South Latitudes* (London: Longmans Green, 1938).

in Manchester where he remained until accepting the appointment with us. Farrington proved to be a conscientious and reliable radio operator.

Through an almost monotonous succession of clear skies and hot days, our voyage on the *Highland Monarch* continued until the sixteenth day of our departure from Gibraltar, when we approached Montevideo, Uruguay. En route to the harbour, we passed the red rusting hulk of the German pocket battleship *Graf Spee* tilted at a ludicrous angle. Her sinking followed the brilliant exploits of His Majesty's ships *Ajax, Achilles,* and *Exeter* in December 1939, forming one of the few bright pages for Britain in the war's early history. Steaming slowly over the shallow mud flats, the *Highland Monarch* churned up a reddish brown wake and entered the harbour amidst brilliant sunshine at 10:30 a.m. on 11 January 1944.

We spent ten free days touring and enjoying Montevideo, that beautiful Riviera of the south. The stopover was not solely for our enjoyment; the *Monarch* took on a cargo of meat from the great *frigoríficos* of the southern cattle country to take back to Britain via Port Stanley in the Falkland Islands. The British residents of Montevideo were most hospitable to the troops aboard the ship (which included our party), the liberality of which I have never previously experienced on so large a scale, for their guests numbered hundreds. We were made honorary members of the English Club, and given all the facilities of golf, tennis, and riding clubs. We were transported on visits of inspection through some of the large nearby industrial plants, taken in special trains to visit 100 miles into the country's interior, and we were entertained at *gymkhanas*, dances, and in private homes. For ten days we were given as delicious, exciting, and stimulating a carnival as one could stand. During our subsequent two years amidst our ice and snow, we all spent hours in happy recollections of these days and eagerly anticipated tasting its happiness again during our return voyage. To those people of this great city who made all this possible—and they were not all British—we owe a debt of gratitude impossible to repay; to all those who made us their friends, and on behalf of all those who shared this delightful experience with me, may I be allowed to thank you.

The loading of the ship was complete on 23 January, and we cast off the mooring lines that afternoon. All but scraping the pier of the harbour basin as we left the port in the fresh breeze that blew upon our starboard bow, we sailed from Montevideo on another day of brilliant sunshine and turned out to sea. As the *Graf Spee* dropped gently over our starboard quarter, we swung south again. We were out of the calm seas of the tropics now, for already there was a gentle roll to it, and a tang in the wind. The sunny skies turned to grey and we encountered the long, black rollers of the "Roaring Forties." We were headed for the Falkland Islands, among the most remote of His Majesty's colonies, but no less loyal on that account. Three days out we encountered fog, and at about four o'clock in the afternoon of 26 January, someone let out a shout of "Land Ho!" and we rushed to the rail to sight the misty outlines of the Falklands low on our port bow. Alongside, we began to see drifting pieces of the seaweed that infests the islands, the kelp from which Falkland Islanders derive their familiar soubriquet of "Kelpers." Flashing in and out of the water were a dozen penguins, the first that most of us had seen outside of a zoo. We entered the broad estuary-like entrance to Port William, and dropped anchor at the Falkland Islands.

CHAPTER THREE

From the Falklands Southward Bound

TO THE NORTH OF OUR ANCHORAGE, THE LOW grass-covered hillside was bathed in sunshine and peppered with sheep, a solitary Nissen hut protruding from the green sward. A mile or so to the south, the coloured rooftops of Port Stanley climbed a gentle slope in serried ranks. The *William Scoresby*, which met us upon our arrival the previous afternoon, now lay tied up to the RMS *Fitzroy* receiving our stores and supplies from the *Highland Monarch*'s winches.

Built in 1931 for the Falkland Islands Company, the *Fitzroy* was 165 feet long and 344 tons net registered. Long before I saw her, I heard a good deal about the *Fitzroy*. Howkins had been at Port Stanley about a year prior to his return to England, and had sailed on the *Fitzroy* twice between Montevideo and the Falkland Islands. He often described the ship, paying particularly vivid attention to her ability to roll about in stormy seas. Farrington and Marr also had some knowledge of her, ensuring that the name *Fitzroy* was a common part of our conversations long before our departure from England. The colony depended almost entirely on her for mail and supplies from the "coast," as the South American ports were locally known. She picked up wool (which is the sole export of the Falklands) from its hundreds of islands in the course of this service. She was ruggedly built and rode the world's stormiest seas under the expert guidance of her young skipper, Captain J.K. Pitt. In time, Tabarin's crew would all know the *Fitzroy* well.

Following the unfortunate loss of the *Bransfield* at Falmouth, her officers relieved those aboard the HMS *William Scoresby*, a naval auxiliary vessel of under 200 tons net register. The *Scoresby*, as she was more generally known, was commissioned in 1925 as a Royal Research Ship (RRS) in the service of the

Colonial Office's Discovery Committee as a platform to mark live whales for a research program to discover the environment and movement of whales from one part of the sea to another. In her early days, she had had a range of between 3,000 and 4,000 miles, and was extolled as being even more unconventional in her motions in rough seas than was the *Fitzroy*. As all of her available space was occupied by fuel tanks, scientific laboratories, and engines, she had virtually no cargo capacity. She was 134 feet in length and designed to reach 12 knots, but her present condition prevent her from exceeding 7 or 8 knots.

The galley wireless reported that we would be off the *Highland Monarch* before nightfall, and our baggage joined the stores flowing into the *Fitzroy*'s hold. The scene aboard the *Highland Monarch* was utterly confused as the troops milled all over the big ship's deck with full packs. After collecting the mail composed during our outward passage, I crossed the *Fitzroy* with Berry and Ashton and climbed down the *Scoresby*'s near vertical gangway where Marchesi introduced us to Captain David Roberts, the general manager of the Falkland Islands Company. Captain Roberts was a ruddy-faced, happy-looking gentleman, and proved a good friend to most of us on the expedition. His hospitality commenced almost immediately when he invited Lamb, Back, Fleck, and me to be his guests at Stanley House for the few days we would be in town.

The *Scoresby* pulled away from the other two ships, and soon moved toward Port Stanley's harbour. The *Scoresby* had a look of desuetude about her, and with good reason, for we learned that she had seldom been to sea during the previous three years. Threading our way through the Narrows, we passed about a dozen aging hulks of vessels from an age gone by—sailing ships that were so badly damaged from the run round Cape Horn that it was uneconomical to have them repaired. Among them was the *Great Britain,* one of the earliest ships to be propelled by a screw and to have an iron hull, which had been a marvel of engineering 100 years ago. With few vessels exceeding 1,000 tons, the 3,500-ton *Great Britain* had been considered gigantic. Her career ended suddenly in 1886 when she was dismasted in a storm off Cape "Stiff" on a voyage from San Francisco. Her greying, wood-sheathed hulk now lay in Sparrow Cove at Port William. Some of the other hulks were still in service, including the *Great Britain*, which until 1933 was used to store coal and other cargo. Other ships were incorporated into the wharf facilities of the little port, making picturesque and permanent warehouses.

In August 1916, Sir Ernest Shackleton described Port Stanley as he found it: "The street of that port is about a mile and a half long. It has the slaughter-house at one end and the graveyard at the other. The chief distraction is to walk from the slaughter-house to the graveyard. For a change one may walk from the graveyard to the slaughter-house."[1] The long, straight street of Port Stanley is still there, and it does not take long to discover the Falkland Islands Company offices, a few stores, the cathedral, the town hall, the secretariat, and the hospital. To the west of the hospital lie the grounds and buildings of Government House, where Governor Sir Allan W. Cardinall, KEB, CMG, resided. Of the 2,400 people who inhabit the colony, more than 1,000 of them live in Port Stanley on the gentle hillside above Ross Road, the principal street. They use peat available within a mile of the town for domestic heating and cooking, and the musty aromas of the fires instantly strike strangers.

Stanley House is one of several homes facing the harbour along Ross Road, and is as fine and comfortable a domestic establishment as one might find in England. On a bright day, the sun streamed through the tall windows of the living room and shone upon the bookshelves of Captain Roberts's well-used library. In the evening, soft lights illuminated it as we sat around the flickering peat fire after dinner one night talking with another of Captain Roberts's guests—Captain Hill, the skipper of the *Highland Monarch*.

Meanwhile, the unloading of our supplies into the *Fitzroy*'s hold continued without respite. She left the *Monarch,* and pulled alongside one of the coaling hulks used by the company to take aboard enough coal for her own needs as well as those of each base for a two-year period. It was decided that the expedition's personnel and cargo would be transported by the *Fitzroy*, and that the HMS *William Scoresby* would serve as an escort. A lighter[2] brought the last of our supplies from the *Monarch*, and they were placed above the coal in the same hold.

We did not see Marr frequently during our stay in this port because he was a guest of the governor at Government House. News filtered through to us that nearly all of us, except Marr and Smith who would sail aboard the *Scoresby* with Marchesi (the expedition's second-in-command), would all sail on the *Fitzroy*. The general plan was for the two vessels to sail directly from Port Stanley to Deception Island where Flett and his men would establish themselves. The two

---

1.   Editors' note: Taylor is quoting from E. Shackleton, *South! The Story of Shackleton's Last Expedition, 1914–1917* (London: Heinemann, 1919), 218.

2.   Editors' note: A "lighter" is a small, flat-bottomed barge.

ships would then take the remainder of the party to Hope Bay and then return to the Falklands via South Georgia to drop off additional cargo and three passengers. Tim Hooley and his family were returning to South Georgia for another two-year term as chief wireless operator. Tim was a tall, lanky, humorous man of probably forty-five years. His name, his blarney, and his good humour all tended to indicate that his Irish connections went deep into the past. His wife was a bright-eyed little woman from Cornwall, and their fourteen-year-old daughter a most attractive girl, for her fair hair and engaging smile harmonized with her modesty and good manners. They were a happy family who were popular with all on board.

One bright and windy morning, Lamb and I went aboard the *Fitzroy* in a little launch that buffeted against the waves that persisted in the shelter of the almost completely enclosed harbour. Climbing up the gangway, we found the well decks strewn with cargo, the steam winches hissing and clanking as hoists lifted more and more crates and cases from the rolling scows moored alongside. In addition to its passenger berths, the vessel's saloon deck contained a tiny smoke room, a galley, and the officers' quarters. The boat deck above contained the captain's cabin, which adjoined the bridge on the starboard side, as well as the radio cabin to port. The bridge was glazed, with the chartroom incorporated into it. Companionways led down to a fore well deck, between the forecastle and the saloon deck, over the two main cargo holds. A third and smaller hold lay aft.

Below decks, I shared a cabin with Flett that was slightly forward of "midship" and not far above the water line. Our single porthole looked forward over one of the main holds. Our doorway opened upon the foot of the main staircase from the saloon deck above us. A double bunk and a small wardrobe occupied the starboard side of the cabin, while a narrow settee and a washbasin lay across the way. There was plenty of space to stow baggage and gear. I am not a good sailor, so for reasons mutually agreed upon, I occupied the lower bunk.

While the loading of the *Fitzroy* proceeded, the *William Scoresby* lay tied alongside the public jetty. She had undertaken many pioneering and exploratory voyages along Antarctic shores in years gone by, and carried the name of the celebrated whaling captain whose *Account of Antarctic Regions* (1820) may be regarded as the first scientific contribution to the study of Antarctic whaling. The *Scoresby* was designed after the style of the "catchers" which whaling fleets use, but was larger, more powerful, and of considerably stronger construction than most. Her bow was specially reinforced to protect against the ice that she so frequently encountered. In this respect she differed from the *Fitzroy*, for though the latter was built 25 percent stronger than the Board of Trade required, she was not particularly adapted for work in the ice.

Having arrived at Port Stanley on the evening of the 26 January 1944, the two vessels prepared to leave on the morning of Saturday, 29 January. Captain Roberts had made arrangements for a launch to meet us at the company's jetty at 6:45 a.m. We clambered over an oil tanker moored alongside, and dropped down the side of the tanker into the trim little launch awaiting us. The cold greyness of the morning was fast brightening into broad day. All of our party stationed ashore were there except Howkins, of whom there was no sign. But then a huge Negro grinned down at us from the tanker's well deck. Just as Captain Roberts decided to wait no longer, we caught sight of a flying figure scurrying round a corner and down the hill toward us. It was Howkins. He had apparently extracted the last drop of sweetness from one of those leave-takings that are always so poignant. We motored out to the *Fitzroy*, the wind freshening in an overcast sky.

The lines were cast off of the coaling hulk as we clambered aboard, and the *Fitzroy* was away with the *Scoresby* following in its wake. After a few last-minute Aldis signals from shore and a few farewell blasts from the *Highland Monarch*, we rounded Cape Pembroke and turned southward along the coast. The round-topped, low-lying hills were a greenish-grey colour in the dull morning light as we sat down to breakfast, the golden-brown peat-water looking like a decanter of whisky. The water was palatable enough, though it did not make good tea.

We called at Goose Green, about fifty miles along the coast, for fresh meat. Quarters of beef and sheep carcasses hung from the shrouds on both sides of the ship, and some hens and a couple of crated pigs for South Georgia gave the deck quite a barnyard atmosphere. At four o'clock in the afternoon, we started out of Choiscul Sound for the open sea, and soon lost sight of the Falklands as we headed for the Antarctic. The ship began to pitch and roll in heavy seas. Clouds of spray dashed against our porthole, streaming down its face until the steward came in to put up the blackout.

The ship laboured along in the heavy seas for the next three days. Sleet and snow fell occasionally as we sailed through the tempestuous waters just east of Cape Horn. Few of the passengers had any interest in anything but the passage of time. On the fourth day the weather moderated, and we could descry the *Scoresby* about half a mile astern. Early on the morning of 2 February, we entered the Bransfield Strait and ran into a fog before noon. The mists lifted late in the afternoon and we sighted the northern extremity of King George Island, one of the islands in the South Shetlands group. Its steep, black cliffs rose from the water's edge to the snow slopes that merged into the low-lying clouds. Having so recently left the tropics, the strong west wind felt cold to us. As we cleared Cape Melville, Bridgman Island became visible to the east, its dark rounded cone just clearing the horizon.

We were all out on the deck the next morning, 3 February, when the ship approached Deception Island. This was our first port of call, as well as the place where Flett would establish himself with Matheson, Smith, Howkins, and Layther. Sailing west-south-west along Bransfield Strait, with Livingston Island off our starboard beam, the jagged cliffs and dirty snowfields of Deception neared. Farrington caught a fine view of the *Scoresby* as she hurried past us toward the harbour entrance. She gingerly approached the 550-foot-wide passage called Neptune's Bellows, and we followed her in just as the clock struck eleven. A fair

Figure 4. The abandoned whaling station at Deception Island, n.d.

wind still blew from the west, and the overcast sky blew flurries of snow as the harbour at Port Foster unfolded.

Deception Island is one of the most curious islands in the world. It is approximately ten miles in diameter and is shaped like a crater with one small sector of the wall collapsed to flood a seaway into its inundated interior. This formation is a magnificent shelter from the raging winds and seas of these latitudes. Since its discovery in 1820, hundreds of vessels have used it as a safe haven.

Deception Island, though probably the most interesting of the South Shetlands group, is not one of the larger islands that string out for 300-odd miles in a northeast and southwest direction. A British trader named Captain William

Map 3. Graham Land, surrounding islands, and Operation Tabarin Bases, 1945–1946.

Smith discovered and explored the north coasts of the islands in 1819, and the rich yield of fur seals began almost immediately. British and American sealers pursued these animals to the point of virtual extermination by the turn of the century. Livingstone, King George, and Elephant Islands are the largest in the group, each being about forty miles in length. After losing their vessel—the *Endurance*—in the Weddell Sea in 1916, Shackleton's party spent several months on Elephant Island before being rescued by the Chilean government ship *Yelcho*. John Matheson's adventure in January 1937 occurred on King George Island. All are typical Antarctic islands with inaccessible rocky shores cut by glaciers, mantled with ice, and sporting few harbours or anchorages.

Deception Island is different. In 1842 the south side of the island was reportedly in full volcanic activity, though no similar observation has been made since that date.[3] Neptune's Bellows lie along this south side, and as we passed between the high sheer walls of reddish-coloured rock that towered up on either side of the *Fitzroy* for 1,000 feet, we turned Fildes Point into Whaler's Bay, not a mile from the Bellows. On shore lay the derelict remains of a whaling station that was abandoned in about 1930 when pelagic whaling began. Large sheets of corrugated iron, loosened from the building frames by the wind, clanked incessantly and ominously. In many places, the sheets had torn off completely, revealing the weathered wooden skeletons of the buildings. Eight- and ten-foot-deep snow filled many of the buildings, burying the contents that had been stored inside.

Enormous weathered and rotted whalebones littered the black-brown beach of angular fragmental lava. Interspersed with the bones lay piles of baleen, the spiny straining apparatus that fringes the mouth of the whale. Years ago, when baleen was widely used for the manufacture of corsets, the piles would have been worth a fortune. Now it lay neglected, supporting a slimy algal growth. The black, granular, volcanic cinder, which cuts shoe leather like razor blades, rose up from the beach into the hills beyond.

Upon our arrival on 3 February, we immediately began unloading Flett's stores and hoisted a Union Jack on the station's flagstaff. There were no docking facilities, for the action of ice and storms left little of the small boat wharf that existed in busier days. Consequently, our two vessels lay anchored about a quarter of a mile offshore. The *Fitzroy* unloaded the first of the cargo onto a

---

3. Editors' note: The volcano last erupted in 1970. See Smithsonian Institution, Global Volcanism Program, "Deception Island," http://volcano.si.edu/volcano.cfm?vn=390030 (accessed 10 July 2015).

false deck of planks supported by two scows that ran together onto the beach where we manhandled each piece of cargo down a narrow gangway ashore.

Flett selected a building for his headquarters that stood near the north end of the whaling station. Like all the other woodwork on the island, its timbers were in fine condition. There was little trace of decay. Where the wood was exposed to the elements, it had a scoured appearance that Lamb described in his diary as a "curious shining silvery look like aluminum." The building was about 100 feet long and twenty-five feet wide, but they intended to use only its north end to conserve fuel. The tables, cupboards, cookstoves, and beds were still in the building and in useable condition. The stores were piled either inside or alongside this building about 100 feet from the beach. Inside, Smith and Berry attempted to arrange the kitchen into some semblance of order and bring it into production. Some of the building's windows were broken but the interior was remarkably fresh and there was no damage that could not be easily repaired.

South of the residential buildings stretched the remains of the whaling factory. Corrugated iron buildings were rapidly disintegrating, surrounding the three inshore sides of a large, open, and planked area, 200 or 300 foot square, where the timbers bore the tracks of the path that whales had been dragged onto shore. The wooden deck was torn, slashed, and worn through in places where the steam saws, knives, flensing tools, and chains had dug into it in the pursuit of the gory task of dissecting the monsters. Inside the cavernous buildings, a mountain of vats, boilers, and piping was rusting into junk.

Twenty years ago, whale oil had been worth as much as £90 per ton, but the price dropped to £14 just prior to the war. Although whaling largely ceased during the war years, since then the price stabilized at £45. In the days when Deception was a busy whaling factory, workers extracted oil from the blubber and cast the remainder of the carcass into the sea, where it beached in the harbour and fouled the air and water for months. Modern pelagic factories make use of the entire animals, producing virtually no waste. Whale liver oil with its high vitamin-B content, bone meal for cattle food, and fertilizer are three modern by-products neglected by earlier whalers.

Deception Island has been a source of supply for almost every expedition that visited it, and ours was no exception. The buildings of the factory included a machine shop and warehouse that were still well stocked. Piles of well-weathered lumber and heavy timbers lay behind the buildings. We carried away a good deal of this lumber, as well as furniture, nails, corrugated iron, alcohol, and even a cast-iron bathtub!

North of the base, the shoreline curled out into a low flat point, containing an almost circular body of water called Crater Lake. Between the lake and the base, the Norwegian whalers had constructed a football pitch. The remains of the goal posts still stood forlornly, with a partially completed foundation for a building near one corner of the grounds.

Behind the group of bunkhouses containing Flett's headquarters, the ground sloped gently upward to an elevation of 100 feet above the sea, and a quarter of a mile from the shore this slope suddenly flattened out toward the wall of the island. A stream gorged a course for itself through the mud, rock, and lava to empty into the sea below the base. To the north of this little stream lay a neatly fenced and gated cemetery. I swung open its rusted gate reverently and walked along its all-but-obliterated paths. Many of the markers were rough hand-hewn wooden crosses, but some were headstones containing the engraved names of those who found this lonely resting place. Most of the names were Scandinavian. One such stone held five names, members of the SS *Bransfield*—a patronymic the same as our own unfortunate vessel. Judging from the numbers of crosses and stones, the cemetery was well filled.

One can also find hot springs along the beach in Whaler's Bay. Scraping a few feet below the surface, even in winter months, emits hot water with a temperature of 190°F. Some of these springs are submarine and subject to irregular flows. When in action, large inshore areas take on a light-yellow opaqueness and small currents develop in the immediate area. In cold weather, this sector produces a sufficient effusion of heat to create a steamy haze over the beach.

Unloading the *Fitzroy*'s cargo steadily continued, with one load following another ashore from early morning until late at night. After the last load each evening we were all dog-tired from the unaccustomed exercise and clambered aboard the ship to turn in. I recollect one such trip at dusk with a heavy load of lumber and supplies aboard the pair of scows for the *Fitzroy*. A strong wind lashed the waves from the west, driving the scows high upon the beach and making it difficult to float them off. The old motor launch was heavily taxed by towing the load, and she barely made headway against the wind. About twenty men clung to the high load, which caught the wind, and as we drifted beam on to the wind they took on a dangerous heel, all but upsetting. But the valiant little engine chugged away and eventually pulled us alongside the ship. The scows rose and fell in the troughs of the six-foot waves, so that one had to judge when they crested, and leap for the Jacob's ladder that draped down the side of the ship and scramble up to make room for the next man coming aboard.

Flett's party gradually settled into the places they would occupy for the coming year. Layther's radio and Howkins's meteorological apparatus were set up in separate rooms. Mr. Hooley gave Layther and Farrington wonderful assistance installing the radio apparatus, and before the unloading was complete they made contact with the naval station at Port Stanley. Smitty, the cook, also made a couple of meals in the commodious galley. There was plenty of room to provide each man with an eleven-foot-square room and each was fitted with beds and bedding as well as private gear and luggage.

By 6 February, all of Flett's stores and the remaining personal gear of the station's new inhabitants were ashore. We bade them goodbye and returned to the ship with Flett, who received some last-minute instructions from Marr and accepted the onerous duties and paraphernalia of postmaster.[4] Almost overnight, Flett seemed to grow out of the chrysalis we had known on the trip out. In assuming the title of magistrate, the old Flett and his jocular smile were replaced by an austere and despotic looking northern islander encased in unapproachable dignity. His new duties appeared to weigh heavily upon him. We went up on deck to wish him goodbye and good luck as he left our cabin with the remnants of his luggage. He climbed over the side into the motorboat and, after a cheery wave of his hand, the boat took him off to his new home.

While at our evening meal, the motorboat returned to the ship and the *Fitzroy* weighed her anchor at 6:00 p.m. As we passed through Neptune's Bellows to re-enter Bransfield Strait, we reached the deck in time to see the whaling station's old buildings disappear round Fildes Point. A fresh easterly wind whipped the waves, but visibility was extremely good and, even from sixty miles off the coast, we had a wonderful view of the Trinity Peninsula in north Graham Land. We swung eastward into the wind and the darkness gradually enveloped us as the closing day found the two vessels setting out for Hope Bay, 150 miles away.

---

4.   Author's note: A special imprint was made on the current Falkland Islands stamps for each dependency. Those for use at the post office at Deception Island read "South Shetlands Dependency of Falkland Islands" and were first used at this post office on 5 February 1944.

CHAPTER FOUR

The North Coast of Graham Land

I WAS UP EARLY THE NEXT MORNING, before six o'clock. It was a still, clear day that had not long broken. We had not encountered any ice on our voyage to Deception Island, so it was interesting to pass a huge tabular iceberg about half a mile square and 100 feet high; its pale blue face changed by the lapping waves into deeper hues. The deep blue sea was almost flat calm, sparsely littered with small floes and bergy bits of ice. As we swung southward into Antarctic Sound, between the tip of the Trinity Peninsula and Joinville Island, the floes began to increase in number and extent, until it became almost impossible to pass between them without brushing against them with the side of the ship. Every floe was swarming with Adelie penguins, which exhibited great curiosity as we passed. Crabeater seals lolled about in groups of a dozen or more on the floes, basking slothful and slug-like in the warm sunshine, paying us scant attention and asking no more than to be left unmolested. Twice we caught sight of the black backs and dorsal fins of a pair of whales slicing the dark water between the floes only a few hundred feet away.

The narrowing throat of the sound closed in upon us as the *Fitzroy* approached the icy bulk of Joinville Island. Farther south lay Dundee Island. In 1935, Lincoln Ellsworth and his Canadian pilot Herbert Hollick-Kenyon took off from here in their exploratory flight over Ellsworth Land to the Bay of Whales.[1]

As the *Fitzroy* pressed southward, the vista ahead appeared to be one unbroken field of impenetrable ice, yet we seemed to continually find lanes of

---

1. Editors' note: Taylor also wrote, "My first airplane flight had been from Calgary to Winnipeg in a box-like First World War Fokker across western Canada one black September night. The pilot of that aircraft was also Hollick-Kenyon."

water through which to pass. I was surprised to look back upon our previous track to find the same appearance of impenetrability. In fact, the superstructure of the *Scoresby* a half a mile astern was the only visible object above the ice. On our starboard beam, the solitary Mount Bransfield stood sentinel at this end of Graham Land. To the south of it, a glacier confined within narrow walls of rock discharged into our destination: Hope Bay.

Suddenly, the *Fitzroy*'s engines shut off and we slid along with the hissing sound of the ice scraping the ship and penguin squawks providing the only other noise. The *Scoresby* came alongside at half past nine in the morning. Captain Roberts and Captain Pitt worried that an onshore wind could pack us into an ice field, and Marr came aboard to consult with the captains. At the end of the meeting, the *Scoresby* set off on an inspection trip to Hope Bay with Captain Roberts, Ashton, Back, Lamb, and Marr aboard. We watched her weave between the strings of brash ice until she disappeared behind the bergy bits. A few moments later, the *Fitzroy* turned about and made northward for the open sea.

Lamb noted in his diary that Marr directed the ship from the crow's nest when they pushed through some brash ice but, for the most part, the sea was remarkably open. They dropped anchor in the bay, fifty yards offshore, at about one o'clock in the afternoon. A landing party spent three hours ashore in search of a landing beach and building site. At the end of the search the ship set out to meet the *Fitzroy* again, arriving at half past seven in the evening. A very heavy swell developed, and the motorboat rose and fell about ten feet as the travellers transferred themselves back to the *Fitzroy*.

Earlier in the day, we had plenty of time to view our surroundings. As we steamed northward into the strait, Active Sound (the narrow opening separating Joinville from Dundee Island) and the southern end of Antarctic Sound seemed to be choked with ice. Rosamel Island sat in the midst of the heavy field of pack ice. Joinville and Dundee Islands were both ice covered, their shorelines comprised of calving ice cliffs. Steep inclines gently flattened themselves toward the summits of the islands to produce a shield-shaped section in each island. Here and there toward the summits, a *nunatak*[2] or two protruded through the whiteness of the cover. The sun beat down upon the pristine whiteness surrounding us with dazzling effect.

---

2. Editors' note: A *nunatak* (a word derived from the Inuktitut word *nunataq*) is an exposed, often rocky element of a ridge, mountain, or peak not covered with ice or snow within an ice field or glacier. Nunataks are also called glacial islands.

Mount Bransfield, which reaches up 3,600 feet on the west side of the sound, was the most impressive landmark of the scene. It was an imposing sight in its glistening setting on the huge glaciated area that mantled it. Along its base, the 100-foot-high ice cliffs continued unbroken to the south as far as Hope Bay. Its pyramidal peak stood out against the skyline. Still farther to the south, a long, white carpet of snow led the eye to more distant mountain ranges silhouetted against the blue afternoon sky.

Hope Bay is a place well known in the annals of Antarctic history. In 1903, three members of the Swedish South Polar Expedition under Dr. Otto Nordenskjöld were marooned at Hope Bay through the loss of their ship, the *Antarctic*, in more southerly waters. The three men, named Ole Duus, Axel Andersson, and Toralf Grunden, were put ashore on 29 December 1902. They intended to sledge southward overland to contact a shore party wintering at Snow Hill Island, which lay 100 miles due south where the *Antarctic* could not penetrate owing to heavy pack ice in the Weddell Sea. The three men hoped to lead the wintering party back to Hope Bay and the ship was supposed to return to pick up the entire party between 25 February and 10 March 1903. While attempting to force a passage through the ice toward the wintering station, however, the vessel was crushed and sank without any loss of life. The party of three men from Hope Bay got as far south as Vega Island by sledge before they encountered open water that forced their return to Hope Bay. When the ship did not return, they began to make arrangements to winter there with only the remains of their sledging rations of European food. They constructed a hut built from the loose stones that covered the area surrounding their encampment. In very cramped and uncomfortable quarters, these three hardy men managed to survive the winter by living almost entirely on the meat of penguins and seals and using blubber from the latter as a fuel source. In October 1903, they repeated their attempt to sledge to Snow Hill Island and on the 12th, and they encountered Dr. Nordenskjöld in the course of one of his exploratory trips at Vega Island. Two of the Hope Bay party suffered from frozen feet, but their general condition was otherwise good. Four days later, they arrived at Snow Hill Island and received care.

The sequel to this incredible tale is even more amazing. Following the loss of the *Antarctic*, the ship's party made their way in open boats through and over the pack ice to Paulet Island. The twenty-five-mile journey required seventeen days to complete. Landing on the island due west of the southerly tip of Dundee Island on 28 February 1903, the *Antarctic*'s complement of twenty men also constructed a house of stones for shelter. Here they lived under much the same conditions as the three men at Hope Bay. In the spring, on 31 October, a party of five men under the *Antarctic*'s skipper, Captain C.A. Larsen, set out for Hope Bay in a small open boat. Upon arriving, he found the stone hut where the men had lived, as well as an account of their experiences and departure for Snow Hill a few weeks earlier. The small boat from Paulet Island then set sail southward for the same destination.

On the morning of 8 November 1903, an Argentine relief vessel, commanded by Captain Julian Irizar and named the *Uruguay,* succeeded in locating Nordenskjöld's party at Snow Hill Island. The ship anchored off Seymour Island and three of her officers, including the captain, walked the fifteen miles to the wintering station. The rejoicing at this meeting was great but could not be completely unrestrained on account of anxiety and fears for the safety of the expedition's vessel and her crew. Unknown to them, Larsen and his men had arrived at Hope Bay on 4 November but were stormbound for three days before the weather allowed them to continue their journey toward Snow Hill Island. On the eighth of the month, they encountered fast ice in Admiralty Sound, fifteen miles short of their destination. Wearily trudging the last snow-covered leg of their journey, they arrived at the wintering station at 10:30 p.m. of the same day that the *Uruguay* located the party, after the ship's officers had returned to their vessel. The happy pandemonium that ensued may be more readily imagined than described. When one considers that this series of adventures occurred long before radio communications were available, the events stand out in their true perspective as a most remarkable concatenation of fortunate coincidences, coupled with a spirit of resourceful hardihood seldom equalled in the history of Antarctic exploration.

We found ourselves sailing away from this historic spot, Hope Bay, on 7 February 1944. Aboard the *Fitzroy,* we caught sight of the plumed smoke from the *Scoresby,* and after several efforts to contact her by radio failed, the ships rendezvoused. Marr, Pitt, and Roberts then began a meeting that continued after we turned in for the night.

The next morning, rumour spread about the ship that a decision not to enter Hope Bay had not yet been definitely made and that we were on our way to Admiralty Bay on the south side of King George Island to spend a few days. In the meantime, the rumour continued, the *Fitzroy* would make another assault on the ice around Hope Bay under perhaps more favourable conditions. However, the galley wireless was wrong on this occasion, for it had been decided not to re-enter Hope Bay and to instead search for a landing site along the coast of northwest Graham Land. A year was destined to pass before our eyes again rested upon this tip of the Trinity Peninsula.

We did not make much progress in these new plans because fog closed in during the morning and forced us to lay hove to for the rest of the day. In the early evening, the fog lifted and revealed the mountains of the mainland to port clothed in snow and ice from sea to summit that cast long, grey shadows upon each other's white capes. We were ten miles offshore and sailing toward the southwest when the fog again closed in, forcing the *Scoresby* to follow well behind.

We lay to almost the whole of 9 February because a heavy fog sat over the sea reducing visibility to all but zero. There was no sign of the *Scoresby*, and every hour or so the *Fitzroy* cut loose with a series of long, frantic blasts upon her horn. She received nothing but the slapping of the waves in return. With monotonous regularity, the ship lifted her head into the air and came down upon the waves with a most resounding smack so that it was difficult to detach the ship's motion from one's attention. In the late afternoon, we heard an answering bleat that gradually loudened, though we caught no sight of the other vessel.

However, the weather improved greatly the next day. Though it was windy, the sky was clear and bright. We had sailed about 120 miles since leaving Hope Bay and breakfast found us lying off Charcot Bay. The bay was enclosed by sheer rock walls and ice cliffs, and it became obvious that there was no spot to land. In de Gerlache Channel, between Trinity Island and the mainland of Graham Land, we passed a small uncharted island which, it was proposed, might be named Fitzroy Island.

To the southwest of our course, and but a few miles distant, lay the Graham Land coast, which Lamb described in his diary as "grand precipitous country covered with snow and ice."[3] In the evening we turned into Hughes Bay still searching for a place to land, and lowered a boat two miles offshore to investigate. Lamb's description of the journey follows:

> as we got near (the land) we found the water thickly
> encumbered by small and large blocks of ice, and even small

---

3.   Editors' note: A copy of Lamb's diary can be found in Lamb, "Operation 'Tabarin' (Base A) Official Diary," 10 February 1944, British Antarctic Survey (BAS), ADG/1A/1944/B.

icebergs. In many places the brash ice was so close that some of us had to fend off the larger lumps from the sides of the launch with spades and boathooks. We passed several precipitous rock islands inhabited by Adelie penguins, and finally, pushing through the brash, made the mainland itself. But the rocks rose sheer out of the water, and the swell was so pronounced, that the water was rising five or six feet on them and rushing down them like a waterfall as the swell subsided; and so we were obliged reluctantly to turn and go back to the *Fitzroy* without having made a landing. It is an unforgettable sight, passing a flattish iceberg rising and falling into the swell, to see it heaving up its gigantic mass slowly, inexorably out of the water, with the sea running off it like a waterfall, and the cracks and hollows of it an unbelievably intense blue.[4]

The following morning, we sailed out of Hughes Bay and continued in a southwesterly direction along de Gerlache Strait. The day was dull and cloudy but the wind dropped and visibility was good. The mountains of Graham Land were wonderfully clear, forming a solid wall along this coast, broken only by the crevasse-riddled glaciers that run down from the high plateau composing the centre of his peninsula. Here and there, the sun shone upon the black and white of the scene, throwing the icy facets of the mountains into glistening relief. The exposed rock faces seemed covered with a light frost, which made the scene one that might have come from a fairyland.

We passed by the massive bulk of Brabant Island on the starboard beam as the morning progressed, and on the other side lay Wilhelmina Bay, studded with islands and bergs. An interminable wall of blue-green ice rises above the water to form the coast of this sector of Graham Land and the cliffs calved quite actively as we passed by, producing much of the brash ice that littered the sea at their foot. High above the ship, gulls wheeled and hovered, while alongside penguins and seals looked up at us curiously. The back of a whale breaking the water was a frequent sight, but they gave the ship a wide berth.

As the sun broke forth, we continued southward well clear of Schollaert Channel until a number of islands to the east of Anvers Island hove into view. Our course altered slightly, and with the *Scoresby* trailing us by half a mile, we approached the

---

4. Editors' note: See Lamb, "Operation 'Tabarin' (Base A) Official Diary," 10 February 1944.

face of Anvers Island over which towered the 9,000-foot eminence of Mount Français. We slipped silently along through the ice-free waters about a mile from the
coast of the big island, as a tremendous cascade of snow and ice ploughed down a
mountainside and plunged into the sea with a thunderous roar.

Gingerly entering Lion Sound, slowly and gently pressing through a string
of brash ice strung across to Lion Island, the *Fitzroy* led the way as the *Scoresby*
closed in upon us. Most of the ice was quite small and the bergy bits grated
noisily along the ship's steel plates. Occasionally, the ship nosed aside a large
and bulkier piece. We were soon in the clear, blue-grey waters of the Neumayer
Channel, which cleaves Wiencke Island from Anvers. Mountains rose steeply
from the shores of the narrow channel, which were the same continuous ice
cliffs we had seen all day.

The fringing glacier at the foot of the 3,700-foot Copper Peak on Anvers
Island calved heavily into the sea with a thunderous roar as we passed below the
mountain. In the midst of the blackness of an exposed vertical face high above
us, a bright patch of green that had the appearance of corroded copper that was
undoubtedly the origin of the peak's name, caught our attention. Pressing along
the channel, we appeared to be heading for a dead end, a cul-de-sac, but there
suddenly opened up a narrow gap in the ice cliffs and our channel widened
into Bergen Bay, the bight at the foot of Mount Français whose summit was
shrouded in clouds by the time we passed. The continuous wall of the southerly
end of this Osterrieth Range of mountains that run along the eastern side of
Anvers Island was most impressive, even though a misty canopy of lowering
clouds curtained the view of its summit.

Soon it appeared as though we were heading out to sea again, for we had
passed the southerly entrance of the Neumayer Channel between Capes Kemp
and Lancaster. Dead on our course lay two good-sized, low, ice-covered islands
of the Wauwerman group, when suddenly we wheeled about, re-entered the
channel, and struck a course toward what appeared to be a series of small rock
piles, barely above the level of the sea deep in the bay between Damoy Point on
Wiencke Island and the north shore of Doumer Island. The anchorage found in
this little arm of the sea was Port Lockroy, used by the early whalers following
its discovery by Dr. Jean Charcot in 1904.

As we approached the harbour, the rock piles revealed themselves to be
a cluster of small rocky islets lying within the sheltering arms of the port. We
entered a narrow passage to the north of this, and stood deep in the bay some

distance clear of the ice cliffs that rise sheer at this point for well over 100 feet. The *Fitzroy* lowered boats, made fast to moorings left by the whalers on Besnard and Smith Points, and dropped a pair of anchors to tighten against the mooring lines. The *Scoresby* then came alongside, and tied up to the *Fitzroy*. A strong east wind blew up and it began to snow. We prepared to establish our base here at Port Lockroy.

The mooring lines from the *Fitzroy*'s stern drew attention to the calling cards left by the vessels that had previously used this port. Names and dates of the "Wilkins Expedition," the "*Discover,*" and the "*William Scoresby*" were painted in large white letters upon the dark faces of the huge boulders which the recession of the Channel Glacier left exposed at the Besnard Point.

About four o'clock in the afternoon, after the vessels had been made fast, Marr, Ashton, Lamb, Back, and I went ashore in the dinghy. We pushed through the fringe of brash that skirted the shore, and landed at Lécuyer Point, that part of Wiencke Island on the south side of Port Lockroy where a small rookery of Gentoo penguins and cormorants is located. Lécuyer Point is a rocky toe of rounded stones worn and weathered by countless seasons of exposure to the wind and ice—an extension of the rocky base that underlies the Channel Glacier. More angular fragments of rock can be found in some variety toward the glacier's face. The country rock is a dull grey microdiorite, and rises to about 150 feet. The flatter slopes of the point were carpeted with a bed of snow into which we sank knee deep at each step, for the temperature was just below freezing, and the snow was soft and sodden. When coupled with the wet snow that blew around us, the prospect of our new home was anything but inviting.

The most impressive feature about the place was the penguin rookery. Thousands of the comical little birds were scattered over every rock and patch of snow, and as we advanced through the reddish-brown deposits that characterize the abode of the Gentoo penguins, the birds swept dignifiedly away from us like the wash from a ship's bow. Now and then a penguin lost its footing, and dignity, for then it propelled itself forward along its silvery breast with feet and flippers flopping over everything that came in its path. As we descended into the lower parts of the rockery, the stench became terrific, for we disturbed the excrement deposits by wading through them ankle deep.

We selected a tentative site near our landing point, forty feet above sea level. White weathered whalebones, which may have lain there for twenty years or more, were scattered along the rocky shore nearby. The site lay on a fairly steep incline, but there were plenty of rocks with sufficient angularity, so that it would not be difficult to build up a stone wall on the seaward side of the foundation. A north or west wind would find us quite exposed, bringing with it the nauseating fumes from the rookery, but we had some protection from the other quarters, and one does not expect to find all one could wish for in the Antarctic.

That evening, having all but decided upon this site, we visited the largest and nearest of the cluster of islets that lay in the harbour—Goudier Islet. We did not go hopefully, but merely to ascertain that we were not passing up a better site. Much to our surprise, we found not one but two better sites that were several hundred feet from the aromatic rookery. One of these sites lay near a rocky beach on the northwest shore of the islets, about ten feet above the sea. The other was on a deposit of loose boulders near the summit of the islet, about forty feet above the sea. Near the former was a small cove in which our dinghies and the small motorboat could moor. We were somewhat more exposed to the winds on Goudier Islet than we might have been on Lécuyer Point, and until the sea froze over we were entirely dependent on the boats for transport. However, the obvious advantages far outweighed these considerations, and despite the fact that one load of stores had already been landed off the pair of scows at a point beside the rookery, it was decided to establish the base on Goudier Islet, the little rocky pile on which Dr. Charcot took his astronomic observations about forty years before our arrival.

PART TWO

Port
Lockroy

CHAPTER FIVE

Establishment
at Port Lockroy

WE HAD ARRIVED AT PORT LOCKROY on the afternoon of 11 February and, like at Deception Island, the unloading of stores began immediately. This task fell under the direction of the *Fitzroy*'s first officer, Mr. F. Jones, who was a most energetic and obliging young man. The scows were towed through the shallow passage separating Goudier Islet from the "rookery," as Lécuyer Point soon became known, and taken round to the west side of the islet near one of the old mooring chains used by early whalers. There was deep water there, so the scows could come along the narrow ledge of rock that formed the shore. There was no room to distribute the stores at this point, so it was necessary to manhandle them up the steep face of rock to the highest point of the islet, forty feet above the sea. Each case of goods coming ashore was handed up the slope from man to man and, at the top of the little hill, we made some effort to sort out those articles that were required immediately (such as tools and radio components) from the general mass of stores. To those of us who had enjoyed the comfort of the voyage out from England, the constant lifting and wrestling with the endless stream of cases that seemed to flow inexorably up from the loaded scows became an exhausting task, and told better than words of our poor physical condition. Indeed, Davies called this part of the islet "Heartbreak Hill." Many a case of fresh potatoes or tinned goods slipped from a pair of tired hands in this odd bucket brigade, spewing its contents down the grey rocky slope and into the sea. After a couple of days, crates and cases covered the relatively flat top of the hill.

This unloading point made the work unnecessarily arduous, and the limited space at the hilltop made it vitally necessary to find some alternative spot to unload the scows. The small boat cove could not be reached directly from the first unloading point we were using, but we found a tortuous approach into it from the north and all the subsequent loads landed at the cove. We continued to use this same approach throughout the year we spent at Port Lockroy. The expansive area contiguous to the beach obviated the need for the bucket brigade, and the discharging of the cargo proceeded at a better pace.

Carcasses of mutton and quarters of beef that we procured at Goose Green on the 29 January came ashore on 13 February and were buried in a shallow snow trench below the construction site. The terrific heat of the sun exposed the meat more each day, however, and the predacious Brown Skuas and Giant Petrels were not long in finding it. At a later date, the meat was moved to a deeper snow pit but the process of deterioration was too far along, and we ultimately had to dump the rotting carcasses into the sea.

As one day followed the next, load after load of stores came ashore. When unloading, the lumber and fittings for the hut received a measure of priority for the first couple of days but general stores began to pour ashore at such a rate that things came on in any order. Soon the entire beach was littered with boxes, crates, and lumber lying in chaotic confusion with parts of the Nissen huts, steel rods, and ancient rusty flensing knives from Deception Island. Except for the tools, hardware, and radio cases, there was little attempt at sorting, piling, or stowing. As a result, most articles were immersed in the multitude of cases comprising our two years' food supply.

In the meantime, Tim Hooley again rendered yeoman service by assisting Farrington to set up the radio. Sockets were imbedded in the rock to hold two steel masts that were double guyed. From these, we suspended the aerial. A small, portable canvas shelter enclosed our gasoline-driven power unit, as well as the storage batteries needed to operate the set. The radio apparatus was temporarily installed on a table before the building even had a floor. We were thus in direct contact with the Falkland Islands three days after work on the house began.

We lost no time pouring the piers for the foundation of our 16 x 29.5-foot prefabricated house. In addition to the lavish scale of materials supplied for this building, we had the lumber, corrugated iron and nails that we collected at Deception Island, the materials from one of two Nissen huts now declared surplus, and the planking from a platform built by whalers of Lécuyer Point. Out of all this, and with the most inexpert labour imaginable, Lewis "Chippy" Ashton succeeded in building a house which was both comfortable and serviceable.

Figure 5. Bringing supplies up "Heartbreak Hill," February 1945.

We began to assemble the "hut" (as it was called on the blueprints) under Ashton's supervision on a bright and clear 12 February. Stringers and joists were laid over pier positions before even the concrete had been poured. Like the pieces of a jigsaw puzzle, we fitted together the 2 x 4 components of the outer walls. Each piece was lettered to suit the markings on the plans and linked to the next by mortise and tenon joints pinned with a three-inch nail. The walls were sheathed with siding over aluminum-foiled tarpaper, and the floor eventually covered with canvas and heavy linoleum. Fitted trusses supported the rubberoid roofing.

While the vessels remained with us, we received considerable assistance from crew members who could be spared from the unloading. Captain Roberts and Pitt also lent a friendly hand. Although we had a fine day at the start of our building operations, a howling westerly wind lashed snow, sleet, and rain at us for most of those days. The last item to come ashore was thirty-five tons of soft coal for the heaters and two tons of anthracite for the cookstove, all in bags weighing about 200 pounds each. The last bag landed on 15 February, but

Marr prevailed upon the *Fitzroy* to lay over for another day because the erection of the building had not advanced to the point where it could be closed in. This delayed departure allowed the crew members to help sort out stores from the utter confusion. The last of our personal gear came ashore and, as we boarded the *Fitzroy* that night, we knew that the two vessels would leave the next morning—weather permitting.

At three o'clock in the morning of 17 February 1944, we roused from our bunks aboard ship and, after a cup of tea, listened to a brief but sincere speech from Back on the merits (to say nothing of the ethics) of building up his medical practice in his new territory. We had one for the road, and nine of us slipped down the side of the *Scoresby* into our little launch. Ashton was at the tiller and, as we swept away from the ship's side, a gust of wind whisked the only pork pie hat in Antarctica off of his head and carried it across the water toward the ice cliffs. We might have caught up with it, but it would have been unlucky to turn back. So we headed for our little cove and walked up the gentle slope to our home. Blair broke a Union Jack from the top of an old flagstaff on the summit of the islet as the two ships sailed away into the dreary grey morning.

We were tired. Since the first landing, the work had continued nightly until ten and eleven o'clock. The preceding night, we slept less than four hours aboard the ship. Under these conditions, our new home presented an unprepossessing appearance at half past three in the morning, with the fresh wind still carrying increasing flurries of snow through the open west end of the building. There was a roof on it but no floor. The windows were merely tacked in and threatened to blow out at any moment. We had no heat, fire, or chimney, but Berry bravely tried to cook in a small enclosure built of crates and boxes just outside the door of the building that was covered with two sheets of corrugated iron weighted down with stones. We began to lay the floor, nailing the boards almost mechanically until the task was complete at about noon. Berry produced bacon and eggs with a cup of tea at some point during the morning, but we stopped only long enough to gulp it down and scrape the congealed egg from the plate. By three o'clock that afternoon, we lashed a tarpaulin over the end of the building to keep the snow out. We dragged a large heater, christened "Big Bunty," aside a stovepipe laid horizontally in an open window frame. A warming glow of heat spread through the place. We turned into our sleeping bags on the floor and slept like lambs in our new building.

The next day we took things a little easier, but continued to work at a steady pace. On 22 February, we extended the north side of the building using the old Norwegian lumber from Deception Island with some of the wooden parts of the Nissen huts. The floor for this section was a very hard type of wood (it was rumoured to be West African). When hammering, its hardness readily bent our Norwegian nails into shapes that became known as "coat hangers." The wood was also warped and not accurately planed, so we usually had to force them into the shape of the previous board by using heavy wooden beams as levers.[1]

While working on the extension that would house our cabins and mess-room, we all lived in the original prefabricated "hut" that had no partitions save the small galley for Berry. He and I assembled an 850-pound Esse cooker from thirty-eight cases of hardware. We had a few bits left over, but the stove worked well, and Berry soon cooked some the most delicious meals imaginable under the conditions. The iron bedsteads gathered from Flett's base were put into immediate use, with five beds arranged along the north side of the room and four more along the galley side. We removed "Big Bunty" after an east wind all but suffocated us by blowing all its smoke back into the room. In its place, Ashton installed a small bogey heater in the centre of the room. Four benches set at two tables straddling the stove completed the room's furnishings. We were cramped, but enjoyed many happy times at this stage of our residence.

The interior partitions of our new extension were made from the sheets of beaverboard that came with the Nissen hut supplies. The partitions proved to be lightproof, but were neither windproof nor soundproof. They did, however, save a great deal of lumber that was, by this time, becoming scarce. We were forever picking over the bits of wood that were left and used many pieces that we had earlier discarded as scrap. Out of this scrap we built another 8 x 30-foot extension along the galley end of the two parts of the building we now had under way. Later, when Marr discovered the whaler's platform on Lécuyer Point, we fitted these oil-soaked planks together to create a third extension that became known as the corrugated iron annex. When lined with iron sheets, this area provided space for general storage and a small area where Farrington kept his motor generator set, batteries, and oil lamps. It also housed the cast-iron bathtub. Our sanitary facilities were housed at the far end, thirty feet away from the attachment to the house. These were gravity operated, and were installed after great deliberations by a specialist.

---

1.   Editors' note: This paragraph has additional content from Taylor, "The Private Journal of Capt. Andrew Taylor, R.C.E.," Taylor fonds, UMA, MSS 108, Box 3, File 11, p. 224.

As we continued building the house, I was introduced to some of the sailors' strange carpenterial terms. They were a little confusing to a landlubber but, once heard, one could quickly pick them up. The floor became the "deck," the front was the "forepart," and the rear was "aft," whether talking about a boat, a building, or a board. Boards themselves were sawn either "fore and aft" or "athwartships," partitions were "bulkheads," and the ceiling was the "deckhead." The outer edge of a piece of wood was its "outboard" side, posts or columns were the "stanchions," pieces of wood and other supplies that lay strewn around outside the house were "overboard," and lost components were "adrift." The kitchen was the "galley," rooms were "cabins," and any kind of cupboard was a "locker" to "store" one's "gear."

After the ships left, additional work depleted our construction gang. Berry and Blair focussed on cooking. Marr and Davies began work on sorting stores because it was essential to get these under cover before the advent of the winter. Farrington suffered an infected finger a few days after our arrival that required treatment several times each day and left him unable to attend to anything but radio work. Back, in addition to attending to bruises, cuts, and more serious injuries (such as Farrington's), was busily engaged setting up his meteorological station. Later on, when he completed his meteorological installation and his practice fell off, he gave Chippie much longer spells of his services. Ashton, Lamb, and I worked fairly continuously at the buildings until they were roughly completed, with Ashton doing the finishing himself.

To sum up our construction progress, the first load of lumber came ashore on 12 February and building commenced the same day. By the 17th, the first part of the workroom building became habitable and it was effectively complete by the 22nd, when work commenced on the part of the building that ultimately became the messroom. About 2 March, we began work on the porch extension that, along with the messroom, was complete by the time the *Scoresby* visited Port Lockroy for the second time on 19 March. Construction on the annex, the last part of the building, began on 29 March and was complete by the end of April.

The building, officially known as Bransfield House, was both commodious and comfortable. The occupants constructed bookshelves, cupboards, tables and other furniture to improve their cabins. Small rugs softened and brightened the floor. It was well worth the effort, for we were much more comfortable in this house than many people who reside in much more civilized localities.

Toward the end of March, Lamb and I erected a Nissen hut just to the east of the house site. We had to keep a sharp lookout on the remaining supplies in order to conserve sufficient materials from being appropriated for the interior furnishings. The site we chose was not as level as we would have liked—one corner had to be built up with stones to a height of about four feet—but this worked out to our long-term advantage. In the end, this adaptation made the hut much more capacious, since it contained no floor and held many more stores than would have otherwise been possible.

Davies and Marr sorted and assembled most of our stores into piles covered with tarpaulins. The canvas, however, became hard, brittle, and very difficult to handle when the temperature dipped to the low twenties Fahrenheit. Davies found that the easiest method of procuring a box out of one of these piles was to open up one corner of the tarpaulin, free it from the ice anchoring it into place, creep about inside, and wrestle the desired case out of the pile. It was, as he put it, "a job for a bed bug." As one blizzard after another roared across the base, cases that were not covered over gradually accumulated a layer of ice and snow until they were literally frozen into a solid mass cemented together by the ice. When the Nissen became available, Marr and Davies began to move the exposed cases. The job was exceedingly slow and tedious because each case required cleaning before it was deposited into the Nissen.

It was June before Marr and Davies had all of the stores stowed. The stores lined each side of the hut leaving a passageway in the middle. Racks hanging from the steel ribs supported the skis, sledge runners, slats, and other lengthy articles. To make the hut impervious to the blasts of driving snow carried by the high winds, Davies spent a great deal of time packing the small cracks and interstices in the building's corrugated iron covering. The sheeting was double nailed for strength and, although the frame of the building withstood some tremendous gales, the joints were not sufficiently tight to keep out the powdery snow that sifted through and covered everything.

The *William Scoresby* visited us twice during this construction phase. The first visit, already mentioned, occurred on 19 March. Although she did not carry any mail for us except messages from Port Stanley, we had all busily scratched off the last few lines for home before winter set in. As at Deception Island, we had our own set of stamps (in eight values up to the shilling) which were first postmarked on 12 February. Two naval lieutenants from the meteorological station at Port Stanley accompanied the ship, and they assisted us at Port Lockroy in attaching the rubberoid roofing to the roof. Before leaving for Port Stanley, the *Scoresby* landed for a few hours at Cape Renard, twenty miles south on the mainland.

The *Scoresby*'s second visit occurred rather unexpectedly in April. When the vessel left Port Stanley on this occasion, its crew did not expect to sail southward beyond Deception Island so late in the season. Ice conditions around Port Lockroy were so open, however, that Marr prevailed upon Marchesi to attempt a call at our base, and the *Scoresby* came through the narrow channels and reached Port Lockroy on 17 April without any trouble. On this occasion, she carried a heavy mail from overseas. Some of the items dated back to October 1943. Although the ship only remained with us overnight, we had time to read our mail and to write off one or two letters to those nearest our hearts. The ship sailed for Port Stanley again the next morning. (A few days later, on 23 April, we heard by radio that the Town Hall in Port Stanley—which also housed the post office and the heavy outgoing mail that the *Scoresby* carried north for us—completely burned down in a disastrous fire. The loss of these laboriously written letters was most disappointing news.)

By the middle of June our base neared completion. Ashton spent a great deal of time fitting and building shelves, workbenches, and cupboards, and these helped tidy the place up. The building was very habitable, divided by partitions into four general areas: the workroom, the messroom and cabins, the galley, and the annex or storerooms. The workroom measured 16 x 28 feet. Ashton built a small darkroom for Lamb along the north wall adjacent to the doorway. Across from this lay Ashton's workbench, while Marr, Lamb, and I each had a workbench on the east end of the room. Toward the opposite end, Back and Farrington had their apparatus.

The expedition had ordered a fairly extensive list of tools in London but they were lost amidst the mass of cases that had been discharged so rapidly out of the *Fitzroy*'s hold in February. Fortunately, Ashton brought ashore a little black wooden box with tools from his own collection, without which the progress of construction on our shelter would have been slow indeed. He used to try to collect the tools each night, but breakages and losses were frequent. To such a craftsman, the sight of our band of "wood butchers" losing and breaking these tools must have been heartbreaking. When we got a roof over our heads, these tools lay about on a table in terrible confusion for weeks during which time little attempt was made to sharpen them or keep them in shape. So one can readily understand Ashton's delight when he eventually constructed a

Figure 6. The biological and survey benches used by Lamb and Taylor at Bransfield House, 1 January 1945.

workbench for himself, complete with both a carpenter's and machinist's vise, a grindstone, shelves to store all of his small materials, and racks to hang his tools. Quite a few weeks went by before he finished sharpening and cleaning the tools to his satisfaction. He stored selected pieces of lumber under the bench, together with odd pieces of hardware too inconveniently sized to store elsewhere. Ashton put in many contented hours of work at this bench. Whenever anything broke, from the lid of a stove to the motorboat, it was Chippie who "fixed it"— and usually fixed it well.

Ashton could contrive to build from materials that, to the rest of us, seemed like absolute rubbish. We were all anxious that everything possible be done to supplement our diet of tinned goods with anything fresh, and the thought of fresh fish was most appealing. With this in mind, Marr had Chippie construct a wire-covered frame fish trap that we lowered through a hole in the ice into the water of the harbour. We used twenty pounds of seal meat as bait but, when we lifted the trap the next day, nearly all of the bait had been consumed by myriads of corn-yellow amphipods that clustered like bees over the remaining bits of protein. The trap also contained one small, diseased, and mouldy-looking fish, measuring about five inches in length. Marr immediately popped the specimen into a jar. This was the only fish that the trap ever caught, for it was moved to another locality about a week later, near one of the off-lying islets (the first of a pair called "Boogie" and "Woogie"). Unfortunately, a gale rose soon after, blowing away the ice through which the trap had been lowered. It was never seen again.

Ashton brought to us skill and industry, for he was a man who could not be idle and happy. It was amazing how, when all the supplies of timber seemed to have disappeared, Ashton still produced a few sticks from some secret hoard of his own that was just sufficient to do the job. For example, he made a pretty flagstaff from a few larch poles that he worked and polished for days. At the top of the poll perched a weather vane that he furnished out of scrap brass. The staff also supported one of Farrington's serials, and the flag ran up to the gaff in real naval fashion.

The east end of the workroom housed the scientific laboratory and library. I had one corner for my survey gear. Marr's corner was opposite to mine, and Lamb had the central portion. The zoological apparatus was fitted onto various stands and racks, involving a mass of test tubes, rubber hoses, funnels, filtering funnels, and cylinders, as well as reams of blotting paper and notebooks stowed beneath the bench which extended completely across that end of the room. There was a window toward the southeast corner of the building on this wall and, except for this opening, a massive bookcase housing the reference library took up almost the entire wall. Marr used half of the bookcase, and Lamb the other half for his books and photographic material.

In contrast to the other desks in the room, Lamb's was always neat and tidy. In one corner stood his microscope. A paper cone marked with the words "Unexploded Bomb" constituted a futile effort to keep inquisitive hands off the instrument. He spent many hours during the long winter evenings classifying his botanical specimens, carefully wrapping each in tissue paper and completely annotating an outer wrapping paper before packing it in the sturdy specimen cases he kept beneath the bench.

It was my good fortune to have the part of the bench that lay beneath the room's only window. In the long midwinter twilight during the months of May, June, and July, the position made little difference. Later in the year, however, when the sun had attained a good altitude, it became a most enjoyable place to work. The window overlooked a beautiful scene stretching above the ice cliffs of the Channel Glacier,[2] Wall Mountain, and the peaks of the Sierra du Fief. When the daylight was insufficient for inside work, we suspended a paraffin lamp midway between our desks.

In the early days of our stay at Port Lockroy, Lamb and I spent one Sunday afternoon building a set of shelves to temporarily store our clothing and other things. We built it on "Heartbreak Hill" where the unlevel surface ensured that the shelf turned out a bit "wonky." After finishing it, we came into the work-room and cleared sufficient stores and cases off the floor to make room for its temporary installation. When we went back out to retrieve our piece of early Antarctic furniture, however, the other lads piled almost everything moveable into the corner of the room that we had just cleared—and then set upon us to eject the shelves and the builders from the room. Fortunately, the structure was strong enough to withstand this tug-of-war. After Ashton erected large book-shelves above Lamb's bench, the latter willed me the "Piano" (as it was dubbed) which was reinstalled near my corner of the room and filled with my survey supplies. Overhead, a couple of map cases known as the "torpedo tubes" hung from the roof above it.

Back's "office" was located at the other end of the room beyond Ashton's workbench. On a table sat his books and meteorological apparatus. A liberal store of pills and medicines filled the shelves above. A pair of mercury barom-eters hung from gimbals on the galley wall, alongside the recording barograph and anemometer. The light was very poor at that end of the room, so Doc sel-dom did any serious work there.[3]

Farrington's radio station was set at the opposite corner of the same end of the room in a little alcove about eight feet in width. The receivers and the effi-cient little crystal-controlled Navy transmitter sat on the bench. The radio had an output of thirty watts, and it is amazing to consider that he used it one night to put a call directly through to London, about 9,000 miles away. It gave ex-tremely reliable service, and facilitated regular daily schedules with Port Stan-ley and Deception Island, 900 and 125 miles distant respectively. Occasionally, Farrington reached our friend Tim Hooley, who had by then returned to his job as chief operator at South Georgia and who related his family's latest news.

---

2. Editors' note: Today, Harbour Glacier.

3. Editors' note: This paragraph has additional content from Taylor, "The Private Journal of Capt. Andrew Taylor, R.C.E.," Taylor fonds, UMA, MSS 108, Box 3, File 11, p. 318.

Twice a day, Farrington put the BBC news through the loudspeaker in the mess-room. In the evening, he often let us hear the lilting music of South American stations, which pleasantly recalled the happy days we had spent in Montevideo.

The messroom and cabins took up the adjacent part of the building, measuring 28 x 19 feet. Except for the cabin occupied by Marr, each room was six foot square and accommodated two men. Although this seems a little cramped, they were actually quite comfortable and served their purpose of providing sleeping quarters and storage space for clothing. Ashton's experience as a ship's carpenter probably had a good deal to do with the efficient use of the space, for there was little to spare, and only one man could undress at a time in the rooms. A double metal bedstead measuring thirty inches wide occupied almost half of the cabin, with cupboards occupying one of the other walls.

Because the occupants fabricated their own furniture, each cabin had an individual character. Ashton's painted cabin was naturally the showpiece of Brans-field House, with red curtains and yellow bunting on the window. Either of these features would have been enough to distinguish it from any of the others, had one not noticed the furniture. Marr's 5 x 12–foot cabin, which he used as a private office and sleeping quarters, occupied the east end of the room. Its furniture was of the simplest design, and comprised of only a table and a small shelf. This seemed to suit him well enough, for he did not allow Ashton to improve it.

The balance of this extension made up our messroom, being about 11 x 20 feet. It was warmed by a small bogey or Quebec heater toward Marr's end of the room, while two small stanchions supported part of the roof along the inside wall. Our nine cups hung suspended from a shelf to one side of the doorway. Other shelves supported our dishes and cutlery. Looking around the room with the two paraffin lamps hanging above the table illuminated, one saw such articles as a gramophone and its stack of records, a bookcase, a fire extinguisher, clock and barometer, one of Farrington's loudspeakers, and a few maps of Graham Land and the Antarctic, as well as the flashlight that Back used for his trips out to the meteorological screen. In the centre of the room stood our ten-foot-long mess table. Along one side of the beaverboarded room that served as a notice board, a variety of cartoons of tropical interest cluttered the wall. Lamb's efforts in this latter respect were the best, and some of his masterpieces were left on the wall as part of the establishment upon our departure.

Berry's galley was in two sections of about 8 x 5 feet each. In one half, Berry worked with his Esse cooker, and his section was seldom invaded by anyone else.

Figure 7. Looking northwest to Goudier Islet and Mount William from the Summer Rookery. The individual in the foreground appears to be Taylor, December 1944.

In the other half of the room, where we melted snow for the water supply and washed the dishes, John Blyth was in charge. His galley stove, the two bogey heaters in the messroom and workroom, and another heater installed in the bathhouse, all burned soft coal.[4] The bathhouse heater burned only occasionally. The others were on from morning until night throughout the year, apart from a brief respite during some mild weather we enjoyed in December and January.

With the exception of a couple of hurricane lanterns used to light the passageways to the outhouse, we lit the base almost entirely by paraffin pressure lamps. These offered a good working light for close work.[5] Unfortunately, toward the end of the winter, when their parts became worn and they began to leak, these lamps produced a terrific amount of fumes that our hermetically

4. Author's note: We were supplied with what Berry proclaimed to be South African coal. There was a great deal of dross in some of the bags, and we used something under 20 tons of coal in the course of our year's occupation of the base.

5. Author's note: Candlelight generally illuminated the cabins.

sealed house did not allow to escape. The windows were completely sealed with ice, ensuring that no fresh air entered the building except when we left the door open. As a consequence, the interior atmosphere was badly befouled in July and August, causing nausea and headaches among us.

We were blessed with good weather for most of the base construction period, although occasional gales swept the area. Once the building was enclosed, there was plenty of inside work to do without losing any time to these blizzards. The temperature dropped rather gradually from the 35°F and 40°F above zero that we enjoyed at the time of our landing, to a little above zero in early June when we had virtually completed the outside work. For many of the construction days, the weather was clear and bright, with no wind and a cloudless sky. On such days we could fully appreciate the beauty of the setting in which our base lay.

Port Lockroy is sheltered in an arm of the sea that ate its way into the west coast of Wiencke Island's 200-foot ice cliffs. It is protected from the open sea to the west by Anvers Island sitting four miles away. Goudier Islet lies deep in

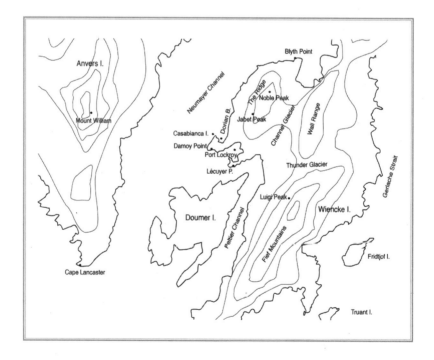

Map 4. Port Lockroy and its surroundings.

the bay among several other rocky islets that just succeed in struggling above the sea level. The visible expanse of sea before us was only a few miles in width, blocked to the north by Damoy Point, which was almost completely sealed in a smooth shelf of ice jutting westward from Wiencke Island, and to the south by Doumer Island, which rose to 1,600 feet. Almost without exception, the entire visible coastline consisted of a continuous wall of ice cliffs. These continually discharged into the sea during the milder season of the year, shimmering blue in the sunlight and sea green in the shadow.

Above Damoy Point, we could just see the summit of Mount Français fifteen miles away. Its distant, snow-covered, and broad-shouldered crest of greyish blue contrasted beautifully with the starchy whiteness of the nearby ice cap in the foreground. Mount Français, one of the highest known peaks along the coasts of Antarctica, forms part of the Osterrieth Range stretching continuously along the east coast of Anvers Island. Toward the south end of this range rises Mount William (4,800 feet). John Biscoe, who named it after his king in 1832, landed at the mountain's base and, thinking it to be the mainland, claimed it for Britain. From a sharp, snow-covered peak, Mount William's blanket of white gently slopes down for about 1,000 feet, terminating in fresh-faced, hanging glaciers. Between the leaning buttresses of rock that give the scene an impression of strength and great ruggedness, these glaciers discharge along their faces and chute down in tremendous icefalls of inexorable power before flowing outward over the fringing glacier at the foot of the mountain and spilling out amidst billowy clouds of snow smoke hundreds of feet high. The coastal glacier flows gracefully down toward the sea, straining and stressing itself as it passes over the convoluting rocks that support it so that huge crevasses mar the smoothness of its surface. On a calm sunny day, the sea mirrored this beautiful scene in colours that seemed even more vivid than the originals. On a calm moonlit night, the whites became greys, the greys became blacks, and this reflection lay tinselled with rippling moonbeams, silver on the surface of the sea.

The ridge of the Osterrieth Range continues northward toward Mount Français, but to the south of Mount William it drops off sharply, passing over two or three jagged crags before rising again to a round-topped, 2,500-foot eminence which we irreverently called William's Rump. From there it descends gently down to Cape Lancaster and the sea. As the eye sweeps eastward from Mount Français, it intercepts Jabet Peak in the foreground, crosses the smooth, moulded line of the Channel Glacier, and then climbs up toward the summit of

Wall Mountain, its flattened face confining the glacier. Wall Mountain is a part of the Sierra du Fief, which runs the full extent of Wiencke Island, paralleling the larger Osterrieth Range to the west. Two breaks occur in the continuity of this range on Wiencke Island: one just north of the midway point called the Nemo Glacier, and the other not far south at Thunder Glacier. Just to the south of Thunder Glacier is the highest point of the Sierra du Fief: the 4,600-foot Luigi di Savoia Peak. The southern end of the range is a most magnificent sight, extending into seven peaks—all over 3,000 feet high—strung out toward the south like the seven dwarfs after Snow White. The white carpet along the foot of Luigi fringes the Peltier Channel and climbs high up the face of the range in many places. Frequent avalanches and icefalls feed it through narrow rock chutes, like sand flowing through the neck of an hourglass. Huge buttresses of rock support the range; the near vertical faces seem black in the distance and, in the sunlight, have a perceptible lustre. If one searches well with glasses, large areas of malachite green- and brown-stained areas are visible on its face, leached and mulcted from its bosom by centuries of time, a challenge to collectors against whom the ubiquitous hanging glaciers, on a hair-trigger support, stand ever ready to unloose themselves upon anyone who dares accept the gauntlet. Above it all stands the "dual crown" of Luigi, as Jean-Baptiste Charcot described it when two of his men climbed to its summit during his first voyage in the *Français*.

On clear sunny days of summer these views reflect the loveliest of images in the water. The almost unbroken line of the ice cliffs marking the shore kaleidoscope along the water's edge. Below it lie inverted mountains. The black and white of rock and snow dominates the scene, but the blueness of the sky and the shimmering greens of the ice seem more intense and brilliant by reflection than in true image.

Even more spectacular are sunrises and sunsets when lurid reds and oranges paint the clouds, cap the mountain peaks, and tint the snowfields with the most delicate pastels. In the evenings, long after we had lost sight of the sun, the colours would slowly change upon the shifting cloud, altering the scene from one moment to the next as shadows climbed higher and higher up the mountainside, until the last red ray skipped past the highest summit and dusk returned. Then a curtain of darkness descended for the night, leaving only the murmurings of the penguins across the water.

CHAPTER SIX

The Winter Months

ON 22 MAY, THE SUN HID BEHIND MOUNT FRANÇAIS'S massive bulk and did not reappear until 24 July. For a period of two months, the best light we had outside was twilight. This period proved to be a most depressing time for us all. For a few weeks, the sun's disappearance had no perceptible effect upon our spirits. By the end of June, however, the continuous series of drab grey days, often made even gloomier by gales blowing for days at a time, proved monotonous in the extreme. We watched the shadow cast by the noonday sun rise higher and higher up Luigi Peak until shafts of light only cleared the top. At our latitude on the rim of the Antarctic Circle (64°50'S), the sun does not normally disappear, for even in the depths of midwinter, during the fourth week in June it rose at noon to an altitude approximately two degrees above the horizon. The summit of Mount Français, rising seven degrees high, rationed sunlight to us that was equivalent to a clear day at a 73°S.

In early July, the mountaintops were again bathed in occasional sunlight, and we watched them emerging day by day. As the days brightened, our spirits welled up from despondency. While out surveying on Damoy Point, a few hundred feet above sea level, some of us felt the invigorating rays of the returning sun on the 21st of the month for a few moments, but it was not until three days later that we saw them from the base.

Prior to the expedition's departure from England, the planners in London anticipated that we would conduct a good deal of scientific work during our first year in Antarctica. Some chaps found opportunities to fulfill this expectation almost immediately upon arrival at Port Lockroy. Back began taking his series of meteorological observations on 1 March. The work involved checking

Figure 8. Sunlight bathing the top of Mt. William, 10 July 1944.

his instruments six times each day. He also gathered information on sea-ice formation, observed passing bergs and pack ice, and took water samples to test for
salinity and sea temperatures. Even before the ships departed, Farrington used
his radio station to transmit Back's reports to the Naval Meteorological Branch
at Port Stanley which used the data in their compilations for weather maps and
forecasts that were transmitted to British ships at sea. In a limited way, Lamb
also made the best use of his opportunities by collecting botanical specimens
from Goudier Islet. This was a very limited area for him, but he was the first
botanist to have visited and wintered in this part of the world. He had high
hopes of extending his gaze over a considerable part of west Graham Land. My
surveying, even more than Lamb's work, depended upon an ability to travel.
The enclosed location of our base, encircled by high peaks and mountains, restricted the survey field. Since we were based upon an island in the midst of an
archipelago, we needed to travel either by ship or over the sea ice to accomplish
much useful work.

It was originally intended that we would land at Hope Bay with our own ship, the *Bransfield*. After establishing a base, we would have begun surveying the islands around Hope Bay with Marchesi's assistance. In addition to being skipper of the *Bransfield*, the latter was also a hydrographic surveyor. Later in the year, as the winter ice became suitable for travelling, this work would extend over some of the same ground that Nordenskjöld travelled through in 1902 and 1903.

The inability of the *Bransfield* to continue past Falmouth in November 1943 had necessitated a new plan, and led to the appropriation of the *Scoresby*. Although well built for polar survey work, the *Scoresby*'s lack of cargo capacity made her a poor substitute for the *Bransfield*. In addition, the *Scoresby*'s previous naval commitments at Port Stanley prevented her from completely co-operating with our plans. If the *Bransfield* had wintered alongside our base at Port Lockroy, she would have been available for our work until the end of the summer and well into the autumn. She also would have been ready for service immediately upon the spring breakup. With the *Bransfield*, we would have had transportation facilities by sea; without her, we had none.

The winter we spent at Port Lockroy was much milder than Rymill's British Graham Land Expedition of 1935 experienced when they wintered at the Argentine Islands, only twenty-five miles to the south. For example, our minimum temperature in 1944 was just −12°, while they experienced temperatures lower than −28°. Consequently, they endured ice conditions that were difficult to traverse, while we found no ice fit for travelling any distance. Although the bay in which our islet lay frozen solid, the Neumayer and Peltier Channels only frozen once during the winter and a gale completely dissipated these ice sheets a few days later. The mild temperatures' implications for our travel, however, were not immediately apparent to us. The end of September approached before we realized that our winter's journey would be confined to the glaciers of Wiencke Island. Until that time, we constantly hoped that sea ice would form and spent many hours preparing equipment and supplies for longer winter journeys.

On such a small islet as ours (its entire length was just over 400 feet), water supply during the summer months became a problem. The large deposits of limpet shells measuring several feet thick told us that black and white Dominican gulls had used the islet as a nesting place for many years, and their excrement discoloured many of the snow beds. We contaminated the only sizeable deposit of snow, located east of the house, with rotting carcasses of fresh meat. After a fresh snowfall, we could skim off the clean snow, but the advantages of this technique were neutralized by its poor yield. In winter, when lumps of glacial ice were frozen solidly in the ice, one could locate a convenient piece and chip away at it for days before exhausting this water mine and searching for another vein. We frequently resorted to this latter source of water during the winter when the interval between snowfalls extended to such an extent that the snowfield became contaminated. During the summer, the problem required a different approach. Our flat beach of stones and boulders, where the boats moored, was usually exposed by the tides twice a day, and bits of suitable ice frequently grounded there. If we happened to find a large chunk, we tied a line to it, making it fast ashore, and enjoyed a supply of freshwater that lasted for several days if a storm did not blow up. We had to be careful not to choose any old sea ice, which of course was salty, for this purpose. In the warm weather, even the glacial ice seemed to absorb some of the salt into its outer surface. There were great lamentations from all hands on the few occasions when the tea turned out salty.

We allowed the fires of Bransfield House to die down each night, except for the base stove in the galley, which burned continuously without having to be re-lit for the eleven months we occupied the building. When we first installed the heaters, we attempted to keep the fires in the messroom and workroom going all night, but we found that the additional heat was unnecessary and that the fumes interfered with our sleep. So one of the first jobs to be tackled each day was lighting these two heaters (the galley staff looked after their own two fires). At first this was done on a more or less voluntary basis, but when the same people attended the job, they eventually tired of the task. Others began to take an interest in the job after getting up to a cold house for a few mornings. Within a month, and without formal organization, each of us attended to these morning duties on a weekly rotation. The chore became known as the "bogey man's job," and generally began the night before with the preparation of kindling for the next morning's fires. At half-past seven on his duty morning, the "bogey man" rolled out of his warm bed, lit up a couple of lamps and the two fires, cleaned out the ashes, swept the floors, and prepared some hot water for the morning wash before the breakfast was ready at half past eight. He then filled the coal boxes (including the galley's), procured the following day's supply of ice and snow, and kept the fires going during the day. Toward spring, when some of us worked outside, Blyth gradually took over some of the snow and coal duties, insofar as they concerned the galley. It was a great thing for the "bogey man" when Ashton spent the preceding day doing carpentry work because it left an ample supply of shavings and firewood.

There were also other chores. Weather permitting, we cleaned out the "privy" once a week. Back seemed to keep a record by which he exuberantly reminded each of our turn to be the "honey man." Davies looked after the galley's requirements by retrieving a steady supply of foodstuffs from the Nissen hut when Berry requested them. His "bogey day" was Tuesday, and each week he carried coal from where the *Fitzroy*'s crew had dumped it near the dinghy harbour to a small stockpile near the house that was even accessible during blizzards. In the winter, after a good snowfall, he used his "handy billy" to pull the 200-pound coal bags up on a toboggan he made, but after the snow disappeared and his footing improved, he reverted to carrying them on his back.

Early in our sojourn at Port Lockroy, Davies and I both had our hair cut clean off our heads, so the problem of haircuts did not bother us for a few months. The others all became dependent on Ashton for this attention. He had considerable experience barbering aboard ship, and took to the task willingly enough. As a rule, each man expected a haircut every month or six weeks, usually in the evenings. In addition, it frequently fell to Chippie to trim the odd beard, for everyone tried to grow one except Davies, Berry, and myself. This is not to say that we three did not grow beards or, for that matter, that the others did. On the one hand, we would often go for a month without shaving, by which time quite a growth accumulated. On the other hand, Back was no nearer to having a beard at the end of our two years south than many of us were between shaves. The others, however, grew a "full set," and we did not see Ashton from behind his beard until our return to Port Stanley in 1946.

Even barbers require haircuts. I had once cut my brother's hair when illness kept him abed for a month, which allowed my mistakes to overgrow. By inadvertently mentioning this to Chippie long before the "Tabarin" barbering problem arose, I found myself cutting his greying thatch one night. The clippers stuck in his hair, and I had to cut them "adrift" with scissors, but on subsequent occasions I must have done a passable job because he always came back to me.

We were fortunate in having a cook of Berry's talent. Given the limited variety of our supplies, I do not think that anyone could have served up better meals than Berry and Blyth. Almost all of the food we consumed came from tins. We had tinned meats: spam, bully beef, tongue, and brisket of beef. Vegetables were usually dried and augmented by tinned peas, carrots, and asparagus;

the latter soon went bad with the frost. Our fruit was both dried and tinned. Dried eggs also caught up with us. In my own experience with survey and army cooks, I never ate as consistently well as I did at Port Lockroy. We ate for eight months unbroken by visitors or fresh supplies, yet the food did not become tiresome. The bread and pastry were excellent. The meat dishes were done to a turn and always served piping hot and perfectly seasoned on hotplates. Many cooks on this side of the Atlantic could emulate their example to advantage.

Breakfast usually began with porridge. This was followed by an omelet of some kind, or else ham or bacon with some "bubble and squeak"—a name given the fried-up remains of the preceding day's leftovers of potatoes and peas or cabbage. Sometimes, in place of this, we would have "dry hash" or tinned sausage with tomatoes. We only occasionally had scrambled eggs on toast because the galley staff considered making toast in adequate quantities to be a bit of a chore. It has always seemed to me that breakfasts are the most difficult meals to make and keep interesting, but Berry did not seem to have trouble accomplishing this.

We were all within shouting distance for breakfast, but Berry sometimes had to call us from outside for the other two meals. He had an army whistle, and in the cold weather he stuck his head out of the galley window to call. When it was warm, he stepped out on the back porch and let off a shriek that always received prompt attention. Lunch, which was served at one o'clock, was often cold meat and potatoes, with fruit for dessert, and sometimes a jam tart. Cottage pies, "sea" pie, and stews also found their way to the table with some frequency. In the evening, we ate our supper at six o'clock sharp. It began with soup concocted from a "stock"—the origin of which was as great a mystery to the rest of us as was the "sponge" from which Berry made his bread. Following the soup, we had Cornish pasties, bacon and beans, fish cakes, or meat cutlets devised from the tinned meats. The vegetables varied from boiled or mashed dried potatoes, peas, dried cabbage, fresh turnips (which kept well in the cold weather as did fresh onions), dried beets, dried or tinned carrots, or beans. For desserts, we generally had a "duff" or suet pudding, as we call it here in Canada, but we sometimes had fruit and occasionally jelly (which was scarce). Coffee frequently appeared with the evening meal as a change from the tea we drank throughout the rest of the day.

Besides the three daily meals, tea was available at 7:30 a.m., 11:00 a.m., and again at 4:00 p.m. We ate like those aboard ship: well and often. Saturday evening, the occasion of someone's birthday, and other special occasions prompted special meals. We anticipated such days with keen delight, and this did much to ameliorate the drabness of our isolation. Like naval personnel, all hands received an issue of rum each night.

On 21 June, as is customary in the "deep" south, we celebrated Midwinter's Day: the day when the sun reaches its lowest altitude. In our case we could not see the sun, since its altitude was less than two degrees. We celebrated our Midwinter's Day well and truly, by sleeping in, skiing at the rookery in the afternoon, and enjoying an excellent dinner in the evening. The menu for the latter event was as follows, and few lasted the course:

Hors D'Oeuvres
Puree of Pea
Fried Pilchards
Asparagus au Beurre
York Ham
Potatoes: Baked and Croquette
Garden Peas
Plum Pudding—Hard Sauce
Macedoine Fruit on Jelly
Mince Pies
Coffee

With a few drinks to enliven the proceedings, we had a most enjoyable day. In the midst of the evening's celebrations, a message arrived for Marr announcing that he had become the father of a son, his first, which gave the party new impetus and carried it far into the night.

We were never short of food-stores, but we subsisted entirely upon tinned goods, except for the meat we obtained by killing seals. We never shot seals for sport; we only hunted them for food. No crabeater seals happened to come our way, but we shot half a dozen Weddells. These huge and ungainly animals, which are eight to ten feet long and weigh about 800 pounds, came out onto the ice through holes they cut themselves or through a tide crack. They were seldom noticed in stormy weather but on mild, though perhaps overcast days, and in bright sunshine in colder weather, they lay like slugs on the sea ice. One could approach to within a few feet of them before they would pay the slightest attention, and even then they rolled over on their backs and looked up with

Figure 9. Lieutenant Commander J.W.S. Marr, RNVR, on skis, n.d.

their huge trusting brown eyes watering before subsiding back into the slumber from which we disturbed them. They have a three- to four-inch-thick layer of fat called blubber that covered their entire body except for the head, tail, and flippers. Even after leaving a carcass for two days, we never saw blubber freeze. Each animal has such a mass of blubber that there is comparatively little meat, considering their size. We found their liver to be almost indistinguishable from beef liver. Their black steaks had a slight blubbery taste, but when smothered with onions they were a welcome alternative to the tinned steak and kidney pudding that few of us seemed to appreciate.

The pelt of the Weddell seal is not fur. It is composed of a greenish-yellow coarse hair (though parts are almost black) with a definite grain that lies toward the tail. We used strips of these seal pelts to cover the underside of our skis. When firmly laced in place, they prevented any backward slip of the skis while pulling heavy loads or in climbing a slope. While cutting the strips, care had to be exercised to ensure that the grain was parallel to the ski, otherwise steering became difficult.

In order to ward off any possibility of scurvy, Back mitigated the deficiencies of fresh foods in our diet by feeding us ascorbic acid tablets from almost the moment we stepped ashore. Normally, these are small, white pellets a little over an eighth of an inch in diameter that possessed a citric taste. For the first three months, while our diet contained a certain amount of fresh meat and vegetables, Back doled us out one tablet each day at the evening meal. As the fresh meat component of our diet decreased, Doc increased our ration from one to two pills a day. Two boxes out of three that we received were of a dingy brown hue and tasted so much like salt that one questioned their value. No one ever had any symptoms of scurvy at Port Lockroy, however, so they were probably effectual enough. Later in the year, those who went sledging also took an Adexolin tablet daily. It had a fruity flavour and was no effort to take.

Given the confined nature of our winter activities, we had a good deal of time on our hands in which we were left pretty well to our own devices. We each had certain household tasks to perform, routine work to attend to, and our own methods of expending our leisure. One of the few pastimes we enjoyed during this long spell of midwinter twilight was skiing, which was all the more thrilling in the half-light. None of us had much experience at it and, having no book of instructions, we learned the hard way. We began in early May when the sea ice around the base was just beginning to form but was not yet strong enough to support our weight. The newly fallen snow that lay over the gentle slopes of our islet offered a good place to learn, and on Sunday afternoons everyone except Berry practised. It was seldom that one of us did not plough face-first through the deep drifts on such a day. Later, when the sea ice bridged the gap across to Lécuyer Point where the rookery had been, we had access to steeper slopes. Within a few weeks, we could all negotiate the run from the 150-foot summit, though the journey was not always non-stop—and some of the interruptions were quite violent. We were rather fortunate in having no serious accidents—except for Blyth, whose injured thumb ultimately caused his return to Port Stanley for an x-ray and treatment.

One fine day in early May, before building operations finished, Lamb, Davies, and I made a day trip onto the Channel Glacier to the east of the base. We each carried thirty-five-pound loads and ascended a steep snow ridge of curious formation from Lécuyer Point. We called it the Knife Edge because it is a sharp razorback of ice and snow with a top that is only a few inches wide during the summer. (The tip of the glacier lies at the confluence of two winds, one from the east and one from the northeast.) It extends southwesterly from the glacier for about 200 feet, and the tip of it overhung the sea in a 150-foot-high cornice. We edged along it until we found ourselves on the glacier and, at an elevation of 300 feet, we stopped to do a little surveying and take some photographs. We continued another mile or so up the glacier until we attained a 700-foot elevation below Jabet Peak and then turned westward toward the long glacial tongue extending onto Damoy Point north of the base. In the bright morning sunlight we had a magnificent view of the steely blue waters of the Peltier Channel that were fringed with glistening cliffs of ice and the snow-capped Sierras. Beyond the end of the channel, we could see Booth Island where Charcot wintered with the *Français* in 1904. Far below, nestled in the shelter of Port Lockroy, lay Goudier Islet and our two little buildings, lost in their own insignificance amidst the grandeur that surrounded us.

Without skis or snowshoes, we trudged wearily down the gentle slope, and the light of day waned as we cleared the base of Jabet Peak with the moon rising from behind Mount Français to the north. We had made previous arrangements for Marr to meet us in the dinghy, and we searched in the dusk for a place where we could descend to the sea 250 feet below us. Yet we could find nothing except the sharp edge of the ice cliffs dropping vertically to the water. We knew that there was an ice formation in the vicinity similar to that of the Knife Edge

Figure 10. Lamb and his "igloo," 14 August 1944.

that, we hoped, would facilitate an easy descent—but it was difficult to locate in the gathering dusk. At last, I thought I could see the top of it, and Lamb and Davies lowered me on a rope down the side of the cliff. My feet touched a more or less level surface, which proved to be what we had been searching for, and the others descended some ice steps that we cut. We began descending the steep slope and met Marr halfway to the bottom. Blyth having accompanied him, we returned to the base in the dinghy.

We also did some local surveying from stations around Damoy Point toward the end of July. We hauled a sledge-load of equipment up the steep but gently rounded slope of the glacier by hauling on a "deadman" buried in the ice near the top of the slope. From this point onward, we were able to ski over smooth slopes down to Darian Bay. Just off the tip of Damoy Point, open water persisted almost across the channel and we saw shags sporting about in the water of Casabianca Islet. We spent several days at this work, returning each night to the base over the sea ice.

Lamb's receptivity to novel ideas distinguished him early on as one of the most inventive members of the base. It was no great surprise to find him constructing an igloo one day in early August, having read instructions in an army pamphlet. He first built a small igloo about six feet in diameter near the Nissen hut, which proved quite satisfactory. Later, he and I built a full-sized one that measured about twelve feet across near some derelict scows that had lain for thirty years above the little beach of Goudier Islet. We smoothed the igloo over the loose snow and made a little tunnel entrance. Just before the snow house was complete, we had a contest to see who could—or rather who could not—get through the small entrance aperture at its base. Interest seemed to divide itself equally between Berry and me, but I managed to squeeze through it, while Berry got stuck in the hole and had to be pulled out by the heels.

Later on, Lamb and Davies went into the construction of igloos on more or less a mass-production basis. They devised a design that required digging several feet into the snowfield before erecting the superstructure on top. The plan required just twenty blocks of snow to roof it in, compared to about sixty for the hemispherical igloo, and they built it in about an hour and a half, compared to five hours for the other. Public interest in this type of igloo waned rather suddenly, however, after Davies found himself excavating the floor directly over a yawning crevasse on Channel Glacier. His construction site was a snow bridge! A few days after completing these igloos, we had some mild weather followed by several days of gales of driving snow. The high hemispherical igloos were completely worn away following the gales, but the low-roofed ones withstood the storms well. Unfortunately, we had never any occasion to make practical use of all this arduous scientific research.

Our base was equipped with two boats: a very sturdily built dinghy (which was also very heavy) and an inboard motorboat. Both were in great demand during the unloading operations from the *Fitzroy*, when several ship-to-shore taxi services operated. Following the ship's departure, we had little time to use them and they sat at their moorings in our little harbour until the frost caught them. We went down one day to chop them free from the ice's clutch, and hauled them over the sea ice onto the rocks of our islet where they spent the winter in the snow banks. We had hopes of having more use of them in the spring when we expected to have time to visit accessible parts of Doumer Island.

These were, as I have said, dreary days. The prospect of accomplishing any worthwhile journey decreased as each month slipped by without the formation of adequate sea ice. We filled the passing days and long evenings as best we could. Lamb remarked in his diary on 7 March that the gramophone had been unpacked and that we "greatly enjoyed the musical selections in the evenings." I think now he would be first to agree that there were times when these selections were a little tiresome. Some chaps chose the same records from the station's collection of 150 each time they played the machine, and we found ourselves anticipating every note and inflection as some tunes wore deeper and deeper grooves into the same records night after night.

We had a good and extensive library of about 600 books. Some were scientific and dealt with the Antarctic. We augmented this collection with our own materials. Farrington had some of the most interesting volumes, dealing with the exploits of Scott, Shackleton, Bruce, Nordenskjöld, and their contemporaries, who led the 1,000 or so men who had wintered in the Antarctic since time began. Nordenskjöld's *Antarctica*, the copy of which belonged to Marr, was in particular demand, not only because we had expected to spend that very winter at Hope Bay, but also because we still hoped to reach Nordenskjöld's country the following summer.

Early in the year, Marr, Blyth, Berry, and Back formed a foursome that played the card game "Solo" almost nightly on the messroom table. For the first few months they all found it of absorbing interest, but as the months crept by it seemed to an onlooker that it became more a duty than a pleasure, each being apprehensive of withdrawing for fear of causing a break in the partnerships that would spoil the others' pleasure. Nonetheless, it expended time and continued, inexorably, night after night.

Davies and Farrington were both great readers, but the latter did not have as much free time in the evenings as most of us on account of radio schedules with both Deception Island and Port Stanley. These tasks often occupied him until nine or ten o'clock. Davies was of quite an ingenious bent, and combined this with a natural facility to work with his hands. Having spent so much time at sea, he was very handy with a needle and palm, and made many of the canvas articles for our sledge journey. From bits of scrap wood, he made up two toboggans that served us well for two years. He worked at Ashton's bench and used his tools with a great deal more care than others did. He was meticulous about returning the tools to their proper places, a habit which Ashton greatly appreciated, as few things upset him more than being in the midst of some of his own work and failing to locate a tool.

Lamb spent many long evenings at his microscope, examining lichen specimens. He, too, was infected with the bug to create something, however, and generally had a job to work at during odd moments. He attempted to make an enlarger for his Leica films by using some of the lenses from a panoramic survey camera, but met with limited success. In trying to overcome the disadvantage of added weight from the sealskins on skis, he devised a small pair of wooden brakes and attached them to the stern of his skis. They were about six inches long and various spectators viewed their trials but, alas, the "galloping mousetraps" failed. Lamb, however, was not generally met by such ill-success in his manufactures and inventions. He made a couple of pairs of fine slippers from sealskin, which he sent home to his wife and son, that would do credit to one of far wider experience in this craft.

Lamb also spent a great deal of time at photographic work, with great success. Ashton and Lamb built a small darkroom along one wall of our workroom. Inside, Lamb installed the photographic apparatus. He was soon busy developing films exposed from the *Scoresby*'s last visit. Lamb did all of the developing and printing of photographs taken by both Marr and Farrington. He also assisted me in handling some ungainly six-foot lengths exposed by the panoramic camera, and helped build a large wooden wheel for the purpose. Lamb had two cameras that he used himself: a Leica 35-mm and a Sanderson plate camera. He obtained some wonderful results with both. Many of the subjects taken with the plate camera were lichens, and showed remarkable detail. He also caught fine views of the surrounding country and was most generous in making prints for his companions.

In the evenings, Ashton was the most industrious worker. He enjoyed making things. After completing a job, he had little further interest in it; but until that moment, there was no time to lose. It was several months before the interior of the house was finished and he had much opportunity to do his own work at nights. About 1 July, however, he began working regularly on his little models. The most fascinating of these were the ships in bottles. He made a little model of a four-masted fore-and-aft schooner that was about four inches long and included riggings, hatch covers, sailing lights, and a little flag flying from a halyard on the jigger mast. Sometimes he even added signal flags. When the little ship was varnished and painted, it looked like a perfect picture. Coloured putty formed the sea in which the ship lay, and included both waves and whitecaps. He even painted hills and clouds as a background. The puzzle to the uninitiated was how he ever got them into the narrow-necked Johnny Walker whisky bottles. He never let anyone watch him fit the ship into the bottle, but took the two parts away with him to his cabin. The next time we saw it, perhaps only a few moments later, the ship was set in her putty sea as prettily as the time we had last viewed it outside of the bottle. He made thirteen of these while we were at Port Lockroy, setting each one into a teakwood stand, and gave one to each of us there, distributing others later to various people at Port Stanley. Each bottle cost Ashton about twelve hours of skillful labour.

Another striking model was a two-masted schooner which Ashton furnished from odds and ends of wood and metal that were only rubbish until he set to work on them. With a nine-inch beam and masts 3.5 feet high, it was about four feet in length to the end of the bowsprit and was fitted with a leaden keel. The hull was sheathed on hardwood ribs, and the little vessel was fitted with an automatic steering gear. Other materials used to complete the model included rifle and shell casings, fish line, and old toothbrush handles. He painted the hull red and used white above the plimsoll line. The officers of the *Fitzroy* and *Scoresby* examined the model with envious eyes when they paid us a call later in the year.

Physically, we were all soft when we arrived at Port Lockroy following our pleasant but long voyage from England. In itself, this fact is of little interest, but it offers the only reasonable explanation for an odd epidemic condition that we all suffered in the early days. In almost every instance when our hands suffered a cut, bruise, or abrasion, a festering sore began. Even Ashton, who was quite accustomed to calloused hands, felt this condition. Back had us wash each evening in hot, disinfected water, but it was nearly a month before the last of these sores healed up. The Norwegian nails we had picked up at Deception Island were made of black iron, and the edges of their square-shaped sections were razor sharp. But they had lain at Whaler's Bay for many years and most of them were rusted to some extent. To these we attributed most of the cuts we received. Whatever the cause of the trouble may have been, the sores left us in March and did not return.

A few injuries were of a more serious nature. One of Farrington's fingers took much longer to heal and eventually had to be lanced by Back in March. During this first month, both Blair and Lamb were down for three or four days with tonsillitis. Shortly afterward, Lamb was again incapacitated by an attack of chronic lumbago. Aside from these ailments, and one occasion when Berry's terpsichorean activities cost him a broken bone in his foot and a plaster cast for a month, we all enjoyed excellent physical health.

We lived under no great mental strain. Yet in such confined and isolated quarters it is natural that tempers are more easily frayed than in more civilized conditions. There were occasional flare-ups, and we had our likes and dislikes among each other. Fortunately, no altercation assumed any serious proportions. We found that dispositions were subject in a large measure to the weather. When we lost the sun in the middle of winter, spirits were low, we became more easily annoyed, and the petty details of a life spent largely indoors occupied our attention. Slowly the days became brighter, however, and with them our spirits kept pace. Finally, when the sun rose high in the sky as it did in November and December, our spirits and morale became quite irrepressible, and practical joking became a daily feature of our lives.

Naturally, each being of different temperaments, we did not all react in the same degree either to the fits of depression or to the spells of exuberance. People such as Lamb, who possessed a remarkably even temper under any circumstances, reacted more slowly to these cycles than most of us. His sense of humour made him the greatest practical joker among us, and by far the subtlest. The absorbing interest he found in his work, and his open mind to experimentation, all coalesced to make even our humdrum life interesting to him. Accordingly, he was not bothered by the petty distractions that agitated some of the others. One of our members reacted much more sensitively to our daily trials and tribulations and had a much more volatile temper that soared up and down almost day by day. We did not live the keyed-up life which one normally experiences in a city or town. There were no telephones to answer, no letters by means of which creditors make contact, no hum and bustle of traffic to dodge, no meetings to attend, and no bridge clubs. The regular schedule of living that became automatic after we settled into Bransfield House made for regular meals, regular habits, and gave the body its best chance to function healthily.

The party received its first clothing issue aboard the *Bransfield* on her intermittent voyage down from the English Channel. The sight of such masses of clothing might have made Buck decide to part company with us at Falmouth! When new arrangements for our departure from England developed, we repacked this clothing, and it was not reissued until we departed Port Stanley. On this occasion we were provided with sea boots, army boots, flannel pants, and a white jersey, as well as several pairs of socks. I recollect my trousers fitting me well around the waist but only reaching a point on my leg midway between the knee and ankle. I found myself wondering if they were not relics of the days of Buck, for they would have fitted a man of his build much better than the comical figure they made of me. The flannel pants looked well on most of the chaps when they were first worn, but after a few days on Davies's "Heartbreak Hill" the wire-bound cases had torn and ripped some of them to expose a greater area of their wearer than of pants.

Later in the season we were issued windproof suits, comprising trousers, a parka of a material like Grenfell cloth, and an inner heavy blanket-wool anorak. This garment was the most useful of all that we possessed. We usually wore it without the inner lining. The two parts of the windproof suit were very light and gave maximum of protection from the windchill, as well as great freedom of movement while working. Other clothing, such as ski boots, woollen underwear, mukluks (sealskin boots), shirts, and sweaters, were all issued on a lavish scale. All but the trousers and a poor woollen balaclava were of excellent quality.

Our greatest interest during the winter was the sledge journey that we hoped to make from Port Lockroy. Plans for it, always a bit sketchy, were at their best on a Saturday night following one of Berry's special dinners, when the "armchair sledgers" gave their imagination free rein. In the early days, before the winter set in, we used to talk of a quick run across the Graham Land Peninsula via the sea ice as a "warming up" trip, before making the main journey, the route of which carried us many miles from our armchairs. But as the mild weather continued, and there was no sign of the sea freezing, our plans changed, and this dash across Graham Land became our principal object. Still later, when July crept into August, and August became September, it was evident that we were not going to be able to use the sea ice to go more than a few miles from the base, for the back of the winter was by that time broken.

CHAPTER SEVEN

The Manhauling Journey of 1944

PREPARATIONS FOR THE SLEDGE JOURNEY BEGAN as soon as the base was safely established. We had no mechanical transport or dogs, so we knew that it would be a manhauling journey. The party would be comprised of four men with Marr as leader, Lamb as botanist, Davies as handyman, and myself as surveyor. The preparations were largely made by Marr and Davies, who manufactured much of our equipment from canvas and thread, using the well-known sailor's palm and needle to make intricate manhauling harnesses, ground sheets, and tarpaulins. Preparing food supplies also occupied much of their time. I was told that they used Scott's 1912 ration schedule but increased his 33.3 ounces per man-day to about forty-one. The ration had little variety, but was comprised of staple foods with high nutritive values and minimal weight including pemmican, biscuits, fats, sugar, oats, chocolate, milk, cocoa, peaflour, bacon, and Marmite (varying in the order given from eight ounces a day of the pemmican to 1.1 ounce of the Marmite). Every item was repacked into tins and fitted into boxes that were about a foot square on their end sections and wide enough to fit across the sledges. Each sledge carried four fifty-five-pound boxes containing about thirty-five pounds of food. In actual practice, we consumed about 28.7 ounces per man-day and a single box sustained two men for ten days.

Lamb and I assembled the two twelve-foot Nansen sledges. They were made entirely of wood and most of the joints were bound together with rawhide lashings with a few connections made with steel clamps. A semicircular "cowcatcher" protected the front of the sledge, and the stern had a pair of wooden handlebars. The runners were about five inches high, and the slatted deck gave approximately five inches of clearance above the base of the runners. There

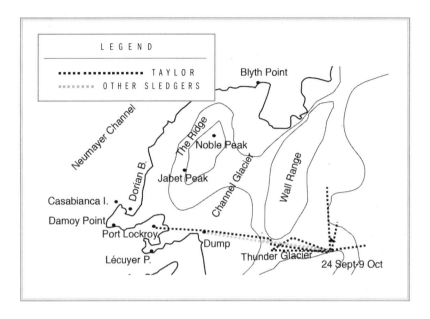

Map 5. The manhauling journey, 22 September to 9 October 1944.

were also grablines along the side for lashing loads. Each sledge had rope brakes that ran under the runners and bit into the snow when in use. When completed, each sledge weighed about seventy pounds.

The sledge Lamb and I used also sported an ingenious ten-pound sledge meter devised by Ashton. It measured distance by counting the movement of a paddle wheel tripped by each revolution of a bicycle wheel. It worked satisfactorily most of the time, but occasionally jammed without our noticing it. We consequently tried to check the distances of our courses by other means whenever possible.

The tents were a design commonly used in polar work: pyramidal with six-foot-square bases to accommodate two men. They were double lined, with four poles at the corners sheathing into the inner wall made of light white balloon fabric. A heavy canvas cover of the same pyramidal shape fitted over this frame. It included aprons or flaps measuring about a foot wide at the base which we anchored to the ground by heaping on snow and banking our sledges. Their entrance was a circular aperture on one face about three feet in diameter. These tents provided very serviceable, albeit cramped, quarters and their relatively small cubical content facilitated easy and quick heating. A two-inch hole at the apex ventilated the tent of the gaseous fumes given off by the cooker apparatus.

The stove used was the ordinary Primus, generally used by polar travellers. It weighed about four pounds and burned paraffin oil, of which each sledge carried six gallons. We had the usual trouble keeping the jet cleared with the little prickers supplied for the purpose but it was our own fault for not straining the paraffin first. Our cooking utensils were heavy black pots and Marr had their handles cut off to accommodate a patent potholder. We also had a small frying pan.

The party was equipped with quite an elaborate quantity of scientific equipment—more than would normally have been necessary for the journey we were about to make. The purpose of taking this additional equipment was to test out plans that contemplated using the *Scoresby* to make a survey of West Graham Land through a series of astronomic fixes at intervals along this coast. The plan entailed using two parties leapfrogging each other as we proceeded up the coast, with the ship surveying the intervening shoreline. Upon each landing, the survey teams would complete their work as soon as possible and use the remaining time before the ship returned to study their surroundings' biology and geology. The plan intended that we occupy a station on the east coast of Wiencke Island to make a complete series of observations of the Danco Coast across the de Gerlache Strait. From this station, useful estimating information could be gathered in addition to the survey itself. If our plan to occupy Hope Bay did not materialize, we expected to execute this scheme as an alternative operation.

When the sledges were completely loaded, each weighed in excess of 500 pounds. Marr set a tentative starting date of Monday, 18 September. On that dull afternoon, with the temperature just below freezing, we moved our sledges toward the rookery over sea ice sticky with salt. There was no wind and it was comparatively pleasant pulling over the level sheet of ice. No sooner did we encounter the slopes of the rookery than we discovered that two men were not sufficient to haul each sledge's weight. We doubled up, and Farrington also gave us a hand getting the sledges to the base of the Knife Edge. Davies wore a pair of *truger* (miniature snowshoe strung with string instead of gut) on his feet. I wore the sealskin-covered skis while Lamb and Marr went "barefoot" to determine which was the most practical footwear for the trip. The sledges were unloaded box by box and taken up the steep 150-foot slope of the Knife Edge and along its razor-like spine

Figure 11. Conducting a survey while the others eat lunch near the base of Wall Mountain, n.d.

for the couple of hundred feet it took to reach the lower slopes of the Channel Glacier. Then we hauled up the two empty sledges and reloaded them.

The next morning, we awoke to a gusty wind, a light snowfall, with evidences of fog here and there. The Boss decided to go on with his plan to pull the two sledges up the glacier toward its summit, establish a dump of stores, and lighten the sledges for the journey ahead. The weather deteriorated rapidly as we skied over the sea ice. By the time we reached the point on the glacier where we left the sledges, the falling snow had thickened and the driving wind made it impossible to see beyond a couple of hundred feet. We would have been travelling blind along the verges of the 200-foot ice cliffs, so Marr decided to return to the base. A strong north wind whipped our faces as we skied down the slopes of the rookery blindly. Fog set in that night.

On the morning of 20 September, we started out to do the job we had intended to do the previous day before a storm broke around us. Ashton came along to help us, as did Back and Farrington about noon. The six inches of snow that fell during our absence from Knife Edge greatly improved the skiing but impeded hauling the sledge. Hooking onto the sledge at 10:40 a.m., the five of us started from the Knife Edge up the comparatively gentle slope of the Channel Glacier. The sledge carried additional stores, including some skis, and weighed close to 700 pounds. The weather had been fine when we had left Goudier Islet, but a bank of fog lay over the glacier, and we soon penetrated it as we gained elevation. At 11:45 we reached an altitude of 610 feet, and Marr decided to make a dump about two miles from the Knife Edge. The temperature was −23°F with a slight wind.

We had a most enjoyable ski run back to the Knife Edge, and tied our harnesses to the second sledge. Back and Farrington again lent a hand. This one slid along much more easily and we were back at the dump at 1:45 p.m., where Marr and Davies sorted over the stores to be left at this point. We took a week's supply of food and paraffin. With reduced loads, our sledge carried approximately 430 pounds of equipment and stores while the other had something under 400 pounds. We had a light lunch of tea and coffee, which Ashton thought far too light for the work we had done, and were back at the base by 5 p.m.

We left the base to begin our trip at a quarter past ten on Friday morning, 22 September. The fog lifted off the glacier and the sun shone brightly upon Goudier Islet. Ashton again accompanied us to lend a hand with the initial part of the day's hauling. A good depth of snow lay over everything, making it beautiful for skiing. As we stood upon the Knife Edge, we looked down upon the ice of Port Lockroy and saw our tracks standing out like a highway from the air. We ran into fog, however, before reaching the dump, and visibility dropped to about 400 feet. Our sledge was the heavier of the two, so Ashton gave us a hand as we swung gradually in a wide arc toward the south, keeping as near as we could judge to the base of the Wall Mountain. It was difficult to keep a course in the fog, but we did not get far before Back—who was following our tracks—caught up with us and helped on the other sledge just as the sun began to break through the fog. He pushed at the stern and they passed us with Back's feet moving in short, quick strikes so that the *truger* threw up a continual spray of snow behind him like water from the stern of a paddle-wheel steamer. We frequently crossed crevassed areas that were carpeted deeply in snow, over which one could hear the hollowness of his tread as we crossed the ice bridges. We hauled our loads at about a mile an hour, and stopped for lunch just after one o'clock. We stood directly below the summit of the Wall Mountain Range, about half a mile from its base, and enjoyed a fine view to the south down the Peltier Channel. We could also see toward the snowfield separating Luigi Peak from Wall Mountain that we subsequently called Thunder Glacier. Six miles to the south, the outline of Cape Errera reminded us of the Rock of Gibraltar.

After lunch, we made for a sloping column of snow that jutted out from the mountain. The other sledge again passed us on this slope, but shortly after rounding it, they came upon a steep sidehill that had to be negotiated before we could descend to the floor[1] of the glacier. They decided to run their sledge straight down the steep slope at right angles to the direction we were pursuing. With Davies and Back braking at the stern, Marr guided the nose of their sledge downward.

In the meantime, we continued on our course. The gradient was not so steep as it had at first appeared, but there was a troublesome side slope that tended to overturn the sledge. With Lamb and Ashton tied to the stern and supporting our sledge from farther up the hill, I remained on the front, and we guided it down the sidehill without much difficulty. We finished several hundred feet farther on our way than the other sledge, and saved fifty feet or so in altitude.

Our self-congratulations were interrupted by loud lamentations from Doc who was squawking at us like Donald Duck. In lowering their sledge down the slope they had run along the longitudinal axis of a crevasse, broken a runner through an ice bridge, and jammed the sledge. Having made a line fast to the sledge we tried to pull it out without success. It had to be unloaded before we could budge the thing. As it was now four o'clock, Back and Ashton left us to return to the base. Lamb and I went ahead to our sledge and began to pull it up the steep incline over deeper snow. Tiring, we made frequent stops as we slowly toiled up the slope.

Marr and Davies, with the lighter load, soon caught up with us half a mile or so past the crevasse. Marr suggested doubling up, and they hitched themselves to our sledge. We started out with renewed vitality for the glacier's summit. We skirted the foot of Wall Mountain to avoid losing any of the altitude we had so laboriously attained, and dragged our sledge to 800 feet above the sea. A hundred feet ahead, a broad ridge led toward the centre of the glacier, and we swung along this, slowly receding from the base of the mountain. The snow surface flattened out; it was so noticeable that it felt like a depression. A roughened surface appeared immediately ahead, and as Lamb and Davies had made a day trip up to this glacier summit a few days previously, I asked Lamb if he had noticed any crevasses in this vicinity on that occasion. Lamb's diary recounts how he suggested to me that:

---

1.   Editors' note: The floor of a glacier is the surface of its horizontal middle.

these large blocks of ice with which the surface was littered were probably derived from ice avalanches from the summit of the mountain beside us: we looked up and sure enough, there was a huge hanging glacier of blue ice perched precariously on the top. We now realized that we were in a dangerous position, and exerted our strength to get further up and out of it with all speed; but it was too late. Less than a minute afterward, there was a report like a gun above us, and from the summit at which we had been looking up to a moment before, we saw hundreds of tons of snow and ice hurtling down the 2,000 feet of cliff face to our left. For some time, probably only a second or two, we stood still in our harness gazing in a kind of fascination at the destruction coming down to overwhelm us; the white curtain dropping at ever increasing speed, with bouncing and hurtling ice blocks dimly seen among it as through a cloud of steam. Some kind of instinct made us throw off our traces[2] and start running, but we had only gone a few yards to the lee [side] of the sledge when it was upon us; we threw ourselves flat on the snow. We felt a tremendous gust of wind blow over us, and everything was blotted out by fine snow forced into one's eyes, one's ears and one's mouth. I covered my face with my hands, and thought of the ice blocks which I had seen coming down; surely it was our finish. Then I became aware that the wind had dropped, the terrible thundering noise had ceased, and one could see again. We had escaped. We picked ourselves up, white from head to foot with powdered snow. My hat and mitts had been blown off me and were lying half buried in the snow about five yards away. The sledge was undamaged. We lost no time in pulling out of that dangerous place.[3]

Nothing but the snow smoke reached the 500- or 600-foot distance we were from the foot of the mountain, despite the sheer 2,000-foot fall. To judge from the lumps of ice strewn about the area where we stood, this had been a small icefall compared to some of the previous ones. We hitched ourselves to the sledge again

2. Editors' note: According to other accounts, the manhaulers were unable to free themselves from their traces. Haddelsey. *Operation Tabarin*, 102.

3. Editors' note: Lamb, "Operation 'Tabarin' (Base A) Official Diary," 22 September 1944, BAS ADG/1A/1944/B.

Figure 12. Camp on Thunder Glacier, n.d.

and trudged on at an accelerated pace for the centre of the glacier and the summit. The sun-gilt cap of a flat-topped peak rose slowly up before us as we proceeded, and gradually the Danco Coast followed it, until we could see the belt of mist which hung suspended over the de Gerlache Strait. We reached the summit and I read my barometer, which indicated an elevation of 1,000 feet. It was six o'clock, with darkness fast closing in upon us, and a strong wind blew coldly through the throat of a glacier from the west.

We were all tired, for this last uphill pull covered a couple of miles and carried us up several hundred feet. Marr decided that we would return to the base at Port Lockroy. We started for the base at a quarter past the hour, stopping at the second sledge for a few moments to rest and eat a bite of frozen chocolate and some dry biscuits. Lamb and I then struck out ahead, following the dimly discernible tracks we had made earlier in the day. It was dark when we reached the dump, and we braked ourselves down the slope toward the steep cliffs of Knife Edge. We located it with little difficulty, and I waited there to guide Marr and Davies while Lamb went on to prepare Berry for the shock of our arrival. Ten minutes later, the others came along, and we skied down the Rookery slopes in black darkness.

Fog prevented us from getting away the following day, so Marr and Davies devised a quick-release arrangement for the manhauling harness. We had discovered the previous day that being anchored to the 500-pound sledge had considerably slowed our getaway when we wanted to move somewhere in a hurry. Some of the other chaps were still skeptical at the time we left them on Sunday, 24 September, and would have been less surprised to see us that night again than they had been the night before. The skiing surface was still good when we left the base at 10:30 a.m., and the sun shone brightly. We made good time back to the place where we left the second sledge two days earlier, and we had our lunch after pulling it toward the centre of the glacier. We were barely finished eating when a heavy black fog began to roll down the glacier toward us.

It did not take long for us to reach the fog. Blindly pursuing a course eastward[4] between the high rock walls that bordered us on both sides, we fortunately caught sight of the first sledge's tracks up to the summit and followed them. Marr and Davies continued down the other side of the glacier by compass, while Lamb and I waited at the summit hoping the fog would clear and allow us to complete my intended surveying. We waited nearly two hours before following their tracks down, making out the misty outlines of the two tents they pitched at 500 feet above the sea. We unpacked the articles we required from the sledge and moved into the tent.

As I previously mentioned, most of our small articles were packed into wooden sledge boxes with hinged lids. One was the ration bar, another contained the stove and cooking utensils, and a third had a radio receiver mainly intended to receive time signals. With these three boxes, the two bedrolls, our clothing, and us packing into the small tent, there was scarcely room to move; Lamb is not a small man, and I am no midget myself.

We prepared our first meal in the half-light provided by a small paraffin safety lamp and the flames of the Primus stove. Davies provided us with a card listing the rationed proportions of the various ingredients required to make a meal: so many "dippers per two man whack," it said. We made cocoa from the water boiled in one pot, and mixed up pemmican and peaflour to make

---

4. Editors' note: Taylor's manuscript mistakenly states "westward."

"lobscouse" in the other. We ate it up hungrily with the few hard biscuits we were allowed, and turned into our sleeping bags for a good night's sleep.

The next morning, we looked forward to our breakfast of cocoa and porridge with some anticipation. After getting up, we rolled back the bedrolls, and dragged in the two boxes necessary to produce breakfast. The meal, according to the ration scale, consisted of cocoa and a plate of porridge made with seven dippers of oatmeal. I had brought in the plane table top to prevent the sheet from getting wet, but then inadvertently upset the top-heavy pot of melting snow in the tent. Lamb showed typical patience when he simply remarked, "What a pity," or words to that effect. It took a long time to get the meal ready, for everything we needed seemed to always be in some box that was outside the tent.[5]

Clouds again hung in the channel, but the day was fine and clear, and Lamb and I went back up to the summit to take the opportunity to take a quick round of magnetic bearings which included Mount Bulcke and Mount Victoria on Brabant Island, fifty miles distant. Following this, we took the plane table and tripod on our backs and went back two miles to the summit of Thunder Glacier, where we had left the range finder the previous day in the fog. We surveyed within the walls that confined the glacier below Luigi and Wall Mountain. Then, with all of the apparatus on our backs, we skied back to camp where we arrived at about three o'clock. We then developed a much better system for cooking the evening meal, by gathering all the food and utensils into a single box and keeping it permanently in the tent.

I also made a survey trip with Lamb toward the south end of the island on the 26th. The day was dull, the clouds were not high, but visibility was fairly good. We could see clearly across the strait: there was no ice in it except for a little scattered brash and small icebergs strung out like a convoy in Flandres Bay. A few miles from our camp, we came to a vertical face of rock overhanging the fringing glacier along the coast. At the base of the precipice, overhung with glaciers several hundred feet thick, the snowfield was riddled with radiating crevasses. It would have taken time to cross such a field and we intended to return to our camp again before dark, so we took up a station not far from the cliffs and extended our survey toward the southern part of the island. We anticipated that the *Scoresby* would be available for some scientific work when she

---

5. Editors' note: This paragraph and the following paragraph borrow from Taylor, "The Private Journal of Capt. Andrew Taylor, R.C.E.," Taylor fonds, UMA, MSS 108 Box 3 File 11, p. 276.

next called upon us, and thus expected to use it to connect the coastal sectors that were inaccessible from ashore.

Lamb and I then plodded homeward, dragging the sledge behind us over the smoothly undulating slopes of the glacier and moving a little closer to the cliffs of ice which margin the shore. We had a good view of the back of our picturesque peak, Luigi de Savoia. Vertical faces of rock lay exposed over the slope that acted like a chute for the constantly calving ice. This made the scene a confused mass of ice and snow, devoid of the individuality that the peak possesses when viewed from the west. A long, sloping tongue of ice ascends to about 3,000 feet, and it was up this slope that French explorer Jean Baptiste Charcot's climbers ascended the mountain. Swinging higher up the slope as we approached the camp, we visited a rock outcrop to collect some specimens. We met Marr half a mile from the camp at about 700 feet and he helped to pull us the rest of the way. He and Davies had gone north from the camp to try to prospect a route through the mountains to the north end of the Channel Glacier, but fog had interrupted them and they were forced to return.

For the next week the weather bound us in place for almost the entire time. If the wind dropped at all, fog enclosed us. Gales blew from the east and west, blotting out visibility with driving snow. In order to conserve our paraffin, we spent much of our time lying in our sleeping bags, and used the Primuses almost exclusively for cooking. The chaps in the other tent suffered the misfortune of breaking the nipple containing the jet on their stove, which required a few hours to repair. We loaned them our stove after completing our meal, and I tried unsuccessfully to extract the part of the threaded nipple that remained tightly screwed into place. I eventually tried jamming in a piece of a nail to reduce the size of the aperture caused by the break. This met with some success, and the stove worked the next day. To pass the time while we were locked in place, we took our meteorological readings every few hours, listened to the radio occasionally, ate, and slept. That was all there was to do.

Lamb took over the cooking job, and I made no argument. He used our cleanest pot to melt water for cocoa. He then excavated about an inch of frozen pemmican from our seven-pound tin with the point of a sheath knife and placed it in the other pot. To this he added peaflour, butter, salt, pepper, and occasionally bacon; the whole then boiled until it thickened into a brown, unappetizing-looking sludge. We rapidly consumed it while it was hot. A few biscuits that were dry and hard as wood completed the repast. This was the big

Figure 13. Taylor using the survey camera, n.d.

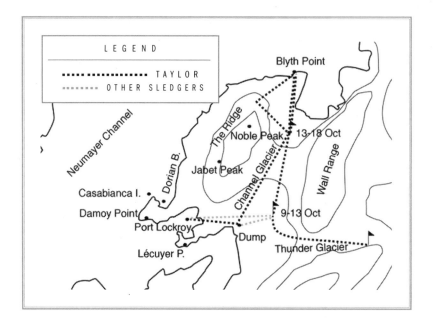

Map 6. The manhauling journey, 9–18 October 1944.

meal of the day, and the pemmican, despite its disagreeable appearance, made a surprisingly filling and nourishing meal. Breakfast, when we indulged in a plate of porridge and a cup of cocoa, was our other hot meal each day. Our noonday snack on the road consisted of a few biscuits and a nickel bar of chocolate, sometimes accompanied by a cup of Marmite prepared at breakfast time and carried in a thermos.

The temperature varied between zero and freezing, and we estimated that the wind velocity rose at times to about fifty miles an hour. The tent walls bellied deeply inward with the pressure on them, occasionally flapping and blattering so violently that we expected them to tear themselves to shreds at any moment. The bamboo poles supporting the tent creaked and bent, as though they might break or lift; we often wondered if we had piled enough snow along the apron of the tent to anchor it in place, or if the action of the wind was eroding it to expose a hole through which it could enter the tent and drive it from over our heads. Although none of these eventualities came to pass, experiencing such a storm in such tiny quarters in the midst of such massive surroundings, with the driving roar of the wind ceaselessly in one's ears for hour after hour, leaves a never-to-be forgotten impression of man's true insignificance. A mantle of humility rests across one's shoulders in the presence of such inexorable power.

About noon on 30 September, the air cleared considerably. Although a fresh wind still blew, Lamb and I did survey work and photography while Davies and Marr went back through Thunder Glacier to the dump to gather additional supplies. Fog closed in about mid-afternoon. We thought that they would continue on from the dump and make for the base at Port Lockroy, but they returned pulling Davies's toboggan at about seven o'clock in the evening. Some of the other chaps from the base had visited the dump and left messages, including one from Lamb's wife.

We meant to continue to survey to the north the next day but a driving wind sprang up before we ventured a mile from the tents, dissipating the good visibility of the morning and forcing us to return. Marr and Davies came over to our tent in the afternoon and the Boss showed us a wire received from the governor of the Falkland Islands to the effect that preparations were being made to survey the west coast of the mainland with the aid of the *Scoresby*, and that a dump of fuel oil would be laid for her at Deception Island.

Three consecutive days of high winds followed a day of fog. On one of these, Lamb injured himself while preparing the evening meal. Grasping the heavy iron pot with the patent potholder, the pot slipped from his grip and boiling water cascaded over his stocking feet. Quickly removing the socks, he applied some salve that we had along, and we bound his feet in lint. In the midst of the storm, Davies and I successfully procured dry bedding for him and fed him some dope. He slept fairly soundly. By morning his feet were badly blistered, but the blisters broke within a couple of days, and he was on his feet again on 8 October. The prompt medical attention they received undoubtedly averted what might have been much worse consequences.

On 6 October, a gale blew all day from the northeast. We were heartily sick of our enforced confinement by this point. The lack of exercise made us a little shaky at the knees when we were compelled, after long contemplation, to go out for a few moments each day to most uncomfortably carry out our nominal daily movements in the face of driving snow. The great windchill of our "southern exposures" ensured that we re-entered the tent with trousers filled with snow.

The bad weather finally broke on the morning of the 7th, and Marr and Davies helped me with our survey gear to a hillside about a mile to the north where we had a good view of the Danco Coast. From an elevation of 750 feet, I measured a series of angles. About noon it clouded over, but we finished our survey work and I took a photograph of the distant coast with the panoramic camera before the northeast wind again blew up. Lamb had a fine hot meal waiting on my return. It was a mixture of pemmican, cheese, and dried potatoes (the latter two items brought from the dump by Marr and Davies). Lamb claimed that it was a Moroccan dish that he called "cos-cos."[6] We had consumed little for lunch and had not drunk anything since morning, so it really hit the spot.

On the 8th, Marr and Davies measured the length of a triangulation base I had laid out in connection with the survey on the mainland. Lamb's feet were sufficiently improved to permit him to accompany me to a knoll atop a small glacier a couple of miles to the north of the camp, where he was anxious to make botanical investigations. We climbed up to 1,200 feet, and the sea beneath us was as blue as the Mediterranean and the sky cloudless. The steep face of the knoll, which we called Snowcomb Hill, supported a rich growth of lichens openly exposed to the violent prevailing northeast winds. After gathering up some rock specimens, we descended the windswept surface of the glacier and were the first back to the camp.

We moved our camp at last on Monday, 9 October. Packing up one sledge, the four of us started the 500-foot climb to the summit of the glacier shortly after eleven o'clock. We had about 400 pounds on the sledge and were at the summit within an hour. Light, new snow overlay a hard, windswept surface, creating conditions that were ideal for travelling. As we stood beside our sledge, an avalanche came tearing down from the very summit of the mountain that produced our harrowing experiences on the 22 September. The morning had been foggy, but the sky cleared a little at about this time, and we could see the top of Doumer Island with Mount William and the Neumayer Channel in the background. Marr and Davies unpacked the sledge in search of Marr's plug of tobacco; he had run out of cigarettes, and in desperation, was smoking plug tobacco in a cork bowl! We were back at the camp just after one o'clock with the fog once again closing in. After lunch, we struck the two tents. This proved to be no easy matter because the tents were engulfed in the weighty snow surrounding them, and when we dug down several feet to clear them, we

---

6.   Editors' note: couscous.

discovered that their aprons were solidly frozen into position. Though the second sledge was more heavily loaded than the first one, it too pulled easily up the gentle slope, and we arrived at the summit in a dense fog through which we could see practically nothing.

Fortunately, after descending the western slope of the glacier a couple of hundred feet, we got below the base of this cloud and into excellent visibility. The downhill slope steepened and we had some difficulty controlling the sledge, which repeatedly threatened to take charge. The escape device recently fitted to the harnesses also let me escape several times most inopportunely, creating delays which were most exasperating as we watched small avalanches—a further reminder that we were not far distant from the scene of our earlier adventure.

We came upon Davies and Marr at the bottom of the slope at half past six and hooked onto their sledge to continue up a steep slope onto the Channel Glacier. We were very tired after an exhausting day; the long pull of about a mile to an elevation of 750 feet was tiring work. We stopped frequently for rests, gasping for breath. The light became extremely poor and one could make out little of the rolls and hollows of the snow surface. Wearily placing one ski-shod foot before the other, and lunging in step one way and then the other, my eye caught sight of the typical misty blue colour formed by light filtering into a hole in the snow. Shouting to the others to stop, I plunged my ski stick through it into a crevasse gaping at our feet. We could dimly make out the outline of its other bank twenty feet or so ahead of us, directly in the path we were about to take. Only a sagging snow bridge suspended across the gap. We did not feel inclined to find a path around the crevasse in the poor light, so we turned the sledge hard-a-port and made camp at 7:30 p.m. Bathed in the red rays of the setting sun, the twin portals of Booth Island received scant attention from the weary mortals for whom the scene was set. We had our pemmican and cocoa supper after erecting the camp and turned in, dog-tired, at nine o'clock.

Marr and Davies paid a visit to the dump the following morning to retrieve food, news, telegrams, and four packages of cigarettes. We learned that a 540-ton Newfoundland sealer named the *Eagle* would assist the expedition and would bring twenty Labrador "huskies" for us. The original Hope Bay plans were therefore likely to proceed. Marr left for the base almost immediately after we hauled the survey sledge up to the camp to send signals required in connection with these plans. He promised to send Blyth up the next day to take his place. In the meantime, we settled down to dinner. Among the food Marr and

Davies brought from the dump was some tea, and we had it with our supper. It tasted good, but we were so unaccustomed to it that none of us got to sleep until long after midnight.

On Wednesday, Davies, Lamb, and I pulled one of the sledges along to the north end of the Channel Glacier, where we meant to camp for a few days. It was foggy but the sledge pulled easily. Indeed, after cresting the summit, we had to put a brake onto the sledge as it was sliding along too quickly. After lunch at the new campsite, we started back toward our tents. It was now snowing quite heavily, obscuring the tracks we made an hour or so before. When we were still a quarter of a mile away from our camp, we discerned the misty outlines of the two tents and closer inspection revealed someone standing beside the nearest one. It was Blyth, whom Back had guided up. We heard all the latest news of the base from Blyth—and enjoyed his cooking.

The snow fell until it was a foot deep, and was followed by wind and more snow, so we did not break camp until Friday, 13 October. It was clear in the early morning, but the snow returned by the time we loaded the sledge. With the additional food that we had been supplied, there was now too much for one sledge to handle, so we had to leave more than 100 pounds behind. We started round the crevasse and up the gentle slope of the glacier but, even with the four of us pulling, the deep snow made the work desperately exhausting. We would rest a few moments and then, after a series of terrific tugs in unison, would succeed in getting our heavy load on the move again, only to stop after another 100 feet, ready to drop from sheer exhaustion. The snow banked up in front of the sledge and our skis broke six inches below the surface.

Few methods of transport invented by man stand lower in any scale of efficacy than does manhauling. The sweaty labour has about it a soul-destroying monotony altogether inconsistent with the powers of observation expected of its travellers. With the weight of the sledge arranged by the harness upon one's diaphragm, one foot is placed mechanically before the other in a lunging stride. Starting out fresh in the morning, things usually go along well enough for the first ten minutes or so. The first halt for a rest is welcome enough, but not essential. As the day proceeds, however, these periods of rest increase in importance until, toward the end of the day, they become almost all there is to look forward to in life! As one weary leg glides forward after the other, the body is lathered in sweat despite the subzero temperatures. One's entire attention is focussed upon the little group coupled to the sledge, and one wonders if perhaps the other chaps are not pulling as hard as they are. Perhaps they are deliberately leaving more of the job to their partners? Will the leader ever stop for the rest which one feels so sincerely to have earned? One's friends, family, life, and ambitions are all momentarily forgotten. All that matters is to rest. In such a condition, one could blandly strike past a wall of gold without noticing it, so eagerly is one's attention focussed upon the need to halt for a rest. Yes, for pure soul-destroying labour, it must be difficult to beat manhauling.

We reached the summit on a compass bearing and started down the other side. There was no need to brake the sledge, for we had to haul it assembled every step of the way. We caught sight of the survey sledge when we closed to within a few hundred yards and, pulling alongside it, set up the tents. We were drinking tea half an hour after our arrival.

It had not been our intention to return for the remaining part of our stores that day, for the snow was still falling heavily and visibility decreasing. When we discovered, however, that some of the cooking utensils from the other tent had been left behind, Lamb and I decided to go back for them. Halfway up the slope of the glacier, we looked back through the driving snow toward where the camp had been and saw Davies following, so we waited for him to come up. The vision of beef and carrot stew, which he knew was at the dump, was too much for his imaginative mind so he set out to fetch back a few tins. Our morning tracks were obliterated as soon as we passed the summit, but we had no difficulty locating the old campsite.

Fifteen minutes later, we had loaded up the toboggan and we were on our way back. Though it was not top-heavy, the toboggan tipped over several times and had to be righted. While the hauling was not nearly as arduous as it had been with the heavier load in the morning, it was still heavy enough and we stopped frequently for rests. For a time, we could see Davies's misty figure half a mile to the west of us. But when we reached the summit, the driving snow thickened and obliterated him and all our landmarks from view. We had to continue on a rough compass bearing. Davies reached the camp ahead of us, and he and Blyth melted snow for us to drink, as one becomes abnormally thirsty when perspiring at the rate caused by manhauling. The Primus was going in our tent, for paraffin was now in plentiful supply and, before we took our clothes off, Blyth came over with a luxurious meal from the dump consisting of scrambled eggs, sausage, and potatoes. We wolfed down the food, and a cup of tea soon put us in the frame of mind to enjoy the storm still roaring and tearing by the camp. To dry out our perspiration-soaked clothing, we turned into our sleeping bags early.

By fitting the phones, separated from the headband, into an empty tin biscuit box, we rigged up a primitive loudspeaker so that we could hear the radio while we were storm-bound. We tied the box to the tent's peak using a shoelace, and its emanations had a decidedly tinny effect. The little portable set had to be "cooked" up to 65°F before it began to operate. Once warmed up it worked well, and we had little static except that occasionally created by the abrasion of the snow particles carried past us by the wind. The aerial was supposed to be suspended between a pair of skis stuck into the snow, which served as supports for the insulators, but we discovered it worked equally well when lying directly on the snow.

The next day was one of wind, snow, and fog in turn, with poor visibility. The following day, however, Lamb and I went off with skis toward the north and slid down the slope where we were camped. We lay about 600 feet above a small bay in the Neumayer Channel—the same one which had given us the impression of entering a cul-de-sac on the day we arrived first at Port Lockroy (and which we have since named Davies Bay on our map). Our camp lay about two miles from the blue ice cliffs which we used to mark its limits, and a quarter mile below the camp lay a series of tremendous square-shaped and cavernous openings, about 100 feet square and bottomless, from our aspect. The ice from the glacier above seemed to flow into this abyss in a smoothly rounded curve. We moved along the steep sidehill slope to the west of the bay, negotiating a track between these crevasses and others lying higher up the hillside. The deep snow gave our skis good grip on the slope, and we climbed up to the tongue of snow that drapes down from Noble Peak toward the Blyth Point, just west of Davies Bay. As we skied down the slope toward the north, we planted a picket at an elevation of a few hundred feet above the sea sparkling below us.

The weather had not improved after we had left the camp. Visibility was good, but the summits of the mountains were obscured so that we could neither complete the survey we intended to make, nor capture the photographs we hoped to take of this area. So, instead of returning immediately to the base, we headed for a rocky buttress overlooking Börgen Bay. We climbed to a point 1,000 feet above the sea where Lamb collected lichen specimens enthusiastically for a couple of hours and took some photographs with his Leica. We gathered a few rock specimens containing what we took to be traces of both iron

Figure 14. Andrew Taylor capturing survey photographs at Blyth Point, 17 October 1944.

and copper. Returning to camp at about four o'clock, we met Blyth and Davies just leaving with a toboggan-load of food and first aid equipment. They had become anxious after our extended absence, and were coming in search of us. Back and Farrington had visited the camp during our absence and left some of Berry's pastry and messages—both of which were welcome. While Blyth concocted a supper of bacon and omelets, we read our messages from home and a copy of a signal that Marr had sent to the governor of the Falklands, requesting that the *Scoresby* pick him up immediately to confer about plans for the next year. With many official signals in the air, Marr did not contemplate returning to our camp, so Blyth remained with us until we returned to the base.

We prepared for additional survey work the next day, measuring a 500-metre base and several series of angles to what we could see of the surrounding peaks. It was not an ideal day for the work because low-lying clouds at about 1,500 feet only revealed the bases of most of the peaks. Marr and Farrington, who brought another toboggan-load of food during the day, encountered heavy snow on the way up, and required about four hours to reach us. By this time, we had stockpiled sufficient food and paraffin for a month, had it been necessary.

Figure 15. The Wiencke Island manhauling team. From left to right: Andrew Taylor, James "Fram" Farrington, James Marr, Ivan Mackenzie Lamb, and Gwion Davies, 29 October 1944.

On Tuesday, 17 October, the four of us paid another visit to Blyth Point. We left the camp at half past ten with a lightly loaded sledge on another cloudy day. The previous Friday, Davies had blistered his heel and was still unable to wear boots, so he wore a pair of mukluks and *truger*. The latter were unsatisfactory and he removed them after half an hour. Nonetheless, he got little purchase on the steep slope we were traversing. At an elevation of about 700 feet above the sea in Davies Bay the sledge became unmanageable and threatened to take charge and drag us all down the slope to our right (which approached an angle of 40°). There was nothing to break the uniformity of the slope except some immense crevasses between us and the ice cliffs. Had we started slipping down, we would have had a Hobson's choice between ending up at the bottom of one of these crevasses or in the icy water of the sea. The beating wind had packed and hardened the surface of the snow to make it much more treacherous than Lamb and I had found it two days before.

At first, with Lamb and me pulling, Blyth was able to hold up the rear of the sledge and steer it more or less along the contour we were following. As we proceeded along the increasing slope, however, this task became much more difficult. Davies attempted to help, but his treacherous footgear placed him at a distinct disadvantage. His feet frequently slipped out from under him, and he instinctively grasped for Blyth or for the sledge. Yet the steepest part of the sidehill still lay ahead of us. We edged along another fifty feet or so with Davies using the blade of the shovel as a holdfast, driving it vertically into the snow so that it supported the lower edge of the length of the sledge runner as it passed each time. We then stopped while he moved the shovel forward to the front of the sledge before lurching our load forward another ten feet or so. It was a painfully slow and extremely dangerous progress. If we made one false step the sledge threatened to swing below us like a pendulum and tug us after it.

At Lamb's suggestion, Davies dug a level platform into the side of the snow bank large enough to accommodate the sledge. We pulled the sledge onto it and let it safely rest before unloading each piece and carrying it a quarter of a mile to the top of the hill. Each of us made two trips before the sledge was empty, which allowed us to pull it without further difficulty. Reloading the sledge at the top, we coasted down the hill toward the point that Lamb and I had flagged on our previous visit. Lamb and I skied down while the other two rode the sledge with the wheel revolving behind them as though they were being driven by it.

The wind blew at about twenty-five miles an hour from the northeast, and made the working conditions extremely uncomfortable by also driving a good deal of snow. Clouds hung over Wall Mountain, Nemo Peak, and Copper Mountain to the north of our station, but Mount Français and the Osterrieth Range on Anvers Island were fairly clear. I was hesitant about waiting for improved visibility, so I exposed three of the panoramic films immediately upon our arrival. Thereafter, we began reading angles with the theodolite from our station, just over the 500-foot mark. We worked barehanded and interrupted the readings several times to get warm. During one of these intervals, we walked down to two outcrops of rock below us. The upper outcrop was devoid of interest, but on the other Lamb found a most luxuriant growth of his lichens. He was very happy collecting them, remarking that he thought it would be worth a special trip later in the year after some of the snow melted from the surface. We climbed back to the station and completed the round of angles.

While we were away, Blyth and Davies disported themselves about the snowfield like a couple of children in an effort to keep warm, for the wind was quite chilling. They dug a pit in the snow, about 5 x 7 feet, to a depth of five feet, in which they proposed we have lunch. The scheme was not a success, however, for the wind blew fine snow in an eddy into the pit and the sun's rays melted the frosty powder. When Davies emerged from the pit, he looked completely drenched with water. A couple of hours later, Davies went into a crevasse up to his waist, and not half an hour following that, Blyth did the same thing only a few yards away from their pit. These two events had a most sobering effect upon their subsequent behaviour.

We finished the surveying at about six o'clock, and it did not take long to reload the sledge and leave the station. By this time, Blyth almost resented the point bearing his name. Following the same relaying procedure we used on the latter part of our journey out, we had no difficulty returning to the camp. We arrived just before eight o'clock and enjoyed the fine dish of stew that Blyth had prepared for us.

First thing the next morning, the last day of our journey, I took a series of sun observations before we broke camp just after noon. Lamb intended to return to this camp a short time later, so we left one tent standing with a good supply of food and two sleeping bags. This lightened our load considerably and we made good time, reaching the summit of the Channel Glacier at 3:00 p.m. It was a beautifully bright and clear day, with a fresh wind from the south. We had an excellent view toward the south as we descended the glacier toward the Knife Edge. The hard and windswept surface allowed us to continue making good time. After pausing for a few moments at the dump, we took our load down the last steep slope toward Lécuyer Point, wondering if we would discover that the ice in Port Lockroy had gone out completely and isolated us from the base. We caught sight of two figures on the rookery below us, and knew then that the ice still held—so we would not have to camp on the rookery while waiting for the others to dig out a boat. We left the sledge atop the Knife Edge, took only a few articles and notebooks with us, and we were back at Port Lockroy by 6:30 p.m. where, once again, we enjoyed one of Berry's civilized meals.

We had been away only twenty-five days. During that time we suffered inconveniences, discomforts, and many more exasperations than would have sufficed for a much longer and more inspiring journey. We had returned with results incommensurate with the effort involved. It was an interesting journey in which to partake, and gave one insight into the laborious methods and equipment that explorers had been forced to use in the early part of the century. It is not a method that should be followed today, especially along coastlines like western Graham Land's. Our complete lack of transport by sea or sea ice, however, had forced us to adopt these methods to make a detailed examination and to survey the comparatively small area that was accessible to us.

We were extremely unfortunate in the weather that we encountered on the journey—one of the worst spells of continuous bad weather which Back's meteorological records registered during the entire length of our stay at Port Lockroy. Out of the twenty-five days we were out, only one was clear, and only six allowed us to accomplish any reasonable work. The high winds that blew with such turbulence were interspersed with days of fog, calm days which had a deafening silence were broken only by the roar of a nearby avalanche.

Travelling along the glaciers that fringe the shoreline is certainly not the ideal method of surveying coasts, as one is forced to attempt to plot the position of a shoreline outside one's line of vision. One may surmise that such points lie vertically below the edge of the ice cliff that verge the course one is following, but it is not always convenient to ascertain this point. In the summertime, with occasional long spells of fine clear weather, a thousand times more work could be accomplished by a single plane photographing every tortuous sinuosity of the coasts in detail that cannot be approached by any other method. Shore parties certainly are needed to establish the ground control required for triangulation and astronomic observing, and to collect specimens of geological, botanical, and zoological interest as each landing affords. Nonetheless, this type of country cries out for the use of aerial photography, and the use of other methods is merely playing at the job to produce very inferior results.

CHAPTER EIGHT

Spring
at the Base

IT WAS STILL WINTER WHEN WE LEFT GOUDIER ISLET to begin our sledging on 24 September, but the lovely weather we enjoyed for a few days following our return made us realize that spring had arrived. Never had Bransfield House looked so attractive. Never had it appeared so neat and clean, for the others had taken care of the spring cleaning in our absence—even the messroom floor was scrubbed so that its rich brown colour was again visible. It made us feel our responsibility for leaving the place so untidy, but Back and Ashton had enjoyed the cleanup. The former took a keen delight in throwing out the accumulated empty cigarette tins, boxes of old nails, bits of sealskin, and other oddments which people had kept in case they "might come in useful some day." This marked the beginning of another stage in our lives at the base, for once this cleanup was done we all took pride in the appearance of the house even though it meant that each of us spent a day every week on our hands and knees wiping the floors. Bransfield House ceased being merely a place to eat and sleep; it took on a "homey" atmosphere and became quite cozy. There was even talk of trying to paint the exterior of the building.

Upon our return, we heard that the *William Scoresby* was due to leave Port Stanley at the end of the month, bring Flett to Port Lockroy to stay with us, and to return Marr to Port Stanley to discuss plans for the forthcoming season with the governor. This was exciting news because it promised to bring what most travellers miss more than anything else: the mail. We observed that the waters in the channels adjacent to Wiencke Island were virtually open, with little or no surface ice during the preceding month, which seemed to promise of a good voyage for the *Scoresby*.

The first night after our manhauling journey, we had some difficulty sleeping on the comparatively soft beds at the base. This difficulty did not persist, however, as our old iron bedsteads could never be mistaken for Ostermoors. It did not take long before we fell back into the routine of the base as though we had never left.

Coming as most of us did from a life spent in temperate climes, and more recently from the luxuriance in the sub-tropics that we had visited on our voyage south, our first impression held this friendliest coast of Antarctica to be entirely devoid of life. The land does not support a tree, a flower, a shrub, or even a sward of grass. No land animal exists upon its snow-covered slopes, for there is no food upon which one could subsist. Along the coast of the Graham Land Peninsula, the mountainous core of the land is fringed with the calving glaciers, and the mountains rise up to the plateau perpetually clothed in ice. Here and there, an exposed foot of rock creeps timidly out from beneath the ice cover at sea level, and it is upon those isolated outcrops that one can land. The 100-foot-high ice cliffs that form most of the coast are alive with slow, glacial movements that occasionally give thunderous indications of their presence by discharging hundreds of tons of ice into the sea beneath them. The sea animals seem to intuitively avoid such cliffs and even the birds know not to nest in them. The entire land gives the impression of stark lifelessness.

As time passes, however, one's perspective gradually refocusses to the scale of this scene. It reveals things that were heretofore hidden by the myopia of a lifetime spent in more civilized conditions. To most people, for example, the study of the botany of such a region would seem a most uninspiring prospect. To Lamb, a specialist in the study of mosses and lichens, it was an exciting challenge.

All can recognize the moss that carpets the forests and climbs up the bases of the trunks of the trees in temperate regions. Perhaps few of us have noticed the lichen—or we pay scant attention to it. Prior to my meeting Lamb, I confess that I never more than casually noticed them, though I had read of explorers using them as an emergency means of subsistence in the far north. These tough, leathery-looking objects cling tenaciously to rocks, boulders, and tree trunks. They seem dull compared to the vivid greens of grass and leaves, and they are invisible to the eyes of the casual observer.

We spent the winter of 1944 on Goudier Islet. It was a winter in which we lost the sun for two months, and even our noonday meals required a paraffin lamp to illuminate the table. It was a winter in which we had a great deal of dull, cloudy weather and many days of gales and storms with winds that tossed our large sledges about 100 feet through the air as though they were cardboard boxes. The winds were such that we saw only a few birds, and those of the hardiest species. When the rising spring sun drew back the carpet of snow enshrouding our islet to reveal the brilliant orange colouring of several square feet of one of Lamb's lichens at the highest point of our islet, many bouquets of flowers have looked much less striking. Against the drabness of all that surrounded it, and magnificently illuminated by a sweltering sun which gave it a setting iridescent with the crystals of snow amongst which it lay embedded, this flaming garden gave us our first promise of spring.

Lamb's diligence and persistence rewarded him with a large collection of lichens gathered from the various localities we visited on Wiencke Island, as well as those collected in the course of his ecological studies of Goudier Islet. Many of the species he collected were new to the Graham Land area, others were new to the Antarctic, and he found a few which were new to science. In addition, he highly prized a few blades of grass that he discovered in a crevice between the rocks of the rookery. His interest also included mosses as well as a variety of marine algae and flora. These specimens were not easily found, but one is amazed at the diversity and luxuriance of some of the growths that the cold rock-faces of the country support.

While searching for and examining some of the marine organisms among the submerged rocks that lined our little boat harbour, Lamb turned over one of the stones and, much to his surprise, found its underside to be alive with zoological organisms. This discovery initiated an intensive search among the surrounding stones by almost everyone, who brought specimens into the house by the pailful in the days that followed. They were surprisingly colourful and odd. After classifying them, Marr set them in a fixative for their return to England. Curiously coloured fish, about four inches in length, were cunningly camouflaged to be all but indiscernible among the rocks where they lay stone-still as we searched for them. Translucent little animals waved spidery arms that contained an iridescent core that gave off a metallic blueness as they vibrated and flagellated before our eyes. We also caught and preserved some large jellyfish measuring several feet in diameter—their undersides were no sight for a tender stomach. Marr's collection included many varieties of shellfish, starfish, and queer-looking worms, and was quite extensive by the time he left.

The birds were the most obvious form of life in the region and we were blessed with about a dozen varieties. The most peculiar and fascinating were, of course, the penguins—the bird so typical of this frozen southland. There was a rookery of Gentoo penguins at Lécuyer Point where we first landed in search of a building site, and we all spent many hours examining those birds in the spring. The penguins largely disappeared from the rookery in April, though rare visitors returned for brief stays during the winter. While caught in a cold snap somewhere down the Peltier Channel in mid-July, we also saw a convoy of about fifty penguins walking Indian-file[1] over the ice toward Damoy Point.

Penguins stand about twelve to fifteen inches high, weigh ten to thirteen pounds, have the usual black back, silvery white breasts, an orange beak, and somewhat light pink feet. They began to return to the rookery in early September and were nesting when we finished our sledging trip. Eric Back found the first eggs about mid-November and returned to the base with a pailful of them the next day. They are considerably larger than a duck egg, being about three inches in length and better than two inches in diameter. Berry tried both frying and boiling them for us, but they were not popular for long because seeing two boiled and peeled eggs' rich red yolks staring through the tough translucent whites like a pair of octopus eyes is not the most appetizing sight to begin the day.

Penguins cannot fly, and have a more ungainly gait when walking quickly, though they can stroll leisurely along with quite a dignified air. In the water, they lose their clumsiness in a symphony of motion that is astonishing to watch. I saw one wheeling and darting about in the shallow water so quickly that it was difficult to follow with the eye. They often swim in groups, and porpoise themselves through the air occasionally to fill their lungs. The penguins in this area fed on krill, a shrimp-like creature that supports the life of many larger whales. They seem to leave their rookery at a regular time each day to feed, taking turns during the incubating period. Few of the seals seem to molest them, at least out of the water, but penguins make a quick and ready meal for a sea leopard.

Their nests are built of small stones about the size of a walnut and, during the nesting season, the females become utterly fearless. I had the tripod of my theodolite set within a foot of a sitting bird for two hours, and for the duration she stubbornly refused to budge off the nest. The males are more inclined to run off on one's approach during the nesting period, but usually return a few moments later. The pair bow and squawk for minutes on end in apparent happiness at their reunion. When a female is chased off the nest, as occasionally

---

1.   Editors' note: A dated term derived from the presumption that North American Indigenous Peoples walked single-file through forests.

happens, she looks first for her eggs upon her return and, finding them still there, bows, squawks and hisses in pure ecstasy before tucking them between her feet and settling down again on her stony seat. Such happiness was only exceeded by a bird that had no eggs in her nest when she left but returned to find one transferred from a bird that had three and who apparently remained ignorant of her loss. Most nests contained two eggs but we frequently saw three and one had four. The first young chicks hatched out about the New Year.

It is also interesting to watch the continual thievery that goes on between these birds at mating time. The nests consist of stones that the birds assemble into piles large enough for the bird to sit over a depression. Altercations begin when one penguin surreptitiously attempts to steal one of these stones from among the hundreds that make up a nest. The owner, noticing this burglary, leaves its nest momentarily unprotected and makes after the thief. During the resulting row, a third bird often makes off with not one but several stones from the same nest. As long as the owner succeeds in retrieving the piece it started after, however, the bird seems perfectly oblivious to the loss of any of the other stones from the nest.

Penguins are most entertaining and inoffensive creatures to watch. One of the most comical sights is when a number of them land on an ice floe. They approach the face of the floe at great speed, dive down deeply just before they reach it, and break through the surface of the water like a huge bobbing cork which has been submerged. They rise several feet into the air, stagger, and fall upon the surface of the ice floe. Upon regaining their balance—which they do almost immediately—they stand as still as a monument for a few minutes, as though they had been there since time immemorial.

We found evidence of polished stones and boulders at the rookery at Lécuyer Point and at Damoy Point. This polishing was accomplished by the feet of uncounted thousands of penguins during their sole occupancy of the island. A white transparent deposit is formed by the birds walking over the stones immersed in their excrement. The polish the stones acquire is exceedingly smooth and glistens in bright sunlight.

Although the penguins were probably the most fascinating birds to watch, we observed other fowl as well. Throughout the winter, our constant companions were a couple of dozen little white birds called paddies or sheathbills. They are about the size of a pigeon, with large blunt beaks that appear out of proportion to the rest of their body, and an ugly face covered with a pink, pimply skin.

With grey feet and legs as well as a fluffy breast, these cheeky little birds fed in the depth of winter upon the garbage thrown out of the galley. During the mating season, we observed pairs of them bowing, scraping, and squawking at one another for what seemed like hours at a time. They have been known to remain in the vicinity of a wintering station, but as a rule they are migratory and fly across the Drake Passage to spend the colder months in South America. They fly with a laborious-looking fluttery motion, spreading their tail feathers into a pretty fan, and one cannot help but wonder at their endurance given the arduous flight over 400 miles of tempestuous seas to complete their migration. Of note, they are the only birds inhabiting this part of Antarctica that do not have webbed feet.

Although fearlessly friendly, they also are timid or cautious and never allowed us to approach nearer than five or six feet. The impertinent, thieving little creatures stole the eggs or young of any other birds that they found momentarily unguarded, and often pecked away at the eggs upon which some unsuspecting penguin or cormorant sat. For all their thieving, however, they remained popular companions. During a visit of one of the ships, members of our base looked on in abhorrence at some of the crew that killed a couple of the birds to eat.

One small section of the rookery was occupied by about 100 cormorants called Blue-Eyed Shags, named for the circle of bright blue that surrounds their eyes. Their part of the rookery sloped down steeply to the sea, a feature that we also noticed at other rookeries. Their nests were built to last from one year to another, and these particular ones were made of pieces of old rope, apparently from hawsers left by the whalers who had used Port Lockroy thirty or forty years ago. The shags cemented together these pieces of rope with some sort of adhesive secretion that made the nests quite solid and substantial. They usually flew singly but fed in large flocks on the water, diving deeply for nearly a minute at a time to catch fish. In flight, they appeared to move rather heavily, with their neck and tail extended in a straight line. One gathers that it is a great effort for them to keep their heads in front of the rest of their body. They are seldom seen over the land because they flew around our islet rather than over it almost every time but, when one occasionally passed over, its ragged-edged wings gave forth a squeaking beat with each stroke.

In the winter, when our harbour was fast in the ice, we saw a similar-sized colony of these shags on Casabianca Islet near the open water of the Neumayer Channel. We judged that they were the same birds from our rookery, migrated these few miles away. They returned to Lécuyer Point in August, ahead of the penguins, and began repairing their nests of the previous year by using pieces of seaweed to replace the frayed bits of rope until the nests were again built up into the form of a truncated pyramid with steep sides.

We shot several shags for food. They were quite long, approaching three feet, and weighed between six and eight pounds. The top of their heads, back of their necks, and backs were black. Their underparts were silvery white, and their black wings had a white stripe. After first hanging them for several days with an onion stuffed into their mouths (which was supposed to take away their fishy flavor), Berry braised the birds. Although we still detected the faint taste of fish, they were quite tasty and offered a welcome change from the tinned meat.

We first noticed shag eggs in early December. They were smaller and more tapered than penguins' eggs, but tasted similar to them when cooked. The young—horrible, naked, snaky-looking young creatures with their long necks breaking through their shells—hatched earlier than penguins.

Adjoining Goudier Islet was a smaller one called Bill's Islet, and after our establishment spread, the gulls moved there. They were the black-backed Dominican Gull, white all over except for their back and the upper parts of the wings—beautiful, clean-lined creatures with a wingspan of four feet. Most of them left us for the winter, but we saw the odd visitor. When we tossed our garbage into the sea each day, the gulls, skuas, and paddies fought noisily until it was all consumed. They performed the most wonderful aerobatics as they chased each other, busily gripping the food in flight, for they always seemed to consider these morsels to be the most delectable.

The four birds I have named were by far the most numerous of all the species we saw at Port Lockroy. In the course of the year, a few vagrant visitors of other species also visited the rookery: Adelie and ringed penguins, to name two of them. They mingled with the Gentoos on these occasions without being harmed and appeared to be perfectly welcome, though they never stayed more than a few days. A few snow petrels appeared during the winter. The dainty Wilson's petrel danced over the water in the spring, and lone giant petrels (or "stinkers" as they were more familiarly known) came periodically. These stinkers had a wingspan of eight feet, and once I saw one gulping down whole pieces of blubber, the smallest dimension of which was three inches. They are hideously ugly and ungainly birds. Some are pure white, but most had darkened spots over their backs and wings. They are gluttonous birds that stuff themselves so full of food that they are often unable to fly and have to disgorge themselves before running awkwardly several hundred feet to attain sufficient speed to become airborne. They collected in numbers from out of nowhere in the winter a few hours after we killed a seal. On another occasion during the summer, we surprised one by approaching within a few feet of it noiselessly in the dinghy. It immediately ran at full speed down the steeply sloping rock and onto the surface of the sea, over which it ran for 100 yards before taking to the air. We did not find their nests at Pork Lockroy and they were never numerous.

Utterly fearless and very strong in flight, the brown or southern skua is known as "the eagle of the Antarctic." It is a dark brown, sooty colour that is difficult to distinguish among the rocks, but we found a few of their nests at Lécuyer Point. When one approached their nest, which are usually singly located as they are not gregarious birds, they immediately gave away its general location by rising from the nest and attacking us in a series of "dive bombings" at what seemed to be prodigious speeds. During the breeding season, they feed off penguin eggs and young. Although skua were always ready to attack and destroy the young of other birds, we saw a pair of gulls give a skua a terrific beating in the air while warding the intruder off of their nest. These gulls totally disabled the bird so that it could not fly and could only swim away along the surface of the water.

The most colourful and prettiest of the birds that visited Port Lockroy was the Antarctic or swallow-tailed tern. It is a small, chirping bird that is silvery grey with a black cap, vermilion bill, and orange-red tail. Its lines are sharply cut and they fly about singly, as a rule. We found a ternery on the west side of Doumer Island, where they were nesting on a terminal moraine—the nests simply scooped out of the hollows in a small bed of gravel and detritus. Lamb inspected the nests with a coat over his head, as time and again they swooped down upon him and struck his head with their beaks. We watched them drive away gulls and skuas, attacking them in pairs and even singly. They seemed to have arranged a series of outpost guards around the ternery, spaced about ten yards from the nearest nest, and equally spaced about the area. As soon as one drew attention to a would-be intruder, others joined from what appeared to be a central pool to attack the stranger in unison.

All of the birds I enumerated, except the sheathbill, were sea birds, subsisting largely for their food directly from the sea. The waters that wash the shores of this little-known continent of Antarctica are as teeming with life as the land is barren. Marr found an amazing quantity and variety of living creatures along the shore of our tiny boat harbour. There were fish to be found in the deeper waters, as well as larger animals: the whales and seals.

For the first month or so following our landing at Port Lockroy, we saw one or more whales each day. On calm days, the noisy exhalation of their breath and huge black backs and dorsal fins cleaving the water made them easy to spot. On one occasion, three of them entered the harbour, then played and sported about in the comparatively small pool of open water beneath our giant ice cliffs for the better part of an hour. This was the only occasion when they were close enough to our shore for Marr to identify them: they were lesser rorquals,[2] one of the smaller members of the whale family, measuring about fifty feet long. One is quite safe among them in a small boat unless the whale decides to scrape its back of parasitic growths on the vessel's bottom. Accordingly, we were very respectful of them while out in our dinghy.

The seals that abound in the district were the crabeater, the Weddell, and the sea leopard. The latter (which was not numerous during our winter at Goudier Islet) is a large, voracious carnivore that measures ten to twelve feet in length, and has been known to attack parties in small boats. Sea leopards are rather dark grey in colour with lighter spots and have a long neck and a head-ful of ugly teeth. They are usually found alone, live on anything they can kill, and have no foes except killer whales. We saw one sea leopard tear a penguin to pieces in the water a few yards offshore, tossing the luckless creature from side to side. In a few moments there was nothing there but a few feathers blown by the wind across a stain of red in the water. The crabeater seal is smaller than the sea leopard, but similar in appearance except that its neck is much shorter and its coat lighter in colour. It is very active and numerous in other localities but we did not see many.

Weddells were by far the most numerous seal species that frequented Port Lockroy. They were usually alone, but we did see a group of three swimming in the water on one occasion. In September and October, two of them gave birth to their young on the edge of the sea ice a few hundred feet from the base. A month later, we saw them teach their babies to swim by pushing them into the water. One of these pups did not take at all kindly to the experience, crying and scrambling until it succeeded in mounting the ice edge that, in October, was not very high out of the water. They do not like the wind or the cold, but

2. Editors' note: Also known as the minke whale.

will come out onto the sea ice to lie for twenty-four hours or more at a time in friendlier weather. The Weddels, which we had the best opportunity of observing, did not appear to bother the penguins or shags while out of the water. They lived at peace with the others on many occasions on the rookery. Several of the stomachs of the Weddells we killed contained the remains of many fish. When we killed Weddells near the station, Berry supplemented our meat ration by frying big slabs of their back muscles as steaks. Some of the chaps at the base preferred to eat the liver rather than the steaks, the former being almost indistinguishable from beef liver.

Though we could not but be interested in the wildlife surrounding us, by far the most active topic of conversation was the weather. Being well housed, well clothed, and well fed, it was the most variable element in our daily lives. Back was our meteorologist, and he made his first observations at 8:00 a.m. or shortly afterward. Before sitting down to breakfast he was inevitably bombarded about the day's weather prospects. He became so fed up with replying to the same question each morning, as each of us in turn straggled into breakfast, that he had Ashton construct a temperature indicator that he hung on the wall and altered each time he took a new reading of the thermometer in the Stevenson Screen behind the Nissen hut. This measure ensured that he merely had to describe the wind, the state of the clouds, and the immediate prospect, in addition to the ice conditions, and whether or not it had snowed much.

It was something of a surprise to me to learn that the winters in this part of the Antarctic were not nearly so severe as those in my former home of Winnipeg, Canada, which is about 15° nearer the equator than Port Lockroy. There are few winters in Winnipeg, a city approaching 300,000, when the thermometer does not dip below −40°F. At Port Lockroy, our coldest day occurred in August, and the best the mercury could do was a paltry −12°F. However, the summers did not rise at all near those of Winnipeg, where temperatures periodically approach 100°F. The warmest day in the year we spent on Goudier Islet was in early January of 1945 when the thermometer struggled up to 45°F. This was the atmospheric Fahrenheit temperature, and it was sometimes difficult to realize it was so cool, with a bright hot sun blazing out of the sky. Back once hung a thermometer on the wall of the house on just such a day and it immediately climbed up above 100°. However, if the slightest breeze sprung up, the heat disappeared in an instant and one immediately felt the atmosphere's chill.

We only recorded subzero temperatures during June, July, and August. The highest mean monthly temperature occurred in February 1945, while the lowest was in June, being 38° and 11° above zero, respectively. For the months of March to October, we averaged three days of fog and four days of gale each month, while we had precipitation on seventeen days each month. Humidity was high—about 90 percent—and the cloud cover was over seven-tenths.

For the same period, observations showed that a wind blew for 80 percent of the observations. This wind became very violent and sometimes exceeded sixty miles an hour. We recorded the highest wind in November, when it rose to eighty miles an hour. The prevailing winds came from the east and northeast; the other prevailing directions were from the west and southwest. Together, these winds accounted for more than half the observations. North winds were the rarest of all. June was the windiest month, for the winds exceeded forty-five miles an hour on eleven different occasions.

Each day, Back also took the temperatures of the sea by scooping up a pailful of water along the ice edge, or through a hole, in which he immediately immersed his thermometer. The water was just over 33°F when he began his measurements in March, but dropped below the freezing point in the month which followed and remained there until the following January. We recorded the lowest mean sea temperature in August 1944, when it went down to 23.2°F; we recorded the highest mean sea temperature the following February, when it rose to 34.7°F.

The atmospheric temperature was much more even during the summer months than it was during the winter, though the winter variations were not diurnal. In summer, the difference between the maximum and minimum temperatures recorded during any single month varied as much as 25°. In the winter, this difference grew as great as 50°. The maximum temperature (45°F) occurred in January 1945. During the winter month of August 1944 we reached 40°F and in July reached only one degree less.

We had no difficulty in keeping the house comfortably warm at all times, even during high gales. A drift formed along the south and east sides of the buildings, almost crept up to the roof, and insulated us from the cold southerly winds. The house was very comfortable at 60°F. Above that, it became too warm.

We did not go to any trouble devising a recording apparatus for measuring the tides, as this had been very thoroughly done by the British Graham Land Expedition at Argentine Island in 1935. However, Lamb made note of exceptionally low tides in connection with a marine organism he studied. In

Figure 16. Port Lockroy personnel posing for a photo on 26 October 1944.
Left to right: James Marr, Gwion Davies, Lewis Ashton, Tom Berry, "Fram" Farrington,
Eric Back, Andrew Taylor, John Blyth.

November, we had a series of very low tides that allowed us to walk over to
two of the neighbouring islets. During this period, collecting along the shore
became very popular, for the days were becoming warmer, and the sun shone
brightly. We gathered all the peculiar marine organisms for Marr that we encountered, and also made quite an extensive collection of erratic geological
specimens. The country rock surrounding us was a grey-looking granite, or
granodiorite, but along the beach we found many stones altogether that were
different than that which comprised the rounded weather-worn boulders along
the shore. All of the latter type were uniformly coloured on their upper surface
with the slime of the sea, and their substance and texture was not revealed until
we broke them open and found broad red bands of jasper, and three-inch horn-
blende crystals which shone and glistened in the sunlight along their freshly
fractured faces. We also retrieved an almost-white stone matted with small red
crystals that were even redder than garnets.

This collecting was not a very exciting task. Only one thing stood between
us and our mail, and that was time. We felt able to afford anything that helped

expend it. There were photographs from the sledge journey to be developed, and a few reports to write, but they did not take long. Several of us gave Lamb a hand at the photographic work by retrieving water, for snow became scarce around the islet. The results of his developing and printing were most interesting to us all, and it was a familiar sight to see someone standing over the tub used for washing prints and fishing them out one at a time to examine the dripping pictures. Ashton helped Lamb to assemble a representative selection of them for transmission back to London on the next ship.

But Ashton was also busy of his own accord. He was slated to go to Deception Island on the *Scoresby* to commence work constructing a prefabricated building to be immediately erected at Hope Bay upon our arrival so that Berry would have some cooking facilities. Ashton consequently packed up his tools into their kits and chests and sharpened and polished them all until they shone as they never had since our arrival at Port Lockroy. Besides these preparations to move, Ashton had another large job repairing one of our boats so that we could put at least one of them into use when a ship arrived. As the motorboat seemed to be the most damaged, he worked on one of the dinghies first, and spent many long hours patching up the holes in its sides with sheets of lead, which he then painted. I gave him a hand with the motorboat, which was a much bigger job because the engine was completely encased in a solid block of ice that had to be carefully chipped away before we could begin trying to turn the engine. When the long-anticipated day arrived, we found—as we had feared—that the motor did not work. We eventually traced the trouble to a faulty magneto, for which there was no spare this side of Port Stanley. But it took a very great deal of sweat and toil to arrive at that conclusion, and the hull was completely patched and painted.

The weather rapidly improved during November. With temperatures never more than a few degrees below freezing and many bright sunny days, the snow disappeared quickly. We did have a few storms, such as the eighty-two-mile-an-hour gale that blew down the pretty flagstaff. On most days, however, the snow melted and little rivulets ran down between the rocks. And at the end of November, it was daylight until nearly midnight.

These days were ideal for photography, and shutter-snapping went on day and night. We dressed up in our working togs when Lamb and Ashton photographed the five members of the sledging party. Later, he took a series of portraits that included each member of the base, and extended the series on fungi to include a number of remarkable pictures of the local lichens. Ashton made good use of his movie camera, too, but he had to make a special filter to subdue the brilliant reflection of the sun's rays off the melting snow.

Besides melting the snow from our rocky islet and stopping our skiing on the rookery, the fine weather set in motion the tremendous movement of the glaciers, which had been all but dormant with the grip of winter's frosts. Miles of ice-cliffed coasts began to break away in massive and thunderous falls into the sea. This created a carpet of broken ice fragments at the base of the cliffs, which drifted about until a gale swept them away. Very gradually, the port began to fill with ice, for the fast ice[3] of winter had long since broken clear. Back and Blyth ascended the Channel Glacier again, and found that the channels were thick with these fragments and peppered with small bergs. The report of this situation delayed the departure of the *William Scoresby* from Port Stanley for a few days, but she sailed on 8 November. Three days later, she encountered "thick continuous pack ice" 100 miles north of Deception Island, and turned back to Port Stanley. So our vigil continued.

Lamb had long intended to return to Blyth Point to continue his botanical studies, and chose to leave on 18 November. There was still a little ice clinging between our islet and the rookery and he, Ashton, and Blyth made their way over the broken blocks. The tide was low, the ice floes were tilted and broken, and the ice tongue was only about ten feet wide. But they reached the tent that we had left above Davies Bay by mid-afternoon and dug their way through the drift surrounding it.

The next morning brought a fine sunny day for visiting the Point, but the side slope approaching it was hard, crusted, and difficult to cross. The crevasses were also larger than they had been on our last visit. Lamb spent the rest of that day making his collection, and they returned to the tent in the evening well sunburnt. The next day was even warmer, and they discarded some of their heavy clothing as they approached the rock buttress Lamb and I had visited on 15 October. Here too, they found much more rock exposed than had been visible on the previous occasion. After further examining this area, the three of them climbed up the side of the slope toward the 1,600-foot summit of Noble Peak. Roped together, they ascended the first 200 feet over a snowfield, up to an outcrop of piled and fractured rock, before reaching an altitude of 1,530 feet in the nick of the high buttress. Lamb was quite thrilled at collecting a sufficient

---

3. Editors' note: Fast ice extends from, and is attached to, the shore.

quantity of lichens to start a fire, and they used this fuel to melt enough water to have a drink and fill two thermos flasks. When they returned to their skis at the bottom of the buttress, Blyth complained about what he took to be some grit in his eye. Lamb, however, suspected the trouble to be snow blindness and bathed the eye upon their return to camp.

In the morning, Lamb's suspicion was confirmed, for Blyth could barely see. Ashton and Lamb trussed him up in his sleeping bag on a six-foot sledge and they began hauling him up the glacier to return him to the base for Back's attention. After crossing the 1,000-foot summit, they found the hauling easier. While descending toward the Knife Edge, they caught a view of the base and learned that their narrow ice bridge from three days before had broken away. Goudier Islet was completely surrounded by water. With one man on each side of him, they guided the blinded Blyth across the narrow ridge of the Knife Edge, and joined arm in arm to slide down its slope to the top of Lécuyer Point.

Spotting only the pair of men descending the glacier slope gave rise at the base to all sorts of conjectures of calamity. Marr, Back, and I rowed over to the rookery and met Lamb and Ashton near the top and learned what had happened. We took Blyth down to the boat and he received immediate attention by the doctor. Blyth's eyes were bandaged for the next two days, and by the third, he completely recovered from his snow blindness. On 24 November, Ashton and Davies accompanied Lamb back to the camp that they had so hurriedly left three days before, struck the tent, and returned with the equipment to the base.

During the sledging trip when we received news about the *Eagle*, we also learned that two zoologists would join the expedition in the new year. Captain N.B. Marshall, REME,[4] of London, would be in charge of the score of dogs being shipped to us from Newfoundland. The other was known to Lamb from an association made at the British Museum of Natural History, with Sub-lieutenant Gordon J. Lockley, RNVR, of Stoke Pages. Upon our return to the base at the conclusion of the sledging, we heard about two additional men, both surveyors, who were being added to our rolls: Captain V.I. Russell, RE, of Edinburgh, and Lieutenant David P. James, MBE, DSC, RNVR, of the Isle of Mull.

On 27 November, we received a signal to the effect that the *William Scoresby* would sail south from Port Stanley on 2 December. The day after she

4. Editors' note: Royal Electrical and Mechanical Engineers.

sailed, she requested an ice report, so Back and Blyth climbed up the glacier on a fine clear day to get it for them. There was no ice worth mentioning around Port Lockroy and the channels were virtually ice-free. We immediately transmitted the happy observation to the ship and, as there was little to do, spent a little time making a last-minute cleanup of our house. We had all written mail intermittently throughout the year, so there was little point in adding to the pile until we received some letters, for all of our letters would go off together. We heard that the ship arrived at Deception Island on 5 December and left for Port Lockroy the next afternoon. People paced restlessly about the house all the following morning, peering out of the doorway every few minutes for a sight of the ship but she did not arrive.

In the afternoon, the wind began to blow quite freshly and Farrington had a report that the *Scoresby* was hove to in a storm at Dallman Bay, about thirty miles to the north of us. Our impatience increased when another signal followed saying that she was continuing the passage and would arrive before long. It was ten o'clock at night when the *Scoresby* suddenly appeared round Damoy Point and anchored to the west of the islet. They lowered a boat and put nine men ashore including Marchesi, Flett, Howkins, and Matheson, together with our anxiously awaited mail—the sorting of which was done in short order and it rapidly disappeared into the cabins of its recipients. Flett and Matheson had both grown quite heavy beards, and the latter was all but unrecognizable. The boat returned to the ship a short time later leaving with us Flett, Howkins, and Matheson. We heard little but the rattle of paper as one letter after another was torn open and read by flickering candlelight all through the night.

On her call at Deception Island, the *Scoresby* put ashore Sub-lieutenant Alan Reece, RNVR, of London. He was a meteorologist who immediately took over the base from Flett who left Deception Island to continue his geological work with us. Howkins, my companion of the *Marquesa*, was being relieved to return to the Naval Station at Port Stanley largely on account of his indifferent health. Matheson was to return to Deception Island while Marr returned to Port Stanley to confer with His Excellency the Governor.

The next day, the Army's dentist from Port Stanley, Captain J. Tomlinson, as well as John Bound of the Falkland Island Post Office Department, came to visit. The former had come down to give each of us a thorough dental examination, and brought along his complete kit of tools including a dentist's chair. He did an excellent job of repairing our teeth and saved many of us untold miseries in the year that followed. Bound came along with sacks full of philatelic mail, and spent the entire day cancelling thousands of sets of the new issue of Graham Land stamps that we brought down the previous January. It was a thankless task that none of the others could have possibly accomplished while the ship was at anchor in Port Lockroy.

Those of us remaining at the base spent most of that day attempting to reply to our mail and, I am afraid, we had little time to entertain our visitors. In the evening, however, Berry prepared another of his splendid meals to which we all sat down. Afterward, the fellowship continued and we sang the songs that sailors probably sing the world over under such bibulous circumstances.

Tomlinson and Bound completed their tasks the following day and prepared for the ship's departure north. At the last moment, Back decided that Blyth's hand (which he had injured skiing earlier in the year) needed an x-ray, so the latter made hurried arrangements to leave with the ship. Bound accepted the mail that we had so laboriously compiled for our loved ones and friends. And just as Marr was leaving Bransfield House, he turned to me and appointed me in charge of the base during his absence. By ten o'clock on 9 December, the *Scoresby* sailed for Deception Island and Port Stanley in an easterly wind that had blown all day long and was still quite strong.

CHAPTER NINE

Moving

IT WAS WONDERFUL TO RECEIVE THE MAIL, and we read and reread our letters until we almost had them memorized. There were also a few newspapers and magazines, and we spent hours gloating over the coloured advertisements in anticipation of our return home. We caught up a bit with the news, for although the BBC gave us the headlines each day, we had received no word about the many items of local interest that filled our hometown papers.

Mail was not the only welcome thing the ship brought down to us. The fresh mutton tasted like food fit for the gods—and negated the need for some of Doc's pills for a few days. We also enjoyed new supplies of fresh oranges and lemons. There were no fresh vegetables, which proved disappointing—but it could not be avoided because Port Stanley's new vegetable crop had not yet ripened.

Last, but not least, there was Gertrude. She was probably the most southerly pig that has ever lived, having come to Antarctica with a companion who remained at the Deception Island base. About six weeks old, it was not long before she received her name and became a great pet, providing us the company of something living that we seemed to crave. Davies adopted her from the first, laying out a bed of straw from some of the packing cases in a little corner outside the house where she could shelter from the wind and bask in the heat of the sun on brighter days. She crept under the house for warmth for a few days after we experienced some high wind and drift snow, but Davies soon constructed a little sty (like a dog kennel) into which she scampered in the inclement weather. On hot days, we often drank our morning tea sitting on a little perch Ashton built near Gertrude's stamping grounds. She snorted about the food that the galley provided from our scraps, and made an extra loud grunt when some thieving paddy tried to steal a morsel. After lunch, Davies sometimes went out to her. If one came upon him unexpectedly, one sometimes heard him talking in an unknown tongue that might have been Welsh, and which may have been addressed to the little porker.

It was no time at all before Gertrude began scampering all over our little islet. She became as sure-footed as a goat and raged after birds when they allowed her near enough to them. In the mornings, when Back went out to take his first met readings at eight o'clock, he invariably left the back door open. Gertrude seized these opportunities to enter the house and run directly for Davies's cabin before Back noisily ejected her upon his return. One day while painting the boats, Ashton completely forgot about our peripatetic pig and, after lunch, came upon a series of grey pig tracks all over the rocks below the house. He later found Gertrude covered in grey paint from the tip of her nose to the end of her tail. He doubted that this coating accounted for all the missing paint, however, and suggested that she drank the greater proportion. Gertrude continued to wear some of this coating until the day she was butchered.

Gertrude probably reached her greatest social success on New Year's Eve. Someone had to "first foot" Bransfield House, and we had little choice in the matter. As the clock struck twelve, we enticed her over the threshold with a saucerful of gin. Young and innocent as she was, she could not be cajoled into accepting the drink, and scampered out as quickly as she entered. We all became very attached to the little animal, and were very sorry when we had to execute her the day before the next ships arrived. Her meat was not grey, nor did it taste of paint, though there were some among us who refused to discover this for themselves.

The Agricultural Officer at Port Stanley, Dr. Gibbs, sent Lamb an extensive collection of plants and flowers from the Falkland Islands and the latter spent a day busily constructing a small garden by spreading the soil and specimens in a hollow in the rocks. He covered the new fauna with wire netting to foil the depredations of birds. A year later, he had occasion to revisit this garden, and found that almost all of the plants and flowers were dead or dying after spending a winter exposed to the cold and snow cover.

Following Flett's arrival and Blyth's departure with Marr, we no longer numbered nine. Berry felt Blyth's departure more than the rest of us because it meant the loss of help in the galley to which he had become accustomed. To provide him some unskilled labour, Flett took Marr's place in the daily roster and each of us, as our day came up, became "galley boy." In addition, one of us took over from Berry completely on various occasions, doing all the cooking and dish washing for the day. As far as Berry was concerned, however, it was a "busman's holiday" for he found himself returning to the galley time and again, like a bee attracted to a honeypot.

Ashton arranged for the *Scoresby* to bring the materials from Deception that he required to construct the temporary prefabricated building meant for Hope Bay. When they arrived, he immediately began fitting together the frames over which he meant to nail the corrugated iron. It did not take him many days to assemble the parts he needed to build the structure that later became known as our "Tin Galley."

We did not face many winds in December, or perhaps it is that the memories of pleasant days engrave themselves more deeply upon the mind. We seized beautifully warm sunny days with little ice about by making short boat trips to nearby landing places. The first of these little day trips took place on 12 December. We intended the journey to last the day, but we went prepared with enough food and camping gear to remain for a few days if a storm arose and prevented our immediate return to the base. Ashton, Lamb, Flett, and I left at 9:30 a.m. and headed the dinghy westward toward Doumer Island over the calm glistening water, crossing two narrow bands of brash ice (or "the wreck of other kinds of ice"). Most of Doumer Island's north shore consisted of steep snow slopes or ice cliffs, but at one point, toward the west end of the island, a rocky point descended from the sea. We landed at this spot a couple of hours later and spent about three hours in the area. We each engaged in our own work with little to distract us except the constant attacks of a few skuas nesting nearby at an altitude of 150 feet. On the west side of the island we found a moraine—quite a recent one, judging from its razor-sharp edges of the grey rock. Below this point, we found the ternery where Lamb had to defend himself from the attacks of these colourful but aggressive little birds who made the still air ring with their strident calls. The exhalation of a whale 100 feet offshore was the first one we saw that year. We had a good view of the snow-covered Wauwermans Islands, set in the midst of an ice-free sea, and then returned along the north shore of the island, keeping well offshore to clear a large berg apparently aground below some ice cliffs. At an extensive rock exposure on the shore of Doumer Island, we found a rock dam constructed by early sealers and estimated that the water pouring over it flowed at a rate of twenty gallons per minute. Aside from the skuas, we saw no birds during our visit but we could nevertheless tell that the site was a temporary penguin rookery by the weathered remains of their occupancy. After this most pleasant day, we arrived back at Goudier Islet shortly after 8:00 p.m.

We took a similar day trip about a week later to Damoy Point, Dorian Bay, and Casabianca Islet. We disembarked from the latter point shortly after 10:00 a.m. Jean-Baptiste Charcot used this low rocky islet that rose less than twenty feet above the sea as a "post office" during the French Antarctic Expedition in 1905. When he left a message that the Argentine vessel *Uruguay* did not happen to notice, the ensuing (unsuccessful) search for this prearranged message started rumours that disaster had overtaken Charcot's party before they reached the Antarctic. In his second expedition four years later, Charcot himself recovered the message intact in the same bottle in which he had left it. The wooden pole marking the cairn housing his message still stood when we arrived forty years later. We rowed over to Dorian Bay and continued our work from Damoy Point. Ashton helped me up to the summit of a knoll at an elevation of 165 feet to do some surveying. From here, we caught sight of two whales breaking the water at two widely separated points. We worked amidst hundreds of nesting penguins and the noise and aroma that accompany such locations on a warm day. Lamb and Flett went collecting above the muddy flat of Dorian Bay, but found nothing of great interest. We were back at the base by 6:00 p.m., having passed another whale as we approached the islet.

We heard no news from the ships between their departure from Port Lockroy on 9 December until their arrival at Port Stanley on the 15th, except that the *Scoresby* lost her lifeboat in a storm while at Deception Island and replaced it with one of the expedition's dinghies. Accordingly, we heard little of the activities of the new members of the party at Port Stanley until after we met them. Apparently Russell, James, Marshall, and Lockley, together with Thomas A. Donnachie (another radio operator from Glasgow), arrived in the Falklands in mid-December and, under Marr, they had all started work on the assembly of our cargo. Shortly afterward, we received a signal stating that the *Fitzroy* would arrive at Port Lockroy on 19 January to embark stores and personnel for Hope Bay.

Christmas and New Year's Days passed off uneventfully. On the former, through the generosity of the manager of the Royal Bank of Canada, Mr. Peat, we shared two bottles of champagne. We also enjoyed gifts of cakes and other foods that the good ladies of Port Stanley sent to us. Apart from these sidelights and the excellent meals prepared by Berry for us on both occasions, the days passed off like many of the previous Sundays we spent on Goudier Islet. Several Christmas signals expressing good wishes reached us: some private, some from the other bases, and one from the governor of the Falkland Islands. Most of us spent both of these holidays busily trying to reply to masses of mail before the ships called again.

We spent most of our time packing gear and equipment for the move to the new base. This task had to be done rather carefully given that the cases could be exposed to the elements for several weeks, so the job could not be hurried. We endured several windy spells during this period—one of which lasted for five days—that confined us to the house more than we had been for the preceding month. On the few good days we had, we often used the dinghy to visit the rookery or some of the nearby points, as Flett continued his geological work in the area. On two calm and bright days, Back and Farrington waded into the waters of the harbour for a swim. They did not remain in the water long—the temperature was only a few degrees above freezing—but they did more than wet themselves.

The heavy fields of pack ice from the far south began to move northward as the end of the year approached. Farrington and I went up onto the Channel Glacier on 7 January with glasses and observed that the sea to the south was one continual mass of thick and heavy pack ice. The pack was studded with tremendous icebergs for some of them must have been miles in extent. Three days later, these bergs began to enter Neumayer Channel, and rapidly clogged the Port Lockroy area with ice. One peculiar berg, with a tremendous arch that ran through it yielding a very thin crown, came in one day and went aground about a mile and a half away. We judged that it was high enough to allow a ship like the *Scoresby* to sail through it, and estimated that its high spire was nearly 200 feet tall. Later, a very large berg entered the southern end of the Channel and drove northward very slowly, moving into the port until we could see at least two miles of its length before it seemingly went aground. It was gone the next day but returned about a week later, ran aground for several days, and then withdrew to the south the day before the ship arrived. The thick field of pack ice that enclosed the area also cleared away at about the same time.

Whether by accident or design (we did not know which), the important signals seemed to reach us on Saturday evenings throughout the year. Back had a theory that the signal detailing the plans for the forthcoming year would arrive on the night of 9 January, and by the length of time Farrington spent at the radio we presumed that this long-anticipated signal had at last come through. He and Farrington did the decoding together, and we listened with bated breath as they read out the results: "an advanced southerly base under Marr will be established at Peter I Island, to which will be attached Lamb, Ashton, Berry, Davies, Farrington, Back. Hope Bay will be commanded by Taylor with Flett and the dogs." Ashton almost overturned the table in his eagerness to examine the maps on the wall of the messroom and identify Peter I Island. All of the others followed, knee-deep in overturned chairs. "Good Lord," he cried, "the bloody island's almost off the map!" Isolated and alone, the island stood almost 1,000 miles to the west-southwest of Port Lockroy, hundreds of miles from any known coast, with blank space on the map to the south. They all stood staring at this ominous solitude, babbling excitedly to each other. The consternation that ensued for the next few moments was almost mutinous! When Back and Farrington could no longer contain themselves, they explained the biggest hoax of the year—and read out the true signal.

Marr in Port Stanley intended to establish an advanced southerly base along the east coast of Graham Land, accompanied by James, Russell, Marshall, and Matheson. I was to be in charge of the base at Hope Bay, with Flett as second-in-command. We would divide the dogs between the two bases, and the stores for the new base would come from Hope Bay's supplies. The receipt of this news gave us plenty to do for a few days. Certain scientific stores required by the new bases were to be drawn from those at Port Lockroy. Some were already packed, while others had to be undone and reworked. In anticipation of our arrival at Hope Bay, we divided the stores into five general categories: food, general hardware, main hut and its hardware, stores shipped from Port Lockroy, and radio stores. When we arrived, Back would act as beachmaster. By this arrangement, we hoped to avoid some of the confusion that had ensued on our landing at Goudier Islet. After marking and addressing each store or baggage assigned to Hope Bay, we left it at a dump near our boat harbour. Upon landing at Hope Bay, our first job would be to erect the temporary galley that Ashton prepared for Berry, then complete the Nissen hut. Finally Ashton would again take complete charge of building the houses, with as much assistance as we could individually give him.

We had time in January to pay more attention to our laundry than was customary for most of us. We rooted through all the old bags and packsacks under the bed and assembled all the dirty gear that had been "mislaid" during the winter. Most of it was so dirty that it could support itself if stood in a corner. Washing necessitated water, so we chopped ice from the piece of sea ice usually moored inshore for the purpose of supplying the galley, and lit the heater in the bathroom. A favourite trick of some of our pranksters was to cover the funnel of this heater with an empty coal sack so that fire did not draw and instead began to fill the bathroom, galley, and house with smoke that Berry (who was sometimes in on the gag) quickly and stentoriously drew to the attention of the luckless launderer. When the fire got "smoking" for several hours, the ice melted into about a pailful of water. We used the water very efficiently; one pail was enough to wash and rinse a whole baleful of clothing. Perhaps it was their seafaring training, or maybe it was the accessibility of the galley water supply, but neither Ashton nor Berry produced a washing with the dark tattle-tale grey found in most of our laundry—the same homogenous drabness that seems to permeate the Antarctic mid-winter.

In anticipation of our departure, we packed up the specimens of rocks and lichens collected during the preceding months and replied to our mail. We watched two little paddies[1] hatch out from a nest most cleverly concealed beneath two of the old whalers' scows . . . and we answered our mail. We watched the fluffy little gull chicks swim confidently about the ice-cold water around the islet . . . and wrote more letters. And we waited for news of the *Fitzroy*'s departure so that she could reach Port Lockroy by 19 January. When the 20th arrived, the Falklands informed us that the *Eagle* had reached Port Stanley from Newfoundland and that all of the ships hoped to sail south on the 23rd.

The weather remained dull but calm, and the pack ice continued to fill up the harbour and all the sea beyond it. In case there was only one copy of some key reference books, several of us transcribed long excerpts out of Nordenskjöld's *Antarctica*, and copied anything we could find dealing with dogs, their training, and handling. The paraffin lamps, again necessary in the evenings, burned long into the night. On the 24 January, word came that the *Fitzroy*, with an oil barge in tow and the *Scoresby* for company, had all sailed from Port Stanley at midnight. The next day, another signal announced the sailing of the

---

1. Editors' note: "Paddies" is the nickname used in the Falkland Islands for Snowy Sheathbills.

Eagle with Marr on board. From the signals that Farrington heard directed to the ships, we presumed that Colonial Secretary Kenneth Bradley, Captain Roberts (who had been aboard the *Fitzroy* on her previous voyage), and Lieutenant Colonel Momber (the Officer Commanding the Falkland Island garrison) were also inbound. All three vessels arrived at Deception Island on 28 January.

For us, the time dragged by. Back gave each of us a complete medical examination and found that, aside from gaining a little weight due to enforced inactivity, no one suffered for the season spent at Port Lockroy. The big icebergs came and went around us, and it was not until the evening of the 31st, after all of the ice cleared out of the channels and the port, that we received further news. The sparks fairly flew between the two bases as Layther sent Farrington a long series of messages concerning an accident suffered by the *Eagle's* skipper, Captain R.C. Sheppard. While on her way south, the *Eagle* encountered stormy weather approaching Deception Island and Sheppard fell from the bridge and landed on his side, fracturing several ribs. Marr rendered first aid by tying a stout bandage around the captain's body. But Sheppard still suffered from violent periodic pains so Marr instructed Back to board the *Scoresby* when it reached Port Lockroy and immediately return to Deception Island. Marr also requested that Ashton join Back and attend to lumber at Deception Bay.[2]

We had breakfast the next morning, 1 February, before the *Scoresby* dropped her anchor to the west of the islet at 7:20 a.m. We were alongside in a few moments. Flett went aboard with Back to reassemble the gear he had left at Deception early in December and, after consulting with Marchesi, they decided that Ashton did not need to return to Deception. The lumber was nearly prepared and Flett could complete any remaining work. The *Scoresby* was only in the harbour for twenty minutes before sailing off again. During that interval, we had time to collect our mail and learn that the *Eagle* would ferry us alone to Hope Bay and that her appearance was not very prepossessing. We returned to the base and distributed the mail.

The *Scoresby* made a quick turnaround at Deception Island on 2 February as she sailed south with the *Fitzroy* that afternoon. It was a dull, uninspiring sort of day, made even more so in the evening when Farrington announced that one of his motor generator sets had burned out. This left only one unit in operation for the ensuing year. It was still dull the next morning, but a fresh west

---

2.   Editor's note: This paragraph borrows from Taylor, "Official Journal, 1944-6," 31 January 1945, Taylor fonds, UMA, MSS 108 Box 5 File 1.

wind blew brash toward the harbour. The two ships sailed into Port Lockroy just twenty-four hours after leaving Deception Island.

We went aboard almost before the *Fitzroy* lost weigh and were warmly greeted by all our visitors, including Marr and Blyth. We were also introduced to the new members of the party. Frank White (a Falkland Islander) and Norman Layther (a radio operator) would become the new occupants of Bransfield House. Gordon Lockley would also join them. He was twenty-eight years old and worked on marine biological research with the British Museum before joining the navy on radar work. He had been through Dunkirk's evacuation as a civilian, and since joining the service had sailed to many parts of the world in various classes of ship, from aircraft carriers on down.

Victor Russell's appearance created a minor sensation. He was wearing a kilt, which we suspect to be the first one ever paraded around Port Lockroy. It was not, however, the first kilt worn in the Antarctic—an honour that went to Dr. William Bruce's Scottish National Antarctic Expedition more than forty years before. Russell was educated at Cambridge and spent several summers on exploratory work in Newfoundland, but was with the Survey Branch of the Royal Engineers in Belgium when he joined Tabarin. He was of excellent physique, being about six feet tall, and proved himself to be a very willing and skillful worker with a most pleasant equanimity.

A red-bearded and slightly built chap who was a year younger than Russell introduced himself as James. Despite the sloppy clothing draping loosely over his well-knit body, David P. James still possessed a somewhat dashing appearance. He came to us following a distinguished career in the navy with the light coastal forces. His ship was sunk under him in February 1943 and he was taken prisoner before escaping from North Germany to Sweden a year later. Prior to joining the expedition, he had been with the Naval Intelligence Division.

Norman Marshall was another Cambridge man, thirty years of age and of a sturdy, if somewhat rotund, figure. Prior to the war, he did biological research with the Department of Oceanography, University College, Hull, but joined the army in 1941 to become a radar specialist. Marshall had a cheery disposition, always ready with a smile and a joke, and on many occasions did much to sustain drooping morale.

We also met Kenneth Bradley and his son, Lieutenant Niddrie, RNVR, a South African meteorologist serving with the naval station at Port Stanley; Alan Carr, the Falkland Islands customs officer who arrived to act as postmaster for another mass of philatelic mail that flooded the postal facilities; and lastly Alan Reece, who had taken charge of Deception Island on Flett's departure in December. We also resumed acquaintances with Captain Roberts, Captain Pitt, and Lieutenant Colonel Momber, all in fine fettle.

I went with Marr to his cabin and he explained to me the forthcoming plan for transferring all the stores to the *Eagle* at Deception for shipment directly to Hope Bay. Two new motorboat magnetos were aboard and the boat that Ashton had spent so much time repairing would come with us because another one had been procured for Marr's party. The other two vessels would land some stores and build accommodations at Sandefjord Bay on the western tip of Coronation Island in the South Orkneys, before returning to Port Stanley. The prospect of having the two bases on east Graham Land created a refreshing and keen spirit of competition.

In the evening, the festivities ashore went off well. Another long sing-song continued until nearly midnight, and Mr. Carr shared his particularly good voice. Then the heavy motorboat from the *Fitzroy* took the party, including the *Scoresby*'s officers, away and pressed through the sheet of heavy brash ice carpeting the calm waters of the harbour.

A fresh wind blew from the east in the morning, and it snowed a little as the working parties from both ships busily unloaded cargo (the first shipment of which arrived ashore while the previous night's entertainment was in progress). Lockley became acquainted with all of the peculiarities of Bransfield House and its location. He also received advice from all quarters. After paying our respects to Lockley, Layther, and White, we departed for Deception Island that evening carrying one of the whalers' heavy mooring chains to tie up the oil barge that would become the *Scoresby*'s source of fuel after we departed for Hope Bay. As the motorboat towed the heavy load along, a beautiful sunset painted the crest of Doumer Island with an orange pastel, and we took leave of Bransfield House with sentimental feelings and memories of the happy incidents we had enjoyed within its rough walls.

The ships sailed early the next morning. We slipped past Damoy Point into the ice-free waters of the Neumayer Channel, stopping for a short time below Copper Peak so that Marr, Reece, and James could visit a small islet and return with some rock specimens from a mile or so offshore. Considering the amount of ice that had filled Port Lockroy only a few days previously, we were amazed at the ice-free waters. While passing the Brabant Island with a fresh wind blowing from the east, we had many birds for company. Cape pigeons wheeled around the ship, dainty Wilson's petrels danced over the waves, and there were also a few skuas. The ship rolled a little as we crossed the open sea in Bransfield Strait, and the sky became overcast as we sailed between the colourful walls of Neptune's Bellows and dropped anchor in Whaler's Bay at 8:40 a.m. on 5 February. The *Scoresby* followed us in a few moments later and dropped anchor off our port side. Some distance away, clear inshore, lay the *Eagle*; beyond her the oil barge sat moored to the shore. With darkness approaching, no one went ashore but Reece.

In the morning, the *Fitzroy* went alongside the *Eagle* to transfer the Hope Bay cargo. We went ashore to meet, among other things, our dogs. Only one had died on the voyage out, which testifies to the care that Marshall (assisted by Russell and James) gave them. The huskies were full of life and seemed to be very pleased to see us. There were not many penguins around the shore of the beach at this point, and all that I saw were dead. It was impossible to prevent the dogs from tackling them. They did not attack for food, for they were not hungry. It was their lust to kill, and they left the bodies of the dead birds strung along the entire length of the beach.

Flett and I met with Ashton, located one of the old piles of lumber, and identified sound pieces that Ashton anticipated needing. Most of our personal gear went ashore off the *Fitzroy*, which anticipated sailing next morning. We found Smith, the cook, in as happy a humour as ever, at the building used as living quarters over the past year. We appreciated the sandwich and cup of coffee he had ready for us in a few moments. The weather had been fine for most of the day, with little wind. The sea and sky seemed full of birds, mostly Cape pigeons, but there were also quite a number of Antarctic terns and giant petrels.

Here we met, for the first time, the red-headed, good-natured new radio operator, Tommy Donnachie. Tommy was from Glasgow, and still retained his "burr." Though only twenty-three, he spent much of his time during the war on armed merchant cruisers. He was a quiet-spoken, genial, and obliging person, and became one of the best-liked members of the party. Lamb and I stayed ashore with Smith, Matheson, and Donnachie that night, and slept on the same sort of metal beds used at Port Lockroy.

It was raining and foggy in the morning but some of us started carrying the timber we had picked over the previous day down to the beach where it would subsequently be picked up and transported by one of the scows to the *Eagle* or to the oil barge. With one man on each end, we carried half a dozen of the long lengths of timber down to the beach at a time. There was too much cargo for the *Eagle* to carry in one load, so the lumber destined for Marr's southerly base was assembled atop the oil barge where it remained until the *Eagle* returned from her first trip to Hope Bay. As Flett and I rounded one of the buildings in the drizzle just before reaching the beach, we ran into Bradley and Marr, who invited us to follow them to the building Flett had selected as the base. We followed them up to the house 100 yards away and into one of the rooms. We sat on the edge of one of the bunks that lined the walls, our clothing dripping from the rain. There was no heat in the room, and no one else was around, for it was barely noon.

We knew that Marr had not been in the best of health when he left for Port Stanley in the *Scoresby* two months previous, and he looked tired and haggard standing before us. After consulting with the colonial secretary, he had decided to relinquish his command of the expedition and return to England. Several months before, he had mentioned to Lamb and me his apprehension about being able to continue working for another year on account of his failing health. He felt greatly the strain of his responsibilities during the establishment of the bases, for he had worked similar jobs throughout the war at Iceland and South Africa. Flett and I were astonished at this sudden turn of events that we had not suspected. We joined Bradley in trying to convince him to reconsider his decision to stand down but he was adamant, saying that he had considered it over a long period of time and that his mind was definitely made up. My own astonishment increased when he proposed that I accept the leadership of the entire party in his place. He forwarded a signal to the governor of the Falkland Islands to this effect that same day, 7 February. Two days later, I received a signal from the governor offering me the appointment of officer-in-charge of Operation Tabarin. I accepted.

Marr intended to remain with the expedition until the new bases were established before returning to Port Stanley on the last ship going north. Our group discussed the wisdom of establishing the second base without the benefit of Marr's experience throughout the winter, and it was eventually decided to amalgamate the two bases into one at Hope Bay. Marr's condition, however, considerably worsened after the *Fitzroy* and *William Scoresby* departed for the South Orkneys. After Back examined Marr, the *Scoresby* was recalled and took Marr directly to Port Stanley where he received hospital treatment before going home to England.

PART THREE

Hope
Bay

CHAPTER TEN

Hope Bay

ON 8 FEBRUARY I CAUGHT A MOTORBOAT going out to the *Eagle* to pay my respects to Captain R.C. Sheppard. Climbing up the dirty sides of the battered old Newfoundland sealer, I found the skipper talking to Back in the saloon. Back had just examined him and expected he would be able to sail the *Eagle* within three days, provided that we did not run into any bad weather, for he was far from well. Sheppard was a fine-looking man approaching fifty, with a good head of silvering hair. A native of St. John's, Newfoundland, Sheppard worked as the harbour master there before joining this cruise with the *Eagle*. Although he had sailed shiploads of food to Britain, he had been at the port for a couple of years and was sent on this as relief from the strain of harbour master work, and this made his accident a rather inauspicious start. We joined the skipper in a cup of good coffee and lobster, which is about the last thing one expects to find on an Antarctic table, and had a pleasant chat. By the time I left, we agreed upon a provisional sailing date of Saturday, 10 February (dependent on another medical examination by Back before we sailed). Second engineer Frank Power took over the motorboat we renovated at Port Lockroy and had it in good running order within a few days so that it could be usefully employed running between the ship and the shore.

The rearranging of cargo occupied much of our time at Deception Island. Even after we learned that only one base would be established, the cargo still had to be sorted so that our stores were complete with the first load aboard the *Eagle* (in the event that the ship could not make a second trip). Ashton and Flett had our party scrounge about the old deserted buildings of the whaling factory, gathering bricks, bolts, nuts, furniture, windows, and other articles, assembling them on the beach, and shipping them off to the *Eagle* or the oil barge.

Figure 17. The *Eagle* at Deception Island, 11 February 1945.

Figure 18. The crew of the SS *Eagle*, 11 February 1945.

We also conducted scientific work at Deception Island. Lamb made the best of the limited time he had at his disposal to gather lichen specimens, which he found growing in much greater luxuriance at Deception Island than at Port Lockroy. He took good views with his camera, and found time to take shots with the larger panoramic camera of Port Foster, as the Deception Island harbour is generally known. Russell also took some sun observations to establish a bearing for Reece's meteorological observations.

There was plenty to interest us and keep us busy, but our departure date depended on Captain Sheppard's physical condition. The *Scoresby* had called for a few moments to take Marr away on the morning of 9 February, and the *Fitzroy* was well on her way to the South Orkneys before Back gave Captain Sheppard his checkup. The *Eagle* had arrived at Deception short of officers, and could hardly afford to lose her skipper's services. I wondered then, and I have often wondered since, what might have happened if Back had not agreed to allow him to sail on the next calm day. The ship's first officer had disembarked at Montevideo due to illness and Robert Whitten, a nephew of the skipper's who had been second officer, ably filled these shoes. The *Eagle*'s other officer was the seventy-year-old Thomas Carroll, an old-time veteran of polar travel who had been with Robert Peary when he made his trip to the North Pole in 1908—a man who could almost smell the presence of any ice his ship approached. So the ship had travelled to Deception short of officers, and it seemed doubtful that she could lose her skipper's services and still continue. Fortunately, this situation did not arise, for Back deemed Sheppard to be healthy enough for duty.

We immediately asked Reece to prepare a weather forecast for Sunday—a day later than originally considered—so that we would have time to finish loading the ship. The weather began to clear on Friday, which improved the prospects of a good weekend. Reece began to assimilate the information he needed to forecast by radio, and Back keenly assisted him.

Saturday was a dull, calm day and, except for some of the personal gear, the dogs, and ourselves, we finished loading the vessel by mid-afternoon. Accommodation on the ship was at a premium, and Ashton temporarily fit some berth space into a small cabin in the forecastle where five men spent an uncomfortable night. About midnight, Reece predicted that the morning would be overcast with patches of fog, clearing later in the day with visibility in excess of thirty miles. There would be a south to southwest wind blowing between force 4 and 5 as well as cloud cover between 4 and 7 tenths. We decided to sail next morning for Hope Bay.

Figure 19. Members of Operation Tabarin on board the SS *Eagle* at Deception Island, 11 February 1945. Standing (left to right): Tom Berry, David James, John Matheson, Victor Russell, Ivan Mackenzie Lamb, James "Fram" Farrington, Thomas Donnachie, Alan Reece, Andrew Taylor, Gwion "Taff" Davies, Charles "Smitty" Smith, Eric Back. Sitting: Lewis "Chippie" Ashton, John Blyth, Norman Marshall, William "Bill" Flett.

The morning broke with some fog and cleared within a few hours. There was little wind. While we had an early breakfast, the dogs, which had been running loose, incidentally located Deception Island's pig through the floor of a wooden building and killed it instantly. We loaded the dogs aboard the ship and tied them to any convenient projection on the deck—the scow, in the boats, anywhere fights could be kept to a minimum. Lamb took some group photographs of the ship's crew and then of the expedition members. After difficulty clearing the ship's anchor, we bid goodbye to Reece and Donnachie and, with Smith accompanying us for the voyage, we sailed out of the harbour at 11:30 a.m.

The *Eagle* passed through Neptune's Bellows and struck a course immediately for the Hope Islands about 120 miles due east just north of Antarctic Sound. Later in the afternoon, we sailed into a beautiful clear sky. Large and isolated bergs scattered across Bransfield Strait but, aside from them, the sea was perfectly clear of ice. It was a perfect day for our trip, and the ship rolled along easily in the light swells at about 7 knots.

We had a good chance to examine the *Eagle*, the last of Newfoundland's wooden sealers. The ship was built as one of a fleet of thirty-nine; her wooden hull was twenty-two inches thick and sturdily braced with tremendously heavy struts and beams for work in the ice. She was a coal burner—and no one had to tell us that latter fact, for her bunkering left the docks clotted with coal. She was rough and dirty from stem to stern, her engines outdated, her running gear defective, and the wooden timbers of her hull weakened to rottenness in places. The "exigencies of war" meant that Captain Sheppard took his "rest cure" on such a ship.

She carried a heavy deck load on this voyage, piled high with timbers, Nissen hut components, crates, a scow too heavy for her derricks to safely handle, and dogs. Forr'ard, a confusion of articles levelled her decks above the rails, all sprinkled with a heavy coating of coal dust. Motorboats and dories squeezed in-between these loads. Little of her black, tarry deck was not hidden by cargo. Lifeboats slung outboard from their davits, and the space they had occupied was as well covered as the rest of the deck.

Tall masts supported the *Eagle*'s inadequate derricks, and the shrouds of the foremast led up a deep crow's nest. Upon this same mast was a fore staysail which we used for a time after the wind freshened. Her superstructure was grey and her hull tarred black. At dinner one evening, Captain Sheppard regaled us with yarns of former days, when her holds and bunkers brimmed with seals through which men waded, knee-deep in meat and blubber, to lie down among the pelts for their rest. Her former history had earned her the sobriquet *"Lucky" Eagle*; her fortune would be well-tested before she again saw her homeport.[1]

We gave a wide berth to the tremendous passing tabular icebergs. Astrolabe Island lay off our starboard quarter as we broke into the sunshine in mid-afternoon. At this time we saw a couple of whales breach a quarter of a mile away

---

1.   Author's note: Among the signals that arrived in late February were some indicating that the government was considering the charter of the *Eagle* for a second season's work, provided that she proved satisfactory at Hope Bay. Captain Sheppard, who formed an attachment with the old *Eagle* that most of us shared, did not feel inclined to wholeheartedly endorse her use for another season. As an alternative, he suggested the procurement of a new diesel-driven wooden vessel of about 300 tons built for the Newfoundland government during the Battle of the Atlantic. He submitted his recommendation and the ship carrying the stores for the party that relieved us in the spring of 1946 was one of these vessels: the *Trepassey*.

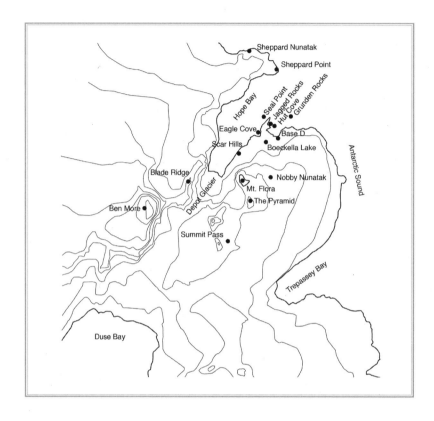

Map 7. The Hope Bay Area.

flinging themselves forty feet or more out of the water, floundering back with a thunderous splash and repeating the performance for us a few moments later.

About midnight, we approached the vicinity of Montravel Rock and the skipper reduced speed in the darkness. The number of icebergs appeared to increase but we discerned no pack ice. Ashton joined Captain Sheppard on the bridge in the early hours of the morning, and we made it well into Antarctic Sound by morning, having avoided any fields of pack ice. We turned into the bay at seven o'clock, and half an hour later we cruised about the bay where a high southwest wind blew gustily for about four hours.

We were now back where the *Scoresby* had been during her brief visit on 7 February 1944. The bay cut into the land in a southwest direction, with heavily crevassed snowfields descending steeply to its almost continuously ice-cliffed northerly shore. At the head of the bay, the picturesque Depot Glacier descended between confining rock walls. To the south stood Mount Flora, a sharp ridge of black rock to the north where Johan Gunnar Andersson had made his amazing fossil discoveries in 1903. The southerly side of the bay had a different character altogether compared to the northerly one, and consisted of small bald rocky hillocks rising steeply from the shore that became more gradual toward the base of Mount Flora, with a massive snowfield farther south. Wind whistled down the Depot Glacier toward us, and tails of snow blew from the blue ice cliffs at its foot. Except for the visit of the *Scoresby* the previous year, no one is known to have visited Hope Bay except for Lincoln Ellsworth who, when returning from his unsuccessful attempt to cross the continent by air from Snow Hill Island, called there in 1935 with the *Wyatt Earp* to pick up the remains of the collection of fossils which Andersson and Nordenskjöld had left behind. In 1909, Dr. Charcot attempted to reach the bay, but pack ice forced him to turn back while he was still sixty miles away. In 1921, Thomas Bagshawe and Maxime Charles Lester had hoped to winter there, but ice conditions also prevented their little whale catcher from approaching and they subsequently wintered in Andvord Bay on west Graham Land, not far from Port Lockroy.

The *Eagle* met fortunate conditions and succeeded where previous attempts failed. When the wind moderated, we launched a dory and quickly located an anchorage in twenty-five fathoms of water, off a little cove along the southerly shore that we subsequently named Eagle Cove. The ship moved in and the anchor bit, but unloading could not begin until we selected a site. We went ashore in pairs, according to a prearranged plan, searching for the most suitable site as quickly as possible. Lamb examined and photographed the old stone hut built by Anderrson, Duus, and Grunden in 1903 before it could be disturbed.

We met at an appointed place at 3:30 p.m. to deliberate. Matheson and I had found a site deeper in the bay than where the ship anchored, and its greatest disadvantage was a rocky beach approach which would be unusable at low tide. Russell and Berry located a potential site in Eagle Cove, and Ashton and Flett discovered a third near the tip of the rocky point (called Seal Point by Andersson) some distance above the water in another sea of penguins. None of our finds seemed ideal. We wandered west of the stone hut after examining Ashton's choice and came upon the site where we ultimately built the base, about half a mile south of Seal Point at the toe of the massive sheet of inland ice that terminated near sea level. The level morainic areas, where rock cropped up at several points, were divided by the bed of a swift-flowing glacier stream. On either side of the stream lay areas about 100 feet square that rose a little higher than the ground immediately surrounding them. The prospective building sites were well clear of the penguins, an attribute which none of the former choices possessed. Immediate access to the glacier was an important consideration for water summer supply, as well as for the dogs and their training. There were fairly good approaches from the sea (despite a few reefs and rocks), and the ice foot was comparatively low: about seven feet.

These two hills became our building sites. The location's greatest disadvantage was its distance from the *Eagle*'s anchorage. The approach was completely exposed to east and northeast winds, which subjected the vessel to heavy swells. We did not then know the prevalence of the wind from the southwest. Matheson, James, and Marshall took a boat to sound the approach to the site and discovered an alternative anchorage a half-mile offshore in twenty fathoms of water. We decided to use this location and informed Captain Sheppard and First Officer Whitten of our choice.

In the meantime, the skipper rested on his bunk. He felt the effects of his preceding sixteen hours on the bridge, became very cold toward morning, and suffered from a painfully sore side. Whitten took complete charge of landing the stores and decided that it was too late in the evening to take a load ashore. In retrospect, he must have regretted this decision as a missed opportunity on the calm first night of our arrival. Many of the crew went into the bay to shoot seals—a favourite sport of Newfoundlanders and, in this instance, a welcome source of dog food. When we got back to the ship, "Skipper Tom" (as the Newfoundland crew affectionately knew Carrol) was busy cutting up a seal on the deck. It took him twenty minutes from the time the carcass was hoisted over the side to strip the blubber and cut off massive pieces which he cast to the dogs. They gulped it down, still warm, the blood dripping from their fangs.

Whitten planned an early scow load containing the temporary galley for the next morning, but the southwest wind blew up about five o'clock and one of the ship's dories broke loose. Our motorboat unsuccessfully tried to catch up with it, and had a difficult time returning to the ship in the teeth of the violent wind. The loaded scow shipped considerable water and had to be unloaded and bailed out. The *Eagle* dragged her anchor several hundred feet seaward before she took a good hold again.

The wind subsided at noon, and we all went ashore in Eagle Cove, walking overland the three-quarters of a mile to the base. Lamb and I walked over to look at the old stone hut. He had taken some photographs the previous day, but had not come across many relics. There was an old tin, apparently used either as a pot or a "smoker" stove for burning blubber, as well as some old rope, cloth, barrel staves, and hoops. The inside of the hut was deep with penguin guano. We found the hut standing wonderfully secure considering the expediency of its construction and its long period of neglect. It was built of loose, angular stones and measured about twelve feet square and 5.5 feet in height. The walls varied in thickness from four feet at the base to two feet across the top. The pole, which had been used with the sledge to support the tent roof, lay along one side of the hut, half buried in the excrement that covered the whole area. The intestines of the walls were stuffed with moss and seaweed, much of which still lay in place, dry and crisp. The floor was covered with the skins of penguins that served as a mattress; the feathers from these skins were still well preserved though many had blown into the cracks between the stones of the walls. An aperture on the north side of the structure formed the entrance, and the occupants used its corner as a fireplace. The "chimney," incidentally, was merely a more open section of the wall through which smoke could permeate. A few small sticks extruded themselves through the cracks of the upper part of the "chimney," perhaps serving as emergency kindling in case the blubber fire went out. In digging around in a hardened pile of soot apparently washed down by years of rain, we unearthed the tin used as the "smoker" stove, still half filled with rancid fat. Above the fireplace in a crevice in the wall, a small, homemade, and broken hammer handle (which, to judge from the location it was found, might well have been the stick they used to stir the penguin soup) was cached.

We left the hut to search for more artifacts. Sixty feet to the southwest, we found five tent pegs, all but one was steel, and fixed the position of the little tent that served Andersson, Duus, and Grunden so well. Alongside lay a light crowbar, about four feet long, buried in the snow. A hundred yards north of the hut, atop a small, rocky knoll, still stood the wooden marker that they had erected to attract a rescue vessel. Although readily visible to anyone landing nearby, from a perspective out at sea the marker was lost amidst the massiveness of its background. The deep red paint was worn off all the weather-silvered wood, except for the parts of the stick that were wedged into the rocky cairn supporting it. In the muck surrounding the hut we found a few more things, including a serviceable

Figure 20. The stone hut constructed by Andersson's Swedish party in 1903 and found by Tabarin personnel upon landing at Hope Bay on 12 February 1945.

Figure 21. The first stores landing at Hope Bay, 13 February 1945.

and well-preserved shoe. Remains of a couple of barrels lay strewn about the place, along with pieces of tin cans that were all but rusted away. A box had been fitted as a frame for a canvas-covered window on the west wall of the hut, and pieces of canvas still adhered to it, the wood perfectly preserved.

We searched the entire area for any sign of a message, but had no success. Presumably, Captain Larsen picked up the message left by the original occupants and Andersson collected many of the other interesting relics in gratitude for their survival through the winter. The hut itself stands as a remarkable monument to the stubborn resourcefulness of the three men who lived within its uncomfortable confines through the windy Hope Bay winters. Its walls stood as sturdily as the day the men evacuated the hut for their momentous meeting with Nordenskjöld at Cape Well Met.

From the site of the stone hut, Lamb and I watched the first scow arrive with its load of stores at four o'clock in the afternoon, so we made our way over to the site of the new base. All hands worked to unload the scow, and Ashton

Figure 22. The makeshift tarpaulin cover on the Nissen hut at Hope Bay, 30 March 1945.

Figure 23. Construction at Hope Bay, 26 February 1945.

immediately began building the "Tin Galley." By nightfall, the walls were up, the door fitted, and the framework of the roof attached. Matheson and four others returned in the dinghy to the ship, which was around Seal Point. The others of us walked over to Eagle Cove to be picked up by the motorboat, which returned us aboard ship with some difficulty.

The following day, we completed the "Tin Galley" despite once again losing the morning to the high southwesterly wind. We even installed the stove so that Berry could cook the evening meal on it. The high wind almost swung the *Eagle* onto a small berg that broke away from shore but, fortunately, the berg just cleared the ship. Some of the dogs were ashore and ran wild amongst the penguins, causing an unholy massacre of the birds. A train of dories and a dinghy brought some of the stores that afternoon, and Back had his beachmastering job well in hand. Toward evening, the heavy timbers for the house began to arrive and a dozen men secured a line around each one, hauling them up the slope to our building site about twenty-five feet above sea level. Russell worked aboard the *Eagle* where he attempted, with difficulty, to send stores ashore to us in the order they were required.

As soon as the "Tin Galley" was complete, we chose the locations for the house and a Nissen hut. All three of these buildings lay clustered together on the north side of the little stream that flowed full-bore. We intended to locate a second Nissen hut on the opposite side of the streambed and to store all of our emergency supplies in it, so that our position would not be completely hopeless if fire destroyed the house. Work on the first Nissen hut began on 16 February, when much of its frame was erected. We poured concrete around its holding-down bolts the next day, and almost got one end attached to this framework when a tremendous gust from the morning wind on 18 February caught it. Despite the ropes that James had used to guy the frame, the structure gently subsided to the ground and pulled the bolts out of the concrete. It took a couple of days to repair the damage, but fastening the curved sheets onto the roof gave the building a degree of strength and solidity. Before the roof was finished, we discovered that we were one bundle of roofing sheets short, and as a result we could not close up the final four feet. Davies and Matheson temporarily wrapped a tarpaulin over the gap and weighted it in place, anticipating that the additional sheets of corrugated iron would arrive on the *Eagle*'s next trip a few weeks later.[2] With the structures in place, stores began to flow into the shelter of the Nissen hut on 24 February.

The main structure, which became known as "Eagle House," consisted of a hodgepodge of buildings that Ashton cleverly fitted together. The main portion comprised two buildings measuring 16 x 38 feet placed side by side. On the west end he appended a 27 x 20–foot addition, while on the opposite end he constructed another 9 x 25–foot addition mostly from pieces of packing cases. The main and central portion contained the messroom. Eight cabins, each measuring eight feet square, as well as another two storage areas, surrounded its perimeter. The long extension toward the front held the engine-driven generator for the radio, a bathroom, storage space for our oil requirements, and the sanitary facilities. The galley, a scientific laboratory, a carpenter shop, and the bos'n's storeroom were located on the opposite end of the house. Ashton began

---

2.   Author's note: This hope was not realized. When we last saw Hope Bay in 1946, this tarpaulin still served the same purpose.

erecting this building on 18 February, and the floor was complete and some of the framework of the walls up when a gale struck on 19 February, collapsing this framework and delaying our progress. The same people who had prepared the original building at Port Lockroy built ours, and they fitted together the studs and panels with mortise and tenon joints in the same manner as that structure. With more pieces involved, however, the jigsaw part of the erection was more difficult than its predecessor. By the end of the month the sheeting was on the roof, and in the first few days of March much of the inner-lining was in place because we were so frequently confined within the building by the weather. After several unsuccessful attempts, we successfully applied the rubberoid roofing on 6 March. Although the building was still far from complete, we moved into it two days later.

Captain Sheppard, unwell from the time of his arrival at Hope Bay, was a convalescent invalid for most of the time he spent there. He was a restless patient, and one day took the new little motorboat called the *Jeanry II* to the northerly entrance to the bay where he tried some fishing. He landed a couple of tasty *notothenia*, a local fish weighing between two and three pounds. We later named the point off which he fished "Sheppard Point." He came ashore once or twice to pay us a visit and to watch the progress of our establishment, but for the most part he stayed on his ship resting on his bunk. Toward the end of February, he caught a cold and the racking cough caused him a great deal of pain. He never complained, however, and was always interested in our problems, though he had to leave all of the landing of the stores in the hands of the hard-working Bob Whitten.

The dogs ran wild for a week or so, roaming about in bands of three or four, chasing penguins, and going far out of sight of the camp for hours at a time. Dead penguins lay strewn all over and the dogs left many partly eaten carcasses around the camp. The animals also contaminated our water supply and any half-emptied boxes of food that happened to be left exposed. In short, they became a considerable nuisance. In an effort to drive them away from the camp area, some of the chaps threw rocks at them. Had their aims been as good as their intentions, several dead dogs would have resulted. Marshall had charge of the animals on their long sea voyage, but since James requested the responsibility at our base, his first task was to arrange tethering lines to keep the dogs a suitable distance from our landing operations.

Davies hated to see the dogs harassing and killing the penguins. He, too, sometimes cast a rock their way—more to scare them than to disable them— for his kindheartedness often included an unfortunate dog being attacked by its fellows. On one occasion, a fight began between three dogs under the house that was supported on brick piers three feet high on the south side. Davies started under the house to tear the dogs apart, as he had so often done before. In the excitement, the dog he happened to be handling turned on him and snapped at his hand. It was not a serious bite, but it drew blood. This seemed to agitate Davies a great deal. Without hesitation, he grabbed the offender by the scruff of its neck and, holding it "athwartships" by the tail, he bit its back. This drastic but effective remedy scattered the dogs. Davies emerged muttering to himself from beneath the house, spitting out white hair that he had pulled from the dog's back.

Low tide exposed a gravelly beach below the ice foot on which we landed the bases' stores. At high tide, there was plenty of water to allow the scow to come alongside the ice foot. Consequently, the scow's arrival had to be timed to suit the tide. The little Port Lockroy motorboat was not nearly powerful enough to handle the loaded scow in high winds, and the magneto still gave trouble so that the engine would not go. Thus, between the tides, the winds, and the inefficiency of the motorboat, we did not discharge the cargo as quickly as we had wished. If there was the chance of a second load catching the same tide, members of the wintering party assisted Back and Davies (whose time during this period was almost entirely occupied with the discharge of the cargo at the base) with unloading the scow on the ice foot. In this way, the area was kept clear for the subsequent load. It also obviated the danger of overloading the ice foot and precipitating all of the stores it supported into the sea.

The greatest difficulty in a high wind was rounding Seal Point before entering "Hut Cove" below the base. As a result, we located an alternative spot to unload some cargo in Eagle Cove, opposite to the ship's anchorage, which the boat could access in all but the worst of weather. Here we unloaded surplus stores that we did not plan to use until the following season. We also placed some oil, petrol, and coal at the site. We anticipated that we would easily transport these stores to the base in the spring by dinghy and, by arranging this alterative point of discharge, we expedited the discharge of the stores and avoided the necessity of constructing a jetty in Hut Cove.

The incessant bad weather forced us to discharge the Eagle Cove portion of our stores before transporting all of Hut Cove's allotment. A consistently high southwest wind caused us a great deal of trouble and annoyance. Since it was an offshore wind, it was exceedingly dangerous for the small boats to get caught in its full blast. On many occasions, on rounding Seal Point into its teeth, there was some doubt that the ship's side could be reached. The boats had to run for the nearby shore repeatedly, rocky as it was, and wait for the wind to subside.

While anchored in Hope Bay, several incidents tested the *Eagle*'s "lucky" nickname. The first occurred on 18 February. The night was clear and fairly calm and we were unloading timbers for the house when, above the hills in the direction of the ship, a massive puff of black smoke showed up against the deep blueness of the sky. A dinghy-load of men set off round Seal Point, and the rest of us dropped what we were doing and ran like mad toward the hilltop half a mile distant. Seeing nothing seriously wrong with the ship's exterior, we returned to the base and finished unloading the scow before using it to return to the *Eagle*.

We learned what had happened upon our arrival. When we had been scrounging our own stores around the old whaling station at Deception island, the crew of the *Eagle* came across several cases of black powder (including some open containers) which they thought might be useful in an encounter with ice. They were properly stored somewhere during the voyage but, in the course of the unloading, one tin was piled loosely on the afterdeck together with several barrels of salt meat, lumber, and other articles. Just what occurred is unclear. Perhaps the breeze carried the burnt stump of a match or a spark from a cigarette. Whatever the case, something ignited the tin of powder and up she went in an explosion that blew the hogshead of meat and other articles into the sky. Fortunately the ship was not damaged, and someone went round in a dinghy collecting most of the articles that took this long route over the side.

A second test of the *Eagle*'s luck occurred the following day when the high winds endangered the ship. Toward evening, the southwest wind funnelled through the glacier at the head of Hope Bay with increasing velocity, and seemed to reach its maximum ferocity just as dusk was closing in. From the deck, one could see it whipping up the spume and spindrift from the crests of the waves in such masses that the whiteness looked more like driving snow across a glacier than the stormy sea it was. Strings of brash ice began to drift past us at good speed. We were anchored close to the south shore, but well out in the bay toward Seal Point. We must have had a good hold with the pair of anchors that were out, for the ship showed no tendency to drag them. However, at about 7:30 p.m., the skipper put a man at the wheel, and started his engines slow ahead, steering to his anchors to take the strain off the cables.

All three ship's officers were on watch as they manoeuvred her round a small iceberg that swept by our starboard side. Two miles away, another slightly larger one approaching at good speed seemed to have struck a course directly for us. The bos'n, grizzled old Tom Carroll, came into the saloon to warn the mate about it at 8:30 p.m. as the wind still whistled through the shrouds. The ship did not pitch, but she whipped and veered from side to side on her long anchor cable.

A few moments later, the skipper took the bridge again. They were all concerned at the rapidly shortening distance between the berg and the ship. In the gathering darkness, the wind seemed to be driving with increasing fury and the berg was headed straight for us, for its bland face extended across the bow of the ship not twenty yards beyond the end of the bowsprit. One looked up at an angle of about 30° to the pulsating vertical face of weather-worn ice. During its approach, the berg had twirled and twisted along its course, occasionally capsizing and rolling forward as its foot found the bottom. The crew had been trying without success to work the ship so that the berg could pass on our port side, and we were about to hit it "amidbergs." If it capsized forward now, it would shatter the ship to splinters.

Old Skipper Tom turned to Captain Sheppard and, shaking his head sadly, said, "Well, Sir. It looks as though this is it, for there is nothing more we can do. This is the end of the Lucky *Eagle!*" But he was wrong. Suddenly, the berg[3] sheered sharply to starboard. Instantly, the skipper drove the *Eagle* full speed ahead, and then steered her hard-a-port. The cold icy mass swept by as our stern swung clear, just missing by a few feet our Port Lockroy motorboat, which hung overside in the davits. As it passed our stern, it went aground for a few moments, rotated upon its supporting foot, and then rolled out to sea. The danger had passed and we had now time to assess the berg's dimensions. It was roughly triangular in section, each side measuring about 100 feet in length. It rose above the water for seventy feet, and from this we estimated that its submerged depth might have exceeded 300 feet. We turned in shortly afterward, as the wind began to abate.

---

3. Editors' note: Taylor's manuscript reads "the wind sheered sharply to starboard." This is a mistake, as James, *That Frozen Land,* 82, reveals.

Figure 24. Enduring the storm of 3–4 March 1945.

The stores had been coming ashore at a good rate toward the morning of 25 February, when the mate aroused us with a load of heavy stores aboard that he wanted Ashton to uncrate. Some were crates of doors and other articles that could be discharged piecemeal, but several parts of the new Esse stove weighed almost as much out of the crate as they did in it. About mid-morning, I attempted to clear a case containing one of the heavier parts of the Esse stove but it stood on end and, in letting it down, I pulled a ligament or fractured a vertebra in my back. I could scarcely walk back to the Tin Galley where Back examined me and prescribed rest. I lay in my bunk for three or four days, at which time I remained unable to stand erect or walk without support. This condition did not change until 6 March when my body was tightly bound with adhesive bandage. This measure brought an immediate improvement but strength

Figure 25. Securing the "Tin Galley" on 4 March 1945.

returned very slowly to my back, and we maintained the bandaging until the following December.[4]

We had abandoned the idea of a second base further south on the east coast of Graham Land before setting out for Hope Bay, but we remained interested in that part of the country. The *Eagle* was tasked to lay several depots around this coast for use in an emergency or by sledging parties. Prospective sites included Snow Hill Island (the site of Nordenskjöld's hut), even further south at Robertson Island, or closer depots across Antarctic Sound on Joinville and Dundee Islands in case any of our party were blown across in a small boat.

---

4. Author's note: I was not wholly incapacitated for that period, but my back's weakness compared to its previous condition was continual.

Russell, who had a complete list of the supplies required for each depot, kept this in mind while the unloading proceeded.

We also hoped that the *Scoresby* would make soundings in Hope Bay and Antarctic Sound. After leaving Deception Island with Marr on 8 February, the ship arrived at Port Stanley four days later, leaving again on 17 February for the South Orkneys. But it was not to be. On 21 February, Deception Island stopped keeping its usual radio schedule and we became concerned. Thus, the *Scoresby* was ordered to proceed to Deception Island on the 27th to investigate the cause of the silence. All of this travelling so occupied the *Scoresby* and rendered her unavailable for work at Hope Bay.

We experienced a great variety of weather in February at Hope Bay: violent gales, rain on a couple of nights, overcast skies, heavy snow, blizzards, and a fine day to end the month. A few days after we arrived, a heavy swell prevented the beaching of the scow and the load had to be towed back to the ship to await better conditions. We lost another half day when a northerly wind blew a thick mat of brash ice into Hut Cove where the motorboat did not have the power to penetrate. Sudden storms forced us to unload the scow at the ship's side on several occasions to prevent swamping and sinking. At every turn the *Eagle's* first mate, Mr. Whitten, confronted difficulties, and unloading was a continual fight against the winds, weather, tides, ice, and darkness. He won the unstinted admiration of us all for the manner in which he met these difficulties.

Time and again these gales sprang up with little warning, so that our small boats became inoperative and people were either unexpectedly marooned ashore or unable to get off the ship. On one occasion, ten men from the crew were unable to return to the ship and slept, or perhaps only lay, in the Tin Galley. Nineteen of us spent that night in a space measuring only sixteen by twenty feet that already contained a mass of stores, furniture, and a stove. Men slept on benches, tables, and even on the floor.

Soon after we landed, Berry established himself around a bogey heater where he managed to warm up hot meals such as stews. He moved into the Tin Galley as soon as it was ready and did a good job under difficult working conditions. His job was even more challenging because Russell was unable to locate the kitchen equipment among the stores in the *Eagle's* hold. Consequently, he fed ten to fifteen people three meals a day for two weeks from a single pot. Fortunately, it was a large one.

Farrington's radio apparatus also seemed to be stored in the bottom of the hold. A small walkie-talkie set came ashore within a few days of our arrival and allowed us to keep contact with the ship a mile away, but we were dependent on Harold "Sparks" Squires of the *Eagle* for messages from Port Stanley that seemed to arrive in unconscionable volume. Farrington's time was entirely occupied coding and decoding the messages so that his services were seldom available ashore. It was almost the end of February before he assembled his transmitter and, with the installation still far from complete, contacted Layther for the first time.

The ice conditions in Hope Bay and Antarctic Sound did not change. Except for occasional brash ice and a few small icebergs (comparatively speaking), the bay remained open. With an east or northeast wind, brash ice from the sound blew inshore, littered our beach, and increased the difficulties of landing our stores. In Antarctic Sound there was pack ice that moved back and forth across the sound, its position dependent entirely upon the prevailing wind. Most of this seemed to occur toward mid-sound and, fortunately, little approached the shore. Icebergs of considerable size, scattered indiscriminately along Antarctic Sound, usually remained several miles away.

After a week of Deception Island's silence, the usual series of conjectures and rumours began to fly about the base. About the best that could be hoped for, to judge from the rumours, was that fire had completely demolished the Deception Island base. When Farrington finally managed to contact Layther directly, the latter told him that Donnachie had reported a fire in one of the generators two days before the silence began. A similar occurrence had likely incapacitated the second generator. As all of the equipment at Deception Island had already been in use for a year, I decided that the more experienced Farrington needed to replace Donnachie on *Eagle*'s next trip to Deception Island. By exchanging the two operators, Donnachie would have the advantage of beginning his season's work with the new equipment at Hope Bay.

With the exception of a large proportion of the coal, most of the stores were removed from the *Eagle* by the end of the month. Until we intercepted the orders for the *Scoresby* to proceed to Deception on 27 February, we anticipated sending the *Eagle* off there with an even larger proportion of our cargo still unloaded. After hearing these orders, we set the *Eagle*'s tentative sailing date at 1 March. At 10:30 p.m. on the last day of February, we unloaded the final stores of personal gear and crates. We then pulled the small motorboat, the *Jeanry II*, ashore and tied the five-ton scow to the ice foot in preparation for the *Eagle*'s sailing the following morning. A gale blew up and the party was unable to get off to the ship, so they returned to the Tin Galley about midnight with some of the crew and waited out the night.

The *Eagle*'s departure the next morning necessitated bidding farewell to several friends. Smith had been of great assistance to Berry, and now returned with the ship to his mates at Deception Island. Russell, as stores officer, also took passage, for Ashton had thought up a great number of additional articles for Russell to retrieve from the old stores around the whaling station. Farrington, with all of his personal gear and radio equipment that he chose from the new Hope Bay supplies, was ready to take Donnachie's place at Port Foster. Flett was also going to investigate the cause of the radio breakdown or, if a second more serious accident had befallen the Deception Island base, take the necessary steps to remedy it as well.

CHAPTER ELEVEN

March 1945

THE NAVAL MET BRANCH AT PORT STANLEY INFERRED a favourable weather forecast for 1 March and the *Eagle* was prepared to take advantage of it. The previous night's high gale subsided about 6:00 a.m., the marooned passengers all ventured aboard, and the ship sailed at noon. We still had a walkie-talkie link with it and learned that the *Eagle* had suffered the misfortune of stripping three teeth off the windlass while lifting the anchor. We planned to contact the ship again at three o'clock that afternoon when Captain Sheppard expected to discuss the possible effect of this misfortune on some of the future plans, as we still intended to have the *Eagle* lay the depots. Although we made contact with Farrington aboard the *Eagle*, he was talking to Port Lockroy and postponed our conversation for another three hours. By this time, the ship was out of range of the small set used by Marshall at our base. The next day, James and Marshall heard Farrington using a radio telephone to speak with *Eagle*'s "Sparks" at Deception Island. However, we still could not contact Farrington. It was not until the fourth day that we finally reached him and received the reply: "All O.K. here, *Scoresby* not here yet. Will contact you tomorrow at 1700hrs."[1]

We were relieved to know that nothing serious had caused the radio silence at Deception Island. As a matter of fact, we had guessed correctly: the second generator failed after fire destroyed the first one. Donnachie succeeded in repairing it and was on the air again just before the *Eagle*'s arrival. Flett, however, anticipated further difficulties of a similar nature and did not alter the tentative

---

1. Editors' note: This paragraph borrows from Taylor, "Operation Tabarin: Official Journal, 1944–6," 1–4 March 1945, Taylor fonds, UMA, MSS 108 Box 5 File 1.

arrangement made before the ship left Hope Bay. Donnachie began to prepare to leave Deception Island with the next ship for Hope Bay.

The *Scoresby* arrived in Whaler's Bay on the following day, 5 March. She brought two new men from the Falkland Islands. Reece received Samuel Bonner, aged fifty-seven, as a handyman at Deception, while the twenty-three-year-old John K. Biggs took passage for Port Lockroy to join Lockley. After dropping Bonner at Deception Island and taking Flett and Donnachie aboard, the *William Scoresby* set sail early the next morning for Hope Bay.

Meanwhile at Hope Bay, 6 March seemed like a good day for Ashton to proceed with roofing the house with rubberoid. Although gales had roared the preceding night, the wind dropped off toward morning. His crew initially made good progress but it began to snow quite heavily at about two o'clock in the afternoon. An hour later, we sighted the *Scoresby* entering Hope Bay. She launched a boat an hour later which came ashore at the ice foot below our base carrying Marchesi, Flett, and Donnachie. We were disappointed to learn that the *Scoresby* was under orders to sail directly for Port Lockroy and then straight back to Port Stanley. We could not use her for any work this year, and her unexpected arrival caught us with no mail for dispatch. Marchesi was only ashore for about twenty minutes before returning to the ship which had not even anchored. In the gathering gloom of an increasingly heavy snowfall, the *Scoresby* sailed into the hazy clouds of falling snow. After leaving Biggs at Port Lockroy, she was back at her berth in Stanley by 12 March.

In the interim, we accomplished a lot of work on the house by enclosing the two original huts and preparing parts of the western annexes. On 8 March, we gladly moved our gear out of the Tin Galley and into the house. The old corrugated iron shack served its purpose well, but had at times been a most uncomfortable lodging. On the 3rd, for example, another gale had arisen toward evening from the southwest that drove a thick blanket of snow. This fine, powdery snow sifted through the joints of the metal sheets, completely covering the south wall of the Tin Galley and immuring Berry's cooking materials on the table three inches deep. The snow blew so thickly inside the hut that we wore our outdoor clothing while eating supper that night. We tried to plug up the cracks in the wall with paper, straw, and even Berry's towels and dishrags, but to no avail. The barometer rose sharply at the rate of about a tenth of an inch per hour, and we estimated that the wind blew at a steady sixty miles an hour (with gusts considerably in excess of that figure). The corrugated iron roof sheets flapped in and out as though they would be stripped off. Fortunately, and quite accidentally, they were laid the right way for the wind to sweep over the joints rather than between them. None of us got much sleep that night, and Ashton sat up from two o'clock on, remarking that "I don't feel very happy about this place; it seems liable to go at any moment." Lamb expanded on this sentiment in his diary:

> When we turned in for the night, the blizzard was gaining force, and rose in the night to a steady fifty miles an hour, rising to seventy miles an hour in gusts. It was about as much as our hurriedly constructed shack could stand, and we lay awake in our sleeping bags wondering whether the next gust would tear the roof off or stave in the walls. Even if one knows that the structure is strong enough to withstand the strain, the continuous raving and buffeting of the wind, hour after hour, has a curiously distressing psychological effect, like that produced by a person shrieking demented threats and abuse at one unceasingly at the top of his voice.[2]

None of us, in short, felt happy about our situation, though some were more fortunate than others in being able to doze the dreary hours by. The temperature outside approached zero, which was about 20° lower than we experienced in March the previous year at Port Lockroy. Fortunately, Ashton incorporated two rather stout wooden braces into the east and west walls when constructing the frame for the building. These beams took the full fury of the wind on the south end, but we knew that if one roof sheet ripped off, the others would follow within a few moments.

The wind showed no mercy until about six o'clock, by which time the barometer climbed from a low of 28.34 to 29.0 inches. Having kept the fires going all night long, Ashton came round to each of us with a cup of tea at seven o'clock. Two hours later it was flat calm and the sun came out blazingly to dissipate what little snow the wind had not blown away. Consequently, the melting snow soaked everything in the Tin Galley.

Following this experience, we strengthened the anchorage to the tin hut in case such a gale returned. We also drew five heavy holding-down ropes over timbers placed longitudinally on the roof. Ashton shored up the outside ends with a diagonally braced, heavy timber frame and Marshall weighted down the

---

2. Editors' note: Lamb, "Operation 'Tabarin' (Base A) Official Diary," 3 March 1945, BAS ADG/1A/1944/B.

shoring with bags of coal. When this work was complete, the Tin Galley was anchored into place by 3.5 tons of coal.

Two nights later (on 5 and 6 March), we endured another gale that was almost as bad as that of 3 March. But for the flapping of an occasional sheet of corrugated iron as it buckled in and out again, there was no movement in the shack that night from the wind and we all slept peacefully. On the nights of 7/8 and 9/10 March, we experienced two more gales that raged all night long and subsided in the morning. We began to notice a pattern. Similar to the day we arrived at Hope Bay, the winds tended to arise, after a calm night, between four and five o'clock in the morning. The ensuing gales blew with velocities up to forty miles an hour, expended themselves, and a calm day followed.

On the evening of 11 March, we heard that the *Eagle* had sailed for Hope Bay late that afternoon. She passed Seal Point again at 10:00 a.m. the next day, just a month following her first entry into the bay. We were pleased to see her again with our second load of supplies, and Russell and the mates were soon ashore to tell us all the ship's news. They had enjoyed another fine voyage, in excellent weather, and encountered no ice at all. Although the ship's windlass was not yet repaired, the Second Engineer had fixed the Port Lockroy motorboat by grafting the magneto coil from an outboard motor onto the magneto of the motorboat. It now ran with power that it had not possessed since we first used it at Port Lockroy. While at Deception Island, the ship's crew had also scraped together all the coal they could find among the wreckage of the whaling station, carried it down to the shore, and took it to the *Eagle* in the boats. They now estimated that the *Eagle* had sufficient coal aboard to allow her to remain in these waters for most of March, and Captain Sheppard was keenly interested in helping us to place the planned emergency depots. They hoped to unload the cargo within a week, as it was not as large a shipment as the first load. Captain Sheppard's health was much improved. He came ashore to pay us a visit the following day, and ate dinner with us in the Tin Galley.[3]

The following morning, heavy swells prevented the delivery of large timbers to the base until mid-afternoon. A strong wind followed, and stopped the arrival of another load. On 14 March, two loads arrived before the wind picked up again in the evening. The Port Lockroy motorboat failed us again the next day, and nothing came ashore, but we put the little motorboat *Jeanry II* into

---

3.   Author's note: Although most of us lived in the house by this time, Berry continued to cook in the corrugated iron shack.

commission on 16 March. She towed three trains of three boats to the base, about nine tons in all—a very good day's progress.

From the time of our first arrival at Hope Bay, Russell oversaw the discharge of the cargo from the ship and tried to first send ashore the articles we needed most immediately. By this time, however, we had such a variety of articles ashore that there was little need of his continuing in this capacity. Accordingly, I told him to come ashore on 18 March. His personal gear, together with a few other articles we were much in need of (such as the typewriter and some of the radio apparatus), arrived on the last load of the night.

A fresh wind blew up in the evening, and the thermometer dropped to −12°F. At Port Lockroy in 1944, the mercury had not dipped to this temperature until about the 1st of May, and this earlier advent of winter caught us unprepared and caused discomfort. During the night, the temperature dropped about another 4° and the wind increased, driving an imponderable mass of snow. Such was the turbulence, as it swept round the house, that it became difficult to breathe. Outside work could not be considered. Even inside, with our fire going, the temperature was just above 20°F.

In the meantime, Donnachie and the *Eagle*'s Sparks had been holding three schedules a day with their walkie-talkie hook-up, flashing messages between the ship and shore—but their traffic had not been heavy. On St. Patrick's Day, however, this arrangement proved fortuitous. Going on the air at eleven o'clock in the morning, we were quite surprised to hear the *Eagle*'s signals coming in very faintly. Generally the call, "Harold calling Tommy. Harold calling Tommy," could be heard in almost any part of the house. That day, some atmospheric interference and the raging blizzard sweeping round the house made it difficult to hear all that "Harold" had to say. We could hear Sparks talking from the *Eagle* in his customary cool, laconic voice, repeating very few words—unhurriedly—to make certain that we heard his entire message. I cannot remember his words precisely, but they were to this effect:

Hello Tommy, Hello Tommy, Harold calling Tommy. Harold calling Tommy. I have a message for you. We are now out to sea. We are now out to sea. In the gale this morning, we were forced to cut the scow adrift to avoid damage to our rudder and propeller. We have also lost your small dinghy. We have lost our anchor and 80 fathoms of cable. We have drifted out to sea and are now in the lee of some land. We think we are to south'ard of you, but we do not know for sure. We have had two collisions with icebergs in the poor visibility, and have lost our bow and part of the foredeck. We cannot tell what the exact damage is, but we do not seem to be taking much water. That is all, Tommy. That is all. Over to you.

With the noise, weak signals, and atmospherics, it took several repetitions to get the entire message. Almost immediately, Matheson, Davies, James, and Russell went out into the gale and walked over to Eagle Cove to search for any of the scow's cargo, but they found nothing and returned within an hour. I wrote out an emergency signal for transmission to Port Stanley and was about to hand it to Donnachie when the *Eagle* came on the air again:

Hello Tommy. Hello Tommy. Harold calling Tommy. Can you see us yet? We are coming into Hope Bay again from the north. We are coming in now. We cannot tell what our damage is without some-one going over the side, which is impossible at present. However, it all seems to be above the water line, and we are not taking much water. We are not in any immediate danger. We are going in again to try and anchor. Over to you, Tommy. Over to you.

With these somewhat improved prospects and better communications, I decided to withhold my signal for Port Stanley until I could contact Captain Sheppard directly. Although the wind still blew wildly, it seemed to be subsid-ing a little and we could see beyond Seal Point—a half a mile distant—where the ghostly outline of the *Eagle* slowly glided past into the teeth of the gale. It appeared as though we could make out the new bluntness to her bow. The violence of the wind increased, however, and again she was forced out to sea before finally working her way into the bay at about four o'clock in the after-noon. They tried to anchor in Eagle Cove, where they had been prior to their accident, and used their spare (and last) anchor tied to a cable on a winch (the windlass remaining out of commission). We heard all of this over the air, almost as it was happening, because Donnachie maintained a continuous watch on the ship. Sparks came on again:

Hello Tommy, Hello Tommy, Harold calling Tommy. We are trying now to anchor in Eagle Cove, but it doesn't look as though we are going to make it. We are now steaming full ahead, and still the anchor is dragging. Captain Sheppard wants to know any information you can give him concerning a possible anchorage off your base. We are thinking of trying to anchor there. Over to you, Tommy, Over to you.

I had James reply directly because he and some of the other chaps took soundings just offshore from our site on the day we arrived. Using this information, he told them to drop their anchor 100 yards east of the twin rocks in the right of our bay (keeping a little farther inshore than the rocks) where they would find twenty fathoms of water. The wind blew as furiously as ever it had. A few moments later, in the cool voice that was natural to him, Sparks came on again:

Hello Tommy. Hello Tommy. Harold calling Tommy. We have now lost our last anchor. We have about given up all hope here now. Captain Sheppard has practically decided to beach the ship. I have an important message for Captain Taylor from Captain Sheppard. He wants you to send all the men you can spare over to Eagle Cove, where the beaching may be made. They are to bring with them ropes and any other tools which they consider might be useful. Did you get that Tommy? Over to you.

I told Donnachie to inform the ship that nine of us would leave immediately while he, Flett, Lamb, and Berry remained behind to look after the base in case the furious wind broke something adrift. Back began collecting first-aid equipment and we dug out some sledges to take with us in the event of casualties. We also warned Berry about possible feeding problems[4] that might immediately develop. Ashton loaded a sledge up with a few tools, some lines, and an empty petrol tin to float the line off to the ship. Marshall, Ashton, and I left with James who, before we had gone more than a few steps, returned to the Tin Galley for some blocks. We did not wait for him, but started out at once (just after four o'clock). While the wind still blew steadily, most of the loose snow blew into the sea, and there was little drift snow flying about. It was not too unpleasant walking, though it was arduous as we sank on each step almost to our knees in our heavy boots. We followed along the shore of Hut Cove to the west of the base until we came to the old stone hut of the Nordenskjöld expedition's camp, continuing westward up the hill beyond it. As we climbed, we

---

4. Editors' note: Taylor uses the same phrase in his official logs, which we interpret to mean "extra mouths to feed."

could see James following about a quarter of a mile behind us. We were puzzled that we saw no one else behind him and concluded that they must have taken a different route to the cove. Deciding to round the rocky knoll, we climbed on the seaward side and were disappointed to find the rocks swept bare of the necessary snow to ease the sledge's passage.

Opposite us, as we turned round, we could see the *Eagle* out in the middle of the bay, facing out to sea. In that hurried glance that we cast her, she did not appear to be moving. As we retraced our steps to cross the hilltop further inland, we met James who informed us that, just as we left, the ship sent another message to the base explaining that Captain Sheppard had decided to attempt to sail the *Eagle* back to Port Stanley. It was a brave decision.

We instantly abandoned the sledge and ran down the slippery rocks past the stone hut and up onto the rocky promontory that Andersson and his men had used as a signal station. Though the weather seemed to be moderating, the gale still blew with considerable violence. The *Eagle*'s masts came into view as we arrived on the rocky knoll, and a few seconds later the ship silhouetted against a background of drift and haze. A heavy sea was still running. We stood on the pile of rocks and waved goodbye and good luck to the *Eagle* and her men. She was making for the open sea in iceberg-ridden waters during a gale with an open bow and without part of her foredeck. She had neither anchors nor windlass, and was not well supplied with either water or fuel. Her intrepid skipper had been in a physical condition for six weeks that would have confined many a sedentary worker to his bed. The *Eagle* had lost her mate on the voyage south, forcing Bob Whitten to fill two jobs by almost superhuman efforts. She had fought the wind, the sea, and the ice—and still found time to land cargo. For all her grimy, rough appearance, she had made a proud voyage.

With anxieties occupying so much of the crew's attention as she sailed away, they would not likely have seen the little knot of four men who stood, braced against the wind, waving them "bon voyage." Nor could they have seen the pride that we all felt in having the *Eagle* and her crew work with us. We would not soon forget them. With the wind still screaming past us, we watched our snub-nosed little ship, her tarry sides white with frozen spray, bobbing out toward the sea until she disappeared behind the ice cliffs of Sheppard Point.

We arrived back at the base just in time to hear Sparks's weak signals apologizing for the *Eagle*'s unexpected departure and hoping that the loss of the undelivered stores still aboard the ship would not cause us difficulties. The message was typical of the ship and her crew, but at the outset of so dangerous a voyage it made us feel very humble indeed.

There had been some parts of Donnachie's radio apparatus that had not yet come to light, and we feared that they were lost in the shipment out from England. In particular, he needed the crystals used to control the transmitter's frequency. He rigged some sort of oscillator as a makeshift solution, but the signals often deviated from their proper channel, making them more difficult for the other station to locate at scheduled times. As he had anticipated, Donnachie now had difficulty "raising" another station with a message to Port Stanley requesting the *William Scoresby*'s assistance and giving the *Eagle*'s course. He eventually reached Farrington at Deception Island, who relayed it immediately to Port Stanley at eight o'clock.

The southwest gale, which for a time seemed to moderate, increased in fury. The corner of the building that housed the radio instruments was at the weather corner—a most drafty place to work because one of its walls was nothing but light, half-inch matchboarding. The temperature outside stood at 9°F, and at the radio desk it was just 5° warmer. Donnachie withstood these conditions at his sedentary task for thirteen uninterrupted hours. Just before he closed down around midnight, he received word that the *Scoresby* was dismantled for a refit but that she might be able to sail the next night.

The uncompleted south wall of the house took the full fury of the wind that continued to blow at gale force throughout the night. Fortunately, Ashton took the precaution of shoring it up on the inside the day before—otherwise the wind might have burst in upon us. The house creaked and groaned all night long, but showed no sign of movement except for an occasional shudder when an exceptionally strong blast struck it. As daylight arrived at five o'clock, I got up to turn out the lamp. Though the wind did not let up in the slightest, the driving snow stopped, and visibility out to sea was fairly good. By this time, all the loose snow from the surface of the glaciers was blown into the sea and there was none left for the wind to carry. There was no sign of the *Eagle*.

Donnachie made contact with the ship at noon next day, and we got the reassuring news that she weathered the gale of the previous night and was in direct contact with both Port Stanley and Deception Island. She reported to Port Stanley later in the day, made light of her damage, stated she was taking no further water, and cancelled the *Scoresby*'s assistance. It was most inspiring news to us all. Coupled with a more moderate wind that produced a bright and calm day by noon, we tackled our construction problems with renewed energy. With the *Eagle* enjoying the same good weather as us, it began to look as though the *"Lucky" Eagle* was going to live up to her name.

The *Eagle* made steady progress toward the north, plugging along at between five and six knots. At noon on 19 March, the *Scoresby* started out to intercept her, returning to port a few hours later with an engine defect. She got away later in the evening, however, as the *Eagle* again battled the gales in the Drake Passage, lying hove for two days. They jettisoned some of their cargo and used lumber, cement, and coal to make temporary repairs to the ship's damaged bow. Much of what remained aboard was still piled on deck until a huge sea came aboard, sweeping everything before it. Midway on her voyage back to port, the crippled *Eagle* met the *Scoresby* and, after losing another twelve hours hove to, the two ships reached Port Stanley on the morning of 24 March with all hands well (except the skipper, whose condition had suffered considerably due to his anxieties and exposure). After Port Stanley crews patched her up, the *Eagle* prepared to sail for Montevideo for permanent repairs on 10 April. Then Captain Sheppard sailed the grimy old sealer northward to her homeport of St. John's, Newfoundland, where she arrived after a voyage of more than 18,800 miles. It is a great pleasure to note that Captain Robert Sheppard was awarded the Member of the Most Excellent Order of the British Empire (MBE) by His Majesty's government for this remarkable voyage.

At Hope Bay, we followed the progress of the *Eagle* toward Port Stanley with anxious hearts. Once she had arrived safely, we began to consider the effect of her sudden departure on our plans. She had unloaded only a third of the cargo when the accident befell her. We therefore lacked the sheets necessary to complete the Nissen hut, the complete supplies for a second one that we intended to erect on the south side of the little stream bed, about twenty-five tons of our coal, some stoves and heaters, the linoleum for the floor of the house, all of our boats (except the dinghy that washed away), much of the lumber required to complete the house, some of our radio equipment, the acid for the storage batteries of our radio and lighting plant, most of our supply of boots, as well as a large assortment of miscellaneous foodstuffs, and scientific gear, the quantities of which were not immediately estimable by us.

Nevertheless, we were not badly off for most things. We had sufficient lumber to enclose our building, and plenty of food and fuel for one year (though not enough for two) at our normal rate of consumption. We had enough clothing and scientific material to carry on most of the intended Hope Bay program.

We hoped that the *Scoresby* would pay us another visit to make up some of our deficiencies of stores, as many of the items would be consumed before the winter was out. But we did not depend upon such a visit.

Dealing with these shortfalls required creativity. Ashton had to be resourceful to stretch his depleted supplies of lumber over the framework of the ambitious building we had under way. But he managed it, as he managed so many difficult tasks. The back portion of the building, including the galley, was enclosed by 29 March. We proposed to fit it out so that Berry could move from his uncomfortable quarters in the Tin Galley, and it did not take long to lay down some old linoleum that had accompanied last year's supplies from Port Lockroy.

We also began assembling the Esse stove, which was among our supplies. The stove was similar to the one we used so successfully at Bransfield House, except that it was a little larger and included a separate firebox intended as a hot-water heater. This additional module operated from a tank under a pressure water system. As we had neither the tank nor the pressure, however, it was difficult to imagine how we could use this part of the stove. Disappointing as this was, our greatest shock came when we discovered that assembly instructions for the stove were for an altogether different model than ours. We stood knee-deep among the intricate-looking mess of cast-iron parts and found no reference to any stove containing the hot-water components this one possessed! The module, moreover, could not be readily ignored or detached from the framework of the entire stove. We were further disappointed to discover that none of the lengths of asbestos pipe that were supposed to constitute the funnel for this stove had arrived. Berry and I began to put things together where best they seemed to fit, and by evening we had the ovens and fireboxes laid, the back of the stove attached, and much of the insulation packed into place. We finished the assembly the next afternoon, and lit the thing after supper. Smoke poured out from almost every orifice, the least of it seeming to find its way up the chimney that we were forced to erect out of tin stove piping. Our best efforts were of no avail, for when we emerged from the galley at the end of our two-hour-long bout with the new stove, the fire was out and both of us smelled like a couple of smoked hams. Neither paper nor wood burned in the firebox with any enthusiasm, far less wood or coal. A black, tarry liquid dripped from most openings that did not issue smoke. It was very depressing. We had two parts left over, but they were only small ones, and one would not have thought that their absence would be enough to create so much trouble and difficulty. The cold stove was covered with a light frost that, upon melting, probably dripped down upon our attempts to make a fire in more or less direct proportion to the heat the fire developed.

We spent two more days on the Esse stove without any positive results until we wrapped the tin funnel with asbestos to conserve the heat and thereby improve the draught. We found a place for one of the two surplus pieces and buried the other among the insulation before putting the top on it again. By this time, Ashton was assisting our efforts, but both Berry and I were in a very poor humour toward each other and toward the stove when we relit it. Fortunately, this time the fire caught. While we were unable to use the hot-water part of it, the stove gave results almost as good as its Port Lockroy counterpart from this point onward.

Ashton and his crew of rough carpenters bent every effort toward completing the outside work on the house and utilized every possible moment of good weather for the job. They poured piers for the remaining portion of the rear of the building. They made the concrete from seawater that was itself thick and pasty at the prevailing temperatures. Thanks to their efforts, Berry moved into his new galley toward the end of the month, and we enjoyed our first meal in the new house on 27 March. The stream near the base provided a copious water supply until about the middle of the month, though it was necessary for Blyth to excavate several feet down into the snowdrift covering it for the last week. Eventually, the stream froze up completely, and he then gathered snow from the nearby glacier for melting in the soyer boiler installed in the galley particularly for this purpose.

By the end of the month the entire party, excepting Matheson and Davies, who lived in a little pyramidal tent across the streambed during the base's establishment, moved into the house. (The latter two men did not move into the house until the following month.) Back erected his Stevenson screen on a little knoll thirty feet above the sea, barely 100 yards west of the base. He began his meteorological observations on 1 March, the same date that he started at Port Lockroy the previous year.[5]

---

5. Author's note: There was nothing remarkable about the month's records, but they were the first of the series. The lowest temperature in the month was 6°F, which was approximately 10° lower than the minimum temperatures experienced at either Port Lockroy or Deception Island in the same month. Probably the most interesting observation was the prevalence and intensity of the southwest wind, the only wind to exceed force 4 (Beaufort's scale) in the month, which it did on thirty-seven of the readings taken.

During this rather interesting phase of our activities at the Hope Bay base, Lamb managed to take enough time off to snap some photographs showing the erection of the buildings (though this was only possible on the days when we were not bothered by the high winds). Under great difficulties, he used Ashton's carpenter shop to develop and print the pictures. Many of these turned out exceedingly well, though the floor of this temporary darkroom was so cold that the dripping solutions from the films and plates soon formed a treacherous icy surface and complicated the execution of such meticulous work. In order to keep his chemical solutions at or near their proper temperatures, he used a small bowl of boiling water beneath his table as an improvised heater. Among the most interesting of the photographs were those showing the conditions of the interior of the house and Tin Galley in these early days of our occupation.

Most of us paid little attention to the dogs but supplying their food was quite a problem for James. He tried to use the penguins at the large rockery adjacent to the base[6] for dog food, but gathering sixty or seventy each day was too big a job. He then tried releasing half a dozen dogs a day, so that at least a proportion of them could forage for themselves without creating too many fights. Nonetheless, the main problem remained: obtaining enough seals to store as a winter food supply for the dogs. We had hoped that the *Eagle* would gather a large number of seals while laying our depots but that proposal was forced from our minds after the ship's emergency departure. The *Eagle*'s crew helped by supplying about a dozen seals, but this was little compared to the hundred-odd that we had hoped they would provide for a winter's store. Accordingly, James cut down his requirements to fifty seals and hunted them all himself. He had some regular assistance from Russell, and the two of them stalked the seals each morning after breakfast. Each walked one direction along the shores of Hut Cove and, by the end of the month, fifteen seals lay in what James termed his "larder" (a tarpaulin shelter at the north end of the Tin Galley). Meals for the dogs alternated between fresh seal meat that was sawn and chopped into solid lumps from the frozen slabs of seal, and occasional hot meals of pemmican and dog biscuits that we cooked on the heater in the house's messroom. Preparing

---

6.   Author's note: The migration of the penguins from the immense rockery at Hope Bay began very suddenly toward the end of February. By the end of the month, the Adelies had virtually vacated the area and were not seen with certainty again until the spring. The Gentoos remained for about another month, and there were still a few scattered about as April began.

the latter stank the place to high heaven. The animals ate at their tethering lines once a day, generally in the late afternoon.

We lost two of the dogs through fights during the month of March. About the middle of the month, a terrific battle took place when a pack of three dogs caught another named "Trot" and bit him terribly before they could be separated. The St. Patrick's Day gale did not help the poor animal's condition, and James brought Trot inside and set him alongside the heater that roared like a blast furnace in the high wind. An inch-thick coating of snow covered the dog's body and all but immobilized him. He lay there all day long, too stiff and sore to eat, drink, or move to do anything but soak up the heat. Once he attempted to lie against the red-hot sides of the stove, and in the evening smelling very "high" he managed to lap up a plateful of water. Next day, the weather improved, and the poor wretch appeared to take more interest in life. A massive and very intelligent fourteen-year-old lead dog named Rover guarded Trot by keeping his charge near the back door of the house lying in the sun. Old Rover, very friendly and popular with us all, stood by his injured friend all day, licking Trot's wounds so gently and caressingly that it was touching to watch. But the attention came too late to have any real effect, and the dog died the next evening.

A few days later, we lost another one named "Wooly." Back made a post mortem on this fine, healthy-looking animal that died after refusing food for five days. Back's investigations indicated that the dog died from a diseased liver possibly caused by food poisoning. This loss brought the number of dogs down to twenty-one from the twenty-four that Marshall brought from Newfoundland.

On 29 March, we were all very pleased to receive a signal from Captain Sheppard including his good wishes and the remark "All hands fine here." It was little to go on, for we know there was many a story between the lines of the signal, but we hoped to receive more information concerning the *Eagle*'s voyage on the *Scoresby*'s next visit. For on the last day of March we were advised that she expected to set sail for the bases on 9 April, and would attempt to bring us some of our missing stores and supplies.

CHAPTER TWELVE

Early Winter
1945

APRIL AT HOPE BAY BEGAN STORMILY WITH A SERIES of tempestuous winds that blew with little interruption for the first ten days of the month. Two gales blew for over forty-eight hours each, the one beginning on the evening of the 5th, and the other on the afternoon of the 9th. The mercury steadily dropped from twenty above on 1 April. By the 8th, we experienced our first subzero temperature, a milestone that Port Lockroy had not reached until June the preceding year. In this context, the gales were not altogether unwelcome, for with the falling temperatures we were somewhat anxious that the inshore ice would form so quickly and thickly that it might prevent the *Scoresby* from reaching us. Indeed, almost as soon as the wind dropped, a skin of ice formed over the surface of the sea. Our house was fairly well enclosed, so we did not mind the winds.

The gale of the 9th followed a fairly heavy snowfall during the calm morning hours, and the wind rose shortly after noon. While James was out in search of seals near Seal Point, he discovered that the wind blew much stronger there than at the base—a phenomenon subsequently confirmed many times. At the base, the breeze began to pick up the newly fallen seven inches of snow and, by the evening, it carried a tremendous load of drift snow. At ten o'clock the winds drove the snow furiously past the building at a velocity of seventy miles an hour. On this occasion, the Doctor was unable to reach the meteorological screen to take his observations; the combination of the wind velocity and the suffocating drift snow was too much for him. I believe this was the only occasion during the two years when the weather defeated him. This wind continued in the night without respite, even increasing in strength.

About an hour and a half past midnight, in the midst of the raging roar of the hurricane, we heard a violent clatter upon the roof, followed for a couple of hours by the scraping noise of something shifting and moving about on it. In the morning we discovered that the southerly aerial mast—a wire-guyed 1.5-inch pipe—was carried away and broken by the fall in two places. Back also found his maximum thermometer broken, some distance away from the Stevenson screen. The winds penetrated into the hallway at the back of the house and deposited a two-foot drift. The loose boards of the laboratory floor also allowed the snow to enter, so that it was all but covered with little conical mounds.

Donnachie's engine-driven generator was temporarily housed in a large, canvas-covered wooden packing case previously used as a storehouse for Ashton's tools. He went out to it on the morning of the 10th and, after clearing it of snow, unsuccessfully attempted to start it. After moving the generator into Ashton's carpenter shop, they discovered its frozen governor. Once this was repaired and Donnachie erected a low improvised aerial, he succeeded in resuming contact with the other two bases in the evening.

The spell of boisterous weather allowed us to make good progress on our new building's interior. We erected partitions around the centre of the messroom, leaving room for the eight-foot-square cabins about the outer walls. The southwest corner cabin housed Donnachie's radio station and Back made use of it to keep his meteorological apparatus and records. The northeast corner cabin was almost twice the size of the others and became known as the survey room, providing working space for Russell, James, and myself. It was eventually well-lined with shelves to contain our equipment and all of the base's stationery supplies. The northwest corner was the same size as the survey room and, besides serving as a passage into our northernmost extension, it was also a general and rather untidy storeroom. The other seven cabins, except for my own, were occupied by two men in the following pairs: Lamb and Flett, Back and Donnachie, Davies and Matheson, Russell and James, Blyth and Marshall, and Ashton and Berry, more or less in that order around the room.

The centre of the messroom was unfortunately broken up by the supporting studs formed by the adjoining central partition of the two huts that were originally erected in juxtaposition. We could not afford to remove these supports entirely, for they carried much of the roof's weight. So Ashton fitted the messroom table into the studding, and we removed one or two studs toward each end of the room to allow for the passage of traffic from one part to the other. With its high barn-like ceiling, cluttered up with half a dozen heavy wooden trusses, the Eagle House messroom never quite equalled the coziness of Bransfield House. Yet it became a very serviceable room that made good use of the available space. With a heater at each end of it, we enjoyed it with comfort.

We had but a single stove in the building while much of this interior work proceeded, and it was difficult to keep the temperature in the house above freezing. The galley, on the other hand, contained two stoves and was kept tightly shut up to protect the baking which went on almost continuously. Temperatures as high as 80°F led Berry and Blyth to work in their shirtsleeves. On windy days the messroom heater burned coal at an alarming rate, for the long pipe and high funnel created a prodigious draft, and there were days when it consumed almost 200 pounds of coal. As we got the house insulated, put dampers in the stovepipes, and installed additional heaters in the laboratory, the survey room, and in a bathhouse, however, much lower fire temperatures heated the house comfortably.

The stove installed in the laboratory was fitted in a rather curious manner. Its pipe extended through the inner partition into the room containing the Bos'n's stores, used almost exclusively by Matheson and Davies. This was a rather unfortunate design on the part of the scientists, Flett, Lamb, and Marshall, for the heavy cast-iron smokestack radiated much more heat into the Bos'n's stores than the heater itself provided for the laboratory. Accordingly, even though little of the heat served them personally, they found themselves lighting, stoking, and cleaning a fire the whole year for Matheson and Davies.

With all these individual stoves and heaters scattered about the building, the possibility of fire was an ever-present danger. We were supplied with four extinguishers but they were unfortunately of the large, cylindrical, foaming water-filled type that contained the following warning in bold letters: "Protect from Freezing." We did the best we could in this respect, but there must have been numerous occasions in the night, after the fires died down and the temperature dropped, when their service would have been most questionable.

We were all, I think, well aware of what our plight could become if fire consumed the house and its contents. Flett was our "fire chief," and he inspected all the fires each night before turning in. He also gave occasional talks on certain precautions he wanted us to take. We tried to store a complete outfit of our basic stores requirements including bedding, clothing, and radio equipment in the Nissen hut so that, in the event of such a misfortune, we would stand a reasonable chance of surviving until a spring relief ship arrived.

While we most anxiously hoped that the *Scoresby* would reach us on her projected trip in early August, we did not entirely depend on her arrival (with much-needed stores). Ashton and I made alternative construction arrangements that we would execute if she failed to arrive. The lack of linoleum was a more serious problem than it might appear at first glance, for the floor of the house consisted of nothing but bare unjointed boards, up against which the high winds whistled with some celerity. We required the linoleum to hold in place the building paper, which was to be used for the floor's insulation. We decided that if this item did not reach us, we would instead lay over the floor large sheets of three-ply veneer we had with us before covering the whole with canvas.

The sudden departure of the *Eagle* on 17 March caught us unprepared, so she carried no mail back to Stanley. Determined that such a thing would not recur, we all spent such time as we could afford preparing a little mail to send off on this hoped-for visit of the *Scoresby*. James and I spent a large proportion of our time preparing a rather voluminous official mail.

We had first received word of the proposed voyage on the last day of March, and got a message alerting us to her departure from Port Stanley on 11 April. Thus, when Friday the 13th arrived and a high wind from the southwest sprang up about noon, we took the half-day off expecting that the ship might arrive the next day. Some intensive pen-pushing resulted. Bearded figures lined the mess-room table, each bent over the lines where they poured out their hearts. The mail was a public service by which Operation Tabarin was not particularly well served. There were long, almost unavoidable intervals when we had no service at all. On the last occasion we prepared our final mail for the season out of Port Lockroy, the post office building at Port Stanley had burned to the ground after our mail reached it, destroying all of our letters. On this occasion, the *Scoresby* did not arrive on 14 April to pick up our mail. In fact, she did not succeed in doing so until January 1946. (Even these letters, written so laboriously and with such urgency, suffered another unfortunate delay, and did not reach their recipients until several months after I returned to Canada in June of that year.)

We assumed from the messages that we received of the *Scoresby*'s departure that it was not her intention to remain for any length of time at any of the bases. We prepared ice reports for the ship in accordance with her requests. But after writing our mail and packing it into the mail sacks, we were astonished to hear that the *Scoresby* had "encountered extensive pack ice in 63°13'S, 57°13½'W." Hope Bay's position is 63°24'S, 56°53'W, which a hurried consultation with the chart soon indicated to be but ten to fifteen miles from the ship's reported position. The signal arrived after dark, but the day had been clear and bright, with excellent visibility despite the southwest wind, and no visible ice to speak of. We just could not understand how the ship could be so near us and encounter a mass of ice that forced her to turn back when there was no sign of its presence from the base. The ship was, at that moment, headed directly for Deception Island on an altered course, intending to land all of its Hope Bay stores there before returning to Port Stanley.

In the morning, James ascended the glacier behind the base to about 500 feet where he had good visibility to the horizon twenty miles distant. He perceived the ice to be virtually non-existent, and landing conditions to be better than they had been for the previous month. Hoping to entice the *Scoresby* to make another attempt at reaching us, we signalled her a report of these conditions. After passing the message, another came from the *Scoresby*, dated an hour previous to our signal, stating that she had encountered pack ice right across the Bransfield Strait, and that she was returning to Port Stanley as of 7:00 a.m. on 15 April.

We were all disappointed at the ship's failure to reach us after being so close to the base. To most of the chaps, the disappointment was two-pronged. They did not receive any mail and were also unable to dispatch that which they had prepared. As much as I agreed with this sentiment, my greatest disappointment was at not getting away the mass of official mail that required so much time to prepare and very largely concerned the plans for the ensuing year. The text of half a dozen impetuously worded signals entered my mind; but before sending them, I asked Donnachie to check the decoding of the ship's position from the earlier of the two messages. It was all well that I did, for he came back a few moments later to sheepishly confess that it included an error, and that the latitude should have been 62° instead of 63°. This placed the ship well to the north of us, approaching the north side of the Bransfield Strait and well beyond our vision. There was nothing further to be done but accept the disappointment that the Fates had prepared for us.

On this same date, the evening of 15 April, we received the first of a long series of signals concerning the health of Bonner at Deception Island. Reece sent this first signal to Port Stanley announcing that "Bonner worried about his ill health which he thinks will recur. He was under the doctor prior to joining expedition and requests permission to return to Port Stanley."[1] The series of messages continued almost up until the day when he was relieved, in early 1946. The signal was sent to the ship on the 16th, but Marchesi decided against turning about again toward Deception Island and the *Scoresby* arrived back at Port Stanley a few days later.

On the 17th, we laid our veneer floor in the messroom. First we laid down a large, brown, treated tarpaulin and tacked it into place. Then we nailed down the sheets of veneer on top of it. On the latter job, we made a good showing in a very short time. After that, we tacked down strips of canvas to make a walking surface. A howling southwester blew at the time, so there was plenty of labour available. By late evening, the job was complete—a very decided improvement. We followed this work in the succeeding days with tarpaulin floors tacked down over the wide-seamed boards in the cabins and, when it was all complete at the end of April, the house felt very considerably warmer.

The *Eagle* brought us three or four large cases of beer privately ordered by five of us. We opened one of them early in the month. Each of the owners received nine or ten bottles and most of us consumed approximately one per day. Back husbanded his very carefully, however, to make the limited stock last for a longer time, and stored his hoard under the bed. He used to chide us for our improvidence as he, the acme of temperance, watched us polish off a bottle, then gloated about the pleasure he would derive from seeing us watch him drink later in the year after ours was all gone. We did not anticipate such a day with much pleasure ourselves, but our anxiety on this score was short lived. After a fifty-mile-an-hour all-night southwester, the Doctor discovered the error of his philosophy when he found four of his remaining six bottles frozen and collapsed into neat little mounds of glass and iced beer on the floor. He consumed the two erect bottles in the evening, and looked the picture of affluence as he sat by the fire in an armchair reading the *Times* for 29 August 1944.

It was an ironic twist of fate that the *Eagle* withstood terrible gales during the unloading of a portion of her cargo and limped back to the Falkland Islands still pursued by gales, while we at Hope Bay enjoyed ten of the finest consecutive days that we experienced in our entire Antarctic stay. After the gale in which the ship suffered her accident, we had not faced another gale until 28

---

1.   Editors' note: Taylor's manuscript paraphrased the message. The original is reprinted in Taylor, "Operation Tabarin: Official Journal, 1944-6," 15 April 1945, Taylor fonds, UMA, MSS 108 Box 5 File 1.

March. With this long spell of calm weather with dropping temperatures began the winter's ice. By 20 March, pancake ice began to form and cemented together with every appearance of permanence. The gale that began on the 28th lasted for three days, however, and dispersed most of the sheet. The lashing of the waves along the shore coated the area between its high and low water marks with ice that extended up over the rocks along the shore, until they were all white with the spray.

The gales lasted throughout the early part of April and swept the new ice off the sea so that there was little to be seen until the middle of the month. Some pack ice entered Antarctic Sound from the north and passed through the sound at the southerly end. In general, however, Hope Bay and the western part of Antarctic Sound were clear of sea ice throughout most of this period. Some pack ice could be seen toward Joinville and Dundee Islands. Toward the south, Antarctic Sound was usually clogged around Rosamel Island.

The permanent freezing of the ice in Hope Bay began on the night of 20 April. Some pack ice entered the bay before that date, but a southwest wind in the morning completely dispersed it (though it did not disperse a sheet in Hut Cove,[2] below the base, and this provided the best evidence that we had some protection from the southwesters). The new ice sheet steadily grew in thickness until the 26th, when a force-8 gale blew up and again swept much of it out to sea. But all of the ice deep in the bay up to Eagle Cove held fast, thus beginning winter's ice in the bay. When the gale subsided after three days, the low temperature caught the sea and ice again almost immediately began to form. Some pack ice drifted into the mouth of the bay from Antarctic Sound, and froze into the new ice sheet where it remained throughout the winter.

We first noticed an extensive field of pack ice in Antarctic Sound on 20 April, some of which pressed in close to Hope Bay. With a light south wind blowing on the 24th, the sound seemed completely filled with pack ice from our observations made at sea level. This included many large bergs. One of these drifted into Hope Bay and nosed its way through the pack toward Sheppard Point, where it apparently went aground. I took some measurements on it with a sextant and found it to be about 100 feet high and over three-quarters of a mile long. The southwest wind blew for the next two days, and the berg was

---

2. Author's note: We tested the ice in Hut Cove toward the end of May and it was 18 inches thick; a week later it had thickened two inches, and this increase continued until the latter part of the winter, when depths exceeded four feet.

gone when the weather cleared. This was only one of many bergs that the sound contained, and was not by any means the largest of them.

Each gale seemed to create a new disposition of this drifting pack ice and the icebergs in the sound. They seldom remained on our side of the sound for long, and this fast gave rise to our first useful observation with respect to ice conditions, an observation which was convincingly affirmed with a long series of similar conclusions. A lane of water existed inshore to the Trinity Peninsula that remained open almost constantly throughout the winter. This fact was further confirmed when each vessel that followed a track between Hope Bay and Deception Island (near the coast at the entrance to Antarctic Sound) succeeded in accomplishing her purpose. By contrast, each ship approaching or leaving Hope Bay from the north inevitably failed.

Marshall and I cut a hole through this ice just east of Jagged Rocks (a couple of black, steep-walled rocks that jutted out of the water) in the western part of Hut Cove in early June. We had read that Andersson, Duus, and Grunden caught fish in Hope Bay in 1903, and in the months of July and August had caught about twenty fish with the most primitive, homemade equipment. Starting to feel the need for some fresh food, we could no longer resist the prospect of catching a few fish. We put down two lines baited with some rotted bacon and went back to pull them up three days later, following a blizzard. Judging by their weight as we hauled up the freezing wet line hand-over-hand, we initially thought we had a good haul. When the last few feet of line came above the water level in the ice hole, however, we realized that the weight owed to innumerable laminar crystals of shimmering ice threaded together like a rope of glistening plates, about two inches in diameter.

We cut another pair of holes a little farther to the east in about five fathoms of water, but still had no luck. A third attempt on 14 June, at a hole cut about midway between the Jagged Rocks and the nearest of the Grunden Rocks (a cluster of high rocky islets which were scattered about the sea), yielded better results. Marshall hauled up the line using seal meat as bait and caught no less than twenty-three fish within an hour. He pulled them in almost as fast as he could replace the bait. In the end, he began to use a small spinner, with equal success. All were of the same species (*Notothenia coriiceps*), about a foot in length, and averaged a little under a pound. Berry cleaned and fried them, and they made a truly delectable meal.

Within a week, fishing became quite a popular pastime and we caught as many as fifty fish in a day. The larger ones were about a foot and a half in length and approached two pounds. We never tired of eating fish, and by Midwinter's Day we had caught several hundred pounds of them. Besides their nutritional value, Marshall made good scientific use of them by analyzing the food they had eaten and by taking a series of measurements on many of the fish, and eventually accumulated a lot of information about them.

Davies did not acknowledge the pleasure in our method of acquiring fish. He watched us stand out on the sea ice in driving winds and drifting snow for hours at the times when they were most likely to bite. We were a little puzzled, one gloomy afternoon, to see him heading for the sea ice with a small sledge dragging along behind him, on which were loaded various items including a pyramid tent and a Primus stove. It was not a particularly nice day, for the southwest wind was just beginning to cause the snow to drift. He took the sledge-load of materials out to a position several hundred yards off Seal Point, stopped, and began to dig a hole through the sea ice. By this time, the depth of the ice approached three feet, and it was no easy task to cut a hole through it with an ordinary axe. When the hole was finally complete, the water flooded it to within a few inches of the surface. Clearing away the excavated ice, Davies set up the pyramid tent over the hole and crept inside it with all of his paraphernalia. He baited the hook and dropped it through the hole. Then he lit the Primus, and put on a potful of snow to melt for a cup of tea. He sat on the box and contemplated the hole. Here surely was the life to live, the way to fish in this country, with the wind driving snow about the base of the tent outside, while all was snug and warm inside and a pot of tea not far off. It was the time for the pleasant satisfaction of a good smoke—but Davies did not smoke, so he querulously looked at the cracked ice that covered the water in the hole and probably wondered why the fish were not biting better under such ideal arrangements. He managed to catch a couple of fish, but it either was not a good day for fishing or the location of the hole was not ideal. With his thoughts thousands of miles away from his fish hole, the surface of the water was suddenly disturbed with a couple of small waves. Then the bewhiskered nose of a seal broke through with a snort. Neither Davies or the seal stayed long looking at each other—probably both were equally disturbed at what they had seen! Davies bolted out the door of the tent. Not long afterward, he repacked the tent on the sledge, put away

Figure 26. Upper Depot Glacier. Blade Ridge (foreground) and Ben More mountain (background) visible, 30 April 1945.

the other articles in the box that served as the tent's only armchair, and trudged disconsolately back to the base.

Even in winter, Eagle House sat in a rather magnificent setting. There was about it an air of spaciousness and freedom, perhaps more imagined than real, with none of the sense of confinement and encirclement that we had felt at Port Lockroy. From the house, we looked northward over the whitened sheet of new ice in Hut Cove, which was joined by that from Hope Bay to reach far out into the sound. Southward, and to our right, the tapering edge of the inland ice rose sharply up the glacier to steep, high ice cliffs that approached 200 feet in height. Below the cliffs lay the Grunden Rocks while along the rough and rocky shore, the beating southwest winds scalloped hard-fluted *sastrugi* (windblown drifts).

When we had arrived we noticed an ice foot about six feet high along the curving shore of Hut Cove, beneath which lay an occasional gravel beach (like the one directly below the base). For the most part, however, the shore consisted of low, rounded, and well-worn grey-black rocks, and its approaches were shallow reef-marked waters. Barely below the surface of the water were many places where submerged rocks lay in wait to tear or break the bottom of a boat. After the ice thickened in the cove to a depth of a couple of feet, these rocks supported huge secretions of ice, around which the tides moved up and down so that the edge of this fixed ice became quite smoothly faced. Relative to the sea ice, this formation appeared to slowly move up and down like a gigantic piston.

We were located on the west side of Antarctic Sound, so that beyond our inshore sheet of fast ice and past the few icebergs that marked the centre of the sound, we caught a distant view of D'Urville Island to the northwest, Joinville Island to the east, and Dundee Island to the south. All were white with their icy mantles, but there were a few nodules of rock that protruded through the ice cap. On exceptionally clear days, a mirage that occurred with considerable frequency made these dark spots seem much nearer to us. The sound was often filled with low-lying clouds that cleared the water by only a few hundred feet, and it was not uncommon under these conditions to see the lower slopes of these islands, ten miles away, with remarkable clarity.

Sheppard Point marked the northerly entrance to Hope Bay. Above it sat a small *nunatak* (the rocky, ice-free tip of a little hill) that we called Sheppard Nunatak. Deeper into the bay, along the same shore, a higher outcrop of rock that we called Andersson Nunatak lay opposite Seal Point. It ran in a north-south direction for a half-mile or so, attaining an altitude of over 600 feet. A deep snow moat was scoured out of the snow along its base on the southerly side and on calm days we often saw the wind billowing drifts of snow which swirled about the base of this *nunatak* from the glacier above it. On dead calm days, it was even possible to hear this wind whistling from a couple of miles distant.

The mountains to the west formed the real scenery of the area. They were the backdrop for our little settlement when viewed from offshore in Hut Cove. Mount Flora stood only a mile or so away, and was by far the most prominent feature of the vista. A rugged-looking mass of brown rock, its sharply defined summit rose along a curving spine toward the north end of it where it attained an elevation of 1,630 feet. Below this crest, and facing the base, a huge amphitheater had been eroded, its walls rising to 500 or 600 feet. Along the inner wall of this saddle-like formation Andersson had made his remarkable collection of Jurassic fossils which indicated a climate that had, at one time, been subtropical. Small ice fields and streams of ice tumbled over the rocks at the feet of the mountain, spilling over the rocky foreshore upon which our base was built (though none were in very active motion). The foreshore, which was about half a mile in depth, consisted of descending hillocks of fragmental rock and boulders, and it was over this area that the huge penguin rookery spread when we arrived. At the foot of the inland ice to the south lay Boeckella Lake, about 135 feet above the sea. This freshwater lake, normally frozen almost to the bottom, issued in summer a stream of water disgorging into Eagle Cove. At the head of Hope Bay, a beautifully defined valley glacier descended steeply to the ice face that formed the end of the bay. Nordenskjöld named this formation Depot Glacier. On either side of it were a couple of well-marked lateral moraines that wove back and forth continuously in a series of gentle curves along the fringes of the glacier. On the south side, the base of Mount Flora contained the glacier. To the north of this glacier, a sharp-crested, scree slope[3] ridge of black rock that we called the Blade Ridge rose gradually up from Whitten Peak near the shore to the ice-capped Ben More[4] which stood upon the inland ice a few miles distant, 3,000 feet above the sea.

The two sides of Hope Bay were remarkably different in character. The north coast was an almost continuous line of active ice cliffs, which made access to the glacier above virtually impossible. The southerly shore was formed of a gradually descending line of hills, known as the Scar Hills, which were about 300 feet in height at the head of the bay, then descended more or less gradually until they petered out at Seal Point. The shore along this southerly side of the bay was, for the most part, formed of inaccessibly steep rock. At various places toward Seal Point, eroded gullies provided ready access to the hills.

When the three marooned men of Nordenskjöld's expedition made their way to Snow Hill Island in 1903, they ascended the sloping toe of the glacier to the southwest of our base. This all-but-inert glacier had almost no fissures or crevasses visible on its surface, and rose rather steeply for the first 500 feet of its elevation. The slope flattened out considerably once this height had been attained, well-marked by a large morainic deposit overlooking Boeckella Lake by several hundred feet. A more gradual gradient carried one up to the 900-foot exposure of a knobby outcrop of rock, which gradually acquired the name of Nobby Nunatak. Once at that elevation, the gently rising field of inland ice led toward the southwest past a remarkably uniform pyramidal peak (Pyramid Nunatak) and so on to the other side of the Trinity Peninsula.

---

3.   Editors' note: A scree slope is a mass of loose stones covering the side of a mountain.

4.   Editors' note: "Ben More" was the name that members of Operation Tabarin assigned to the mountain that eventually became "Mount Taylor."

While we had a good view seaward to the east and northeast, comparatively low hills surrounding our base provided some protection from the raging southwest winds. The rocky hillocks of the rookery were covered with snow following any heavy snowfall, but the winds soon whipped them clear again. At times during the late winter, there was much less snow covering the area than there had been in March. There was a tendency for this wind to bare the summits of the rocky hillocks, and to fill in the hollows. The tortuous bed, followed by the stream out of Boeckella Lake down into Eagle Cove, drifted almost full.

Russell and I walked over to Eagle Cove one day in early May, where the hurriedly discharged stores from the *Eagle* remained, and found many of the boxes containing foodstuffs still lying exposed above the snow. Almost all of the coal, petrol, and paraffin barrels, however, were completely buried. The sacks of coal were, in many cases, frozen hard to the rock on which they lay. We hauled a few cases of meat back to the base, following the route along the streambed to Boeckella Lake, and thence downhill to Eagle House.

On 7 May, we began work on moving the twenty-five tons of stores at Eagle Cove to the Nissen hut about a mile away. It was the first time that we harnessed up any of the dogs, so we all gathered to see what was going to happen as James and Russell harnessed up a team of six. The dogs were led by "Captain," and his henchmen included "Jimmie," "Jack," and "Popeye." They were the best set we had, and we dubbed their group the "Big Boys." Popeye had suffered a severe trouncing from Captain when they were younger. The beating appeared to have knocked much of the spirit out him, so that he was slightly ill-tempered and eccentric. The other two animals were a pair of short-legged animals that were Matheson's favourites: "Jack" and "Ginger." The latter was reputed to be a lead dog, but he did not show much evidence of this reputation as he immediately made a beeline for a position underneath the back steps. Jack scuttled along behind him for the same spot, their traces drawn taut and tangled. The team was unmanageable with these two in it, and they had to be released.[5]

---

5. Author's note: Matheson seemed to feel rather keenly the poor showing of his four-legged friends Jack and Ginger when they were first harnessed to the sledge. A few days later, he attached the pair to our manhauling sledge so that four men and the two dogs could pull a heavy load of paraffin over the hump. The two dogs, no longer frightened for their lives, pulled very well indeed, and Matheson was quite cheered by the result of his efforts. Having lost all our precious boats upon the departure of the *Eagle*, Matheson was almost disconsolate without them. These two friendly little animals seemed to help provide him an alternative interest.

Figure 27. Davies with the "Chromosomes" team on the Hope Bay sea ice, July 1945. Note the *sastrugi*.

After becoming re-accustomed to pulling, the remaining animals moved several loads during the day. The dogs made a fine sight as they flashed over the brow of the hill above the base and dashed madly down the steep, snow-covered slope, with one man lying flat on the sledge atop the load and the driver standing on the runners at the back, clinging to the handlebars with his clothes and whip flying in the breeze. The loads were about 300 pounds each and more than a ton of stores moved this first day, some by the excavators manhauling a twelve-foot sledge. We had the extremely good fortune of encountering a carboy of acid beneath the snow, which Donnachie badly needed for the radio set batteries as well as for the wind-charging outfit (which we had heretofore been unable to consider installing).

Digging out the stores was a laborious chore. As we excavated the articles, we piled them on the snowfield, about sixty feet above the sea at a point where the dog teams could easily load them. It was not long before we dug out enough paraffin, petrol, and alcohol (for biological work) to last us throughout the year. The balance of the stores remained buried, to be taken round to the base next year when they could be readily moved by dinghy (after we were re-supplied with small boats). The coal, still frozen to the rocks, was difficult to dislodge with our hooks and crowbars without tearing the bags and spilling the contents.

On 18 May,[6] we added three more animals to the "Big Boys" team: a little bitch named "Beauty" and a couple of well-grown pups called "Shaggy" and "Jack." The latter eventually went by "Colonel" to avoid confusion. On 26 May, the remaining dogs, "Mutt," "Jeff," "Sydney," "Rover," and "Widgeon," were connected to a sledge, but one could not stretch the imagination to call them a team. Rover was a powerful old animal, and had taken Widgeon under his wing, while the other three were a group in themselves. The dogs pulled well on the road, but the driver had constantly to be on the alert to prevent them fighting. This team became known as the "Odds and Sods," and four of the five of them worked as part of a team throughout the winter.

On the day that the Odds and Sods went into commission, "The Drinks" (a short-lived team consisting of "Whisky," "Gin," "Bitters," and "Punch")[7] disappeared. It was not the first time that this happened, for Punch, their leader, was of an itinerant nature. The other three dogs followed Punch closely, and he was often tied up to prevent his wanderings. On this occasion, however, he managed to escape by slipping his collar over his head. They had been away for several hours at a time previously, and no one ever saw where their excursions took them. There seemed little prospect of locating them by a search, so we did not worry too much about them the first day. After a strong southwest wind blew for the next two days and they failed to return, however, we became apprehensive that we had lost them for good. Perhaps they had run out onto the newly formed ice toward Sheppard Point and had been swept out to sea on a sheet of detached ice? On 2 June, we presumed that this had been their fate and wrote them off. Months later, in mid-July, Russell ascended onto the glacier above Sheppard Point, and found dog tracks that were hard and elevated above the snow field. He suspected that they belonged to "The Drinks," and we concluded that they had gone for a run past this point and become lost somewhere beyond it. The loss of this team brought the number of our dogs down to seventeen before any of the real sledging (for which they had been brought) had even begun.

---

6. Editors' note: This date was determined using Taylor, "Operation Tabarin: Official Journal, 1944–6," 18 May 1945, Taylor fonds, UMA, MSS 108 Box 5 File 1.

7. Author's note: These dogs all arrived at the base with those names, which we presumed they acquired on their voyage south.

Our ill luck with the dogs at this stage did not end with this loss. Four more dogs were gone on 2 June. Fortunately, we heard barking that seemed to come from near the ice edge toward the entrance to Hope Bay near Sheppard Point. Russell, James, and I took a light sledge with some tools and dog food and went on skis in search of them. Turning past the field of hummocky pack ice frozen into the bay, I caught sight of the four of them about half a mile distant in the pack. We left the sledge and went after them. They met us on the way. James still hoped to find some trace of "The Drinks," so we continued toward the ice edge to discover what had attracted them—for they were covered with blood. The dogs preceded us, and we found them worrying the life out of a seal, about 200 feet from the water's edge. Later, they made off toward the water, where a great deal of running about and barking took place. There was another seal in the water, extending its head up through a hole in the young ice alongside, apparently intending to land. We saw no sign of "The Drinks," and with so many distractions about, had some difficulty catching the other dogs. Given the stiff southwest wind that blew, the ice edge was not the healthiest of spots. We lost no time, once the dogs were caught, tying them up and leading them back to the sledge outside the field of pack ice.

A few days later, we harnessed the two remaining teams to continue hauling the stores. Lamb introduced the two odd dogs, Jack and Ginger, into the Odds and Sods. This short-legged pair got along reasonably well with most of the other dogs, despite the fact that they had shown such a marked reluctance to work with them. A furious gale from the day before had tossed several of the twelve-foot sledges about and even some small eighty-pound cases of food stores. The wind had also scoured away the snow in many places to a depth of two feet, leaving a hard surface in which the *sastrugi* were undercut on the windward side, leaving an overhanging lip (nearly a foot in depth) to the southwest on most of them. The dogs dashed down the slope from the base toward the sea ice where we now hauled our stores from Eagle Cove. The reluctant pair of dogs lost their footing and were dragged along the slope. Ginger unfortunately caught one of his legs in the overhanging lip of *sastrugi* when the sledge passed over, and the latter's momentum caused his leg to break about the upper joint. The animal suffered greatly, and James considered that it was best to dispatch the dog, which he did with a shotgun.

The last of our series of misfortunes with the dogs occurred on 1 July. By that date, the gales had blown huge drifts about the house so that the dogs had

Figure 28. Pretty's pups, July 1945.

easy access to the roof at all times. Two of them, Rover and Widgeon, took up their permanent residence on it for a while. The Odds and Sods team were all tied on a wire tether down below the house where they fed each night. On this particular evening, we left the dogs happily consuming their seal meat and all seemed to be well. About 10:00 p.m., however, we heard one of them on the roof. On investigation, it proved to be Widgeon, who was howling most mournfully. Almost the entire team was loose, and old Rover lay dead down by the ice foot with Mutt, Jeff, and Sydney prowling about. Old Rover had been a great favourite, for he was good-natured, friendly, and a good worker who would shamble along with his great, shaggy head wagging from side to side. He had had the heart of a lion, for which the other dogs all had a good deal of respect. None of them ever deliberately tackled him alone and there did not seem enough blood about him to have caused a fatal injury. Back's theory (substantiated by a postmortem that he conducted with James the next morning) was that he died of heart failure, given that he was somewhere between twelve and fifteen years of age. We did not hear the fight on account of the strong wind that blew, but Rover must have given his customary good account of himself for Mutt walked about next day with a large lump on the side of his face, and Sydney had a badly wounded nose.

Although old Rover was popular with most of us before he died, he had earned discredit in the Doctor's eyes by interfering with the meteorological observations. Doc had installed a sun recorder—a spherical glass ball which focused the rays of the sun onto some light-sensitive paper—on the roof toward the front of the house. Rover saw the roof as his domain and spent much of his time there, but apparently he mistook the sun recorder for a tree. His emanations froze upon the glass ball, altered its refractive index, and affected the observations. In order to discourage the animal, Doc spent some time fitting a series of boards, with hundreds of nails through each so that they projected hundreds of points outward, around the base of the sun recorder. Doc called this apparatus his "Anti-Rover Device." The invention was not a complete success, however, because we caught old Rover lying quite happily upon the nails on several occasions. He was a tough old animal.

The loss of Ginger and Rover brought the census of our dogs down to fifteen. Of these, "Lady" suffered a bad wound on her foreleg that refused to heal, or even grow fur, so that she limped about on three legs all the time. The fourteen active dogs we had left provided us with two teams of seven dogs. Fortunately, their number suffered no further depletion before the main sledge journeys.

Early in April, we anticipated that some pups were on the way. Russell and James spent most of the first half of that month preparing and building kennels to house the new families. These little shelters were built from large packing cases in the space between the house and the Nissen hut, but some were submerged in a huge drift that formed on the lee side of the house and were not uncovered until the following spring. Beauty, Captain's friend, produced the first litter. She did not avail herself of the new maternity home, but gave birth to a fine pair of pups (subsequently named "Hobbs" and "Hinks")[8] in the tent that Davies and Matheson inhabited during the early part of the base's

---

8. Editors' note: These names almost certainly refer to Arthur R. Hincks and William H. Hobbs, whose vigorous debate concerning the first explorer to see the Antarctic mainland attracted considerable public attention during the late 1930s and early 1940s (David Winston Heron, "Antarctic Claims," *Foreign Affairs* 32, no. 4 [July 1954]: 665). We wish to thank Peder Roberts for bringing this reference to our attention.

establishment. On 28 May, Pretty produced a litter of five, four of which were bitches. These were her first pups, and she chose to bear them in the Tin Galley. Unfortunately, two of them were crushed to death before morning, and James brought the mother and pups into the house as the wind again approached the force of a gale. They grew up there in the house for about the next two weeks before returning to their birthplace.

Most chaps helped at one time or another hauling stores from the cove to the base and, in the course of this work, acquired some familiarity handling the dogs. We had hoped to be able to drive them and, to this end, Davies retrieved walrus hide whips—each about thirty feet long—from the stores in the Tin Galley. In practising with them, it was more customary for the driver to feel the weight of the broad, thonged end of the lash. If we were fortunate enough to hit a dog, it was seldom that we struck the one at which we had been aiming—which did more to confuse than help the dogs in their training. Lamb gave himself a terrific belt in the eye on one occasion that coloured up beautifully and lasted several days. The whip was of some effect for steering the dogs if the driver could sweep it toward them from the side because they immediately veered away from its direction. We never did become very proficient with the whips and, as a result, we didn't succeed in driving the dogs at all throughout the winter. Instead, the teams had to be led by a man at all times.

Moving stores proved to be a blessing in disguise, for it provided work and healthful exercise for most of the chaps at the base during a period of dull, gloomy times when the sun retreated lower in the sky with each successive day. This forced us to go out on several occasions when we would probably have stayed inside, thus receiving the fresh air we so frequently neglected to take.

During the long period we worked on this task, we faced a number of gales and high winds that filled in our entire excavation, forcing us to begin the whole job from "scratch." Nevertheless, by alternately digging and hauling, in addition to repairing the sledges (for we had some casualties among them), we steadily ate into our task. As a rule, we managed to make two or three trips in the morning, and another in the afternoon, having to stop early on account of darkness. The loads varied between 300 and 600 pounds, depending on the surface we encountered on the sea. The trips went on with little respite, except on the days when the wind was too high. On Midwinter's Day (21 June), we worked long enough to make two trips with each team, and on the last one completed the task (though a few barrels of petrol still lay buried in the snow).

Davies and Matheson handled the stores that we moved from the cove to the base. A large dump of coal along the ice foot below the base remained buried in up to ten feet of snow, so the two storekeepers spent much of their time digging the sacks out of the deep drifts formed to the northeast of our newly erected buildings. As they uncovered coal and other stores they made room for them in the Nissen hut and Tin Galley, the latter of which was lined with a heavy tarpaulin and used by James largely to prepare and store dog food. It smelled to high heaven of seal meat, so we moved much of the coal to the bottom of the central aisle of the Nissen, which Matheson described as the "bilges."

We were kept well informed via Port Stanley of the progress of the arrangements for the succeeding year's continued occupancy of Hope Bay. During March and April the signals required considerable attention. Of the personnel already in the south, only Russell, Reece, and James entertained any thoughts of remaining another year (and James did not entertain his for long, as some business arrangements made on his behalf in England forced him to alter his decision). Most of the remaining members of our party already were spending their second year in the Antarctic and looked forward to their voyage home. In this connection, we jotted down the dates of important events in the history of our expedition along the length of a large thermometer, drawn upon a sheet so that each inch of it represented a month of the expedition's time. As each month passed we inked in its section of the red thread. The title, "Wings for 1946," appeared in big bold letters at the top of the thermometer. In between the title and the inked-in sections, personnel pencilled in prognostications. These forecasts, such as "Ship finally breaks through the ice to us," and the last one, "Frozen in," at times seemed to have a ring of truth too true for comfort.

We listened regularly to the BBC news each day, and were in the midst of moving stores when the war with Germany drew to a close. The news of the German Army's capitulation in the west was cause enough for a spontaneous celebration. On 8 May, we listened to the historic broadcast of His Majesty the King to his people, of whom we must have been among the most remote. Berry put on a special dinner in honour of the occasion, and we toasted "The King," "Mr. Churchill," and "Sweethearts and Wives." Later on, Berry concocted a punch in an effort to enliven the proceedings, but the wanton spirit of celebration that should have been present among us was noticeably absent. Perhaps our thoughts returned too readily to other places and other people with whom we would have given so much to have spent this of all days, to some whom we would never meet again. It was a day of gratitude and reverence.

The red line of "The Thermometer," as we called our calendar, reached mid-May when a party composed of Back, Lamb, Davies, James, and Russell ascended the east shoulder of Mount Flora one Sunday. At that time of year, the sun rose just before nine o'clock and set at two o'clock. On that particular morning, the sunrise was beautiful and lasted for the better part of an hour. The sun clothed the mountain's rimy covering with the softest of pastel pinks to rich and riotous vermilions before breaking through above the horizon. The ascent up to this part of the mountain, which is something over 1,000 feet above the sea, was not difficult because a snow slope led up to it from the east, and when the party reached the top. Russell, Lamb, and Back had been up to it once before at the start of April, and on that occasion Lamb found the plateau at the top to be richly carpeted with lichens, making a good collection of botanical specimens before returning to base. This was an excellent point from which to make sea-ice observations because it provided a good view of Antarctic Sound well to the south of Rosamel Island, and we used it for this purpose on numerous occasions.

On a different Sunday, another party of six men and seven dogs ascended the Pyramid Nunatak up the grey rocky slope of its northwest shoulder, the summit of which was found to be 1,900 feet by aneroid. Here they obtained an even better view that included the vista to the southwest along the Crown Prince Gustav Channel. Ross and Vega Islands were readily distinguishable from the thirty-foot-square summit. After eating lunch at the top of the Pyramid, they descended its western slope along a somewhat easier route, and returned to the base about a quarter to five, just as a rising southwest wind began to make itself felt.

Preparing the first newspaper to be published at Hope Bay—the *Hope Bay Howler*—was one of the last tasks to be performed before Midwinter's Day. We had with us a little hand duplicator that reproduced typewritten material with rather indifferent results, and we used the machine to prepare 100 copies of the paper at the end of each month. The editor and the contributors were generally anonymous, and eventually our paper included news items from the other two bases, sent in by radio through the *Howler*'s correspondents at Port Lockroy and Deception Island. None of us would claim that the six- to ten-page sheet had much literary merit, but all hands always looked forward to its production and perhaps it did something to broadening our horizons beyond the small circle in which we moved. The cover sheet was the same for each issue and consisted of a rough coat of arms that included a loaded sledge, a seal peeking through the ice, and a pair of pennants crossed over a bottle labelled "Gordon's Dry Gin." The latter commodity was conspicuous by its complete absence from the base because Berry, expecting to find a number of additional cases among the stores, generously had donated what turned out to be our sole case to the Deception Island base in February.

PART FOUR

The First
Sledging Journey

CHAPTER THIRTEEN

Preparations for Sledging

BERRY BROUGHT OUR TEA TO US IN BED on the dull, gloomy morning of 21 June, Midwinter's Day. With it came the first issue of the *Hope Bay Howler* stamped with the wrapper of the "Hope Bay Publishing Co. Ltd." The first issue was ten pages (with the cover and two cartoons taking up three pages). It included a good deal of twaddle on everything in general, including an article on fishing and another, with a more serious predisposition, on the SS *Eagle*. In common with most papers, there were letters-to-the-editor, some efforts at rhyme, and a few advertisements, such as:

WANTED: Bright young man for the Antarctic. Must
have knowledge of botany, zoology, ornithology, surveying,
taxidermy, geology, oxometry, etc. German and French essential.
Must be able to type, operate a wireless set, light fires, clean
drains, build houses and drive dogs. Some knowledge of Huntin'
Shootin' and Fishin' expected. Salary despicable. Prospects nil.
Please write and state any additional qualifications.

HOUSING SHORTAGE: Buy one of our collapsible Nissen
houses. Easy to erect. Quicker to take down. Apply to Messers.
Taylor, Lamb, Flett, and James. Sole agents for Antarctica.[1]

---

1.   Author's note: The four names in the last ad were the four men involved in erecting the Nissen on the occasion of its subsidence through the force of the southwest wind on 18 February.

VOL. I   № 1

THE
HOPE BAY

HOWLER

● 21· June, 1945 ●

Guaranteed Circulation 100 copies.

Figure 29. The *Hope Bay Howler* cover, 21 June 1945.

In this, and in most of the subsequent issues, Lamb contributed the back-page cartoon filled with the doings of a curious-looking species of short-legged, fuzzy-coated men and their short-legged, snub-nosed, fat little dogs. In this particular issue, he produced a caricature lampooning some piously written words on the means of stopping a dog fight. This initial issue received a rather mixed reception, as some of the facetiously intended remarks were none too guardedly written and struck rather close to home in some instances. Later issues avoided this difficulty and the paper became quite popular, with the Doctor contributing the greater proportion. It was well worth the effort.

After making two additional trips to retrieve additional supplies from Eagle Cove that afternoon, we came back to the base and sat down to another of Berry's really big dinners. It was what he termed an eleven-course meal that he and Blyth spent considerable time preparing over the preceding week. It

Figure 30. The messroom at Hope Bay after dinner on Midwinter's Day, 21 June 1945. Taylor's face is visible between the vertical boards.

took an hour and a half of steady eating to get through it. Lamb and I prepared a menu to commemorate the occasion. The dinner began with hors d'oeuvres, and worked through an assortment of soups, fish, meat pies, seal meat, puddings, jelly, and mince pies. Lamb took a flashlight photograph of the members of the base just as we finished the meal. At the end, everyone was so full that the ensuing evening was not nearly so lively as anticipated.

Without any definite directions for the scientific program at Hope Bay, its planning remained in a very fluid condition for many months. The area promising the most interesting results was the east coast of the Graham Land Peninsula. Our experience of the previous year at Port Lockroy, however, led us to anticipate that the Crown Prince Gustav Channel would not freeze sufficiently to allow us to travel to its northern end until late in the autumn and, consequently, we would have to avoid dependence on the sea ice in this channel for at least the first journey. Governed entirely by this factor, we initially planned to make a journey from Hope Bay along the summit of the Trinity Peninsula and find a route down to the permanent sea ice farther to the south. While making these plans, we still had twenty-three dogs with which to arrange our transport and hoped that a ship would place supply depots in the area to the south.

With the subsequent loss of a proportion of the dogs, as well as the failure of the ships to lay any depots away from Hope Bay, we modified our plans. On 16 May, we had a meeting and decided that the midwinter days were of extremely short duration for a scientific trip. Much more information could be acquired by carrying it out at a later date—on or about 10 August—when light conditions would improve. By leaving just before mid-August and returning before the equinoctial storms, we hoped to escape the weather that so seriously handicapped us on the previous year's journey.

Our May meeting, however, left several additional factors undecided. The itinerary of the trip was not definitely settled. Later, we considered the possibility of making our first trip directly to Snow Hill Island through Sidney Herbert Sound, mainly to investigate whether the *Wyatt Earp* or even Nordenskjöld had left useable supplies there. We would have then left two of the four men at that base while the other two returned to Hope Bay for a further load of supplies. In view of the surface conditions we later found on this part of our route, it is just as well that we did not attempt this proposal.[2] These changing plans and proposals extended over a period of several months, but they did not greatly affect the general preparations for the journey, which went steadily, if slowly, forward throughout the latter part of June and all of July.

Nor did we determine whether our numbers of travellers could be as great as the six who wanted to go on the journey. Before the middle of July, it was decided that not more than four of us would make the journey: Lamb, Russell, James, and myself. The contributions that each member of our party would make toward the preparations for the trip, as well as their duties on it, were also established at this time. All of us would be equipped to carry out a compass survey of the areas we passed. We would all keep diaries throughout the journey, for there were bound to be days when the experiences of the party might not be uniform for all hands. Lamb would arrange the assembly of the camping equipment, cooking utensils, Primus stoves, paraffin, and methylated spirits. On the march, he would continue his botanical work while also carrying out geological observations and collecting specimens as opportunities offered. Russell's task was most important: preparing the food supplies and packing them into suitable sledge boxes. On the trail, he would be responsible for obtaining the time signals for our chronometers and observing the glaciers that came within our view. My own task was to prepare the working charts and survey gear that might be required. I was to plot the survey notes each night of the journey, make observations on the physiography of the region, and also to help Lamb with the collecting.

We assumed the base was completely established when the stores from Eagle Cove were all moved to the base. We then turned our attention for the first time to some of the scientific work. Back had steadily pursued meteorological observations since 1 March, and James made a series of general observations regarding the sea ice conditions. Marshall had also kept his eye on the birds and seals, and took sea temperatures at every opportunity. Flett had taken some time to examine the rocks, measuring the strikes and dips of the sills and bedding planes that abounded at Hope Bay. His geological specialization was petrology, and he gathered as many rock samples as the snow cover permitted. These were not of great interest to most members of the base, but they were of tremendous interest to Flett. Despite these activities, there had been little collecting and no

---

2.   Author's note: An abscess which bothered James a few days before we were ready to leave caused the temporary consideration of the journey being made by only three of us, but Back managed to clear the trouble up before the day of our long-delayed departure.

surveying. There was much to be learned of the geology, botany, glaciers, and tides of our immediate neighborhood.

Geologically, Hope Bay is probably best known for the magnificent collection of fossils made by Dr. J.G. Andersson in 1903. I found the indistinct impression of a fern during the days we occupied the Tin Galley. In mid-April, Flett found a few fragmentary fossils near Boeckella Lake. But it was not until 8 July that a party climbed up the face of Mount Flora below its summit and located the bed of shale where Andersson found much of his collection. It was at an elevation of about 950 feet by aneroid, and the parts of the beds we inspected seemed to be largely comprised of a mass of large stems with no leaves from which the species could be readily identified. On our way back to the base, we passed below a large moraine near Boeckella Lake and decided to climb up it to inspect the fragments of some shale among the debris. In this shale were many clear impressions of small fern-like leaves, and we gathered up a selection of them just before the darkness closed in around us. There was no time to make more than a cursory examination of the area.

Donnachie and I returned to this moraine two weeks later on another bright and sunny Sunday. We spent quite a successful couple of hours collecting many pieces of shale that showed the clearest impressions of plant stems and leaves of various different species. Many of the latter were readily identifiable from the illustrations shown in the scientific reports of the Swedish expedition. The leaves varied from a fraction of an inch to part of the frond of a fern measuring ten inches in length and six inches across the base. Most of the leaves we found bore a fern-like appearance, but some resembled coniferous plants, and one or two seemed to be of a deciduous type. This find added great impetus to the collection of fossils by members of the base. It became a popular sport and kept Flett extremely busy cataloguing and packing the specimens for shipment back to England. This interest increased in popularity as temperatures moderated and created more pleasant working conditions.

Lamb was so critical in selecting his specimens that we seldom retrieved any lichens that were of interest to him. He did not, of course, create this impression when receiving such botanical gifts, but appeared most grateful and was always prepared to give a learned exposition on the species in question. On more than one occasion on passing Lamb's window (particularly at Port Lockroy), I was almost struck when he tossed the specimen in question out the window, at the base of which subsequent visitors will likely find a small mound of lichen-covered stones of a great diversity of species.

There were few birds about in this part of the winter, though June was the only month when we did not notice any evidence of Gentoo penguins (despite the fact that they left the rookery early in April). Andersson chronicled the localities occupied in the large rookery by the relatively small colonies of Gentoo penguins, and the locations of these colonies were unchanged. This same fact applied to an area on the side of the glacier to the east of the base, which Andersson marked on the map as the "resting place" of the giant petrel. We noticed sixty or seventy of these birds in that area when we arrived, and they were seldom seen "resting" at any other place in the vicinity. By June and July, however, the stinker was a very infrequent visitor that we only saw on four occasions in the two months.

We did not see shags or cormorants frequently in this area; and those we did observe were generally "on the wing." The gulls, however, seemed on the increase, and it was not unusual to count between forty and sixty at one time. There were about the same numbers of paddies scavenging all they could find around the base, as cheeky as when we first encountered them the previous year.

Seals were not numerous during these months, a fact that enhanced the value of those cached in the snow during February and March. Most of these were deeply buried in drifting snow, and the exact position of some became a matter of some conjecture. Many had been left on bare rock where they were killed and we had the same experience digging them out and releasing them that we had had with the coal bags at Eagle Cove. The pelts froze to the rock so securely that the frozen flesh tore free from the skin before the joint with the rock gave way. Despite the cold, however, the blubber still possessed considerable resilience.

We succeeded in getting a few seals in this period, however, to help eke out the dog food situation. On 17 June, Flett spotted a seal about a mile offshore in the direction of Sheppard Point, and an expedition quickly formed to dispatch the animal and bring back the carcass. James went a little in advance with the guns and killed not one but two Weddells lying beside a hole in the ice. The ice was between three and four inches thick at this point. Back, Russell, and I arrived with the "Odds and Sods" a few moments later, loaded up one of the seals, came back for the second one, and returned with it to the base after dark. The spot at which we found these seals had been open water two weeks previously. A gale from the southwest blew for the next two days. When the visibility cleared, the part of the ice where we found the seals was swept out to sea.

June was one of the stormiest months on record, and the mercury stayed continuously below the freezing point. We experienced two gales in the first week of the month, both reaching force 10 (sixty miles an hour). The first one lasted for twenty-eight hours while the second blew for forty-three hours, during which the wind velocity exceeded fifty miles an hour for more than twenty-three hours without respite. The prevalence of the southwest wind was marked in the month of June; 57 percent of our observations indicated a wind from that quarter.

The following month showed a much wider variation in temperature. The coldest day of the year was 22 July, when the noon reading dipped down to −22°F, while we read a high of 39°F above at midnight 10–11 July. The wind was not nearly as boisterous as it had been the previous month, with force 8 being the maximum recorded velocity. It is of interest to compare the 1.7°F monthly mean at Hope Bay with the mean temperature for the same month at Port Lockroy (13.3°F) and Deception Island (9.0°F).

The observation of the sea ice in this midwinter period was not an exciting pastime, for the hard frosts caught the surface of the sea and there was little movement of the ice or change in its limits. Hope Bay, of course, solidly froze for the winter. There was only a light sheet of ice across the sound, however, with many leads and patches of unsafe grey ice, so that a few hours of the strong southwest wind was all that was needed to open up large areas of the Antarctic Sound. There was little movement of either the pack ice or the icebergs in the sounds at that time of the year.

On the afternoon of 20 July we heard a tremendous roar that prolonged itself continuously for about five minutes. At the time, some of the chaps were out ice fishing, while I happened to be in the house. The roar signalled the slow subsidence of about half a mile of the ice cliffs along the north side of Hope Bay opposite Seal Point. The fall cracked the three-foot thick bay ice with a series of sharp reports but, as far as we could see, it was not the cause of any of the ice in the bay detaching itself and drifting out to sea. The shift created a huge cloud of snow smoke, traces of which were still visible half an hour later. The wave created by the fall caused the ice along the shore below the base to rise and fall violently about three feet. It was two days before some of us walked over to view the effect of the hundreds of thousands of tons of icefall. We found that the confused mass of ice from the cliff roughened the surface of the sea for 300 yards out from the shore. The freefall propelled the large blocks of glacial ice underwater until they lost their momentum and buoyancy forced their passage upward through the over three-foot-thick sea ice. A large, isolated piece that had projected farthest out from the ice cliff apparently lacked sufficient force to break the sea ice open, and instead created a congested area of about 100 square yards where sea ice broke and burgeoned upward to a height of about four feet.

Our surveying activities began in June with a long series of astronomical observations for latitude and longitude as well as local large-scale surveys. We selected a place about 300 yards to the west of the house where we hoped that our magnetic observations would be unaffected by any metallic objects round the base, and where Russell and I frequently observed the stars. Along the surface of the ice of Hope Bay we measured a 3,000-yard-long baseline, which we first used to calibrate our sledge meters and later employed to triangulate a network of control points over the area. Our sledge wheel was simply a bicycle wheel that rotated within a wooden frame attached to the rear runner of the sledge. The sledge meters that came with our supplies were simple cyclometers, such as are used on the bicycles that wheel around the English country roads. The meters were small things made of aluminum and brass and, after testing and breaking about a half a dozen of them, we found that their average life expectancy was about two hours and concluded that there was no alternative but for Ashton to reassemble the arrangement we had used the previous year at Port Lockroy. This he did, rearranging the parts so as to have a direct drive on the spindle of the bicycle wheel. Though the wheel tilted a little with the eccentric load, on the whole the latest model of Ashton's sledge meter gave extremely accurate and satisfactory results throughout the winter. The one failure, which is subsequently recorded, had nothing to do with the excellent workmanship Ashton put into this job. We would certainly have found ourselves at a decided loss had we not had this improvisation to use as a sledge meter.

By the time the latitude and longitude observations were complete and computed, we established that Hope Bay was located approximately twelve miles south of the position previously assigned to it. The result of twenty sights gave a latitude of 63°24'S and a longitude of 56°59'W. We had intended to set up a concrete monument to mark the position where we took these observations. Toward this end, Ashton manufactured a suitably engraved brass plate about nine inches in diameter; but our departure from Hope Bay occurred with some precipitancy, and we never erected the monument.

Figure 31. Sledging past the Pyramid Nunatak, 16 July 1945.

We also made a range-finder survey of the coastline around Hope Bay. In the course of this work, Russell found a small islet near Sheppard Point that he called "Cambridge Islet" after his alma mater. A few days later, James and I were extending the shoreline to the east of the base. There were low, rocky islets clustered close in to the base of the steep, blue ice cliffs that rose to such an altitude along this sector of the coast, and James evened the score with Russell, naming them the "Oxford Group." We gathered rock specimens from each of them, but as we moved toward what appeared to be the most easterly of the islets, some distance past any of the others, a strong northwest wind began to blow. We could see large floes of considerable extent breaking away from the shore ice and sweeping out into the sound toward the south, so that we were less than half a mile from the rapidly approaching ice edge. While a couple of hundred yards from our objective, we turned back to the base. A few days later, a strong west wind swept the ice of this entire area out to sea.

We had for some time intended visiting the Depot Glacier in order to set out some stakes as reference points to measure its motion. We chose to set out on this excursion on 16 July, leaving the base with the "Big Boys" at half-past nine. The day was bright and clear, with the temperature holding near zero. Two of the bitches, "Beauty" and "Pretty," with the former's three-month-old pups "Hobbs" and "Hinks," accompanied us. James did his best to prevent the dogs from starting out, and again tried to send them back from Nobby Nunatak, but they refused to go, raced and jumped around the sledge, and proved a considerable distraction to the other dogs in the team. We swung round the Pyramid Nunatak and made for the summit of a small glacial pass with its elevation of 1,460 feet. From this point, on so clear a day, we had a magnificent view of the country to the south through which we expected to travel when our sledge journey began.

In the distance, but dimly distinguishable from the sky, we saw the rounded summit of Mount Haddington with the black cliffs of Vega Island in the foreground. The Crown Prince Gustav Channel appeared to be solidly frozen, and many bergs were discernible in the direction of the Bay of a Thousand Icebergs (although we did not have a full view of the latter). There also seemed to be unidentifiable islands lying in the channel, giving it more than the suggestion of an archipelago. A gentle downhill slope lay before us into Duse Bay, and there were many sharply pointed *nunataks* protruding above the snow toward the southeast.

We continued our journey over one or two small crevasses, rounded the westerly of the two *nunataks* that marked the pass we entered, and obtained a good view of the Ben More heavy ice cap. Its freshly broken face hovered above the smooth pearly faces, lightly tinged a blue-green colour, down which the icefalls roared. A small glacier separated this mountain from the south end of the Blade Ridge on the same side of Depot Glacier (the latter ridge being a dark scree-surfaced wall of diorite having a remarkably uniform angle of repose). We tied the dogs up at a point overlooking the glacier, and set about the job we came to do. By theodolite, we lined up half a dozen stakes across the glacier. We noted small crevasses in the glacier that were all well spanned by glazed ice bridges. From his observation, Russell concluded that we would discover little movement in the glacier when we re-measured the stakes in the summer. The centre of the glacier measured 1,000 feet in altitude by aneroid.

We returned to the sledge at three o'clock and ate our lunch of frozen sandwiches, cheese, and biscuits. A frozen thermos flask lid prevented us from adding a hot drink to the meal. Half an hour later, we started our homeward journey. The two little pups paddled along behind us, but became quite exhausted and could not keep pace with the bigger animals on a downhill run. When they were about half a mile behind us, we waited for them to catch up and took them aboard the sledge for the balance of the journey. The glacier surface over which we travelled was pure ice for a good part of the journey, and the dogs and sledge fairly rattled over it. Not until we were east of the Pyramid did we encounter any *sastrugi*, and they were not large enough to bother us. It was not quite dark enough to obscure the sound, for a good moon shone and we could see quite large patches of open water between the young, grey ice and the stronger white surface of the sea. Russell did not ride the sledge, but towed along on his skis on a rough and riotous ride in the semi-darkness. Everyone enjoyed the day, the dogs not the least of us, and we arrived back at the base with appetites little short of ravenous.

Though no tide-recording apparatus was supplied with our stores, there was a job to be done obtaining these records. We left the design and manufacture of a suitable device to Ashton. We approached Back for the use of one of his eight-day meteorological clocks to use as its driving mechanism, but the Doctor was not keen on parting with his only spare at this particular season of the year, for the clocks on his self-recording apparatus inevitably gave trouble when the temperature dropped below zero—and just as inevitably stopped when the mercury dropped to ten below. Though it was quite a comedown, Chippie began to design a gauge utilizing an old alarm clock as the driving mechanism. It was based on a twelve-hour chart, meaning that the charts would have to be changed on the machine twice daily. This was quite a contract to carry out given the certainty of being out on the sea ice in a southwest gale for some of these changes. The plans and construction of the gauge began toward the end of July, incorporating the micrometer stage of a microscope and an empty dried milk tin as the recording drum. Before the end of the month, we tested the mechanism in the cold, and immediately discovered the clock's tendency to stop in low temperatures. Cleaning and re-lubricating the clock with graphite seemed to improve it. We then encased the whole apparatus in a wooden box and fabricated a hand-turned 11.5-inch wooden wheel. The gauge's operation depended on the wooden wheel being rotated by a counterweighted wire rope round it, the other end of which was securely anchored on the sea bottom. We then made preparations for its installation on the sea ice so that the month's records might be procured in August and September.

About the end of July, our station also began taking soundings in Hope Bay. Following the experience of the *Eagle* earlier in the year (and the obvious reluctance of other vessels to spend much time in our harbour), we also needed to take soundings in the harbour. Had we possessed a boat, we would never have considered this job in midwinter. The *Eagle*'s sudden departure, however, robbed Matheson of the chance to undertake this job in the spring after the ice went out. But we were virtually marooned, and if this work was to be done before our departure, Matheson had no alternative but to take a series of soundings by arduously cutting through the sea ice with an axe or some other tool.[3] We had tried to manufacture a couple of ice drills, but neither proved very satisfactory. Digging a hole through ice that was more than three feet thick was back-breaking labour. On the ice, we laid out a grid for Matheson to work to, and he and Flett plotted the results each night, including the bottom findings brought up by the tallow on the homemade lead.

Not once in the two years we spent in this part of the Antarctic did any of us catch sight of the celestial phenomenon know as the *Aurora Australis*, or Southern Lights, observed by so many south polar expeditions. Back was keen to catch a glimpse of it; Russell, Lamb, and I spent considerable time on clear nights

---

3.   Editors' note: Most of this paragraph's text originally appeared in Chapter 16 of Taylor's manuscript.

employed on astral observations. But none of us ever spotted this heavenly display. We did, however, notice one or two interesting solar and lunar phenomena from the Hope Bay base. We observed, for example, remarkably brilliant mock suns over the glacier near Andersson Nunatak at three o'clock on the afternoon of 21 April, just as the sun set on a clear, fine, and all but windless day. The southerly one was pure white light and quite dazzling, while the other, not quite so bright, was tinged with the colours of the spectrum. The two mock suns were level with the altitude of the sun, and there was no sign of any above the sun, which just cleared the glacier by a few degrees. A most peculiar prismatic effect occurred on the morning of 11 July. Just before nine o'clock, before sunrise, of course, an altocumulus cloud of considerable extent lay just north of the zenith. The most easterly tip of this cloud took on an iridescence with all the colours of the rainbow. The colouring lasted for more than half an hour, and the iridescence spread until it covered an arc of 15° along the cloud in the projected direction of its eastern tip, which appeared to be the focal point of the sun's rays, tending to fan out beyond it. The colouring increased in brilliance, then disappeared quite suddenly as the sun rose into the bank of clouds that lay along the horizon. The red sunrise dispersed the clouds about half past nine.

We were kept constantly informed of Bonner's physical condition at Deception Island since the *Scoresby*'s approach in April. It became apparent to Reece even before this date that Bonner's physical condition caused the members of that little base considerable anxiety. It would have been a good thing for the base and for Bonner had it been possible to evacuate him back to Port Stanley at that time. But, as was remarked in the July issue of the *Howler*, "In spite of rumors to the contrary, Samuel Bonner would like to state that after due consideration, he has decided to remain in the South Shetlands for the next four or five months." On 23 June, however, Bonner suffered a stroke. Smith tried to awaken him in the usual course of events, but Bonner did not respond immediately. Apparently this was not unusual, for Reece had all but relieved Bonner of all duties about the base. Bonner frequently did not get up with the other members of the base for breakfast. About an hour later, Smith again called Bonner, and after receiving no response, went in to give him a shake. Reece went in to examine him and became alarmed after finding Bonner lying on his back and breathing heavily through the mouth. His eyes were open, but glassy and unseeing. The station flashed the details of his condition to Back at Hope Bay, who immediately diagnosed the condition as a cerebral hemorrhage and prescribed treatment. Bonner came out of his comatose condition five hours later, and in a couple of days made a complete recovery.

Back kept in constant touch with Reece throughout the winter concerning Bonner's condition, providing frequent advice and treatment. On about the fifteenth of each month, we sent the government of the Falkland Islands a message that was variously known as our "Next-of-kin" or "Omnibus Telegram." Each base compiled its own, which generally read "all well here," but the one from Deception Island always added the words "except Bonner, who is as well as may be expected." These signals, we later discovered, were a real comfort to most of our relatives at home since they were the only substitute for any regular mail from us.

The back injury I had suffered on 25 February had not healed completely, and I was a little apprehensive of my strength to withstand the rigours of a sledging trip. It was still bound in an elastic bandage, and strength had returned to it very slowly. A week after the accident, I had been unable to lift a five-pound weight; a month later, I could sustain only fifty pounds. The decision to delay our departure until the longer days of August, therefore, also favoured my back's slow return to strength.

July was busy, largely devoted to getting our scientific work at the base underway and to completing preparations for our upcoming journey. It was a happy month, with brightening skies and brightening interests. No one dared suggest that any of the chaps had the "Channels,"[4] but they were definitely taking an interest—and a long-range interest—in the future. The July issue of the *Howler* contained the following advertisement, perhaps of more than passing significance:

> SITUATION VACANT. Wanted, as soon as possible,
> lady typist, aged 18 to 25. Good looks and good shape
> will receive good pay and overtime, but in a pinch,
> any old bag will be paid for services rendered.

James gradually completed the manufacture and assembly of all the materials needed by the dog teams, and also overhauled the two sledges that would make the first journey. The one Lamb and I meant to use was twelve feet long. It was the same sledge that he and I had been so laboriously attached to during the previous year's manhauling over the glaciers of Wiencke Island. I recommended

---

4.   Editors' note: "The Channels" is a nautical term that refers to the euphoria many sailors feel when they know they are about to reunite with their families.

that James use a nine-foot sledge because he broke a number of the larger ones on the Eagle Cove haul. This was, we later realized, a mistake, for our loads were far too big on the early part of the journey to be carried on such a short sledge. However, James rebuilt his sledge and stiffened up its runners. At the end of the sledging it was in much better shape than the larger sledge.

The dogs developed a worrisome condition in July. The problem first became apparent about the tenth of the month. They began to lose their hair and large areas of their bodies became exposed and completely bared. The white fur that remained was a red, rusty colour. Great long messages flashed back and forth between James and the agricultural officer at Port Stanley, the messages seeming to consider all of the diseases dogs could contract under such circumstances. I do not think that the name of the trouble was ever actually pinned down, but by the time we completed this exchange of information, and following a Lysol treatment, the ailment had run its course, and the dogs made quick and complete recoveries.

James also looked after the manufacture of the harnesses from codline and lampwick, making sufficient quantities to provide each team with a few spares. Harnesses for individual dogs were marked with the dog's name so that each animal wore the same harness each day. James also strengthened the tethering lines made earlier in the season. The last of his responsibilities for the sledging trips concerned the preparation of a box almost completely filled with materials for effecting sledge and ski repairs in the field.

The food stores prepared by Russell followed the diet and rations used by the British Graham Land Expedition of 1934 to 1937 fairly closely, with minor adjustments to suit our bulk supplies. The following was the man-day ration scale as it was ultimately prepared:

Biscuits...3.1 oz.
Cocoa 0.6
Oatmeal...2.0
Chocolate 2.4
Pemmican 5.6
Sugar..3.2
Milk Powder...................................2.0
Butter..5.6
Nescafe 0.4
Tea 0.4

Dried Apples 0.4
Dried Onions 0.2
Pea Flour 1.6
　　27.5 oz. per man per day.

During the first week or two of the sledging trip, Lamb and I found this ration scale to be far too filling. In the later stages we could have eaten it without
either discomfort or difficulty. We found that two little items, the dried apples
and onions (which were particularly effective at making seal meat much more
relishing), did a great deal to dispel the monotony of the fatty ration.

Lamb assembled two boxes of utensils, one for each tent. The kits contained a pot and pan, one Primus stove, and other items such as the alcohol for
lighting the stoves, candles, matches, and eating utensils. Each complete box
weighed about thirty pounds. We were each also supplied with a bag containing
medical supplies, such as bandages and dressings, a set of surgical instruments,
and a good supply of Number Nines,[5] which were never required.

The tents supplied in 1945 were slightly larger than those we had utilized
the previous year, being seven feet square instead of six. The roominess provided by this extra foot in each direction was amazing. The canvas of these new
tents was not quite as heavy as their smaller counterparts, nor were the poles
nearly so strong, being made of turned wood instead of bamboo.

I prepared the survey apparatus for the trip, including some additional supplies that were not normally necessary. These included tables and materials required for one of the two men to work out and plot the information gathered at
Snow Hill Island while the other returned to Hope Bay for supplies. A second
reason for this additional equipment was precautionary in case the ice carried
us off to sea, so we brought a small sextant among these extra items.

We hoped to be able to keep in contact with Hope Bay by means of a walkie-
talkie radio that could be installed at Snow Hill Island if a party remained there.
Despite the deprivations that arose from various incidents, we still possessed two
sets. One had suffered an immersion in the seawater during the landing of the
stores. Donnachie readied the better of these two sets and tested it by making
contact with Farrington at Deception a few days before we left the base. We arranged a code for the transmission of our signals by radio telephone, maintaining twice-a-day listening watches. In the event that the station lost radio contact

---

5.　Editors' note: "Number Nines" is slang for a laxative.

with us, it would send signals containing important messages on the evening schedule each Monday.

Before leaving Hope Bay, we also carefully culled all the information we could gather out of Nordenskjöld's book *Antarctica*. We were especially interested in materials relating to the disposition and contents of any depots that party left behind in case we found ourselves in a position to make use of any of them.

We assembled a dump of stores for the journey at Nobby Nunatak, and by the end of the month had a pile of 900 pounds of man food and dog food that eventually constituted the load for our seven-dog teams. Consequently, only about 250 pounds had to be taken up the steep slope on the day we left the base. By hauling up a few hundred pounds of these stores at a time, we had virtually completed our preparations for the journey by the end of July, then spent about a week waiting for suitable weather to begin the trip.

CHAPTER FOURTEEN

Start of the First Sledge Journey

WE WERE AWAY ABOUT HALF PAST TEN on 8 August. Russell and James were in charge of the first sledge, pulled by the "Big Boys," while Lamb and I had the other team known variously as the "Odds and Sods," "Odds and Ends," and a name bestowed on them by Lamb: "The Chromosomes." It was a dull gloomy day, the temperature about zero, with little wind and a heavy carpet of snow covering everything. Given these heavy surface conditions, we were particularly fortunate that the sledges were comparatively light because of the loads we had already hauled to Nobby Nunatak. Seven dog teams pulled each sledge, but we had the assistance of Matheson, Back, Donnachie, Marshall, and Davies to get up the heavy initial slope of the glacier. The incline flattened out considerably once we approached an elevation of 500 feet, and we arrived at Nobby Nunatak just after noon as the other team pulled away with their full load.

We packed the remaining stores onto the sledge and, still assisted by the other chaps, the two teams continued up a flattening slope toward a pass between two *nunataks* we called Summit Pass. It was about four miles from Eagle House and rose to an elevation of approximately 1,500 feet. We reached it at four o'clock. Here we bid goodbye to our friends, who left us to return to the base.

The two dog teams were not well matched. The "Big Boys" were a powerful set of dogs, well-built, spirited, and a cohesive unit governed indisputably and led by a fine-looking brown-coated animal named "Captain." They pulled a top-heavy load, 100 pounds heavier than ours, on a nine-foot sledge with comparative ease. On the other hand, the "Odds and Sods" were formed from the dogs who did not assimilate into either Captain's team or the one where "The Drinks" originally formed the nucleus. A scrawny-looking black and white animal named "Mutt" held a rather shaky supremacy over the others. There were three factions in it. "Dainty," "Mutt," "Jeff," and "Sydney" formed a tightly knit unit, between which there was considerable individual animosity; all were black and white animals except Dainty, our lead dog and Lamb's favourite, who had a light brown coat. Two of the other dogs, "Pretty" and "Jack," black and white too, tolerated each other but possessed a wholesome respect for the first-named four. The last of the team, "Widgeon," sorely missed the companionship and protection of the recently departed "Rover," and further suffered from the result of a dog fight a few days earlier at the base. He limped along on three legs, one forepaw lifted clear of the surface of the snow. There was little spirit left in Widgeon, and he was of no use at all at this time in hauling his share of the load. The other dogs had no hesitation setting upon him, which they frequently did, but they seemed to do it more to build up their own morale than to inflict any further harm on Widgeon, as he lay snivelling at their feet. Just before we were

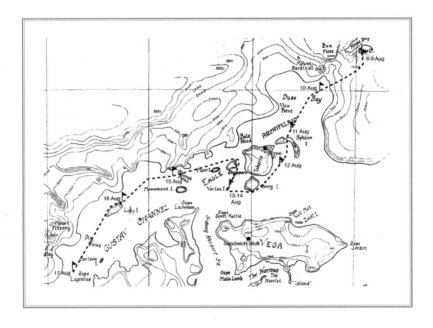

Map 8. The first sledging journey, 8–17 August 1945.

about to leave the pass, Mutt, Jeff, and Sydney had a terrific battle, which all three seemed to enjoy. The only casualty was a chewed-up trace.

Lamb and I took our team ahead from this point, following a tortuous contour for about a mile toward the broad summit of a snow ridge extending eastwars from an ice-sloped *nunatak*. We made camp for the night a short distance farther on, having travelled just over five miles that day. The two dog teams halted near each other but were far enough apart to prevent them from getting together for a fight, for there was a never-ending feud between them which lasted for the entire journey—and, indeed, continued after we sailed for home. After unlashing the straggly looking loads on the sledges, we set up the two tents within thirty feet of each other. We placed in each tent a ration box, utensil box (which included the Primus stove), and bedrolls. We also kept the survey box for our tent, and sent the radio box to the other. The sky cleared toward evening, and the temperature was −7°F. James, appointed as radio operator, tried to contact Donnachie at Hope Bay but was unable to do so, owing perhaps to a fault in the transmitter or maybe the "skip distance" phenomena of these shortwave sets. The dogs were quite tired from their unaccustomed exercise and rested peaceably (though supper-less) chained to their steel-wire tethering line. With intermittent light snowfall and fog closing in around us, darkness enfolded our camp 1,000 feet above the sea. The night was calm, with the mercury at −13°F.

In the morning, with blue sky overhead and prospects of a better day ahead, we packed up all our gear except for the tents. We were ready to break camp at half past eight, but the southwest wind began to blow threateningly, and within an hour a heavy drift blew, reducing visibility to well under half a mile.[1] By mid-afternoon, the velocity of the wind approached forty miles an hour, with the barometer rising sharply. We did not move, but lay in our sleeping bags all day long with the Primus stoves burning more perhaps than they should have burned; for we felt the cold, which reached −5°F in the tent, toward evening.

The temperature dropped that night to −17°F. Soon after sunrise, the light southwest wind dropped and we enjoyed a bright, sunny day with perfect visibility. The northern end of Crown Prince Gustav Channel spread out below us, with Andersson's Bay of a Thousand Icebergs slightly to our right and

---

1. Author's note: The bitch, "Pretty," succeeded in getting loose from her chain in the morning but, surprisingly, made no attempt to return to her pups at Eagle House a little over five miles distant.

well-filled with bergs in the distance. The topography of the land ahead was rather confusing, confirming our belief that it constituted an archipelago rather than the peninsula shown as Cape Corry on the older maps. To the right of the southwesterly course that we were about to take, several miles distant from where we stood, the massive, ice-capped face of black Ben More rose up its full 3,000 feet. To the left, the ice cover of this tip of the Trinity Peninsula draped down to meet us past a scree-faced outcrop of dark rock protruding through the white sheet of snow and ice.

The surface was good as we started out from our camp, with the other team leading. The dogs raced down the slope with both Lamb and me riding the heavily laden sledge at a brisk pace. This continued for about two miles. Then we approached a steeper slope and it became necessary to attach our improvised steel cable brakes to the sledge to retain control. The brakes worked almost too effectively, for though they controlled the sledge's speed through the soft snow to some extent, we began to cross bare patches of ice where they bit so deeply that the sledge stopped dead and could hardly be budged to get under way again. We crossed crevasses occasionally, though they were generally well bridged and those that were open were less than a foot in width. As we approached the sea, a weather-worn face of ice lay to the east with several crevasses radiating from it. Russell and I prospected a route across them and down onto the sea ice. We crossed over an ice bridge spanning a five-foot-wide crevasse, and then encountered an open one that was a couple of feet in width. The dogs passed these with comparative ease but bogged down in the deep snow of a thirty-foot-wide rift below them. We had to partially unload in order to ascend the short slope up onto the sea ice. For the next quarter-mile we passed through a field of drifted pack ice before we came upon the smoother surface of sea ice where we stopped for our usual lunch of two hard biscuits and a little frozen chocolate. Looking back on the course we followed, it seemed as though we had accidentally found the only approach to the sea ice for a mile or two in either direction along the shore. Most of the shore consisted of undulating ice cliffs from thirty to fifty feet in height, the inland ice being rather badly crevassed along the fringe formed by the tops of these cliffs. Southward, we could see another snow slope up which one might have ascended from Duse Bay (as the Bay of a Thousand Icebergs was named on the Admiralty charts). This route lay at the base of some steep, ice-capped black cliffs that were snow-fringed along the base. It may well have been where the three men returned to Hope Bay forty or so years ago, and where a drift formed by a blizzard caused them the loss of their camera.

The day was still quite beautiful. Though the temperature was well below zero, there was hardly a cloud in the sky. We made our entry into Duse Bay through a little embayment along its northeast end. Into this part of the bay we saw a large number of icebergs frozen into the surface of the sea that gave the place its original picturesque name. Close inshore to the point where we stood there were a few bergs, but they were old and weather-worn into fantastic forms. One of the smaller ones had a square tower rising from one end of its mass like an ancient Norman church. Another was crowned with a sharp, pointed, whitened spire that rose into the air for twenty or thirty feet. A third had a large hole like an eyelet, forty feet above the sea. They were all worn grey and abraded by the blasts of hundreds of blizzards, while parts of the ice forming them were a dirty green colour.

To the south, we could distinguish the even, black cliffs of Vega Island. Beyond it, in the distance, rose the flattened summit of Ross Island on Mount Haddington. Between these features and Duse Bay lay high islands composed for the most part of snow-free brown rock. To the southwest, we observed a confused mass of islands and headlands, the lower parts hidden by intervening icebergs. This made the choice of our route somewhat problematic, for we did not want to encounter a peninsula in that direction that might force us to backtrack with our heavy loads.

With one man pulling in a man harness on each sledge, we made another two miles over the rather soft snow surface before camping on the sea ice that night at about four o'clock. We had not made a much longer distance than on the first day of our journey, but we were now "over the hump" because we were down on the sea ice. Fortunately, the older maps were in error concerning our route, for we found the distance between Hope Bay and Duse Bay to be eight instead of twenty-one miles. The sun set by the time we made camp, with the sky to the southwest blood-red and the temperature at −30°F. Before the tents were up, however, Russell's feet were frostbitten.[2]

---

2. Author's note: Nordenskjöld's Snow Hill temperatures were much below Back's corresponding records at Hope Bay. The fact that the line of demarcation between these differences in temperature was so marked, however, was an interesting observation. While we had a minimum temperature in the night of −35°F, Back was recording −6°F at Hope Bay, about ten miles away.

The morning of 11 August was again bright and sunny as we left the camp-site at half past nine. Although the snow surface was hard, it was badly cut up with *sastrugi* and frequently caused the sledges to upset. The day was hard on both men and beasts, largely because we were so badly out of condition. In the bright sunlight, a noticeable mirage raised every bergy bit of ice up until it seemed to have assumed the proportion of a tabular iceberg, making the interpretation of the topography even more difficult as we found ourselves heading into what appeared to be a cul-de-sac. With the rather limited supplies we had for the job at hand, we could not afford to spend several days exploring the fjord-like feature that existed ahead of us. Rather than take any chance at having to retrace our steps, we altered our course from the southwest toward the south. We meant to pass to the south of that feature shown on the map as Cape Corry, and struck a course for a high, black rock cliff atop the west end of Vega Island. It had a central seam of white lying horizontally in it, and Lamb immediately gave it the name Sandwich Bluff.

In the afternoon, the mirage became even more marked. It made us all but certain that no passage existed toward the southwest, though there could have been a route over a low col or glaciated pass. The mirage tended to make any distant irregularity in the ice look like a cliff face, elongating all the details vertically like the astigmatiser of a rangefinder.

We passed over distorted pressure ridges, through a field of old and roughened pack ice cemented into the surface. During the crossing, our sledges upset repeatedly. Some pieces of the ice contained fragments of rock, and one small berg was covered black with a layer of it. But we were too tired to walk over and investigate it, and too busy keeping the sledges on the move with evening approaching. As long as the sledges remained in motion, the dogs pulled with enthusiasm. As soon the sledge slowed toward a halt, the dogs turned their heads round and looked back over their shoulders, stopped their own forward progress, and allowed the sledge to stop. To get it moving again, we had to draw back on the traces to have the dogs pull forward more or less in unison. Then, just at the instant when this pull became effective, we pulled sideways on the bow of the sledge to unfreeze the runners. If we were lucky, the procession began again; if it failed, we repeated the procedure.

We used the "Odds and Sods" team to break trail. Lamb drove while I pulled, and more often than not we required James for pushing. The dogs were heavily overloaded, as they had no reserve power at all for the heavy spots.

Widgeon, with his injured leg, had not eaten a bite of the dog pemmican placed beside him each night since we left; he still only trotted alongside the other dogs, his trace slack all the time. The other dogs all ate their food up as soon as we threw it to them. Sydney, in particular, consumed his voraciously in just three gulps.

We camped half a mile short of a brown, rocky bluff toward the north side of Sphinx Island at four o'clock, having covered a little over seven laborious miles. In the morning, we rearranged the loads so that the other team had the twelve-foot sledge and a larger proportion of the load, for they had romped along easily in our tracks all day and stopped on several occasions to allow our team to get some distance ahead of them.

We started off for what appeared to be a narrow channel between two islands, but when we approached it we discovered that they were connected by a narrow isthmus of snow-free land about 100 feet in height. We lost some time crossing this hurdle, after which we again found ourselves on the sea ice with steep hillsides rising along the islands to either side of us. We were still headed for Cape Corry, in calm, bright weather. All morning we observed clouds of snow drifting about the cape from the southwest, such that they completely obscured the bases of the cliffs that bound it and left the summit brilliantly illuminated in the afternoon sunshine. When approaching this wind zone, we had noticed "whirlies" driving round its perimeter; at sea level, they were about twenty inches in diameter and revolved counterclockwise with the cloud of snow they carried whirling into a broadening vortex high into the sky. Though the temperature approached twenty below the night before, the blizzard brought it to five above so that none us became frostbitten in the storm. By three o'clock, we headed into this drift. The wind blew at force 7, carrying such a blanket of snow that the dogs showed a distinct aversion to facing it and soon lost interest in pulling. We travelled just over five miles that day before we halted and began to pitch camp.

We had the greatest difficulty erecting the tents, due to inexperience, and it was all that the four of us could do to get each tent standing. We tied a guy rope from the apex of the tent to the heavily loaded sledge, now firmly clamped in the drifts swirling about it, and then proceeded to make the base secure. We weighted down the south side of the tent with ration and paraffin boxes in addition to the usual snow and hoped that the tent would hold. With the force of the wind catching the canvas walls of the tent like a sail, we had made a poor job of erecting the shelters. When we crept inside, we found ours to be 4.5 feet square. Lamb and I, who are both over six feet tall, suffered some inconvenience folding ourselves into suitable shapes in which to try to sleep for the night. The snow that drove into our bearded faces froze and brought tears to our eyes so that our faces were encased in ice so rigid that it was almost impossible to speak intelligibly, even within the shelter of the tent, until the inch-thick clots of ice were peeled off.

After spending a most uncomfortable night in beds far too short for us, the storm blew itself out by morning and the temperature descended to −10°F. We had a bad upset after starting off, and it took us half an hour to extricate the sledge from the position in which it was wedged. James came back a mile to help us get under way again. Things went well for the remainder of the day, and we had the finest of weather with a clear blue sky, little wind, and the sun shining metallically down upon us.

Figure 32. Sandwich Bluff, Vega Island, 13 August 1945.

We found Cape Corry to be a high, steep-walled island with a moulded dome of snow that poured down the side in places in small, hanging glaciers. Although the island had a thin ice cap that overlay its flattened top, the cliffs were sheer and precipitous with little snow lying about them. Approaching the island, the surface of the sea began to improve for sledging and we found ourselves making good time over hard, windblown snow.

When rounding the southerly end of Corry Island, two other islands appeared ahead of us in the Crown Prince Gustav Channel. We set our course just to the north of the nearer one. To the south, we could clearly see the black, precipitous walls of Vega Island, Devil Island, and Cape Well Met.[3] We encountered a very disturbed zone of rough ice just to the west of Corry Island containing great white icebergs. At the base of one of these James spotted a seal and walked over to dispatch the animal with both the .22 rifle and a service revolver. The rifle, however, did not shoot at all, and though he pumped half a dozen revolver bullets into the quivering mass of blubber, the animal succeeded in disappearing down a tide crack.

Having made about eleven miles, we camped at 4:15 p.m., just to the north of the small high island of red rock toward which we had set our course. James had not had any luck with the radio up to this date, and he was unable to receive or send any signals. In the evening, Russell managed to get a time signal to use in conjunction with the round of eight stars that I observed. The temperature was −13°F. It was almost midnight when we turned in to our sleeping bags for the night.

We didn't move the next day, 14 August, on account of a gusty, southwest wind that blew up in the morning. Though the sun was out, the conditions were so similar to those that we had encountered before the gale struck us two days previously that we waited a couple of hours to judge what the wind was about to do. It grew steadily worse, with many whirlies that drew the snow up into the air in such well-defined vortexes that they inspired Lamb to call the nearby island Vortex Island.

We spent the day plotting up the survey notes that we had made since leaving the base. We also worked out star observations, as there had been some difficulty with the chronometer after we had made the observations. Lamb and

---

3.   Author's note: These reminded us of the meeting of Nordenskjöld with the small Hope Bay party in 1903. The rock formation Lamb named Sandwich Bluff on Vega apparently overlooks Cape Scott Keltie.

James also laid a small depot of supplies on the east[4] side of Vortex Island at the base of the long scree slope. We would return to this point on our homeward journey and the depot meant that we would not have to haul these supplies around for the whole trip. Among the articles left were two-and-a-half days' man food, three-and-a-half days' dog food, one of our two sledge repair boxes, three pairs of skis, a gallon of paraffin (which would fill the stove seven times), and a few other odds and ends such as the rifle, the boat tarpaulin, and related parts. The surface that we were travelling over was so hard and smooth that the others felt inclined to leave their skis to lighten the load. Russell took his, as he had found that they were much easier on his frostbitten feet, which were becoming very tender. I refused to part with my snowshoes—the only pair we had with us—in order to break trail for the dogs if this proved necessary. Furthermore, I did not consider that my weakened back could stand much walking in soft snow without them. My back had given me considerable discomfort for the previous few days, possibly due to the arduous, unaccustomed exercise to which it had been subjected.

Before departing, Lamb collected a rock sample from the depot site which he claimed was composed of rock almost identical with that found at Deception Island: a brown agglomerate, of which the island is largely formed. Around the vicinity of this depot we also found evidence of penguins, demonstrating that this point was accessible to the birds at certain seasons of the year.

Visibility was poor this day, and we could barely make out the misty outline of Corry Island. We camped along the tidal zone, where the ice was broken up into many flat-surfaced pieces. Offshore, the surface was rough and hummocky with many bergy bits frozen into the surface. We expected to start out toward the southwest through this the next morning, with lightened loads, and hoped to make better time. In the night, the temperature fell to twenty below zero.

The 15th of August broke dull and gloomy, but the sky cleared later in the day and we headed into the teeth of a bitter westerly wind. The rough, hummocky surface persisted for a couple of hours as we left Vortex Island and passed north of Sheppard and Marr Islands.[5] We again viewed the channel between Corry and Tabarin Islands, which we had seen earlier from the east. To the north of that, we caught a glimpse of what appeared to be an even wider

---

4.   Editors' note: In the next paragraph, Taylor's original manuscript inconsistently stated that the depot was located on the northeast section of the island.

5.   Editors' note: This is a different route than described in James, *That Frozen Land*, 126.

Figure 33. Vortex Island, 15 August 1945.

Figure 34. The Vortex Island depot from the sledgers' camp site, 15 August 1945.

channel between Tabarin and the mainland of the Trinity Peninsula. We were in a small archipelago of islands—which we called the Eagle Archipelago—that were of a rather more complicated nature than our single journey through allowed us to completely solve. It seemed likely that had we continued on our course toward the southwest across Duse Bay, we would have found a continuous passage along the coast instead of having to veer farther toward the south in order to round Corry Island. Almost dead ahead of our course lay one of the largest islands in the area. It was distinguished by a prominent pillar of rock at the west end of its high summit that we named "The Monument" when first glimpsing it from twenty miles away above Duse Bay. We continued to call this island Monument Island, though it seems now probable that this was the one to which Nordenskjöld had appended the name of Red Island.[6]

The islands in the archipelago all had a decidedly similar appearance which made their identification especially confusing at first sight. They were generally high, between 500 and 1,500 feet. Except for Corry Island, as well as small parts of Marr Island and Tabarin Island, they had no ice caps. They were remarkably snow-free, their soft rocks friable, and settled into long slopes and mounds that from no great distance looked like nothing more than great mounds of rich, red earth. Their shores were, for the most part, fringed with long, high slopes of scree and rock debris. High up the slopes there frequently appeared to be a horizontal layer of harder rock that presented a fresh-looking vertical face, probably measuring fifty feet thick. Corry, Monument, and Marr Islands had extensive flat summits formed by this high sill; but on Sphinx, Tabarin, and Sheppard Islands, active erosion left little evidence of the rock sheet that once overlay them. Moreover, much of these three islands were lower in altitude and more readily accessible.

Just opposite Monument Island and along the track we were following, we encountered two massive boulders on the sea ice. They were about three feet in diameter and seemed to be granite, a rock quite foreign to anything we had encountered in this region. They lay side-by-side within a few feet of each other, a mile or two from the nearest shore, and must have been transported there by sea on an ice floe that had at one time formed part of the support for a moraine. We saw no other such deposits at any place near this part of the archipelago on the sea ice.

We had had quite a good, hard, windblown surface on which to travel for most of the day but in the late afternoon, as we approached the shore in the lee of the mountains of the Trinity Peninsula, the depth of snow increased

---

6. Editors' note: Today, Monument Island is, in fact, known as "Red Island."

considerably. We had intended to camp close by a rocky point of the mainland, but the heavier surface sapped the dogs' energy so we made camp a mile or two short of our objective. The temperature was −26°F.

The coast of the Trinity Peninsula exposed to our view at this camp presented a huge field of gently undulating snow that sloped down toward the sea. Numerous small, pointed *nunataks* indiscriminately pushed up through this surface. Each was remarkably alike in shape, being of a general triangular pyramidal section with sharp edges out of the black rock from which they were formed. Behind this foreground that extended from five to ten miles inland, the rocky face buttressing the Graham Land Plateau rose sharply, with the plateau edge forming an active ice cap of milky-blue above the cliffs. At this point, the elevation of the plateau was a little over 3,000 feet, and was cut by a rather vaguely defined glacier that nicked the skyline quite deeply and then spread itself broadly out over the snowfield below the escarpment. This glacier was probably two miles or more in width across the plateau, was all but free of large-crevassed areas, and fell in gentle folds toward the sea along a slope that appeared to increase a little as one approached the shore. There were places where the white glacial slope fell gently to the sea floor, yet the ice cliffs frequently terminated at the shoreline. These were not high, and were badly fissured in many places.

We began to make out the character of Ross Island from this camp. The area differed markedly in character from that to the west of the great channel in which we now found ourselves. There were high-rock, ice-capped promontories that were snow-free along their slopes. They were deeply cut by large glaciers seemingly descending from the summit of the island, which at times was difficult to distinguish from the sky with which the great snow cap readily blended. To the east of the northerly tip of Ross Island, we could see where Cape Lachman marked the entrance to Sidney Herbert Sound where Nordenskjöld and his small party from Cape Well Met had been the only men ever to pass.

Our team was not standing up very well to this arduous travel. Of the seven "Odds and Sods," three were already crippled. Jack and Mutt both seemed to have contracted some sort of rheumatic pains in their legs which stiffened them up a great deal and obviously caused them a great deal of suffering. Widgeon was still hobbling along on only three legs. Russell and I also noted an indication of further trouble when we discovered that the soles of our sealskin boots already had holes that allowed the inner duffel slipper to show.

In the morning, we tried to continue along the course from the night before, but the depth of snow increased as we approached this shore of the mainland so that, within an hour, we found ourselves stuck. We stopped so often that we made little progress and were obliged to alter course farther offshore, toward a high island six miles ahead of us. In our notes we named this Long Island. Although it is some distance away from the location shown on previous maps, there is little doubt but that this is the island Nordenskjöld referred to as Herrström Island.

The condition of our dog team necessitated my manhauling with them again, so I found myself on a long trace in man-harness ahead of the lead dog for the rest of the day. It was a most uncomfortable day, with the thermometer at −10°F and a southwest wind between force 4 and 5, blowing drift snow into our faces. Visibility was probably ten to fifteen miles, but the clouds were down to 1,000 feet and the light was diffused, making even simple walking a matter of inconvenience. We made slow progress through a field of small bergs, after which the surface began to improve a little. We gradually worked into a field of broken pack ice further roughened by pressure ridges. We arrived at the island at three o'clock in the afternoon, having made seven miles from our last camp. With the force of the wind increasing, we made camp on the northwest corner of the ice foot. The sky in the distance to the north and to the east was clear, and the temperature dropped to −30°F that night.

It took us an hour and a half to pass down the west side of Long Island the next morning. With the sun out and the temperature rising to −10°F toward noon, it became quite warm. There seemed to be some confusion about whether we were heading into a little bay similar to the one we had encountered when crossing Sphinx Island. James bet me a bottle of beer that we would have to retrace our steps. Fortunately, this did not prove to be the case. The obstacle turned out to be a string of grounded icebergs with pressure ice and ridges across the direction of our travel on the sea ice, creating fissures from six inches to six feet across. Eventually, we found our forward movement blocked and were forced to turn more to the east—a direction that brought us quite near to the island again.

Lamb, James, and I walked over to the low, beach-like south end of this Long Island and collected geological and botanical specimens. Though the area was readily accessible from the sea ice as far as the birds might be concerned, there was no sign of the place ever having been used as a penguin rookery,

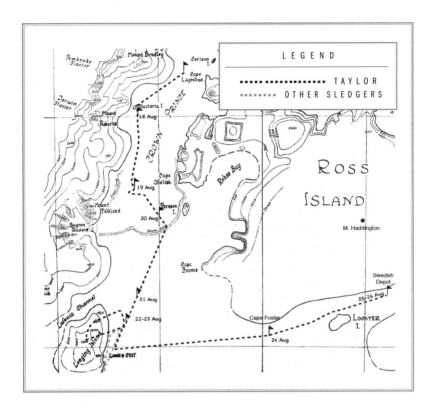

Map 9. The first seldging journey, 18–26 August 1945.

indicating that the channel at this point was seldom if ever open. The part of the channel we were now about to march along was permanently frozen ice, possibly of a glacial nature, as some of the grey, discoloured bergs amongst the field of those which littered this vicinity indicated.

We resumed our course toward the southwest and were obliged to make another detour to avoid having the dogs spot half a dozen seals sunning themselves below a large tabular iceberg. The seals were too distant to tell their species with accuracy, but they looked like Weddells. No matter how big our load might have been, had the dogs caught a whiff of these animals they would have wheeled off with a power that they seldom displayed. We continued for a couple of hours, weaving between the high, fresh-looking, starchy-white walls of many icebergs. They were so numerous along this part of the coast that Ross

Island was almost continually obscured from our view, while we caught but occasional glances of the mainland. After extending for four or five miles, the field of bergs came to a gradual end and we once again found ourselves out in the open. We spotted Carlson Island hugging the Ross Island coast, and along the mainland the topography seemed to simplify from the confusing mass of pyramidal peaks that had lined the foreshore to the north. The colour of the rock also seemed to alter slightly, from the coal blackness that we first encountered to a very dark brown. The peaks, however, still possessed the same sharp-edged faces. We began to head for a low, rocky foreshore, passing en route below a towering peak that we called Mount Fitzroy.

The surface continued to improve, being hard and windswept, as we approached the object of our course. Accordingly, we made good time. James and Russell both rode on their sledge to keep behind our team, while I went ahead. We passed within half a mile of another dozen seals that the dogs fortunately did not "wind." I made the best time I could on the hard surface; my speed was the governing factor this day, as the dogs were pulling their loads easily. We could not drive the dogs in the true sense of the word, as they had not been trained to travel by commands. Furthermore, Russell did no unnecessary walking because his frostbitten feet bothered him a little, and they were blistered on both the toes and soles. Arriving at the rock outcrop, Lamb and James scrambled up the 150-foot slope, and the former made the collection for which this halt had been arranged.

While Russell remained with the two dog teams, I went ahead to reconnoitre a route through a mass of small icebergs lying off the little bay that indented itself into the coastline to the south of the outcrop that the others were visiting. The rocking of one of the bergs pressing up and out exuded its foot in a mass of puffy-looking ice that had the appearance of popcorn from a distance. The wind blew lightly from the north, and the sky above us remained partly overcast, though it was clear blue to the west. We passed through the field of bergs with no difficulty and came out upon an excellent surface, altering course a little toward what we took to be another lot of seals. "They" turned out to be just a few lumps of black ice, however, and we travelled on to make camp to the south of a large berg at 4:15 p.m. We had travelled more than eleven miles that day, in weather mostly just below zero. The coastline had been one of continuous low ice cliffs, frequently crevassed.

The sun rose in the morning at 7:15, promising another good day. The temperature was about ten above, and the snow surface was an even, hard, and crusted one that sustained the sledges very well. It took us a couple of hours to keep clear of another field of bergs and, on clearing them, we headed for a small, rocky island several miles away, deep in a little bight of the mainland shore. After an hour, Russell took James's place in breaking trail, but could not manage it because his frostbitten feet seemed to have worsened. He had to ride the sledge for the remainder of the day, so I took his place ahead and Lamb followed with our team. All of our dogs seemed to have recovered from their rheumatism, if that is what their trouble had been, but Widgeon was still hobbling along with his three legs and slack trace.

Along the mainland, the elevation of the Graham Land Plateau rose gradually and now stood at 5,000 feet, the steep cliffs of the escarpment being also much higher than they were farther to the north. Two large glaciers spilled down from the plateau between ill-defined bastions; they were lacerated with large crevasses that were clearly visible from ten miles away, the disturbed zone of the glacial ice extended continuously across the fringing glacier of the coast where complex ice faces disgorged the ice upon the frozen sea. Ice cliffs still predominated along the shoreline, but there were many places where the massive white sheet flowed evenly into the sea.

A little to the left of our first course, we could make out the spindle of rock that gave Cape Obelisk its name. There was a remarkable mirage effect in that direction during the morning, when it almost seemed as though we could see the ice cliffs of the barrier before our eyes. The island that we approached (which Lamb subsequently named Alectoria Island after the predominant lichen he found upon it) was farther off than we initially judged it to be. As we approached the shore, the snow became deeper so that one sank halfway to the knee at each step. We found this condition time and again when approaching this coast; the snow along it inevitably deepened as one approached the shore. We arrived there just after 1:00 p.m., and Lamb set out to climb its 350-foot summit.

Half a mile ahead, James discovered and killed two seals. We made camp early, at 3:00 p.m., in the lee of a large iceberg. I used a ski stick as a splint to repair a broken leg of the tent, while the two teams were taken back separately to where the seals had been gutted. Being the first meat of any description that the dogs ate in two weeks and their first fresh meat in months, they really gorged themselves. They came back with dripping bloody coats, their traces dyed as deeply as themselves, and with full bellies curled up in the drifting snow and fell contentedly asleep. We had Weddell steaks in our tent that night, the tenderest seal meat that I have ever eaten (and much better than London's wartime meat). One of the animals had contained a fetus about 2.5 feet in length with a pelt of the softest fine fur. James brought it back with him, but we had no time to deal with it and, consequently, it froze stiff by morning.

Our progress brought within view the vast expanse of the Weddell Sea, beyond which seemed for the moment to be an unbroken field of featureless ice (except for a couple of isolated bergs). We were approaching one of the most distinctive features of all this northern part of East Graham Land, which we named Mount Falkland. It had been within our sight since we left Vortex Island, and we gradually came nearer to this broad-backed mountain that lay at the entrance to what Nordenskjöld named Sjögren Fjord. The mountain, which was about eight miles in length and rose to well over 3,000 feet, stood fairly isolated from any other high peaks. It was not snow-capped, and the slopes were largely ice-free, though a valley toward its eastern end supported a small glacier. The high back of the mountain ran roughly in a direction northwest-southeast, and it did not have the sharpness of outline of the smaller *nunataks* to the north, indicating that it had been exposed to the elements for a much longer period of time than the others. It was a friendlier-looking mountain than most that we saw because it had no hanging glaciers or heavy icefalls to warn one off. We almost expected to find a little settlement nestled at its foot.

The fresh meat of the night before had a marked revitalizing effect upon the dogs, who were restless all night long. They made plenty of noise that kept us awake for long intervals, and they terminated their behaviour by a free-for-all fight in the morning before we got under way. Their harnesses and traces were stained red from the "blood bath" of the night before, and some of the whiter animals had coats of the same unusual hue.

The soft snow in which we camped extended throughout our morning's march, with the temperature just above freezing. The sea surface was almost free of bergs and rough ice, but layers of snow whipped over it by the winds generally covered it. Occasional areas laid bare a hard snow surface sculptured off in flukes a foot or two long, making a white marble-like surface. It was pleasant to walk upon "barefoot," to use Davies's expression, but skis or snowshoes were completely unmanageable. For the most part, the snow surface was barely strong enough to support one's weight, and it made walking a most exhausting task. The day was bright and sunny, with only a light wind from the south, but in the morning to the north a smoky haze filled the channel.

Our course took us close to a very disturbed area of glacial ice along the shore that had discharged a considerable amount of ice of a dark green colour. Many of the pieces were full of stones and mud that had undoubtedly come down from the mountains above the coast. We did not go more than a few hundred yards before noticing that we were passing over a very undulating surface. Another 100 yards brought us to the brink of a chasm that was, in my estimation, a couple of hundred feet across and about seventy feet deep. The walls of the chasm were rough though weather worn, and its bottom was snow-filled. In an effort to avoid this chasm we headed further offshore, and made camp at 3:30 p.m. when the temperature had dropped to about twenty below.

Russell was on his skis this day, and he said that his feet had improved considerably. Another hopeful feature of the day's march was that all of our dogs were pulling a little better, perhaps owing to the fresh meat. Even Widgeon and little Jack made an effort to pull about as much weight as their share of the dog pemmican.

The sky was clear, and in the evening I observed a round of eight stars to locate our geographic position. By this time, we had a fairly comfortable routine to carry out these observations. With the theodolite tripod set up alongside the tent, I went out warmly wrapped to work in the thirty-below temperature. I shouted out the readings to Russell who took the notes from inside the tent where he also had the chronometer. I set the telescope near the star and gave him a series of warning shouts of "Coming up!" When the star was right on the cross-hairs I yelled "On." He noted the time, and then I made the readings on the instrument's micrometers by flashlight. It took about two hours to gather pointings on two stars in each compass quadrant. Much of the work was, of necessity, done barehanded, and I was ready to enjoy a cup of cocoa inside the tent by the time we finished. In my experience, the hands can withstand considerable exposure in these low temperatures without too much discomfort so long as the wrists are kept well covered.

Trusting that we had now avoided the undulating ice surface of the day before by adopting an easterly course, we set out in the morning for the south with the sky clear and the mercury at −26°F. We had not proceeded very far before the surface again began to roll in long waves a quarter of a mile or so in length with an amplitude of between sixty and seventy feet, as near as one could judge, for the slope was noticeable to the extent that the dogs had to make quite an additional effort to reach each crest. We had been anxious to have a brief though close view of Sjögren Fjord but the morainic deposits strewn over the glacial ice on which we crossed proved the fjord-like feature to be a glacier (and not an arm of the sea), so we altered our course again toward the southeast in order to avoid what might have been the worst of the roughened surface. We passed immediately below the east end of Mount Falkland, which rose well and massively above the surrounding snowfields, with slopes comparatively gentle from all aspects.

Just to the west of our initial course, the ice was bent into all sorts of unusual knobbly shapes, marking what appeared to be a continuation of the large chasm that we had avoided the previous afternoon. The southeasterly course took us over rougher and steeper slopes, but by noon we seemed to have passed through the worst of it and began to see a steadier horizon once again. When we descended into the troughs of these huge ice waves, everything sank out of view. A mile beyond the place where we stopped for lunch, and just opposite Persson Island, we stopped to examine an extensive morainic deposit about 600 feet in length. The rocks were of an igneous character, similar to those that we had found upon first approaching the gigantic tongue of ice on which they lay, for that indeed was the character of the southerly end of Crown Prince Gustav Channel. We saw the confluence of about seven glaciers between the east end of Mount Falkland and a *nunatak* that buttressed the opening on the south side. Five of these glaciers were well-defined valley types that extruded the tongue of ice into the perpetually frozen channel. Without exception, the ice in this area was of great age.

We passed over a greatly improved travelling surface in the afternoon, which became reasonably flat again. As we proceeded, the snow cover diminished until we found ourselves slithering around on patches of bare pebble-surfaced ice. Just before 4:00 p.m., we came to the brink of another chasm that had a bearing almost due east and west, and that seemed to be running in almost a straight line for the southerly side of the outlet from the glacier system. It was about 100 feet across, with rough, jagged-looking sides, and again contained a bed of snow in its valley. The banks of the chasm rose fifteen or twenty feet above the level of the surrounding ice. We had to alter our course still farther to the east, and made camp half an hour later at no great distance from Persson Island to the south of Cape Obelisk.

The two chasms that we encountered that day appeared to mark the shear zone between the glacial ice in active motion and the permanent ice that is relatively fixed. The first of the two chasms that we encountered was close inshore to the westerly delimitation of the channel and roughly paralleled the shore, running in a relatively straight line northward from the toe of the massive mountain containing the glaciers. The second of these chasms seemed to turn northward a short distance beyond our camp, passing to the west of Persson Island, and indicated that the glacial ice flowed northward into the channel. We referred in our notes to the glaciers as the Sjögren System of Glaciers, to perpetuate the name Nordenskjöld originally gave to the feature.

Just before we were blocked by the second of these great chasms in the ice, we had passed over a rather peculiar morainic deposit consisting of a series of large boulders three to four feet in diameter. These boulders were set upon the ice at more or less regular intervals of several hundred feet, laid out in an almost continuous straight line from the confluence of the glaciers. The due east bearing of this "beaded" moraine was the same as that of the chasm, and it extended into the channel far beyond the point where we intercepted it. We followed it inshore with binoculars as far as could be seen and, considering the extension of it eastward from our point of interception, we estimated it to be at least six miles in length.

We made a little over nine miles in the day. Being Monday, in accordance with previous arrangements made before we left Eagle House, James tried to intercept any signals that Donnachie might be sending from Hope Bay, but he had no success. He did hear the first news broadcast since our departure from the base, however, and we were all astonished to hear of Japan's capitulation following the apparent entry of the Russians against them. Surely we must have been among the last civilized people on the earth to hear this news, five days after it happened.

Our good fortune with respect to the weather continued on 21 August. We had another fine day with a light breeze blowing from the north. The north wind raised the temperature (which had dropped below −20°F during the night) gradually throughout the day, and it was above zero by nightfall. We continued travelling toward the east and again intercepted the curious string moraine that we had seen the previous day as it extended for a mile or so toward Ross Island. When it seemed as though we had passed the worst of the roughened ice surface, we turned south again. In half a mile we came to another rift and I went ahead of the teams, locating a route across it with no difficulty.

In another mile, we came to an additional pressure zone in the ice. It was larger than the one we had crossed earlier in the day, the ice being forced up into

Figure 35. Rift on the shelf ice facing the southwest side of James Ross Island, 21 August 1945. Note the scale of the ice obstacles relative to the human figure.

the weirdest contortions along its length. At the bottom of the long, rolling surface, there was an open crack about twelve inches wide between the lips of the ice bridge over the crevice. Six to eight feet below the surface of the ice, we saw a level sheet of black ice covered with fine, long crystals of ice more than an inch in length. It was as though the sea had found its way into this fissure while it formed and the heat from its creation caused the crystals to develop. The bearing of both rifts crossed on this particular morning was approximately northeast and southwest, the more southerly of them turning in a broad arc northward toward Persson Island. We had little trouble crossing the gap.

We altered course toward the south and made for a rocky headland about twenty miles ahead, which we took to be the point that Nordenskjöld had called Cape Longing. A low pass or channel lay between gently moulded hills of snow on our right. The quantity of morainic material scattered over the ice noticeably lessened as we continued southward. We had exceedingly good travelling conditions and covered fourteen miles in the day with little interruption.

Widgeon still hobbled along beside the other dogs with his three good legs, and began to eat a little food. Russell was also on the mend. Having used skis for the past several days, his frostbitten feet seemed to have almost completely recovered. It said a great deal for his personal fortitude that he never allowed us to lose even a part of a day on his account, despite the sufferings his feet caused him.

Since our departure thirteen days previous, we had finished three of our five tins of paraffin—if one included the tin still cached for our use at Vortex Island. With half of our ration period behind us, we found ourselves in a position to make some geographical discoveries of more than passing interest—but without adequate supplies to pursue them safely. Had we had but another two weeks' stores in hand, there would have been no question of our turning back at Cape Longing. Although there was still the possibility of continuing as far as Cape Sobral, we could not hope to go farther. The decision of when to turn east remained open for another day.

The surface of the ice greatly improved throughout the day, though it was still slightly undulating. It was a windswept surface, flat and featureless, with no ice or bergs of any nature. The sledges slid easily over the hard, wind-packed *sastrugi* pointing toward the northeast. The snow was quite deep, for we could push the ice axes down to their hilt without difficulty. We plodded mechanically forward across the uninteresting area, our eyes glued to the snowy cap covering the point for which our course was set: the channel between the snow hills approaching us from the southwest that was almost certainly filled with glacial ice. As time slipped unheedingly by, our minds were active enough—but not concerning our physical activities of the moment. We thought of the halt for the night, of the food that our stomachs began to crave, of bedding down in our sleeping bags to rest for the night, and of things far distant from the south end of the Crown Prince Gustav Channel. We made camp at 4:45 p.m.

We were almost ready to move by 8:00 the next morning. A beautiful blue sky lay to the south and the southwest but, toward the west, jagged-looking dark clouds stretched their forked tongues eastward across the Graham Land Plateau, and began spilling into the north end of the channel. At sea level, we could see little toward the north beyond Cape Obelisk on Ross Island. The temperature rose twenty degrees to 34°F with the freshening of the wind. At 10:00 a.m., the barometer rose but slightly, and the wind force was only 3.

James thought it improbable that the weather would get any worse, so we started out half a mile later. The heat in the wind softened the snow so that the sledges still slipped along easily while a man on foot broke through the hard crust. As a result, the dogs easily caught up with me. In an attempt to improve our progress, we tried to drive them. It went fairly well for almost an hour, with Mutt leading because Dainty's trace was tangled and shortened. But Mutt seemed to tire of being in front of his two companions, Jeff and Sydney, so he sat down. We extended Dainty's trace and tried to drive her, but she tended to veer to starboard out of the wind, so I had to go ahead of them again.

The wind continued to freshen, and we had not gone more than four miles when it blew a good force 6 and still rose while blowing a good deal of drift snow about. It seemed as though we would soon be in for a repetition of the experience we had had on the 12th, when we had barely erected the tents against the force of the wind. So we called a halt and set up the camp. This time, we had no great difficulty with the tents. We fixed the two windward back corners first and then weighed down the windward apron with snow. When the guy rope on the windward side was secure, it was quite easy to attend to the other two poles that held together to make a temporary pyramidal frame. The camp was up by 2:00 p.m. and the wind immediately began to abate; at 3:00 it was quite calm. By 4:30, the wind veered from the northwest to the southwest, and again blew stiffly.

We observed morainic boulders all day to the east of our course, and the surface over which we had sledged was quite undulating; at times we sank so low and sharply that all the view to the north and west was completely lost. We were still six miles from the rocky headland that we figured must be Cape Longing. Above it, the great ice sheet rose up to form a white shield-shaped hill to the south. Eastward, the dark rocks of Lockyer Island crept out beyond the silhouette of Ross Island, behind which lay a higher mass of ice: Snow Hill.

All of the dogs were, by this time, becoming noticeably hungry on their pemmican diet. They eyed us enviously when we ate our frozen chocolate and hard biscuit, growling at each other as they picked up the crumbs. After walking with us since leaving Hope Bay, Widgeon began on this day to use his foot again and did a little (very little) pulling.

The wind blew all night long, but when we arose at 7:00 a.m. on 23 August, a glorious windless day awaited us. The sky was quite cloudless and the visibility was excellent but for a light blue distant haze. We decided not to move our camp on this day, but to split up into two parties; James and Lamb heading forward to Cape Longing, while Russell and I went westward into the deep channel, the mouth of which we had passed the day before.

With the "Big Boys" hitched to the sledge, we struck off on a course just west of north. We ventured but a mile when we found ourselves on the brink of another rift in the ice. It was wider and deeper than any which we had passed previously, being about 100 feet across and sinking in the centre like a catenary to a depth of fifteen to twenty feet below the level of the surrounding ice. I went on ahead of the team and found a drift out of the trough up where we ascended to its westerly lip. Half a mile farther on, we came to another rift, fully 100 yards across, which we crossed with little difficulty. When we found a third rift twenty minutes later, we decided that we could make better time by travelling over the slopes of the snow hill on our left, so we struck a more southerly course. We crossed a series of small rifts inshore before crossing a series of small tide cracks. Ascending the hill to an altitude of 200 feet, we had a good view of the disturbed area of ice to the north over which we had spent the past few days in travelling.

Altering course to almost due south, we headed the dogs for the summit of the hill, stopping to take aneroid readings every half hour. The snow was hard-packed and made an excellent surface upon which to walk. We saw no loose snow anywhere on the hillside along our ascent, all of the surface being composed of hard, fluted *sastrugi*. It was 2:00 p.m. when we reached the 1,300-foot summit that treated us to a truly magnificent view.

Sixty miles to the south, with the aid of binoculars, one could see in surprising detail Robertson Island and the Seal Nunataks, with Lindenberg Island in the foreground, the dark mountains serving to emphasize the petal-like shapes of the snowfields. Many of the islands appeared to possess a moat-like feature to the west. The escarpment of the Nordenskjöld coast presented an almost unbroken face, the cliffs of the ice cap suspended over a precipitous rock wall, much steeper than that farther north. The rock surfaces also seemed to be much more sharply defined and jagged than those we were accustomed to seeing.

From Cape Sobral, a zone of very disturbed ice extended eastward for at least fifteen miles. There was no definite sign of any barrier ice cliffs to the south. A shadowy line marked a rifted area extending northward into a fjord between our point of observation and Cape Sobral. From the centre to the opposite side of the ten-mile-wide feature that also marked the mouth of Larsen

Bay, a smooth and even surface lay over the ice. Being on the lee of Cape Sobral from the southwest winds, we did not doubt that its snowy surface was deep.

We had a good view of the sea from where we stood, and there was no sign of open water anywhere. Even at so great a distance as this view presented, we could see to the south a disturbed area of ice lying north of the Seal Nunataks. We saw another turbulent area of ice skirting the south side of Ross Island, beyond which rose the Lockyer and Snow Hill Islands. Altogether, it was an inspiring view on such a beautiful day, particularly with the knowledge that no one else had enjoyed it since time began. We took a few photographs and some compass bearings before leaving the summit at 2:45 p.m.

The dogs took us on a wild ride down the hillside, descending the slope at so great a speed that we flew across a couple of wide crevasses before we had time to notice them. As we tore down the slope, we tried to pick out the location of our two tents on the plain spread below us but their white canvas blended so perfectly with the snow surface that, even with glasses, they were utterly indiscernible. We took a shortcut down a steeper face than the one we had climbed, headed in the general direction of the camp, and caught sight of the tents when we got to within a quarter of a mile of them. In poor visibility or a blizzard, we would have never found them. We reached the tents at 4:00 p.m., having travelled about fifteen miles.

The others came in an hour later, having experienced the same difficulty in locating the camp owing largely to the undulations of the ice. They also had enjoyed a successful day, starting out on the prolongation of the previous day's course for Camp Longing's rocky cliffs. After travelling for four miles, they found themselves in the midst of rough ice with frequent rifts and crevasses and a great deal of old weather-worn ice rising twenty or thirty feet above their heads. Obliged to leave the sledge a quarter of a mile off the cliffs that they set out to reach, they scrambled on foot the balance of the way over the rough ice to the slopes of rock debris at the base of the laminar cliffs. Here Lamb found traces of fossil plants and, after much searching, he located the bed of slaty shale just above the top of the sloping talus from which they emanated. He took a representative collection, remarking that he thought they were of the same period as the Hope Bay fossils. This was the first sign we had of sedimentary deposits on the mainland so far south. Viewed from a distance, these cliffs (which we named Lamb's Cliffs) and those near Cape Sobral appeared to be almost identical, so that there is every likelihood that the rocks of that cape will also prove to be sedimentary.

Figure 36. Below "Lamb's cliffs" on Longing Island from the north, late August 1945.

We had seen enough of the icy mass above Lamb's Cliffs in the afternoon to convince us that there was every probability that Cape Longing, like Cape Corry, was not a cape but an island. Our view was, admittedly, not complete, for there was a small extent of the coast to the northwest that was "dead ground" to us. Yet the channel to the northwest appeared to be continuous, and if this was in fact true, then most certainly, Longing was an Island. We believed that such was the case.[7]

The day had been most interesting, and whetted our appetites to extend our travels into the fjord behind Larsen Bay. Our plans were now clear; we would head for Snow Hill Island in the hopes of replenishing our supplies. If we could do this, we would be back to continue our work to the south and west of Longing Island; if the supplies were not there but the house proved to be habitable, we would leave two men at Snow Hill while the other pair returned to Hope Bay with both dog teams for additional supplies.

7.   Editors' note: This assumption proved to be correct. Cape Longing is, in fact, an island.

The next day (24 August) was a perfect one for travelling, and we made good time in the crisp morning air toward Cape Foster, traversing more than ten miles by noon. As we approached Ross Island, we could clearly make out the typical character of its southern part—the ice cap formed a hanging glacier over precipitous black walls. At the foot of these walls, the calving ice from this fixture fed a flat, fringing glacier. Most of these lay in well-marked embayments, the arms of which were rocky, snow-capped promontories that were much broader than those farther north.

As we continued toward the island, the snow surface softened and deepened, slightly slowing our progress. Nearing the big island, the ice became much rougher, with many small rifts and crevices in it. Some of the latter were four to six feet across. We fell into a number of them, and at the bottom we saw a sheet of black-looking ice covered with the same long, spiny crystals that we previously saw down such cracks. Crossing one of these fissures in mid-afternoon, Lamb and I both distinctly heard the bleating of a seal, though we could not see it. At about the same time, Russell claimed to have seen what he thought was a seal about a mile to the south of our course. In the course of the day we made eighteen miles, taking two-hour spells in breaking trail for the dogs. We camped in soft, two-foot-deep snow just short of Cape Foster.

On the 25th, we left camp at 9:30 a.m., with the temperature the same as it had been the day before: –17°F. The soft snow that we encountered late on the previous afternoon continued for a mile or so after we passed Cape Foster. We entered Admiralty Sound at 10:30, however, and found ourselves on another hard, windblown surface of snow. We enjoyed good travelling conditions up to the time we stopped for lunch at 1:00 p.m. Numerous rocks and boulders lay scattered over the sea ice, and we crossed two massive pressure ridges of considerable age. The presence of a growler with the rippled surface so typical of sea-washed ice strongly suggested that this point was close to the northerly extremity of Lockyer Island. (The balance of Lockyer Island's coastline is formed of precipitous cliffs of dark red rock, having a rather laminar appearance. At both ends of the island, ice from its white cap tumbles steeply down into the sea in broad rough-faced glaciers.)

We made camp on a firm, two-foot-deep snow surface over the sea ice that was just off the point on the map that Nordenskjöld had marked as his Depot Cape. Our hungry friend, Sydney, ate ten feet off of our rawhide whip as we made camp, and got a beating with the remainder. On 26 August, the southwest wind blew and we spent the entire day in camp. Visibility was less than 100 yards on account of the blanket of driving snow roaring along. By mid-afternoon, it was a gale, and our hysterical young bitch Pretty chose that moment to create a diversion. It was her habit to become impatient at being tied up, to leap into the air to the end of her chain, and to accompany each leap with continuous shrieking and yowling. Most of the latter, fortunately, was lost in the wind. In performing one of these leaps, she pulled out the ice axe that served as an anchor for the tethering line and, in a moment, we heard the entire ravenously hungry team swarming over the sledge in search of food. Putting on our windproof clothing as quickly as possible, we dived through the tent door and went out into the storm to disentangle the mass of dogs, wire, and chain. It was not too bad a tangle, for we caught them in time to prevent its completion. We administered a beating on Pretty when she resumed her antics. After putting more snow along the apron of the tent to replace what the high wind scoured away, we returned to our frozen bedrolls where we passed the time reading the parts of *Antarctica* that referred to this particular area. Each time we heard Pretty again during the night above the raging wind, two silent prayers shot heavenward from our tent that the ice axe would hold so that we would not have to repeat the job in the darkness of the night. They worked: it held.

CHAPTER FIFTEEN

Nordenskjöld Haunts

FOR THE WEEK THAT FOLLOWED, WE FOUND OURSELVES in an area in which our link with the turn of the century permeated every phase of our lives. As we approached Snow Hill Island, where the Swedish South Polar Expedition wintered under Dr. Otto Nordenskjöld from 1902 to 1903, we were within sight of scenes that their eyes rested upon daily—and which no one but those aboard the *Wyatt Earp* had seen since. We camped in places where Nordenskjöld and his team camped and were about to visit the station that served as their base, where even the tools they used in the construction of their shelter still lay. It was impossible to divest ourselves from this strong connection to the early history of this part of Antarctica.

Absorbed with anticipation of what the next few days might hold for us, we set off from our camp on the morning of 27 August with the southwest wind blowing strongly on our backs. Not the least of our interests was the possibility of finding sufficient food and fuel to replenish our supplies and so allow us to continue southward down the coast of the mainland.

Russell made the first direct contact with relics from the Swedish Expedition. Russell set off on skis toward Depot Cape, a mile to the northwest of the camp. He made fast time toward the "far-projecting promontory" on the "solid slope of the hill" that, according to Nordenskjöld's description, overlooked the location where Ole Jonassen and José Sobral transported the depot by dinghy in a stormy trip during March 1902. At that time, Nordenskjöld recounted, they had "dog pemmican, four boxes of sledge journey provisions, a tank of petroleum, etc.," but they used most of these supplies on their main southward journey that same year. When Jonassen and Nordenskjöld passed Depot Cape on their momentous

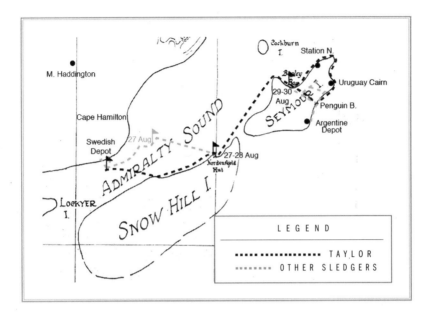

Map 10. The first sledging journey, 27–30 August 1945.

journey culminating at Cape Well Met in 1903, they deliberately left the remnants of this depot untouched so that it might serve as a reserve "in the event of
the ice in the channel breaking up."

Russell had some difficulty locating the depot, and it was not until an hour
after arriving that he found the top of a small cairn barely protruding through the
snow covering the hillside. Digging down into the cairn, he quickly located a tin
box that held the provisions, seemingly in perfect condition, the joints all soldered
to make the box completely waterproof. The years of its long exposure took their
toll, however, for when Russell lifted the box out of its position, he discovered that
the bottom of it had rusted away and the contents tumbled out. There was a great
variety of food within it, including about four dozen large biscuits, tins including
butter, sardines, and pemmican, and paper parcels of dried fruit, tea, sugar, dried
vegetables, and other things. In all, the food weighed about sixty pounds. Most of
the contents were still in near-perfect condition, and many were marked with the
name "Beauvais of Copenhagen"—the firm that apparently supplied the stores to
the expedition more than forty years before.

Russell could not carry off all of these articles while on skis, so he selected representative samples of those in tins, bottles, and paper bags.[1] Despite the biting wind and subzero temperature, it did not take Russell long to make the trip back to the tent. Once inside, he and James set to enjoy a feast of these ancient provisions before breaking camp and following Lamb and I toward Snow Hill Island. The sugar, though congealed into a block, was particularly welcome and tasty; the biscuits were not so successfully preserved. The weather was still unsettled, but they decided to move on at about 2:00 p.m. They made good time in a rising wind, but the tent was something of a task for two men to erect in a high wind, so they stopped below Cape Hamilton after travelling a couple of hours.

That same day, Lamb and me departed from the Lockyer Island camp in the morning. The sun was shining and the barometer was steady, but the snow drifted heavily and the dogs did not enjoy working at all. Nuzzling its snout out into the sea ice below Cape Hamilton, the wrinkled surface of Rabat Glacier[2] flowed down from the highlands of Ross Island. A great square tower of rock stood at the south end of Cape Hamilton's cliffs, and from its top, a stream of snow was issuing like smoke from a factory chimney. We skimmed over the hard surface at a good pace, with the drifting snow writhing over it so thickly that it completely obscured the surface at times. Straight ahead of us we sometimes caught a glimpse of Basalt Peak. To the east of our course, the haze occasionally cleared sufficiently to afford a glimpse of the Station Nunatak nestling on the pristine slopes of Snow Hill Island. We soon lost sight of Ross Island, as the blizzard wind whipped up its velocity to forty miles an hour. But objects became more readily discernible on Snow Hill Island. The wind dusted down the slopes of the island into the trough in which the wintering station lay, blowing before it huge billows of snow. We formed the impression, even at a distance, that the Snow Hill Station was the windiest locality in miles. On that account, wind velocities recorded there might tend to be higher than the representative winds of the area.

We entered a still windier zone, and the surface of hard, glazed snow became even better as far as travelling was concerned. With the strong tailwind behind us, we made excellent progress for a couple of hours. The drifting snow decreased, despite the higher wind, for apparently there was little loose snow left on the surface. By 2:00 p.m., steering on a compass bearing, we found ourselves in the midst of

---

1.   Author's note: With the box now punctured, none of the food that remains is likely to be in an edible condition when next it may be seen.

2.   Editors' note: Perhaps Howarth Glacier today.

a series of pressure ridges, with many angular fragments of fresh-looking pack ice frozen into the surface that caused the sledge to capsize frequently. For an hour or so it became difficult to tell what we were heading into, and almost impossible to choose a course, for the visibility closed down to about 200 yards as we approached the island. In an hour, we passed the worst of the drifts and came upon a surface composed largely of clear glare ice that, except for occasional shallow snowdrifts matting it, was very slippery. An hour later, we could again see our two landmarks, the Basalt Peak and the Station Nunatak.

We threaded our way across the slippery surface between some small bergs and over a series of pressure ridges just as the sun, which had blazed down upon us all day long, sank behind a bank of clouds to the west. Heading over the glassy surface, Lamb rode the sledge in the high wind as it crabbed along at an angle of 30° to our course. The almost complete absence of snow over the surface of the sea ice in this vicinity is certain evidence of the high winds that sweep along this part of Admiralty Sound.

In the dull twilight, with the wind roaring past our ears and the Basalt Peak gauntly and forbiddingly gazing down upon us, we rounded the end of the low ice cliffs that enclosed the site of the wintering station. The surface of the little cove below the house was brown with a layer of rock dust deposited by the winds. The grit of this sandy surface made the sledge pull a little more heavily. At the end of the cove stood Nordenskjöld's Snow Hill Station, set on a little terrace with slopes as clean and uniform as a railroad grade.

We had so avidly read about this house that many of its comforts were as firmly fixed in our minds as its location. All day long we had doggedly battled the wind and the blinding drift, and I would not deny that at the end of the day there was in my mind a picture of a good coal fire to be built in the house, round which we could sit pulling at our pipes with a glass of "hollands" in our hands while the damp sleeping bags hung suspended from the rafters to dry and warm.

The dogs pulled the sledge up onto the ice foot. Lamb and I gingerly walked over the sharp-edged stones, still mindful of the gaping holes the size of our fists that had by this time worn through the soles of our sealskin boots. We climbed up the little pathway worn by Swedish feet to the doorway of the building, trying to imagine what the interior of a building might look like after withstanding forty Antarctic winters without glass in the windows. It was as well that we noticed this latter deficiency on our approach, for the three feet of snow that buried most of the interior's contents was a most dispiriting sight, as the wind roared by in the gathering darkness.

Figure 37. Nordenskjöld's Snow Hill Station, late August 1945.

We glanced through the open window on the west side of the house into the room that served as a messroom. This room had held the last happy party on 8 November 1903, when Captain Larsen entered it following his trying trip from Paulet Island via Hope Bay. The table still stood in its place by the wall, but its back was broken by the weight of snow it had been called upon to support. A red flannel table cover hung on a doorknob, and its folds draped down into the icy clutch that held all but the top foot of it. Chairs stood where they had been last used, with their legs completely submerged in the mass of snow the building contained. One might almost say that there was more snow inside the building than around it, for the gravelly surface was whipped bare by the incessant blasts of the southwest winds.

Another window on the north side of the building allowed us to catch a glimpse into one of the cabins. A mound of snow filled the lower bunk, as though a white blanket covered a body. The names of each bed's former occupants—Bodman and Ekelöf—were deeply carved into the two bunk-boards. The whole place had an air of the utter desolation that had sole possession of it for nearly half a century.

We had seen enough. Our illusions were dispelled and we disconsolately retraced our steps down the little hill, passing a few heavy iron tent pegs on our way. The dogs were difficult to rouse, and utterly disinterested in moving a step further, but we could not erect the tent where they lay. Ill-temperedly, we lashed them into action. They climbed up a great fluted slope of snow—the hardest snow we encountered in two years and all but indistinguishable from ice. With difficulty, we found a place flat enough to pitch the tent, and just as we were about to erect it, we discovered that we had lost both our tent pegs and a small bag of medical supplies in the course of our day's march.

There was no immediate need of the latter but it was impossible to put up the tent without pegs. I walked back toward the dark old house, through which the wind whistled and moaned eerily, and gathered up five of the heavy iron tent pegs that Nordenskjöld may have used on his two great journeys. They served to guy our tent for the remainder of our trip back to Hope Bay, even if they were hard to knock into the icy surface that formed our "feather mattress." We had our usual pemmican supper and turned in to concentrate on sleeping on our hard beds, with the temperature at −15°F.

By morning the wind had dropped considerably and the sun shone cheerfully from a cloudless sky, the mercury being a little lower than it had been the day before. After a quick breakfast, we went back again to have another look at the house, so full of snow and history. The ferocity of the wind had torn off the tarpaper that was once strapped down over its surface, and snow had entered the house through the broad gaps in the boards that formed the walls. The two great struts that bolstered the north end of the building against the prevailing winds were still solidly in place, while at the other end one frayed rope still helped guy the building from the roof. Below the wooden props that formed the building's northerly buttresses, an array of open boxes lay scattered about. They were, for the most part, filled with snow, but wisps of clothing broke through the surface. Two carboys of what we presumed to be acid, still half-full, stood alongside.

The two doors in the passageway that led into the building were frozen ajar in the ice along the floor, so we made an unconventional entrance into the building through the window of the cabin used by Bodman and Ekelöf, ducking our heads as we passed through the doorway into the messroom. The round seats of the chairs, barely clearing the surface of the snow filling the room, made puzzling-looking objects at first glance. Opposite the position occupied by the table stood the remains of the little heater—described by Gösta Bodman and

Erik Ekelöf as "difficult to get it to burn, but . . . once it had begun to do so, it soon became red hot, and gave too much warmth." It may have been difficult to get it to burn in 1902, but it would have been much more so at this time, for the stovepipes above it were rusted through, barely hanging together by the seams. Alongside the heater, Ekelöf's intricate-looking bacteriological apparatus still occupied the same position illustrated in *Antarctica*, with the racks for his smaller apparatus sitting above it. In one corner, toward the west end of the room, sat the table where the great Swedish scientist did so much of his valuable work, and it extended across the window with shelves full of glass tubing and photographic materials extending right up to and onto the ceiling. The tabletop was still littered with tubes, racks, and bottles. The table legs, as with every other loose thing on the floor of the room, were tightly clamped in the ice.

Shovelling the snow off the messroom table, we found dishes and cups from a last hurried cup of tea. We also found the remains of the recording anemometer that contributed some of the most interesting scientific results from the Snow Hill Station. It had either fallen or been wrenched off the wall and its electrical coils were loosened from the frame, but the paper tape on which the recordings were made was still in place and in excellent condition.

Lamb looked into the kitchen. The old iron cookstove was ready to fall apart, but various pots, pans, and dishes remained intact. There was no sign of any paraffin or fuel oil on the site, nor did we find any edible food worth mentioning. The best we uncovered was some tea that was only beginning to deteriorate. In the galley, just to the left of the main entrance, we found some solidified cocoa as well as some pastry that Lamb reported as fine in appearance but rancid.

In the room next to the galley, which Ole Jonassen and Gustaf Akerlundh had occupied, the same blanket of snow and ice covered everything. In the lower bunk was an old wooden box all tied up and ready for shipment, but apparently left behind in the hurried departure of the occupants. It had apparently belonged to Akerlundh, for, as the front of it was beginning to disintegrate, the haft of a wooden sheathed knife protruded, marked with the initials "G. A[h]." Most of its contents were held fast in the grasp of the ice that also clutched the box itself, but I managed to free a frozen roll of papers which later proved to be disappointing as simple advertisements for acetylene stoves and lamps. There was also a good deal of clothing, most of which seemed to be in near-perfect condition. The only other article that I managed to release from the ice was a small collecting bottle containing a variety of fossil shell specimens.

After a brief look into the cabin that Nordenskjöld and Sobral had occupied, we turned our attention to the large loft that ran the full length of the house. We swung up into it through a trapdoor in the ceiling, bordered by almost two feet of soft snow. We then had to shovel some of it down into the room below in order to make room to work. We shovelled away enough snow to expose several open boxes strewn about, but with the exception of a few dozen candles that we took with us to use on the continuation of our own journey, they contained little of great interest. We also found many bottles and scientific chemicals, boxes of corks, long rolls of recording tape for the anemometer, a couple of penguin skins, a very few tins of food, some rope, and more clothing. In addition, one corner contained an improvised bedstead, presumably used to alleviate the overcrowding in the little building toward the end of the Swedish party's residence.

While the building was still structurally sound, our investigation proved it to be a complete shambles. The paper used to seal the inside and outside of the walls from the inclement weather had been torn away so that both the walls and the roof leaked badly. There were hardly any windows left in the place, and 1 to 1.5 feet of solid ice paved the floor.

These observations allowed us to decide our future plans almost immediately. There being neither food, fuel, nor shelter, all of our projected plans became impractical immediately. We had to abandon any ideas we had harboured of continuing our survey any farther south, the state of our supplies precluding the option of leaving a couple of men at Snow Hill Island to work out the scientific results of our travels to this point while the other pair returned to the base to bring out additional loads of supplies. Our immediate plans crystallized into an immediate return to Hope Bay, with a brief visit to Seymour Island en route. Once we made this decision, the balance of our visit at Snow Hill resolved itself into little more than awaiting the arrival of Russell and James.

The house was a melancholy place in such a state, when one considers the historic events that occurred within it during those early days of Antarctic history. We were glad that our inspection was finished. The remains of the astronomical observatory still stood toward the north end of the little hill where the house had been erected. A few pieces of the observatory, including most of the roof, had blown away and lay strewn about the foot of the hill along the shore of the little cove. In one corner of the observatory's frame, a bleached white section of the guy rope

Figure 38. The remains of the observatory, late August 1945.

from a tent with the bowser[3] still attached supported a small seal pelt. Outside the building, the mummifying body of one of the dogs rested on the hill's slope.

More pieces of tent rope were scattered about the litter that once formed the meteorological screen, now recognizable only by its latticed door. There was no sign of the anemometer that had been "removed to a little hill just below our dwelling-house,"[4] but there were various articles scattered about the bare, stony ground around the house. These included many tins of food (all blown), as well as various tools, including a double-headed adjustable wrench, a geological hammer, a keyhole saw, a wooden block plane, and a small hatchet. All of the latter were in reasonably good condition, so I collected them to take back to the base as

3.   Editors' note: A petrol or water dispenser or tank used to refill a cistern.

4.   Editors' note: Nordenskjöld and Andersson, *Antarctica*, 142n.

souvenirs. There is little doubt that these tools had been used to build the house, and that many of them had been used in the work carried out away from the station.

Near the shore of the cove below the hill, not far distant from the remnants of the astronomical observatory, lay four-gallon cans with the embossing "Tidewater Oil Company of New York." We considered that these were part of the supply of fuel that originally belonged to the artist Frank W. Stokes, who had accompanied the Nordenskjöld expedition in its earliest days.[5] Next, we climbed up the little terrace behind the house to attempt some collecting. Lamb wore his rope-soled shoes that, though quite heavy, equipped him well for climbing. My ragged sealskins had holes in their soles almost big enough to allow the insoles to drop out and the sharp-edged stones cut the thin sealskin readily, so I had to limit the scope and range of my travels. Lamb discovered the retreat where Nordenskjöld had retired to work in private at this favourite and convenient patch of fossils. A large sledgehammer stood against a stone at the summit of the sandstone slopes, with fragments of broken fossils strewn over the surface of the ground beside it. There were many rather poorly preserved gastropods and a few ammonites. The gastropods were about an inch and a quarter in diameter, while the ammonites measured about three inches across. These spiral fossilized shells varied in thicknesses from a quarter- to a half-inch.

A small gravel-surface plain divided by a frozen stream bed spread out to the south of the house. Fossils were comparatively frequent over this area, which was confined to the south and west by the steep fifty-foot high face of a glacier. Toward the north end of it, the flukes of the *sastrugi* were so deep that a man could lie within one of them and be completely concealed at a distance of about thirty feet.

Above the western shore of the cove below the base, we saw some remarkable examples of geological architecture that Nordenskjöld had described in his book. Vertical walls of basalt, remnants of dykes several feet thick, stood out of these banks of rotting stone that composed the shore. As I examined the lichens below them, I spotted the other team approaching from the direction of Cape Hamilton. I whistled a signal to Lamb at the tent, and he had some cocoa ready for James and Russell when we met there a few minutes later.

---

5.   Author's note: On the last day of the *Antarctic's* presence at Snow Hill Island, Nordenskjöld wrote that "it was determined that the wintering party should take over the supply of petroleum which Mr. Stokes had brought with him for the purpose of warming up his hut" (ibid., 106).

They too, had pictured the luxuries in which Lamb and I would wallow, and were shocked to see our tent up. They had to inspect the interior of the house themselves before they could bring themselves to realize that they would be sleeping in their tent again that night. We listened to a few critical remarks on the site we had selected to pitch the tent before we all helped to put it up. James broke the handle of their shovel on the hard snow of our camp and had to go in search of an old one from the Swedish Expedition, which was much weaker though still useable with care.

It was not until we were about to leave the place that the thought came to mind that, in all our searches around the base at Snow Hill, we had seen no sign of either sledges or skis. The Swedish team had probably used these items to transport personal baggage and specimens to the *Uruguay*, the vessel that eventually rescued their expedition. Nor had we seen any mark, sign, or stores left at this place by the American vessel, the *Wyatt Earp*, which Ellsworth had used in 1934 and 1935. As I sat in the tent in the evening, sewing tapes onto duffel slippers to wear over my flimsy sealskin boots, I could not but think of the limited stores we saw to that point and how hard a year the Swedish party would have suffered if circumstances forced them to winter at Snow Hill Island for a third year. The temperature, as we rolled into our sleeping bags, was $-20°F$.

A light wind blew from the southwest shortly after midnight but the weather was quite calm in the morning and the temperature about $-15°F$, with the bright sunlight holding forth the prospect of a good day. We suffered the misfortune of breaking the cork in our thermos flask by trying to remove it while frozen, however, so we faced the prospect of no drinking between break-fast and supper each day for the balance of the trip. This was a most annoying and aggravating experience at first, but we later grew not to mind it.

At 10:00 in the morning of 29 August, we left Snow Hill Island and headed northward toward Seymour Island. For a mile or so we found more of the glare ice that we had encountered upon our arrival at Snow Hill, but as we passed below Ekelöf's Rocks (curiously sculptured sandstone relief which decorates the face of the island) hard, windblown snow covered the surface. My inten-tion had been to run up the east side of Seymour Island to inspect the depot at Penguin Bay, but as we arrived opposite the channel separating Snow Hill from Seymour Islands the surface became extremely rough and broken so that it seemed better to remain to the west of the island and take advantage of the good surface on which we were travelling and making good time.

Furrowed with erosion, the sandstone cliffs that marked the southerly headland of Seymour Island gave way, through a broad sweeping arc, to a series of hummocky knolls, between which snow-filled valleys led gently down toward the sea. Gravel bars lay half a mile offshore that frequently contained fossils, but we did not stop to make a search of this area. We stopped for lunch just short of Cape Bodman, close inshore where a bank about six feet high marked the well-defined shore with what might have been a raised beach.

After a cold, dry lunch, we steered farther offshore along the course we followed and over a hard, windblown surface marked deeply with *sastrugi* until we stood below the khaki-brown face of Cape Bodman. As we rounded it, we opened up to view the north end of Seymour Island, with its flat 700-foot plateau fringed along the shore by sharp-edged dun-coloured hills separated by long snow slopes rolling down toward the sea. Turning almost due east, we kept close inshore and struck deeply into the bay between Cape Bodman and the northern part of the island. The bay was covered with a large sheet of snow-free ice, remarkably free of growlers and other interruptions in its surface, and made peculiar by the dark brown rock dust that drifted off and covered most of the land lying to the southwest. It was not sufficiently gritty to impede our progress to any noticeable extent, however, and we hauled slowly along until the two sledges had been pulled up over the tidal zone and onto the shore. There we made camp, surrounded by the brown, sandy hills that form almost all of the topography around this part of the bay.

The previous night at Snow Hill Island, James had tried to conduct an observation for position but he was unable to keep his instruments level on the tidal zone. So, with the temperature hovering steadily near −20°F, I observed a series of eight stars at Seymour Island. An astronomical program such as this took something over an hour to complete and, when the job was over, I enjoyed the heat thrown by the half dozen Swedish base candles that Russell and Lamb used to warm the tent.

The bamboo poles that formed the frame of our pyramidal tent were about eight feet long and had to be lashed into the sledge load longitudinally. We had worn several small holes into the thick outer canvas cover during our sledging on 27 August which, in themselves, were of no great importance. The weakened area that they formed, however, was significant, and we had to repair the worst of them with two patches that evening before we encountered another wild wind. Even in the light wind that sprang up, handling the sail needle and thread for more than half an hour proved an uncomfortable diversion.

At 6:00 in the morning on 30 August, the thread of mercury in the thermometer lying beside my bedroll read −20°F. It was a fine, clear day, with little wind. We intended to spend at least the morning exploring the island and searching for the stores depot that Nordenskjöld had left at Penguin Bay. Russell remained at camp to look after the dogs and to give his frostbitten feet a rest. Lamb and I left at 7:30 a.m., with James following in our tracks an hour later. We directed our footsteps toward a deep and narrow valley, not far from our camp, that cut the island transversely in an east-west direction. We threaded our way through a series of low sandstone hillocks whose arid aspect reminded one of the "badlands" of the western states. Climbing up a gentle slope as we entered the valley, it was not long before we reached its summit, about 150 feet above the sea.

At this point we separated. Lamb struck off northward to ascend a "hogs back" of sloping sandstone that led up to the plateau forming the dominant feature of the northern part of the island. I continued eastward along the twisting valley as it led down toward the sea again. Except for a small section near the summit sheathed in bare ice, the floor of the little valley was covered with snow. A long drift descended from the higher lands to the south while high winds swept bare the valley's steep northerly slope. This outlet eventually took me down onto the sea ice midway along Penguin Bay. Bold rocky cliffs extended toward the north and to the south lay the same low hummocky hills that we had seen opposite the coast to the west. I had not taken the trouble to examine Nordenskjöld's description of his depot before leaving the camp, so I did not know exactly where it lay. My search, extending over the lower slopes along the coast adjacent to the north of the valley, disclosed no sign of the fossils that were said to exist in high numbers near the depot, so I felt quite certain that it did not exist at this part of Penguin Bay. After examining 100 yards or so without result, and assuming that the more accessible part of the island might be farther north, I wrote a message in large letters in the snow beside my tracks to inform Lamb or James that I intended to follow the coast northward. If travelling conditions were good, I might continue walking around the north end of the island before returning to camp along the west coast. Since we had intended to leave the camp and strike off for Cockburn Island about noon, and it appeared likely that my return to camp might extend itself beyond twelve o'clock, I felt it prudent to leave this message of my intentions where it might be seen by anyone following my tracks.

My walk took me along the base of the steep sandstone cliffs that bordered the northern part of Penguin Bay for several miles. The sea ice was remarkably level and undisturbed by growlers or bergs close inshore. A mile or so out to sea, however, began a belt of rough ice. Beyond that, I saw numerous tabular bergs before the horizon lost itself in a band of low clouds. I was glad that I had left my snowshoes at the camp, for the surface of whipped snow on the sea ice was quite hard and my feet seldom punched through it. High above me I caught sight of Lamb's figure, also walking north along the eastern fringe of the plateau. He seemed to be on the edge of a precipitous drop and I could see him stop occasionally to pick something up. When he was about half a mile distant, I called and shouted in an effort to attract his attention and inform him of my plans, but to no avail. He could not hear me, and apparently was unable to see me, so I continued northward.

At last, after following the seamy sandstone cliffs for several miles, their summit began to drop steadily, though not smoothly. I passed round the last point of land that had obstructed the view in the direction of my march. There, the land broke into long sloping hills and valleys of soft, crumbling, brown stones with little snow. A rather distinctive valley came into view. While scanning it closely for any sign of the depot, my eye caught a leaning staff of wood jutting up from a pile of stones around its base atop the next hill. The moulded lines of the knoll were covered with masses of fragmented stone and pebbles, and its summit lay 100 or 150 feet above the sea. As I climbed up a gentle slope toward the mast, I picked up a few beautifully fossilized molluscs about three inches in diameter. Every detail of their intricately marked surface was perfectly preserved. I was in a hurry to get back to the camp as near noon as possible, however, and there seemed little time to stop too long to look for fossils.

Arriving at the hilltop, a wooden staff about seven feet long and less than two inches in diameter was firmly fixed into a cairn of large stones. It inclined to the east and some letters were carved into it. The edges of the characters that faced toward the southwest were worn away, undoubtedly blasted off by the sand and snow carried by the high winds. Removing a heavy block of stone at the base, I found a rusted tin about six inches in diameter and three inches deep that almost fell apart as I extracted it. Inside the tin was a mass of frozen sand from which protruded a piece of paper containing the letters "A.A.E." Gently peeling back the sand revealed another word—"Uruguay"—beneath which lay the remains of a little wooden pillbox containing a firmly folded sheet of paper

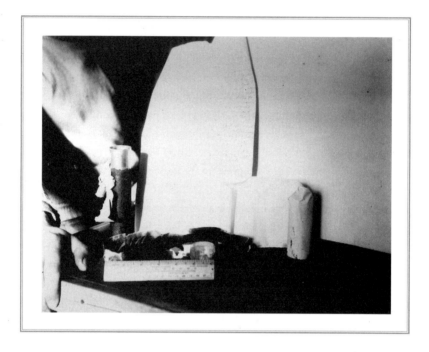

Figure 39. The Argentinian documents retrieved by Taylor and his team. The photograph was taken shortly after their return to Hope Bay.

that still appeared to be in quite good condition. The paper was ruled into small squares by blue lines as though it had once been part of a notebook. I did not take time to examine its contents there, apprehensive that I might damage it in its frozen condition. So, after a quick glance to see if there was anything else within the cairn, I replaced the block of stone.[6] After another hurried examination of the immediate area to make certain that no depot existed at this point, I left the signal mast standing as firmly as it had for the previous forty-two years before hurrying down to the sea ice.[7]

6. Author's note: I took photographs of both the cairn and the tin containing the papers before disturbing each of them.

7. Author's note: Since I did not have any receptacle with me, I was unable to leave a message recording my visit to the cairn.

After my return to the camp that day, the inner paper from the little wood-en pillbox was thawed out, dried, and carefully unwrapped inside the tent. It contained the following message:

Les sousigues, de l'Expédition Argentine de Secours,
commandant Capt. Julian Irizar, ont reconnue cette station le
7 Novembre, 1903, en trouvant seulement un pointe indiquée
avec des pierres et au milieu une canne en bois avec le signature
de Andersson et Sobral; faite une enquête complète et minitieux
dessous et autur de pierre ont y trouvé aucun, écrit.

Jose Garrachategui   Felipe Fleiss
....
Doctor   Lieutenant

Judging from the date, the *Uruguay*'s officers had deposited the note while their vessel searched for the Swedish Expedition, and before they found other evidence that their search might prove successful. They would have conducted their search with charts based almost entirely upon the observations made by Sir James Clark Ross's 1842 expedition. (Except for Larsen's observations, little additional information had been added to the map since that time.)

Venturing down once more onto the sea ice, I continued to follow the shoreline northward around the next point of land half a mile beyond the cairn. Here I found a long, sweeping shore backed by high sandstone hills eroded into numerous small valleys set back a little from the flat foreshore. I walked along this curving beach that had many fossil shells but no complete specimens because, it appeared, the waves battered them into fine fragments. Toward the northwest end of the bight along this part of Seymour Island, I climbed up 100 feet on two occasions to inspect what I thought to be possible depot sites. After finding no signs of human activity, I threaded my way through an extensive field of pressure ice off of the island's northern tip.

Rounding the cape at this point, I started back toward camp along the western shore. Here, the dun-coloured hills rose almost sheer from the sea up to the plateau, banded and studded with orange-coloured rocks. A wide and well-marked valley rose into the hills a mile to the south, the southern slope of which climbed directly to the plateau. The sandstone cliffs all along this sector of the coast fell gently to the sea. Three miles from the north end of the island, vertical cliffs marked the shore, rising up to 100 feet, eroded by vertical fissures into uniform sections. The cliffs were over half a mile in length and they sloped wavily down on either side of their summit so that, from a distance, they bore resemblance to gigantic vertebrae.

I took a direct southward course over fairly level ice that turned dark brown as I came within half a mile of our camp. I reached it at 2:00 p.m. Lamb had returned half an hour ahead of me, but the other two had taken a team of dogs and headed into the valley where I had begun my twelve-mile walk earlier in the morning. A bank of clouds approached us from the north when the northwest wind, which had blown stiffly for most of the day, began to subside.

After our separation that morning, Lamb had climbed up to the plateau collecting as he went along. James joined him before he reached the top. He found no sign of any botanical life on the plateau, at least over that section which he examined, so he descended to the east end of the same valley where we had started together earlier in the day. Not seeing me there, he concluded that I had returned to camp and walked about a mile southward above the eastern shore of the island. Along the way, he collected beautiful fossil specimens including pieces of wood, teeth, and a peculiar pencil-like fossil that he called a belemnite. He returned to the mouth of the valley along the sea ice and thence to camp, arriving around 1:15 p.m.

While awaiting the return of Russell and James, I took a walk over the ground to the west of our camp and found fossils in great variety and profusion over the surface. I picked up pieces of ammonites and coral. It was a great pity that we were not better supplied for our visit to Seymour Island, as we certainly could have spent more time studying its interesting geology.

It was about 5:00 p.m. before James and Russell returned to camp, and they had much to tell us. Fearing that an accident had befallen me when I failed to return to camp on schedule, they set out with the dog team to rescue me, following the transverse valley across the island. At the other side, they had missed my tracks leading northward and thus missed the message that I had written in the snow to allay such concerns. Instead, they turned southward toward the south end of Penguin Bay, where they stumbled upon the cairn and wooden cross marking Nordenskjöld's depot. They returned with a small, unopened canister that had been attached to the cross. Unfortunately, they had no camera to record their find. The only implement they had with which to attack the stores that had frozen into a solid mass, moreover, was an ice axe.

Only after our return to Hope Bay did we open the little tin canister, measuring approximately 1.5 inches in diameter and six inches long. A wooden stopper wrapped in thin rubber and sealed with electrician's tape covered the opening. The wood was weathered silvery white and the tape brown, but it had proven an effective seal. Inside the tin, carefully wrapped in thin parchment-like paper, lay a perfectly preserved document written largely in English. The message was written on sheets of double foolscap, the left margin uncut. It read as follows:

> Republica Argentine,
> Armada Nacional.
> On board the *Uruguay Argentine Navy* the 10th day of
> November of the year one thousand nine hundred and three.
>
> The subscriber, Commander of the *Uruguay* in his voyage to the
> Antarctic regions to relieve the Swedish commission directed by
> Doctor Nordenskjöld, having arrived to Cape Seymour depot,
> and being so lucky as to find Doctor Nordenskjöld, and all the
> rest of the commission as well as Capt. Larsen Commander of
> the *Antarctic*, has decided to sail back with all these gentlemen
> on board going to Paulet Island to pick up the *Antarctic*'s crew.
>
> In Cape Seymour Depot we leave the provisions as described in
> the adjoining list for the use of those persons reaching this point
> in need; in other depot which we shall leave also at Paulet Island,
> we shall leave also the same kind of provisions but in greater
> quantity, as well as a report on the probable route which the
> ship will follow.
>
> (Signed) Julian Irizar
> ....
> Commander
> November 10, 1903.
> (Rubber Stamped) Armada Nacional
> Canonera Uruguay

The second page, written partly in English and partly in Spanish, contained a complete list of the depot's provisions. With their ice axe, Russell and James, apparently considering us to be "persons in need," began their attack upon these stores, assembled by Sir Ernest Shackleton. According to James's own account, the depot

> was in two separate piles. In the first one we managed to open a box containing a Primus of similar manufacture to our own. It was in good condition except for rust around the nipple. Some Primus prickers attached to it were in perfect condition and we took two back, as we are short. In the same box were the remains of some tools. A cold chisel and a knife proved of help in attacking the other pile, which was clearly of food.[8]

At first it seemed that we were going to find nothing left in fit condition to eat, as the boxes we unearthed contained rusted tins, whose contents were unrecognizable. The first useful discovery was a case of corned beef, eight of whose twelve tins were unblown. We then found a case of rice, a case of beans, and a case of sugar, all of which were on the point of rusting through, and had contents spoiled at one end and good at the other. Our final discovery was a case of drink. What it was was impossible to say, but the fact that the liquid was liquid strongly suggested something alcoholic.

It must have taken James and Russell some time to consider whether to bring back more Primus prickers (which weigh a fraction of an ounce each) or the dozen bottles of "Bagley's Hesperedine." The label on the bottles read "M.T. Bagley's Hesperedine, Orange Bitters," but was largely written in Spanish that we interpreted to indicate some sort of stomach medicine. They took no chances. With a decisive imprudence typical of dog drivers, they martyred themselves by choosing the heavier load. The fluid was frozen almost solid but none of the bottles were broken. While the temperature outside was almost −20°F, we warmed up a bottle over the Primus stoves that night in the tents and lay back in our sleeping bags with half a mugful of the heartwarming liquid.

It was a pleasant conclusion to our visit to Seymour Island, a day when little planning was all knocked galley west to produce results more interesting than we could have ever hoped for. We found two documents, replenished

---

8. Editors' note: James's diary, 30 August 1945, BAS, ADG/1D/1945/K1.

some of our supplies with liberal helpings of the Penguin Bay Depot, and also added some specimens to our collections. Together, these gains almost made up for the disappointments at Snow Hill Island.

CHAPTER SIXTEEN

Polar Rationing

THE TEMPERATURE INSIDE THE TENT at 6:00 on the morning of 31 August was −15°F. A belt of low clouds approached from the north. I barely managed to get a bearing onto the north shore of Cockburn Island before fog intervened, rapidly dropping like a curtain to ground level and reducing visibility to considerably less than 100 yards. Light conditions became very puzzling; one lost almost all sense of perspective and could not intelligently guess whether his next step rose or fell in elevation. We left Seymour Island at ten o'clock and travelled blindly forward through the fog on the compass bearing.

After crossing a half-mile stretch of sea ice browned by Seymour Island dust, we came to glare ice interspersed with shallow patches of snow that were like the surface over which we had travelled on our approach to Snow Hill Island a few days previous. The sea ice was remarkably free from bergs and pack ice; its clean, patchy surface made for excellent travelling during the first three miles of our route. I was in the lead and stopped frequently to take bearings. Lamb followed closely behind with our team. James and Russell followed about the same distance behind Lamb with the other team, but the fog was so dense that they were, at times, lost to my view. It was easy to get off course, but we must have moved generally in the right direction, for a few minutes after Russell took the lead from me at noon, the high-rounded summit of Cockburn Island became visible through the mists. Gradually, as we approached the island, the straight-lined slopes of rock debris that buttressed its steep walls came into view. After passing over a thinly snow-covered surface, we arrived in the lee of the island where sand covered the sea ice and caused the sledges to move forward stickily.

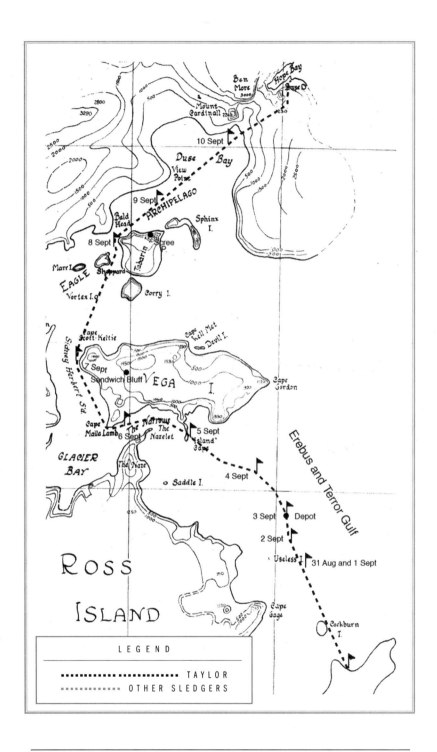

Map 11. The first sledging journey, 31 August to 10 September 1945.

As a breath of warm air wafted in from the north to drive the temperature up to 18°F in a period of just a few minutes, the fog dispersed for ten minutes. The grit-covered sea was almost bereft of snow. The bows of Sir James Clark Ross's two ships, the *Erebus* and the *Terror*, had once ploughed the waters that this ice overlay. He had landed on Cockburn Island on 6 January 1843 to take "formal possession of the island and the contiguous lands." Sir Joseph D. Hooker also made a botanical collection that for many years afterward represented the vegetation of the most southerly land visited by man. If for no other reason than the historical association of Cockburn Island with Hooker's work, Lamb was anxious to stop long enough to examine the area at least superficially, and we continued along toward the north end of the island. We had almost reached the point where he wanted to take his collection when a blast of cold air from the south struck us. Fog engulfed the island again, and within a few moments, the temperature dropped to −8°F.

Lamb set off to make his collection along the lower slopes of the embankment that rose up into the fog while I examined parts of the same area for rocks of geological interest. I found no signs of fossils during my search. When I returned to the sledges, the dogs of the "Big Boys" team were eating the whip down to its last few feet and gnawing a six-inch-diameter hole into one of the boxes on the sledge in search of food. Had they been able to read, they would have selected some other box for their depredations, as this one—marked "Sledge Repair"—contained nothing more delectable than some wire and tools.

Despite the chilling southwest breeze, the fog persisted and Lamb returned to the sledges after an hour. Had the weather been better he might have worked longer, but it was most uncomfortable and dispiriting on such a day. We were all pleased to see him return. After a bite of frozen lunch, we left Cockburn Island in the fog and started off on a northward course calculated to clear Cape Gage by a few miles before swinging toward the northwest to parallel the coast of Ross Island. The depth of the snow covering the ice increased steadily as our march progressed. About a mile from Cockburn Island, I discovered that our sledge meter's pointer had malfunctioned after we took the reading during our long halt for Lamb's collecting. It indicated a distance of eight miles when the time interval told us that we had travelled one mile. There was nothing at this stage to prevent the slightest touch of hard snow or ice from altering the reading of the meter's pointer because we broke the meter's glass face at Cape Longing and lost the protecting cover somewhere between Lockyer and Snow Hill

Islands. It seemed to operate satisfactorily during the afternoon but became completely unreliable as the snow deepened later in the day. Consequently, we were unable to use the meter for the balance of our journey back to Hope Bay.

The barometer dropped steadily all day long and began to settle late in the afternoon as the southwest wind whipped up. We were in for another "blow," so we camped rather early at 4:15 p.m. after covering an estimated 11.5 miles. The snow drifted heavily as we set up our tents in deep snow.

We enjoyed switching from our steady pemmican diet to the Seymour Island stores. James also gave us some of the stores which Russell had taken from the Depot Cape, so that we existed largely on the forty-year-old stores that Shackleton had yearned for during his epic drift on the sea ice following the loss of the *Endurance* in 1915.

The wind ceased about midnight, and by 8:00 the next morning the temperature inside the tent was above zero. The fog was still with us and visibility was less than 100 yards. I was particularly anxious to revise Nordenskjöld's survey along this coast and decided not to move in case the visibility improved later in the day. We ate a breakfast of 1903 bully beef and beans which was quite good except that the beans did not have enough time to absorb sufficient moisture before freezing. They consequently remained somewhat hard even after having been "cooked" and we suffered indigestion for the balance of the day.

Russell and I spent the morning catching up on our survey notes. Toward noon, the fog lifted so much that we could discern the lower slopes of Cockburn Island. But the improved visibility did not last—the barometer continued to fall and the wind intensified. By mid-afternoon it became quite violent, shifting the temperature from a high of 23°F to −6°F, so we did not move camp.

For the previous few days, we had used the candles from Snow Hill to warm the tent and conserve our dwindling supply of paraffin by contriving a "smoker." On this day, the wind from the northwest blew through our ventilating aperture and prevented the fumes from exiting the tent. As a result, Lamb and I suffered from terrific headaches all day long. Between our indigestion and our headaches, it was not a particularly happy day. We both lost our appetites, however, and saved almost one full day's rations. This saving subsequently proved to be to our advantage.

On 2 September, the visibility improved a little, though not to the extent I had wanted for our survey. As our paraffin resources were down to little more than a quart for the two tents, we could not afford to spend any more time waiting for the weather and decided to continue back to Hope Bay. The south-west wind blew strongly during the night, but it was quite calm when we left our campsite at 9:00 a.m. The surface was good for a mile as we approached a string of small icebergs stretching out toward the northeast. As soon as we entered the area beyond them, however, the dogs were taxed by deep and soft snow. We were down to about two days of dog pemmican, but expected to pick up another full box within a few days with the rest of our supplies at Vortex Island.

A short distance beyond the line of the bergs, we came to a low rough and rocky islet about 75 x 150 feet in extent and no more than twenty-five feet above the sea, which we named Useless Islet.[1] We took a sample of the rock that seemed similar to the granodiorite on Goudier Islet at Port Lockroy. There was no sign of any botanical life but there was plenty of evidence that birds used it.

From the time of our departure from Hope Bay twenty-six days previously, we had seen no birds. At various times throughout this day, however, we saw about a dozen white birds, which we took to be snow petrels, flying toward Ross Island. By this stage in the journey, we hoped to find a seal, and took the presence of these birds as an augury that the animals could not be far distant.

We turned to a more northerly course in an effort to avoid the deepening snow but there was little if any improvement. Two of our party members lacked adequate equipment to travel over such a surface, so they floundered about be-hind the sledges. It was tiring work. The sun shone dimly through a haze for most of the morning, but in the afternoon the southwest wind began to rise and we anticipated another gale. The runners on Russell and James's slightly heavier sledge broke deeply through the light snow crust, forcing them to unload part of their load and relay the last mile as the drift began to lift. Lamb and I decided to make camp at 2:00 in the afternoon after only covering an estimated four miles while we waited for them to bring up their load. We had just finished making things snug in the rising wind when it suddenly dropped and the sun came out. It was, however, too late in the day to break the camp and move on, so we settled in for the night and thought about the stores we left in the little depot on Vortex Island thirty miles away.

It was −20°F when we got up on the morning of 3 September. The night had been calm, and we had a pretty sunrise at 7:15. We left the campsite at 9:00, proceeding due north with the dogs floundering in deep, powdery snow that rose to their bellies. Lamb and I broke trail with our team for a couple of

---

1.   Editors' note: Today known as Lonely Rock.

hours in the bright sunshine. I went ahead on snowshoes to break a trail for the dogs while simultaneously manhauling the sledge with the animals at the end of a long towline. It was heavy going. The frequent stops soon led the dogs to lose interest in the work and forced us to move the heavily loaded sledge under our own power. The other sledge moved along easily in our tracks but James and Russell were unable to take the lead because their shorter sledge was unmanageable in the soft snow. They tried it once, but could only progress a few hundred yards in an hour. So we went ahead again, and the stops became more and more frequent as the snow deepened. The pair of snowshoes that I had not discarded at Vortex Island now proved invaluable, as they broke a wide enough track to give both the dogs and the sledge a little footing. Skis, by comparison, were almost useless for this purpose. Toward noon, the sledge meter produced another dud reading and convinced us that we could no longer depend upon it where there was the slightest chance of anything, even deep soft snow, brushing its face and moving the pointer.

On this day, we had our first good view of the northeast coast of Ross Island. The steep, black-faced promontories remained out of view, but the glaciers did not seem to have the same deeply-eroded embayments that characterized most of the island. We also saw ice cliffs at many places on the island for the first time. Half a dozen snow petrels flew by us, and we also sighted four paddies that we felt indicated the presence of nearby seals. All of the birds flew in a southwesterly direction toward Ross Island.

We were painfully slow in approaching the south side of Vega Island. The high-rounded snout of Cape Gordon jutted out toward the east. As the skyline slowly ascended westward toward the summit of the island, one gathered that great snowfields blanketed the island's south side. The summit of the island terminated in a high cliff before sloping down westward toward Sidney Herbert Sound, which, at our distance, was just a confused mass of hills.

The snow that we travelled through was more than three feet deep in many places and had little sustaining power. These conditions once again forced James and Russell to relay their load in the afternoon. With our dwindling supplies of food, dog food, and fuel, it became increasingly evident that any prolonged delay, such as a long storm extending over several days, could have disastrous consequences. We estimated this day's progress at less than three miles and the snow, if anything, seemed to deepen. With the heavy pulling and reduced rations, the dogs began to show signs of weakening. The reduction in

Figure 40. The stores depot left on the Erebus and Terror Gulf. Cape Gage is visible in the distance,
4 September 1945.

their loads became an immediate necessity, so we prepared to leave a depot just north of a string of bergy bits and pack ice containing articles such as the radio, theodolite, empty paraffin tins, ration boxes, and all personal gear that we could do without for the remainder of the journey. We expected to return along this part of the coast to complete its survey and therefore hoped to retrieve the dump of stores at that time.

The hungry dogs each consumed their last half-pound of pemmican that evening. Unless we were fortunate enough to encounter a seal, they would only have the forty-year-old bully beef we brought from Seymour Island until we reached our depot at Vortex Island. With the food from the old depots, we had about five days of man food on hand, but prepared to ration ourselves to make it last longer. There was little paraffin left in the tin to supply our fuel requirements. It was only sufficient for cooking; there was not enough to provide warmth or to dry wet clothing. The latter purpose was definitely necessary, as a foot of slush and water lay between the soft snow and the ice.

When we got up at 5:30 on the morning of 4 September, the temperature inside the tent was –30°F. By 8:00 a.m., James recorded an atmospheric temperature of –40°F. Since the minimum recording thermometer broke at Hope Bay during the winter, we had no record of the absolute minimum during the night, but it is most probable that it was lower than –45°F. This was the lowest temperature that we recorded on this journey.

At the commencement of the most disappointing day of the entire trip, we rose early to begin sorting our stores. Our troubles began when James announced that both he and Russell had suffered frostbitten feet while packing up and arranging their part of the depot stores. James suggested that we delay our departure until later in the morning in case it warmed up, for the sun shone brightly in the clear air. We waited an hour or two until the temperature warmed up to –25°F and, by 11:15 a.m., we arranged the dump of stores that we hoped the operation would only temporarily abandon. In addition to all of the stores we had decided to leave the previous night, we left behind some carpenter's tools that we thought would be useful to rehabilitate the building at Snow Hill, various bulky and heavy relics from the Swedish wintering station, and several bottles of Bagley's liqueur that we took back for the other lads at the base. We estimated that we left behind between 300 and 400 pounds of weight. The only things we continued to carry that could not be considered essential for returning to Hope Bay were the boxes containing the geological and

Figure 41. Facing north under the tough conditions, 4 September 1945. The centre of Vega Island is visible in the distance. Note the dogs lying in the deep snow.

botanical collections. James was anxious that these, too, be left behind, but I did not consider that their 150-pound weight would seriously prevent us from at least leaving them on land rather than the sea ice. Had they lain on the ice for several years, they would most certainly have been lost, whereas they could lie safely on land at some conspicuous point for someone else to pick up at a much later date if circumstances prevented us from doing it ourselves.

Just before we left our camp and depot, Russell took a round of compass bearings so that our party could find the location at a later date. With our lightened loads and bright, sunny, and calm weather, we had high hopes of travelling faster and farther than we had during the previous few days. In retrospect, we might have paid greater heed to the travails Nordenskjöld and his men experienced traversing the same area in mid-October of 1903:

> The snow grew deeper and deeper, and in the glorious sunshine we had, everything sank lower and lower, and before long it grew heavy on skis, even unburdened as we were. The sledge was turned into a snow-plough; the dogs sank past their bellies and our party moved

at a snail's pace and we were at last obliged to give up all thoughts of going round Cape Gage, and tried instead to keep nearer in toward land, ere the going proved quite as bad. . . . We had unheard-of labour, and even on skis, one sank deep into the snow.[2]

The snow we encountered remained very deep, and the going was still slow and heavy. We changed sledges again, and I went ahead with Russell to help manhaul the sledge pulled by the Big Boys (and guided by James). This queer hook-up broke a deep trail that the Odds and Sods' sledge followed under Lamb's guidance. Despite these measures, we made considerably less than a mile an hour in the first two hours on the trail. On changing course westward to make for a promontory that appeared to be an island south of Vega Island, the snow—more than three feet deep—became heavier, cleaner, and softer. Under these conditions, the sledge runners sank and submerged the deck, making our load act more like a plough than anything else. Lamb began to fall a little behind in this softer surface, so I detached myself from the front sledge and went back to manhauling the other. By the time we had caught up with the front sledge again, we found the big sledge completely bogged down and unable to move. The snow seemed to deepen further, and one sank almost to the waist without skis or snowshoes. When handling the sledges from the rear, it was easier to move behind it on one's knees, being dragged along while hanging onto the handlebars, than it was to attempt to walk. When one's foot reached the bottom of the deep snow, it found slush that immediately froze into a solid cast of ice when exposed to the ambient temperature of −30°F.

Feeling sorry for ourselves after making a disappointing 3.5 miles, we made camp in the morass of snow at 4:00 in the afternoon. Our depot at Vortex Island was still twenty-five miles distant, and since we had used the last of our Primus fuel in the stoves as we finished setting up camp, it became a matter of some importance that we reach our little cache. Russell and I thus set off on skis and snowshoes to break a trail northward toward Vega Island in the hope that it might harden overnight. We also hoped that we might find an improved surface for travelling by getting farther away from Ross Island and closer to Vega. By this time, we had no doubt in our minds that Ross Island's bulk sheltered the drift snow coming from the southwest. Unless occasional winds compacted the snow, it had no strength. It was also obvious that the

---

2. Editors' note: Nordenskjöld and Anderson, *Antarctica*, 312.

weight of the deep snow depressed the ice into the sea and produced the consequent slush underneath the drift.

As Russell and I plodded northward toward Vega Island, the darkness began to close round us. For a time, it seemed as though the surface was improving. At the end of two miles, however, we had to admit that it was still very poor and soft, and we prepared to retrace our footsteps back to the camp that we had left James and Lamb to complete. We expected to have a good start in the morning if a night wind did not fill in the trail with snow. It was dark when we returned to help the other pair complete the camp.

I helped Lamb tie the dogs to their tethering line. Each team received one tin of Seymour Island bully beef divided seven ways. It was a particularly pitiful meal for the animals considering the work of the last few days, but we only had two tins of this meat left so we could feed them only one more meal until we got a seal or reached Vortex Island. It was not a particularly happy situation and James requested that Lamb and I visit the other tent for a "meeting." Russell was in his sleeping bag, feeling the cold of the unheated tent rather more than the others of us. James seemed apprehensive that evening, and rather startlingly proposed to spend the next day undertaking a reconnaissance trip to find out if the deep snow persisted. If it did, he proposed that we begin a return trip to Snow Hill Island where, when we reached it, he thought that we could repair the house sufficiently to live in, using the wood of the building for fuel, and could live on dog meat until seal and penguins became available.

This proposal struck me as much more drastic than others that came to my mind. Besides the fact that we were now considerably closer to our supplies at Vortex Island than to Snow Hill, this proposal seemed to me to possess many other disadvantages. It meant discarding the collections that we had made on this journey (for they would have to be abandoned in order to facilitate our return to Snow Hill), sacrificing the preparation (in the south) of the scientific results of the journey (which we anticipated doing at Hope Bay immediately upon our return), and sacrificing all the dogs for next season's work (for we presumably would have eaten them). Certainly our troubles would but begin when we got to Snow Hill, and our continued absence and radio silence would cause considerable anxiety both at the base and at home. In order to accomplish our rescue, an expedition would have to be organized to assist us, with all the attendant publicity that goes with an adventurous failure. Furthermore, we had no assurance that a ship would be able to get through to Snow Hill this year or next. (After all, the *Antarctic* had not managed it in 1902.) For these reasons, I quickly decided that we would continue northward. Even though the deep snow would continue all the way to Vortex Island, we should get there almost as quickly as we might expect to reach Snow Hill. Our progress northward would also increase our chances of finding a seal. Once at Vortex, our troubles would be over, for there were three and a half fillings for each Primus in the depot.[3]

The only immediate result of the discussion in James and Russell's heatless tent was a noticeable mood of despondency that did not ameliorate as Lamb and I crept out into the darkness, fell into the deeply worn trench-like path between the two tents, and waded through the deep snow and slush back to our own cold tent. The temperature was about −35°F, and the slush solidly encased our feet in ice by the time we reached our own tent. Consequently, the simple matter of taking off one's boots occupied about twenty minutes of knocking the scales of ice from the duffel slipper coverings by whaling them with the handle of an ice axe. We had our supper of bully beef and pemmican, hanging the wet footwear in the peak of the tent so that most of the ice would melt off as the meal cooked.

A bank of cloud covered the sky as far south as Cockburn Island in the morning, causing the temperature to jump up to −15°F. Lamb and I went ahead with our team, following our snowshoe trail from the night before. It was frozen and gave the dogs a good footing, but Lamb (following behind the sledge in his "bare feet," as Davies would have said) plunged through the light crust at almost every step. We travelled steadily, however, until we reached the end of the trail at 10:40 a.m. During the entire time that we travelled through this great snow "bog," the dogs hardly ever left the prepared trail and gave the impression of being harnessed in tandem rather than in the fan formation that we actually used. They all lost their tendency to play and jump over each other's traces, so there was no need to untangle the lines as we usually did at each of our hourly halts.

Russell and James caught up with us shortly afterward and took the lead over the unbroken snow surface, just as the sun broke through the cloud cover. It shone so brightly that, for the first time that year, we wore snow goggles to avoid the glare that developed around noon. We made slow progress and had an early lunch due to an "affair" between two of the animals—a surprising occurrence given their weakened condition.

---

3. Editors' note: Taylor extensively quoted from his sledging journal for this paragraph and added his own retrospective commentary in parentheses.

In our team, Mutt and Sydney had walked with slack traces alongside the other dogs for several days and lost all interest in pulling. Jeff began to exhibit the same failing. Strangely enough, Widgeon, the dog who had suffered from a lame leg for the greater part of the journey and who had done little useful work up until this time, was now one of the best dogs in the team. Dainty and Pretty did wonderfully well, though the latter was little more than a walking skeleton. Jack, though generally a lazy little creature, also pulled more than his own weight. The situation in the other team was much the same. Jimmie was the worst of the lot and Popeye and Captain also began to lose interest in their work.

While the others stopped for lunch, I went ahead with the snowshoes to break a trail for a couple of miles on a course slightly more westerly in the hope of finding a better surface. Heading for the east end of the island that was almost directly on our course for the previous four days, the soft snow continued. As I approached the island, however, the snow surface that had been completely flat and featureless began to show slight effects from the wind, and a little farther on occasional patches of hard snow protruded through the surface. I hurried back to pass the good news of improved conditions to the others who had, by this time, gotten under way. I am afraid they did not put much reliance in my optimism, for we had often made this same observation and been proven wrong. I hooked onto James and Russell's front sledge. Lamb continued to perform the Herculean task of handling the other sledge single-handedly without complaint, and usually kept well up behind the other sledge. In this manner we covered almost five miles: the best day's travel we had had since we passed Cockburn Island. Yet it had still been a laborious day's travelling. In the last half-mile of our travels for the day, we encountered a remarkably improved surface that was quite hard for quite extensive distances. The depth of snow between these hard patches, moreover, diminished to something under a foot. Although we had not overcome all of our difficulties and possessed no more food or fuel than when we started out that morning, we all felt more optimistic of our prospects and were almost certain that we had overcome the greatest obstacle to our returning to Hope Bay. We made camp at 5:00 p.m. to the east of Ross Island.

We estimated that our sledge loads were now both under 400 pounds and knew that, if the dogs were better nourished, they would have pulled swiftly across the good surface all day long. Even in their present condition, the improvement in our travelling surface held out the prospect of a good day's travel that would bring us closer to our Vortex Island depot only twenty miles distant

Figure 42. The Naze, 7 September 1945.

from the camp we occupied that night. Having made a positive advance toward our goal, and with the temperature still −30°F, we turned in to our sleeping bags in much higher spirits than we had felt for several nights.

At 6:00 on the morning of 6 September, the sky was overcast, the temperature almost zero, and the southwest wind began to blow. Half an hour later the wind brought considerable fog. We would not normally have travelled on such a day, but it had been several days since things had been normal and our shortage of fuel forced us to have less respect for the weather. A few moments after we left our campsite on the stroke of nine, we crossed a series of tide cracks and found ourselves gradually rising above sea level up a gentle slope that had been imperceptible from the camp. We were on a low spit of land, probably thirty feet high and a quarter of a mile in width, which connected the "island" that we had been camped beside to Vega Island, making the former into a cape. To our left, this cape rose up in a high, rocky mass nearly free of snow. To our right, a rocky point with brown talus slopes jutted out from Vega Island. After crossing this little isthmus, we soon found ourselves down on the sea ice again, weaving a course between a few small, grounded icebergs on a surface that continued to harden. We made good progress nevertheless. Beauty delayed the other team for a while with one of her love affairs that had recently been of quite frequent incidence. The fog blotted out most of the landscape and we were again reduced to travelling on a compass bearing. We occasionally caught a glimpse of the high rock wall to our right, but for the most part we could see nothing except the snow a few feet in front of us. For a time, the sun shone dimly through the mist to give us a bearing, but it did not last for long.

After two hours' travelling, we began to catch an occasional view of an island well to the south of our course. We could not, however, see any part of either Ross Island or the narrow throat of Sidney Herbert Sound that should have been dead ahead of our course. The wind began to rise, the snow drifted, and for a while we crossed over a softer surface. We soon found a good surface by altering our course closer inshore toward Vega Island and, despite the wind, we made good time.

Our good fortune did not last long. The velocity of the wind rose, and the fog changed to a blinding drift of snow. An Antarctic blizzard was upon us and our course went into the very teeth of the wind. As the wind rose, the drift increased and completely obliterated all our landmarks. Even the sledges, which were 100 feet or less apart, became separated a couple of times. Fortunately, there were occasional momentary lulls when the wind dropped and visibility improved sufficiently to allow us to see where we were going. The fiercely drifting snow, however, forced us to camp shortly after 2:00 p.m., as it whirled about our feet like a living mass of whiteness.

With the wind at its height, blowing fifty miles or more an hour, the combined efforts of the four of us succeeded in erecting one of the tents, into which we crept for a smoke and a respite from our labours before starting to erect the second one. An hour after our arduous exertions to set up the tents the wind began to drop, and by 5:00 p.m. there was little of it left worth mentioning. It became dead calm four hours later.

We had no food to feed the dogs that evening: a cruel circumstance considering that they had dragged our sledges an estimated nine miles that day. Our own clothes were wet from perspiration and the blizzard, but there was no heat to dry them. If we estimated distances correctly, however, we had the satisfaction of being only eleven miles from the depot. The temperature in the evening was −10°F.

On 7 September, the weather treated us to another fine, calm day, with the mercury about –20°F. We looked back eastward upon the route we had followed through the blizzard the previous day, and could still see the spit-connected promontory that was close to where we had camped that morning. Westward, Vega Island projected in a point about three miles distant; on the other side we hoped to find Sidney Herbert Sound turning toward the north. Far beyond this point, the eye caught a snow-capped feature with black, rocky cliffs not unlike Corry Island's, with valleys penetrating into the interior on both sides. Unable to navigate with any great accuracy since the sledge meter stopped working, we were uncertain whether one of these contained the passage that led into Sidney Herbert Sound.

The hard surface allowed us to make good time to the promontory three miles distant, where deep snow surrounded a zone of pressure ice and grounded growlers. As we approached the cape, the Naze (a huge, brown, rocky knoll largely covered with snow that includes steep cliffs to its northwest and scree slopes along their bases) lay to the south of us. Gradually and slowly, we worked our way round the base of the hill to our north. As we mounted the top of one of the pressure ridges, the entire north end of Sidney Herbert Sound came into view with our Monument Island distantly set in the middle. It was good to set eyes again on so familiar a landmark.

Proceeding northward along the sound, we soon came to the end of the pressure ice that seemed to predominate toward the eastern side of the sound. We soon found ourselves upon a smooth, flat surface of soft snow no more than a foot deep. The dogs were failing fast at this stage from starvation. James had to place Jimmie on his sledge at eleven o'clock in the morning because he was no longer strong enough to walk. In our team, Mutt could not totter along after four o'clock in the afternoon. Russell came ahead to help me manhaul, for we were again breaking trail with the Odds and Sods team, even though it was hardly able to pull its own traces.

High, craggy rocks of brown and black raised themselves above the mantle of snow fringing the lower slopes of Vega Island. Toward the north, we recognized the black and white horizontal formation Lamb had named Sandwich Bluff. Across the sound, Ross Island extended itself in high, black cliffs and occasional grotesque formations of rock into Cape Lachman at its northern tip. We passed another series of small bergs in mid-afternoon and continued to hope that we would find a seal among them. It was of little use, for much of the ice

Figure 43. David James breaking open the depot they left at Vortex Island, 8 September 1945.

frozen into this part of the sound had an ancient appearance. We made camp at 4:45 p.m. below some high black vertical cliffs just short of Cape Scott Keltie.[4]

James wanted daylight to kill one of the dogs to make food for the others, for they had not received their ration of pemmican for five days and had not eaten anything at all for two days. He decided that the victim would be Mutt. Leading the tired but faithful old animal out behind the tents, he sent three bullets from the revolver crashing through his skull. When the dog didn't drop and still staggered about after James bashed in his head with the butt of the revolver, a fourth bullet dispatched the tough old animal. Unable to repress the flood of memories of the service he had given us so willingly, it seemed a murderous manner of repaying such loyalty. In the darkness, James distributed the parts of the dog's carcass to the other thirteen animals who barked incessantly when they caught the smell of Mutt's blood, causing a curious echo to reverberate from the cliffs above us. There was little meat on the poor, starved animal, and it took but a few moments for his companions to consume him.

4.   Editors' note: Today, Keltie Head.

We warmed our bully beef over some of Nordenskjöld's candles, as we had done for several nights to spin out the little paraffin fuel we had left. The temperature outside was –25°F when we hung our frozen footwear up toward the apex of the tent to thaw so that we would be able to wring the water out before putting them on in the morning. We all suffered from frostbitten feet from wearing wet footwear in these low temperatures.

As we left our camp on the fine, clear morning of 8 September with a temperature of about –15°F, we could see Vortex Island six miles away. For a mile or so the surface was a little soft, but then we found a good, hard, windblown snow top where we could slide along at a good pace—with Lamb and me contributing more than half of the motive power for our weakened six-dog team. The other sledge followed along behind us, pulling its load unaided. At 11:30 a.m., the other team diverged from our course and made for the east end of the island while we rounded the west. James and Russell reached the depot ahead of us and, when we arrived, were already busy digging it out. Russell made a search around the iceberg near where James had attempted to kill the seal on 13 August but found none this time.

Lamb and I helped James extract the skis, ration box, dog food, and our precious half-tin of paraffin. The latter contained seven fillings for the Primuses, and since we arrived with a little remaining from our last filling of the stoves from five days before, we expected to be well off with this commodity for the balance of the trip. Loading these articles onto the two sledges, we turned northward between the two islands of Tabarin and Sheppard. The hard, windblown surface over which we began this course soon gave way to large, rough *sastrugi*, after which we entered a field of hummocky ice for an hour or so. Coming out of this roughened area, we headed for a sharp, distinctive peak at the northwest tip of Tabarin Island, which we named Horn Peak, and then came upon alternating surfaces of glare ice and thin, windblown snow. We camped a few miles short of our objective at 5:15 p.m. On Sheppard Island, to the west of the camp, lay a little bench at the foot of a long, snowy slope, and I decided that this might make a convenient locality to establish a base camp when we returned at some later date.

As we erected the tents with the temperature above zero, we were treated to a glorious red sunset. After tethering the dogs out on their chains, each received—to their astonishment—not one but two blocks of pemmican. They fell upon them ravenously, and the blocks were gone within a few moments. Sydney,

Figure 44. Andrew Taylor (left) and Ivan Lamb (right) at the end of the first sledging journey, 11 September 1945.

being the most impolite of them all, gulped his two down and then tried to intimidate Pretty into giving him one of hers. Inside the tent, we also enjoyed a heavy meal of pemmican. Even more than the food, however, we enjoyed the heat from the Primus stoves in the tents for several hours in the evening until we were thoroughly baked. It seemed like the transcendence of pure luxury.

Our trip verified that a channel separated Corry and Tabarin Islands. At our location, the former had the same high, precipitous walls we saw along its eastern side; toward the northwest corner of the island, the black-brown rock fell less steeply to the sea. Occasional icefalls drained the ice cap of the island into the sea along its western coast. Tabarin Island sat between Corry and Sphinx Island and, with the exception of its northern end, was lower in altitude than Corry. The snow cover on Tabarin Island flowed down in gentle folds toward the sea, unbroken save for occasional *nunataks* set in its starched-looking cover. At its northern side, two peaks rose considerably above any other parts of the island.

Although we were up at 5:30 in the morning on 9 September, we did not get off to our usual start. We all enjoyed a feeling of utter relaxation and restfulness, as though regaining our paraffin ended the anxious part of the journey. There now seemed to be all the time in the world to cover the last twenty miles to the base. The temperature read 5°F as we lay in our tents absorbing the heat.

For a short time, it was bright and sunny as we packed up and left ahead of the other sledge, which was again delayed by intimacies between a pair of their dogs. Not long after we left the old campsite at 10:15 a.m., the wind began to blow up from the west and drifting snow weaved over the surface as rising clouds covered the sky. I still manhauled on the long trace. Although our six dogs were much better after two nights of feedings, they were still very weak. Jeff and Sydney hardly pulled their traces. As we rounded the northwest corner of Tabarin Island, however, the team seemed to "wind" a seal, for they began to pull so assiduously that I had difficulty in keeping ahead of them. Shortly after this sudden interest in their work began, James and Russell caught up with us; their bigger and more powerful team apparently caught the same incentive. James said that they had felt ill and groggy in the morning, possibly from eating a tin of Nordenskjöld's forty-year-old meat paste that they had brought from Depot Cape. Their condition had not improved during the morning, and James noted that if they became much worse they would be unable to proceed any farther.

Figure 45. Victor Russell and David James at the end of the first sledging journey, 11 September 1945.

They kept on for a little, however, as we passed a large iceberg half a mile or so to port of us. Lamb spotted some birds circling round its base, and the dogs began to show a decided interest in that direction. The wind rose steadily while great white clouds billowed toward us over the mountains of the Graham Land coast. By this time, we were within sight of Ben More as well as the Depot Glacier above Hope Bay, and the surface ahead of us appeared to be excellently hard for travelling toward Duse Bay. In view of the threatening weather and James and Russell's indisposition, however, we decided to camp near the big berg, hoping to find some seals along its base. While Lamb and I began to set up the camp with the force 7 wind, the other two went round to the north side of the berg where James discovered and shot three seals in short order. After erecting the tents, we took the dogs over to the gutted seals where each team had a carcass to itself. They wallowed around the opened seal, still tied to their traces and the sledge, eating steadily and voraciously for half an hour until they completely satiated their starved appetites. After the privations they suffered, it was a fine sight to see the dogs able to have all of the food they could consume. When they could eat no more, we tethered them out on their lines beside the tents where they lay down and almost immediately went to sleep.

Lamb brought back about twenty pounds of steak and liver along with thirty pounds of blubber (the fatty wall comprising an insulating layer around the animal, three inches in thickness). By perforating the walls of a tin to provide a draft, we created a blubber "smoker." We filled the tin with two-inch-square cubes of blubber and, after some difficulty, we ignited the cubes. This produced good heat, with plenty of soot that blackened everything exposed to it. We also cooked the steaks, which were extremely tough. We had only covered four miles during the day, but finding such a complete source of supply for our needs made our short move relatively unimportant because we were again completely self-sufficient. The warm west wind shot the temperature up to 35°F, and the sky cleared toward late afternoon as the barking of an occasional dog re-echoed off the high face of the iceberg.

On the morning of Monday, 10 September, soot from the blubber smoker covered everything in the tent, including our face and hands. Breaking camp at 10:00 a.m., we passed a dozen scattered seals as we set out in a straight line toward the head of Duse Bay, where we descended onto the sea ice a month before. To the north of Tabarin Island we found a fine, hard surface passing below the long, white glacier slope that draped down from the high summit near the

Figure 46. The "Odds and Sods" dog team consuming a seal on 9 September 1945. According to Taylor's notes, the dark spatter toward the left beside the sledge was seal blood blown by a high west wind.

northeast tip of the island. As we travelled down the channel, we spotted two relatively low but extensive outcrops of rock that marked the westerly entrance to Duse Bay on the mainland of Graham Land. Making steady progress, we soon made out the rock outcrop ahead of us as Summit Pass, on the tip of the Trinity Peninsula, where Davies, Matheson, and Back left us on our first day out from Hope Bay. Gulls, snow petrels, and giant petrels flew about us as we entered the roughened area across the bay, where small bergs and hummocky ice studded the sea ice. We still made excellent time, however, because the surface continued to be firm and hard.

We passed through several miles of this rough ice before crossing pressure ridges that transversed our course. The sun shone brightly down upon us all afternoon and the temperature rose to as high as 30°F. The dogs pulled almost as well as they normally did on this improved surface and, just as dusk closed in at 5:30 p.m., we set up our camp at the foot of the glacier separating us from the Hope Bay base. As we closed up our tent for the night, Russell brought over the dregs of a bottle of Bagley's and a solitary candle as a present for Lamb to celebrate his birthday. The evening also marked the last time, after over 100 such camps, that Lamb and I occupied the same tent.

The last day of our sledge journey was 11 September. The sky was clear and sunny as we left James and Russell's tent standing with a few odds and ends required for the next journey that would depart in a few weeks. The sledges crossed the shore rift of the glacial ice without incident and we all manhauled the sledges to help the dogs up the steep initial slope, which extended up about 200 feet. From this point onward, the gradient became easier and, with Russell and me continuing to manhaul, we made good progress on the hard surface.

We first saw the drifting tails of snow streaming off the summit of Ben More from the west, and it was not long before the clouds of drift snow from the mountains of Graham Land caught up with us. Although the sun continued to shine down brightly and the temperature remained at 20°F, the wind began at 10:30 a.m. and blew at gale force by 1:00. Nevertheless, we made steady progress toward Summit Pass.

Soon after we passed the summit of the glacier, the surface became covered with snow and the dogs found it a little more difficult to traverse for a mile or two. We paused for a moment in the shade of the Pyramid to take a few photographs. The sea was quite open in Antarctic Sound except for little fields of brash ice which patched the deep blue colouring of water. The snow thinned as we progressed down the gentle slope past the Pyramid. When we approached Nobby Nunatak, the snow cover had all blown away leaving only bare, slippery ice. In the high wind, the sledge swung downhill and crabbed at a dangerous angle toward the east, causing numerous upsets. On one such occasion, the handlebars on our sledge came completely adrift; we lashed it together temporarily and made erratic progress down the hillside. As we passed Nobby Nunatak, Russell and James rushed past us to be first back at the base. We came down the last 400 feet of elevation in good style riding over a good bed of snow, and reached the base at three o'clock in the afternoon.

It was a very pleasant homecoming for the four of us. We had a busy couple of hours scrubbing ourselves and changing into clothes that were relatively clean, while Flett dispatched a signal to the Governor of the Falkland Islands informing him of our return to the base. We enjoyed the comforts of dry clothing and bedding—and plenty of food. I don't think I ever appreciated Berry's cooking quite so much as I did at his supper table that night.

PART FIVE

The Second
Sledging Journey

CHAPTER SEVENTEEN

Interlude

AFTER THE FOUR OF US RETURNED FROM THE JOURNEY, our appetites were insatiable. We seemed unable to exist between meals without a few slices of bread or a bun or two. Hunger even disrupted our sleep, and we only managed to last through the night with the aid of chocolate bars. Our ravenous appetites lasted continuously for about a week; we could eat double helpings of everything that came out of the galley. Though I cannot speak for the other three, I know that I lost fifteen to twenty pounds during our absence from the base, and it took ten days of assiduous attention to my newfound appetite before I noticed any recovery. It was unfortunate that we lacked a scale to keep an accurate record of our weights before and after the journey; it might have produced some interesting statistics.

With the exception of a great deal more snow and less ice on the sea at Hope Bay, we found the base much as we had left it. As a matter of fact, the ice in Hut Cove blew out to sea with the same wind that blew us into Eagle House. It was as well that we managed to return the day that we did, for this wind persisted and increased in fury for the next few days. Accordingly, it was quite conceivable that we might have found ourselves exasperatingly storm-bound for days, just across the 1,500-foot height of land separating our base from Duse Bay.

In order to avoid an otherwise inevitable accumulation of office work toward the end of our year at Hope Bay, I had arranged in March that monthly scientific reports be prepared and turned in to me each month before the 10th of the succeeding month. This proved to be no great hardship and did much to fill time between April and July when we were not as fully occupied as we were during all of the other months of the year. I regularly received these reports until the end of July, and spare copies were prepared for storage in a steel box in the

Nissen hut as insurance against the ever-present danger of their destruction by fire. (Incidentally, the same hut also held spare clothing and equipment, including that required for setting up another complete radio station, for if fire ever caught Eagle House there would have been little or no chance of extinguishing it in the prevailing high winds.)

Now there was much to be done to prepare the records and information we gathered during our sledging journey. Just before lunch on the morning following our return, we held a meeting where I allocated the work that each of us would contribute toward completing this program. The plan was to have it done by the end of the stormy period, which we anticipated based on our experience at Port Lockroy in September and October 1944.

The specimens of lichens, algae, and mosses that Lamb had gathered during the sledge journey kept him busy for several weeks, as he worked at drying, describing their occurrence, and packing them up so that their delicate fibres arrived at their destination undamaged. He wrote a brief report on the botanical features of the area through which we had travelled. His greatest chore, however, was developing and producing prints from all the films taken throughout the journey.

Flett examined the geological specimens. He was greatly interested in the petrological specimens and only passively so in the paleontological ones, but he willingly looked after all of them for us. With Ashton's assistance, he deciphered our hurriedly written field notes, which were necessarily brief and scribbly due to cold fingers as well as the wartime paper shortage that even extended to the Antarctic. Packing up hundreds of rocks and fossils was a big job, and they filled quite a number of cases in the end. In addition to the geological report accompanying this work, Flett gave great aid to Lamb producing the photographs.

James was responsible for two reports. One concerned the condition of the sea ice we had passed over. The other concerned meteorology of the area that we had covered during our trip. The former was a rather dull subject but the latter subject had many points of general interest, the principal one being the marked difference in temperature between the East Graham Land area and that of the other bases during the same period. The average temperatures for the months of August and September 1945 combined for each of the three bases were as follows:

Port Lockroy   19.0°F
Deception Island   17.5°F
Hope Bay   13.5°F

The average temperature we experienced in East Graham Land between 8 August and 11 September was −5.7°F. Particular days show simultaneous temperatures respectively at Hope Bay and in the field as follows:

10 August	−8°F	(Hope Bay)	−35°F	(Duse Bay)
20 August	3°F	(Hope Bay)	−29°F	(Mount Falkland)
30 August	24°F	(Hope Bay)	−18°F	(Seymour Island)
7 September	2°F	(Hope Bay)	−30°F	(Cape Scott Keltie)

The even manner in which the respective barometric curves at Hope Bay and in the field followed each other was remarkable; every little change in the one simultaneously reflected in the other. The southwest wind that prevailed so regularly at Hope Bay was also prevalent over the entire area. Another noteworthy point was the cloud cover we enjoyed throughout the trip, which had the remarkably low average figure of 3.3 tenths. By comparison, the mean at Hope Bay for the same period was 5.3 tenths.

Russell compiled a glaciological report based on his observations during the trip. The section in which he described the complex configuration of the Sjögren Glaciers and the shelf ice that extended out into the sea from it proved particularly interesting. He also computed the astronomical reductions for positions we recorded on the journey. It was meticulous and toilsome work, and he also relieved the monotony by acting as water boy for the photographic firm of Lamb & Flett. This latter task required him to supervise the continuous melting of a tubful of snow, as well as its supply from the drifts that all but inundated the house at the time.

We also packed remnants of food that we had purloined from the Ross and Seymour Islands into a wooden box for shipment to London. From the provisions laid at Depot Cape by Nordenskjöld, Jonassen, and Sobral on 13 March 1902, there was an assortment of tea, prunes, salt, cloves, apple rings, and butter that we sealed in a glass jar after sterilization at Hope Bay. We also packed rice, beans, and bully beef (the latter treated similarly to the butter) from the Argentine depot on Seymour Island laid on 10 November 1903, and placed four unopened bottles of Bagley's "Hesperedine" into a similar box for whatever purposes government officials determined necessary.

Lamb, Russell, and James also prepared copies of the diaries they composed in the field, or extended their brief notes into full accounts. These contained different points of view of many incidents that we experienced in common, reflecting the different interests of each writer. There is much within them for persons with the time to study their contents.[1]

Aside from typing the journal I had written in the field and preparing a general survey report, my work largely consisted of plotting the survey notes. The task slowly evolved into our map of the area. Much of the information that I used to compile the map at this stage came from photographs taken especially for the purpose. They did not produce the results I had hoped for because Russell's and Lamb's cameras froze up and became completely inoperative in the low temperatures that we experienced, while James lost his camera near Longing Island. Consequently, I took almost all of the photographs used for this mapping work with Marr's camera. After calibrating the camera at Hope Bay, a transparent scale permitted angles to be read off the photographs directly. With these angles, I triangulated the location of features where we had not taken measurements on the ground. By using the sea horizon, which was well depicted on most pictures, I also used vertical angles to fix spot heights to distant features.

Ashton carried out a most interesting piece of work during August, September, and October. As previously mentioned, we hoped that our year at Hope Bay should produce a four-week cycle of the tides—preferably a continuous graphical record. Ashton spent considerable time devising an instrument for the purpose using the micrometer stage of a microscope in conjunction with an alarm clock as a power unit. He completed the instrument's construction about mid-August, set it out on the sea ice of Hut Cove, and collected his first useful record on 14 August. The machine gave good results for about a week before colder weather toward the end of the month caused it to produce intermittent readings. The machine's design required the changing of its paper charts every twelve hours, which was an unpleasant task with an offshore wind and the ice edge but a few hundred feet distant. The station acquired the last record from

---

1.   Editors' note: The British Antarctic Survey Archives holds copies of all three diaries: AD6/1D/1945/K1 (Appendix S, R and Q). James subsequently published large portions of his diary in *That Frozen Land: The Story of a Year in the Antarctic.*

Figure 47. Checking the tidal gauge, 15 October 1945.

the drum of this instrument on 9 September, when a strong gale blew from the west and blew the ice upon which the gauge sat out to sea.

Fortunately, Ashton seemed to have anticipated this event by beginning two weeks previously on the construction of another machine using a meteorological clock and part of a carpenter's clamp. This made a workmanlike and satisfactory job, and yielded five weeks of readings. The series ran continuously, measuring twice-daily tides and indicating a maximum tide of nine feet with the springs. Furthermore, the machine required almost no attention once it was enclosed in a tent to prevent the drift snow from interrupting its operation. Each chart depicted the tides for a complete week. The correlation of the information measured on this instrument, coupled with observations of the motion of the sea ice in mid-sound, indicated that the northerly currents into Antarctic Sound were flood tides.

As I mentioned earlier,[2] Matheson began on this laborious task in July, and it was well under way when we returned from our sledging. He made his own lead and filled the hollow base with tallow to bring up samples of the clay, sand, and gravel from the bottom. Ashton improvised a couple of ice drills for him and, with the axe (and help from Flett and Marshall), Matheson dug through a total of more than 300 feet of solid ice in about eighty holes. The deepest water sounded lay about half a mile west of Seal Point, measuring 110 fathoms. From the information Matheson assembled using these primitive tools, he produced a chart showing the submarine contours of the southeast shore of Hope Bay as well as Hut Cove, and determined a better anchorage in the latter location.

We had received little information from the other two bases except for their contributions for the *Hope Bay Howler* which continued to appear regularly on the 21st day of each month. Given their fewer numbers, the teams at Port Lockroy and Deception Island spent a much larger proportion of their time on domestic duties, menial chores, routine observations, and radio schedules. At Hope Bay, we interpreted the lack of any definite word concerning Bonner's condition as an indication that his health had not markedly worsened. Only those who were at Deception Island realized the strain they all bore from living continuously with a man who was not only ailing but, as it transpired, dying among them. While they gave Bonner every consideration that their limited facilities allowed, there can be no questioning that his illness and enforced relaxation created a tense atmosphere and caused the other three personnel to shoulder heavier domestic and handyman duties. In this respect, as Reece remarks in one of his reports, Bonner's illness altered his position at the base from a partner to a definite liability. In the cold light of reason, the Deception Island base would have operated more efficiently and harmoniously without the ailing man. By the time this was discovered, however, there was no means to transport him to a hospital where he might have received adequate medical attention.

While we were at Port Lockroy in 1944, we had enjoyed no success at fishing. Layther persisted, however, and on 9 July he caught his first fish. Before the end of the month, the station's personnel landed some large *Notothenioid*, the largest of which weighed more than four pounds. This success continued through August and September, with many of the fish weighing more than three pounds.

---

2.   Editors' note: See Chapter 13.

Frank White, at Port Lockroy, seemed to utilize the available game to a much greater extent than the cooks at either Hope Bay or Deception Island. We all enjoyed the fish that was conveniently available at all of the bases in 1945, for there was also an excellent fishing ground off Fildes Point near Neptune's Bellows that Matheson used in 1944 at Deception Island. Besides such piscatorial delicacies, shags and penguins made regular appearances on the Bransfield House table, and were popular with all hands. The shags, as I mentioned previously, had a slight fishy taste. The penguins, which have deep and tender breasts, made excellent eating with just a touch of gaminess to add to their flavor. For some reason, the penguins never seemed particularly popular with Berry, though we had relished eating them on several occasions while out sledging. White also made good use of the seal meat that we handily procured, for boredom with steak and kidney stew or herrings in tomato sauce are important factors for making even greasy seal meat more appetizing.

The most important incident that occurred at Port Lockroy during this season was the procurement of the pup of a crabeater seal (*Lobodon carcinophagus*) from the nearby sea ice on 22 October. Few babies of any species can have made the wires burn up such as Lockley did with the advent of this little seal. They sent off one signal after another in an effort to get unmistakable instructions from the government naturalist at Port Stanley about how to preserve this zoological specimen that they claimed was unique. Incidentally, the naturalist, Dr. J.E. Hamilton, had been magistrate of the South Shetlands two decades earlier. In the end, the furry little seal was skinned and dissected; its more important parts were preserved for subsequent shipment and examination.

October and the early part of November was a tempestuous period with little sunshine and much wind at Hope Bay. It also brought heavy snowfall. Before the end of October, twelve feet of fresh snow had fallen at the back of Eagle House. Five gales blew October behind us, but in the first week of November we experienced the longest gale of the year. For seven days, the wind blew continuously from the usual southwest quarter without dropping below thirty miles an hour. Most of this time it blew in excess of sixty miles an hour, and reached a top velocity of sixty-nine miles per hour. The temperature in this storm varied from 2°F to 24°F.

With respect to the sea ice, 17 August seemed to mark the beginning of the summer break-up at Hope Bay. For several months up to that date, the Antarctic Sound was more or less completely frozen over, with young ice containing occasional leads that opened up in gales or warm weather. From the high observation spot at Nobby Nunatak, we saw the close heavy pack press up toward the south of Rosamel Island. Northward, the frequent presence of "Arctic smoke" indicated the presence of open water not far distant. Hope Bay itself was tightly frozen along a line southwest from Sheppard Point. Continuing winds during the middle of the month swept most of the ice away from Antarctic Sound, and toward the end of the month there were indications that the heavy pack ice, which so consistently seemed to hug the shore of Joinville Island across the sound, was dispersing.

In September, the winter ice continued to move. Hut Cove cleared out on the 11th and almost presented its summer shoreline by the end of the month. The mass of pack ice that had frozen into Hope Bay in April still held firm at the end of the month, but the ice edge receded to a position well within Seal Point. This tongue of pack ice did not escape until 21 October, by which time drifting ice from the south filled much of the sound. It was not completely ice-free for the remainder of the month. At times, heavy pack ice containing many bergs completely chocked the sound. Previous observers suggested that this condition might be coupled with the break-up of ice in the Erebus and Terror Gulf, but our experience in this gulf led us to conclude that the source of this pack was likely more distant. Fridtjof Channel opened up on 19 October, and remained so.

The distribution of the pack ice along the sound at that time of the year largely depended upon the winds. The southwest winds even cleared away an unbroken field of pack ice extending eastward from Hope Bay for about five miles within a few hours. As the prevailing wind is the southwester, it would appear unlikely that Hope Bay would be blocked for long under similar conditions. In fact, the longest period that ice made the bay inaccessible during October 1945 was four days. The southwest wind also tended to sweep a pathway clear of ice close in to the Graham Land shore.

The rather sudden breaking out of the ice in Hut Cove on the day of our return from the sledging trip led to the loss of one of our pups and the near loss of a second. On 14 September, one of Lady's little pups romped along the ice foot below the base, which was about twelve feet high at low tide, before slipping over the edge and into the water without anyone noticing. By the time we became aware of its plight, the little pup had swum about sixty feet offshore. This made rescue impossible, and the poor animal drowned in the freezing water. The next day a second pup, Reuben, suffered the same experience. About four o'clock in the afternoon, we were all aroused by the shout "Dog in the Drink!" We rushed out to see Pretty's pup struggling through a thin layer of ice coating the surface of the water near Jagged Rocks about a quarter of a mile from the base. Hastening over with poles, ladders, rope, sledge tarpaulins, empty paraffin drums, and anything else that might prove useful, we broke a path for him through the thin layer of ice toward the heavy fast ice. After a stout effort by the little pup, which had been immersed in 29°F water for fifteen minutes, Blyth reached him and hauled him out. Reuben was taken back into the building, rubbed down vigorously, dried, and warmed. For about an hour, the courageous little animal shivered continuously and sobbed spasmodically. He dried out by the time we finished our evening meal and seemed almost happy again. By the next day, he frolicked about as usual, completely unaffected by his "dunking."[3]

With the passage of the winter months, the birds and animals began to recapture Hope Bay from the gulls and paddies. We had been surrounded by white pigeon-like paddies or sheathbills throughout the winter, but when the opening of the sea presumably broadened their area of interest in September, their numbers shrank from about forty at the beginning of the month to less than ten at the end of it. By October, they were lost in the hordes of Adelie penguins over the rookeries.

About forty black-backed or Dominican gulls had flocked around our station before our sledging party departed in early August. Their numbers dropped the following day and, for the balance of the season, our station's inhabitants observed no more than a dozen on any single day. Presumably this reduction bore a direct relationship to the dog food that usually littered the area surrounding Eagle House while the dogs were present. When the penguins returned to the rookery, the gulls became much more frequent visitors, and increased in number to almost 100. Though we discovered no eggs, they nested along the Scar Hills deep in Hope Bay. Despite the lack of shag rookery within our range, the gulls appeared again in August, and numbered about forty by September. Fewer were seen in the month that followed when their own distant rookeries reopened to the sea. In November we seldom caught a fleeting glimpse of one.

---

3. Author's note: Following this incident, Matheson constructed a raft made of steel drums lashed to a twelve-foot sledge in case of another emergency. He and Donnachie later let themselves out on a line to our old fishing grounds to try their luck again; the raft was a success, but the fishing was a complete failure. Fish were caught periodically up to the end of November, but never with the same success we had had in June and July.

Although these other birds were of ornithological interest, their numbers were completely lost in the living sea of Adelie penguins that inundated the area in October. Four solitary penguins made a brief appearance on the fast ice of Hut Cove in early September, but they did not stay. The real invasion began on 8 October when the first few permanent visitors arrived. By the 11th, hundreds of Adelies were ashore, popping out of the water along the ice edge of Hope Bay near Seal Point, and tobogganing along on their silvery breasts into the bay as far as Eagle Cove. There they began their ascent of the rookery by waddling awkwardly up the snow slopes that rose from the shore. By 19 October, we estimated that there were 50,000 of them.

Donnachie found the first Adelie eggs on 4 November during a comparative lull in a long storm. He later returned to the rookery with Back and Blyth to collect eggs by the hundreds, and sledged them back to the house in a large wooden box for domestic consumption. By carefully and continuously marking the remaining eggs in the nests of the same comparatively small area of the rookery, the team ensured that it only collected fresh eggs on future trips.

The gentoos, which probably constituted only one percent of the penguin colony, were within earshot of the base by August. We observed a few ashore near the Grunden Rocks on 19 September; others landed near Seal Point by 7 October. They reoccupied the same three scattered areas along the fringe of the huge Adelie rookery, and nested by 19 October. We found the first egg on 16 November.

We observed only one other species of penguin at Hope Bay: a solitary, vagrant ringed penguin that arrived in November. We had hoped to catch sight of the great emperor penguin, one of which had been captured at Snow Hill Island by the Swedish Expedition in October 1903, but the birds denied us this experience despite our vigilance on our travels and at both bases.

A great variety of petrels also visited Hope Bay in relatively small numbers. We found the fluttery little Wilson's petrel for the first time on 17 October, and we discovered eggs by 10 November. We saw up to thirty silver grey petrels daily after 6 October, but their numbers markedly shrank in November. A few Antarctic petrels visited Hope Bay on 11 September. Beginning in early September, flocks of up to 150 snow petrels flew by toward the east, coinciding with almost simultaneous sightings of them in the Erebus and Terror Gulf. After a lull, many more snow petrels arrived during the first week of November, but few were subsequently seen except those that wheeled high about the northern slopes of Mount Flora (where they were probably nesting). We first noticed the

Figure 48. Lamb's comic, "It is all for the sake of science," from the *Hope Bay Howler*, October 1945.

giant petrel or stinker in the spring on 5 August, and by September there were forty of them with us. Most were of the dark or intermediate plumage, but one in every twenty birds was pure white. Finally, pintado petrels (more commonly known as Cape pigeons), which abounded by the thousands in the harbour of Deception Island, came to Hope Bay slowly. In the last week of September and the first week of October, we occasionally spotted single birds. After 9 October, they came in flocks of up to nine, and these visitors increased during November, when about forty were around. Few skuas were about, with the first arriving on 12 October. From the 15th, they were a continuous presence and numbered up to eight, nesting at widely scattered points just above Eagle House in November.

The only other bird that we saw at Hope Bay up to the end of November was the Antarctic tern, the same species that we had observed at their rookery on Donner Island in 1944. The first appeared near the end of September, and by the last week of October we saw them almost daily. Their scarlet colouring stood out as they flew swiftly about, and we first found one of their eggs at a nest along the north slope of Mount Flora on 18 November.

Seals had been rather rare around the base during the winter, but they became more numerous later in the year. Two Weddells were killed in August and three more in September—helping us to eke out a dog food situation that had been none too good at times during midwinter. In September and October, the seal meat shortage ended, for in the two months we spotted forty animals and killed crabeaters and sea leopards. The acquisition of one of the latter species settled an argument that had prevailed throughout the winter. Until 25 October, both Marshall and Matheson maintained that all of the seals previously killed at Hope Bay had been Weddells. Those of us who had spent the previous year at Port Lockroy disagreed, and the long neck, broad shoulders, and fierce powerful jaw of the sea leopard that we caught settled the point unmistakably.

The measurements that Marshall made throughout the year on the temperature and salinity of the seawater continued. He took the former measurement several times a month through the ice. The sea temperature in August read 29°F, and by November it only rose by one degree.

Meanwhile, publication of the *Hope Bay Howler* continued, albeit with deteriorating print quality. Lamb's cartoons were a regular feature—and also became progressively worse. The jokes and attempts at poetry continued "cornily," the former generally depending on some little-advertised incident of camp life for their point. The October issue was typical. The cover page was the same as the initial issue, while the back cover featured Lamb's cartoon titled "It is all for the sake of science." Between these covers were four closely typed pages of script subdivided into sections including editorials, letters to the editor, a feature entitled "Keep it under your Bowler" (dealing with security), news from both Port Lockroy and Deception Island, an article about "How I came to the Antarctic" (one of a series which had provoked the suggestion that an article on "How I got out of the Antarctic" might be much more interesting), a few advertisements, and public notices dealing with topics of current interest.

With the approach of spring, there was much to attract our gaze but little time to enjoy it. Lamb and Flett produced large quantities of photographs and it was difficult to pass by the tanks that they used to wash the prints without steering for a glance. Outside, the little pups silently and irresistibly entreated one to stop to pet them. It was Davies's chore to look after them, and he fulfilled the role with typical thoroughness. He carefully prepared their hot meals each day, and even took them off for a run up the slope to Boeckella Lake. They ran and tumbled along together, taking more than a casual interest in the penguins as they bounced along like string-connected fur bags.

Despite the pressure of other work, Russell found time to make a day trip up to the head of the Depot Glacier with Back and Donnachie on 26 October. There was little indication of any movement since they had set out across the glacier in July, but the two easterly stakes had disappeared completely. (We presumed that they were submerged beneath newly formed snowdrifts.)

With the possibility of our departure for home in the not-too-distant offing, we prepared a complete list of our stores in October. The list consisted of two sections: those expendable and those that were not. It took James about a week to get it ready. Just as he finished it we received a signal from London asking for just such a list, so we were able to furnish it immediately. In the subsequent months, we entered expendable items against the list each week, so that by the time our relief actually arrived we were able to turn over a complete inventory of the remaining stores at Eagle House.

At a post so completely isolated as Hope Bay, the slightest rumour concerning conditions "outside" that might affect us personally was sufficient to start off a flood of conjectures. All too frequently, such floods let loose without even the basis of rumour. By October, we were starving for news of the plans regarding our relief. We longed to see faces other than those that we (at times all too intimately) encountered each day. Naturally, our thoughts spanned the distances between Antarctica and our respective homes; they dwelt long and often on memories of the comforting companionship of loved ones; they anticipated our return to the sources of these memories; and they caused us to ruminate at length (and with some frequency) on the "order of our going." There is little doubt that our isolation created a condition of exile as well as considerable mental strain, and it was fortunate that there was so much to keep us actively employed, both physically and mentally, throughout our second year of solitude.

It would be pointless to deny that some ill feeling developed between certain individuals, but these sentiments simmered beneath the surface and were sufficiently controlled to ensure that they seldom bubbled up. Like catalytic agents, the gentle kindliness of Lamb, the friendly helpfulness of Davies, and the bantering good nature of our youthful doctor, did much to ameliorate and assuage the ruffled tempers of others—and made those of us who fell short contemplate our faults with shame.

Definite word of London's plans for the immediate future would have done much to relieve our internal strain. By the end of October 1944 at Port Lockroy, we knew the *Eagle's* planned role and that Reece, Lockley, Russell, and James would join our party. We also knew that Marshall was on his way south with a score of dogs for us. At the time, we found all of this news extremely interesting. At least momentarily, this information broadened the sphere of our interests beyond our own myopic horizons and served the important psychological purpose of diverting our attention from each other's shortcomings.

In 1945 at Hope Bay, however, we were told nothing. The prolonged silence probably reflected security concerns, for there was no other justification for it, but we were never provided with a rationale. The lack of news created an "edginess" that added to our internal difficulties. It kept the door of idle chatter ajar, and prolonged facetiously worded conjectures that were not without an element of serious truth—a truth sometimes dismal to contemplate. Some utter pessimists among us asseverated that the lack of news indicated that no action was being taken toward our relief, and that we might be abandoned for yet a third year in our icy surroundings. Observations concerning this situation found increasingly frequent vent in succeeding issues of the *Howler*. The comments grew from gentle hints in August that the "sport of fossil hunting" was producing many heavy boxes that could double as "ballast" on the relief ship,[4] to acidulous remarks in October noting that the willingness of those at Port Lockroy and Deception Island to transmit news to Hope Bay stood "in marked contrast to the sluggishness or rather gross neglect which characterises [*sic*] our correspondents further afield."[5] For the most part, these comments reflected the general feeling on the subject.

This complete lack of news concerning our projected relief influenced our plans for the second sledge journey in two respects. The first involved the importance of keeping in radio contact with the bases during our sledging journey so that we could head back to Hope Bay immediately if it learned that a ship was making a typically brief call at the station. The second point concerned the journey's locale. We could either carry out our original intention and travel along the summit of the Trinity Peninsula,[6] or we could conduct a more intensive examination and survey of the islands in the area

---

4. Editors' note: *Hope Bay Howler*, 21 August 1945, UMA, MSS 108 Box 9 File 24.

5. Editors' note: *Hope Bay Howler*, 21 October 1945, UMA, MSS 108 Box 9 File 26.

6. Editors' note: See Chapter 13.

through which we had passed on our previous journey. Assuming that Tabarin would continue for another year, the Hope Bay party could anticipate having infinitely better dog power than we possessed. This expectation, coupled with the likelihood that we would learn about our relief ship's arrival on short notice, made the latter plan much more appealing. Consequently, we decided to go back into the Ross Island area and examine its north end along both coasts, as well as the islands adjacent to it. Retrieving our stores from the sea ice of the Erebus and Terror Gulf became our secondary objective.

Davies immediately took charge of the preparations for this journey, while the other three of us continued our scientific work. He made up the food supplies first, on a more liberal scale than we had on our earlier trip. James and Matheson helped him get the sledges and tents ready, while Back, Marshall, Matheson, and Ashton helped move the stores up the long slope of the glacier at various times in mid-October. By the time we were ready to leave the base in early November, the initial sledge loads were very light indeed.

CHAPTER EIGHTEEN

The Second
Sledge Journey

AT ABOUT NOON ON 9 NOVEMBER, THE TWO DOG TEAMS started up the glacier slope behind the base. Snow lay heavily over the surface, and we stopped for frequent rests. In the single track made by the sledges, a couple of men followed along pulling a lightly loaded, six-foot sledge that we planned to use for manhauling around Sheppard Island. On the Big Boys team, "Jimmy" (who had an injured leg) and "Beauty" (who was almost due to pup) had been left at the base. "Pretty" also had some maternal expectations and did not accompany us. We filled the depleted ranks in the two teams with three young dogs, "Hobbs," "Hinks," and "Reuben," so that each team still comprised seven dogs.

The weather had been fine and clear earlier in the morning but clouds subsequently hid the sky, and it became a dull and murky day as we reached Summit Pass at 2:00 p.m. We ate lunch there with Back, Marshall, and Matheson before they returned to the base. We attached the short sledge to the stern of that pulled by the Odds and Sods and slipped downhill at a good speed toward Duse Bay, enjoying brilliant sunlight within a few minutes of leaving the pass. The snow was only a few inches deep over a hard crust and we rode the sledges down the long 1,200-foot slope onto the sea ice without incident by mid-afternoon. Here, we found the surface to be even better, and the dogs raced along our southwesterly course with their tails high in the air. After travelling four miles from where we descended from the inland ice, we encountered a pressure ridge in the ice of Duse Bay that was apparently formed by the southward thrust of the ice out of the bay.

At this point we saw the first of many hundreds of seals that we would encounter on this journey. We passed within a few hundred feet of ten Weddells that did not take the slightest interest in our procession. The surface was good beyond the ridge, and by the time we camped on the west side of the bay (below an extensive outcrop that we named View Point) the following day, we had covered sixteen miles. The teams easily pulled our 850-pound loads, and we had been able to ride the sledges a considerable portion of the way. At the camp, the dogs contentedly tore at the seal meat that Russell and Davies[1] had cut up after catching a couple of seals nearby. We enjoyed the tender steak for supper while a few gulls and skuas hopped curiously about the carcass. It had been a perfect day for travelling, with the mercury barely below freezing and almost no wind. We turned in to our warm, dry sleeping bags with appetites completely assuaged and the comforting feeling of a day of accomplishment.

The weather in the morning was no less perfect. We left the dogs tied up beside the standing camp and went off to look at the nearby rocky outcrop. Davies and I loaded the big camera onto the hand sledge and began ascending the snow-filled hollows between the outcrops. Before reaching the 500-foot summit of the hill, we halted three times to collect the lichens that grew in great profusion. On that bright and clear day, we took in the magnificent panorama that inspired us to name the spot View Point. The view stretched from Summit Pass, through the east and the south quadrants, and toward the west to include the summit of the Stanley Glacier on the Trinity Peninsula. The sea was studded and roughened with hundreds of large and small bergs. Between our vantage point and the rugged cliffs of Vega Island in the distance, the northerly exposures of some of the islands of Sphinx, Tabarin, Sheppard, and a little of Marr Islands were all markedly different from the others in general appearance. Each was characterized by long banks of rich, earthy-looking slopes that were all but completely free of snow. I photographed the scene with the large panoramic camera. With field glasses, we could clearly see dozens of seals over the starchy whiteness of the sea's surface. We descended the hillside by a slightly different route, and were back at the camp by noon, where we found the birds still gorging themselves on the seal carcasses. The sun beat down upon us and it seemed breathlessly hot inside the tent. A couple of terns flew northward past the camp as Lamb and Russell returned. They had ascended some 450-foot black cliffs that stood belittlingly over the camp and had found a fine view of the northwest arm of Duse Bay.

---

1. Editors' note: Davies assumed James's place on the second sledging team because the latter still suffered from frostbite that he had acquired during the first journey (James, *That Frozen Land*, 177).

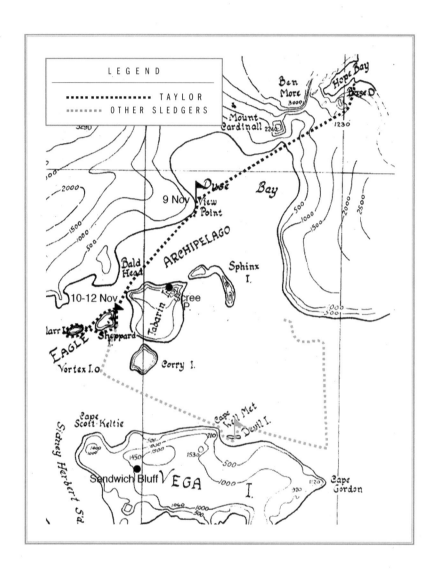

Map 12. The second sledging journey, 9–12 November 1945. Insufficient records exist to accurately re-chart Russell and Davies's trip back to Hope Bay.

After lunch we broke camp and by two o'clock in the afternoon we were on the move again. We took a slightly more circuitous route around the southwest-erly entrance to Duse Bay, where a dozen seals huddled inshore enjoying the heat. With Davies and Russell leading, we struck a course for the left tangent of Marr Island and remained well to the north of the flat-topped mass of brown rock that formed the westerly tip of Sphinx Island. From the east end of Tabarin Island, a high, flat, combed-black scree peak rose up over 1,500 feet with a little glacier draining down to the west of it from the small ice cap. The western part of the island's shore presented an almost uniform straight cliff nearly 1,000 feet high and continued for almost two miles. Black and brown layers banded the cliff's face down to the bank of loose rock that submerged its base. This face of Tabarin Island was typical of many miles of cliffs along the shores in the area.

As if to mark the end of Tabarin Island as we approached, there rose a distinctively shaped high nodule of rock that we referred to in our notes as "The Horn" or "Horn Peak." It extended above the snowfield behind it, clothed about its base in long slopes of loose rock. The red rays of the setting sun set off the foliations of the high face of the rock.

To the north of our course, the rocks of View Point descended in elevation toward the west, petering out into the sea along a series of rock cliffs that were a couple of miles in length. Their termination marked the entry of a deep bay filled with bergs close inshore. The shoreline appeared to be comprised almost entirely of ice cliffs. Many crevasses lacerated the surface of the glacier above them and ended in great dark gashes in the ice face.

The dogs made good time as we travelled over a pie-crust surface that covered nine inches of soft snow, and we soon found ourselves entering the passage between Sheppard and Tabarin Islands. A considerable snowfall had completely buried the hard-glazed surface that we had sledged over two months before, and there were few signs of the irregularities that we had noted then. After covering ten miles, we pulled up onto the little shelf on the east side of Sheppard Island and had a mild celebration to honour Russell's birthday.

The sun shone brilliantly in the morning as Russell and Davies left Lamb and me with the tent and drove the two teams southward toward the east end of Vega Island. Everything that they did not require for the return trip to Hope Bay had been unloaded. The only exceptions were a few things that they needed to run a survey along the north side of Vega Island, as they planned to pass its way before following the south shore of the Trinity Peninsula (to where we had descended the inland ice onto the surface of Duse Bay). They then planned to follow the same route we had often followed back to Hope Bay, and expected to return to Sheppard Island in five or six days with another full load of supplies.

Figure 49. Lamb and tent at Sheppard Island, 11 November 1945.

Figure 50. Davies with the "Odds and Sods" leaving Sheppard Island, 11 November 1945.

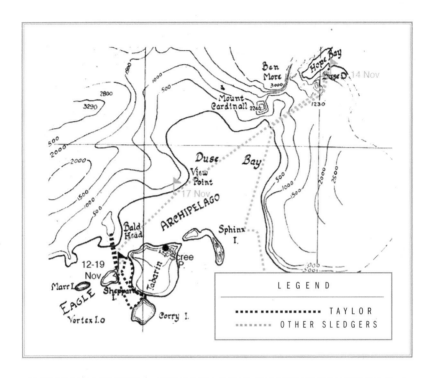

Map 13. The second sledging journey, 13–19 November 1945. Insufficient records exist to accurately re-chart Russell and Davies's trip back to Hope Bay.

They took the weighty load of specimens that we had collected the previous day at View Point with them, and left our camp at 10:30 a.m. on another day of brilliant sunshine.

Our tent sat upon a shelving foreshore of flat scree slopes that were richly vegetated with mosses and lichens. From a slight indentation in the shoreline below us, a little valley ran steeply inland up to the higher reaches of the island. A massive hill marked the northeasterly tip of the island while, to the south, a broad snow slope led up to a rocky eminence.

From the camp we had a good view of the western slopes of Tabarin Island. The greater portion of its slopes were solidly encased in ice that flowed smoothly down to the sea. The northerly part of the slope was high and made of ruggedly broken rock, but toward the south only a few black *nunataks* broke the island's white cover. An ice sheet drained down from a summit near the

Figure 51. Marr Island, n.d.

northeastern part of Tabarin Island. At the south end of the island, the same sheet lay over a flat-topped black rock that had snow-free slopes.

Corry Island is more massive than Tabarin Island. The high-combed summit of Scree Peak on the latter juts up 2,000 feet above the sea, and Horn Peak is well above 1,000 feet. Yet the southern end of the island is low (a little above 400 feet). Corry Island, on the other hand, has a remarkably uniform appearance. It has a flattened, shield-shaped ice cap that lies over 1,200 feet above the sea and most of the island is only a little below this elevation. From the shore, the deposits of fragmented rock that fall from the high cliffs rise up steeply. The island's rocky walls rise sheerly above these slopes to the ice cap, which is still active in several places. Icefalls occur with frequency and hide the brown rock faces in a curtain of roaring, shimmering white.

We climbed up the little valley of Sheppard Island that started from a point behind our tent. It was snow-filled, but its gently sloping walls were peppered with morainic material. Lamb and I separated at the head of the valley, 300 feet above the sea. He headed southward while I climbed higher toward the summit at the northeastern tip of the island. The top of the hill was over 400 feet in height, and was composed of a crumbling, light-brown-coloured agglomerate. The beds of these formations lay exposed in weather-worn nodules; their edges were well-rounded so that they were pillow-shaped and most of the interstices were filled with mud and crumbling rock. In damp places up the hillside, one sank ankle-deep into the muddy slopes. I watched for signs of fossils, but saw none; there was little of interest except a variety of erratic, volcanic rocks.

There was a fine view of the northern part of the Trinity Peninsula from the island's summit. The point was higher than any others on the island, but one could see comparatively few rock exposures because the top of the island to the west consisted of a long, dished depression filled with snow. I subsequently tried to capture the view in a photograph using the panoramic camera but the light conditions were never sufficient.

We returned to camp and I attempted to contact the bases using Donnachie's "sea-dipped" walkie-talkie radio without success. The transmitter functioned well enough but the receiver was dead. We turned in to our sleeping bags early, inconvenienced to some extent by a terrific sunburn that had attacked our faces and particularly our lips. It caused no little discomfort, and encouraged a state of lethargic drowsiness.

There was no wind, nor were there any clouds when the day broke on 12 November. The sun beat down mercilessly and soon drove the temperature up above the freezing point. We loaded collecting equipment onto the small sledge and struck southward from the tent at 11:00 a.m. to investigate the other islands in the archipelago at close quarters. We planned to "circum-ambulate" Marr and Sheppard Islands along a track that would take us in a large figure eight. Within half an hour we descended over the zone of tide cracks onto the sea ice and then turned westward along the south side of Sheppard Island. Pulling the sledge over the light coating of snow that carpeted the sea ice while wearing snowshoes was a pleasant pastime. We stopped below a geological formation that Lamb took to be a "Basalt Plug," comprised of an unusual columnar jointing of hexagonal basalt similar to that found at the Giant's Causeway in Ireland. We gathered a heavy specimen. The remainder of that day's journey took us across the mile-wide passage between Sheppard and Marr Islands, and to the north side of the latter over sea ice (which was glare ice in stretches). At the west end of Marr Island, we crossed through a field of hummocky ice, followed along the south side of Marr Island and the north shore of Sheppard Island, and arrived back at camp at 7:00 p.m. With the exception of sighting about a dozen seals, the trip was of little interest because all of the rock we inspected was the same basalt tuff common to the area. A stiff, cool, easterly breeze also sprang up to make most of our day's trudging a little uncomfortable.

Temperatures remained slightly above freezing for the next couple of days, and a blow from the southwest prevented much useful work from being accomplished. Packing up our mass of geological and botanical specimens helped to pass the time. The radio, fortunately, decided to work on the 13th, and we were able to maintain constant contact with Layther at Port Lockroy, thus learning of events at Hope Bay. The next day, for example, we heard that Russell and Davies had arrived back at Eagle House after encountering the anticipated rookery of penguins. Lamb remarked that this was a rather circuitous route for news to travel in order to inform us of conditions existent but a few miles distant at Vortex Island. The information had travelled from Vortex Island to Hope Bay by dog team, and from Hope Bay to Port Lockroy to Sheppard Island by radio. The news, however, was a rather interesting corroboration of our earlier observations and conclusions.[2]

On 16 November, a gusty southwest wind blew all night long, but diminished in intensity toward noon when the sun came out. After lunch, we set forth across the channel to examine more closely the west side of Tabarin Island. In the course of our previous passage through the archipelago, we had only touched upon two of the islands from a distance. Most of the other islands had appeared to be of sedimentary origin, which was one of the principal reasons we arranged to spend these few additional days examining them in detail. Therefore, we found it more than a little disappointing that each island was formed of the same basalt tuff agglomerate that varied in proportions and shades from black to red-brown. The rich, earthy-looking appearance of the rounded, low-lying hillsides inevitably proved to be crumbling piles of the same rock, and the fossils we had expected to find were elusive and indiscernible.

The geology of Tabarin Island proved to be no exception. On the island, large pieces of rock had detached themselves from the heights and littered the ice along the shore. We wove a devious course between them, and Lamb periodically climbed up the hillside to add to his botanical collection. Toward the south end of the island, we passed round the scree slopes that margined the shore and came upon a low, ice-cuffed face lying opposite Corry Island only a few hundred yards away.

---

2.   Editors' note: This paragraph of Taylor's manuscript lacks dates. The supplemental information is from Lamb's diary, UMA, MSS 108 Box 6 File 17.

It took another day before we got over to Corry Island, which was composed of the same uninteresting rocks. At two places, large sections of the 1,000-foot cliff had collapsed and deposited twenty- and thirty-foot-high segments on the shore. Pools of water lay along the base of the cliff. We saw a few seals off to the east and felt a chilling wind from the same direction as we started back westward along the shore. Along the way, we passed below a huge cave in the face of the cliff that opened a couple of hundred feet above the sea. It appeared to be about 100 feet across and thirty feet high, with a snowdrift carpeting the entrance. The imperative of getting back to camp to keep a radio schedule, however, kept us from climbing up to it.

Our trail took us along a seal track, and we followed it for two miles before meeting the seal that had probably made it. Considerably agitated by our approach, the creature breathed heavily and moved with great energy, darting first toward us and then away from us until we passed, trying repeatedly to force its way down tide cracks to get into the water. I watched it for a couple of hours after we had passed, and it lay stone still after its anxiety had subsided. There is little doubt that we had frightened it—the only occasion that I ever saw this reaction from a Weddell.

On 18 November there was no wind and clouds were down to 300 feet, with the temperature high at 38°F. We did not succeed in contacting the base. After juggling the tubes around we finally got the radio working, but Layther's listening watch was over so I got no reply to my call. We updated our notes and packed specimens before starting off toward the mainland to the north. Before we travelled a mile, we met Russell and Davies with the two dog teams. We stopped to have a chat and to hear all the base's news while warding off a playful pair of pups named Rebecca and Rachel who had replaced Dainty pending her *accouchement*.

Russell and Davies's trip back to the base had been good, but they had been severely sunburnt in the brilliant sunshine. They had followed the north coast of Vega Island past Cape Well Met to camp beside Devil Island and the penguin rookery that Nordenskjöld's men discovered in 1903. After replenishing the supply of fresh eggs, they had crossed the northern extremity of the Crown Prince Gustav Channel to the mainland coast, which they followed for a short distance before running into the foul weather we also had experienced on the 13th. The two lightly loaded teams had made good time while

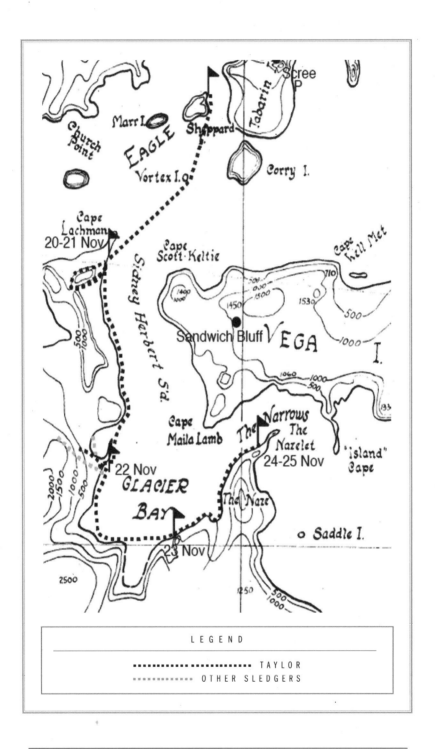

Map 14. The second sledging journey, 20–25 November 1945.

Figure 52. Photograph from Sheppard Island of Vortex Island (foreground) and
James Ross Island (background), n.d.

following a rather erratic course.[3] Returning to Sheppard Island with heavy
loads, they had passed View Point by a mile before camping beside some seals,
and romped along the rest of the way in fine fettle up to the point where we met.
After arranging for Russell to meet us with a team that afternoon to hand back
the rock specimens we hoped to collect, he and Davies continued on toward
the camp while Lamb and I proceeded on our way toward a high, bare, rounded
hill on the mainland that we called Bald Head. In the meantime, the sky had
cleared and it was bright and warm.

On skis we made good time across the two-mile-wide channel, arriving at the
headland at about 1:00 p.m. and ascending the hill to an altitude of 400 feet. It
was largely composed of morainic deposits and there was an immense variety of

3.   Editors' note: Davies and Russell arrived at Hope Bay on 14 November, unloaded their
eggs and specimens, reloaded, and proceeded back to Sheppard Island on 17 November.
See diary entries for these dates in: Taylor, "Operation Tabarin Official Journal, 1944–46,"
Taylor fonds, UMA, MSS 108 Box 5 File 1.

volcanic rocks. We soon amassed a weighty collection, but Lamb was disappointed at the limited variety of lichens. In the brilliance of the day, however, we had an excellent view of the northerly ramparts of Tabarin, Sheppard, and Marr Islands, and we took bearings on each (as well as a series of photographs) before descending the hillside to keep our rendezvous with Russell. After loading the sledge, the dogs made fast time over the hard surface of the sea ice and we came upon Davies butchering a seal off the northeast tip of Sheppard Island. The dogs willingly hauled a load of the dripping meat back to the camp for their supper, as well as for our own.

The same day, we read a letter from Flett that told us all the local base news. In the evening, I made a good contact with Layther to pass back to Flett word of the dog teams' arrival. We were about 200 miles distant from Port Lockroy, and conversed as easily as one would over a city telephone.

We did not start out on the day that followed because the weather looked so unpromising, but it was not a waste. We had ordered a bivouac tent by radio, and set it up on the snow slope above our camp. Then we moved into it all the stores that we were not taking with us on our initial trip, including the three boxes of specimens we had assembled since Russell and Davies's trip to Eagle House. We kept out twenty days of supplies.

On the 20th, we set out from Sheppard Island for our trip into the Erebus and Terror Gulf. Clouds enclosed our island's 500-foot summit, which I ascended to retrieve the big camera. There was no wind, and the temperature was about −10°F. We swung out over a good surface onto the sea ice at 11:00 that morning and headed for Vortex Island. Again we found the hummocky sea ice (which we had encountered in September) to be well covered, and the dogs made light of their heavy loads over the firm and crusted surface. Within two hours of our departure we approached the summit of Vortex Island, enshrouded in mist.

We heard the squawks of penguins along the slopes that banked the east end of the island long before we actually caught sight of them. Between 300 and 400 birds nested there, covering plenty of eggs. We collected about four dozen eggs. Davies was the most adept at gathering them, for he quickly evolved a very workmanlike technique for the job. Warily putting one hand down near the unsuspecting sitting penguin's tail, he quickly and firmly grasped its tail while gently upending the bird so that it slithered forward off the high nest more or less on its chin. Before the penguin regained its dignity, Davies quickly whipped the eggs off the nest into a spare mukluk. Most of the birds seemed to accept the loss philosophically, but one of them was quite upset and pecked at Davies's

Figure 53. Fossil splinters of wood in fossil valley near Cape Lachman, 21 November 1945.

legs and then at the bootful of eggs. Davies beat a wary retreat, muttering Welsh imprecations upon the culprit's head.

We had not stopped at Vortex Island principally to collect penguin eggs. We arrived, instead, to collect the dump we established there in early August that included the boat tarpaulin and its spreaders, the .22 rifle, the sledge repair box, and the ski skins. The great boulder above the little cache was easy to find, as was the boat tarpaulin we had left to cover the articles. We had used some heavy boulders to weigh down the margins of the tarpaulin, and melted snows froze around them so that the entire cache was almost one solid mass firmly clamped in the ice. We broke up the boulders that we had used as weights and picked away at the ice with knives and axes without respite, but three hours passed before our combined efforts freed our effects from the grasp of Vortex Island. It was impossible to avoid making holes in the tarpaulin, and Davies later counted sixty-five perforations. Throughout the entire operation, the penguins kept up a continual noisy objection to our depredations, their nests being but a few feet away.

The tarpaulin was extremely heavy due to the many pieces of ice that still adhered to it, but we added the stores to our sledge loads and were away at 3:45 p.m. We headed southwest toward Ross Island at a point just to the south of Cape Lachman. Large patches of the snow were covered with a light brown coating of rock dust—a substance that we even encountered several miles distant from the nearest land, where high winds had obviously transported the deposits. The surface of the sea ice became a hard-crusted snow, but there were many large *sastrugi* that indicated the terrific sweep of the wind along this channel. We spotted more than twenty seals scattered about the ice over the course of our day's travel.

We were several miles beyond Vortex Island when an agitated lone penguin that had been following us eventually caught up and may be said to have attacked the Big Boys team. A terrific altercation ensued, in the course of which a few feathers drifted through the air. Strangely enough it was Colonel, rather than the penguin, that came out the worse for wear. The latter apparently felt that honour lost from the theft of the eggs was more than satisfied and dignifiedly strutted back the several miles toward the rookery on Vortex Island.

When approached from a distance, Cape Lachman has the appearance of a high, broad, precipitous headland that is quite bold and massive in extent. As our little procession neared this impressively black and monumental feature, however, it became apparent that a low, rocky tongue extended from its base for probably a mile or two distant in a northeasterly direction. This black, rocky foreland, largely snow-free, ascended toward its tip at 400 feet and ended in precipitous cliffs. As we approached the broad col made by this curious edifice, our good travelling surface changed to glare ice and made our skis completely unmanageable (and unnecessary). A flooded tide crack gave way when we were nearly on the shore and our sledge lodged for a few moments in the water. We succeeded in freeing it with little difficulty and drove the teams up onto a long, low, snow-filled valley, camping 100 yards inshore at 7:00 p.m. Having made eleven miles despite the difficulties we had encountered at Vortex Island, it did not take long to get the tents up between the muddy shoulders of the valley formed of morainic stones. The sun broke through for the first time during the day and gave us a pretty view of Corry Island as we looked down the little valley.

In the morning it took us a short time to send off a couple of signals to Layther, for no conversation could be held because the receiver did not work. The day was dull with a slight breeze from the east as three of us set off to inspect the northerly tip of Ross Island. Davies stayed with the dogs at the camp and began the dispiriting task of repairing the tarpaulin. Lamb left the camp first and headed north toward the inclined plane that rose to the headland over the tip of Cape Lachman. He says in his diary that "in places on this stony expanse there was moderate vegetation consisting of a dominant moss and a number of lichens, and I made a representative collection, and took a sample of the agglomerate rock which crops out here and there." The "moderate vegetation" that Lamb described would be all but indiscernible to most people, but his sharp eyes made his trip successful.

Half an hour after Lamb left, Russell and I set off on foot[4] southward along the west shore of Sidney Herbert Sound. Below the high, broad cliffs that constituted Cape Lachman's most conspicuous landmark, the wide col that connected it to the tip of the cape spread out into a broad coastal shelf. The surface was comprised of small fragments of angular rocks interlarded with a high proportion of mud, and though the stones within this soft matrix were quite variegated, the same basalts and tuffs that we saw so often were much more common.

As we went south, we rose along a gentle incline with little to no snow. About half a mile inshore at an altitude of 150 feet above the sea, we walked past a little pond measuring a couple of hundred yards long and perhaps fifty yards across. The lake contained some ice, but water ran freely from it in little rivulets toward the sea. In one place a steep cavity cut through the muddy soil to a depth of about fifteen feet. Near this lake we found a couple of poorly preserved fossil casts made by a shell, but they were by no means common at this point.

We were about two miles south of our camp when, after climbing over a couple of rocky hills about 300 feet high, we found ourselves standing on the verge of a broad valley measuring about a mile across. At a distance, the slopes along the far side of the valley seemed to be of a markedly different character than any other outcrops we had seen on this sector of Ross Island: they were light yellow in colour and, in places, were well stratified horizontally. We encountered the nearest of these outcrops before reaching the base of the valley, and found a very light, sandy soil on its surface that was covered with a layer of black pebbles and small boulders. I split open a couple of nodular stones that I found, but there was no sign of fossils within them. Shortly afterward, I came upon a small outcrop of limestone and found many well-preserved traces of plant remains within some

---

4.   Editors' note: Taylor's manuscript says that he and Russell "set off" but Lamb's journal entry for the 21st mentions that they made this trip without the sledges (Lamb, "Operation 'Tabarin' (Base A) Official Diary," BAS, AD6/1A/1944/B).

of the pieces that I split. Yet there seemed to be no identifiable leaves. Strewn over the ground were six- to eight-inch-long fragments of fossilized wood with clearly discernible annular rings. Some of these fossils and fossil surfaces were exposed in places, and their near-white, weathered exteriors showed the details much better than the freshly broken rocks. At various places there were lengths of small fossilized trees measuring several feet in length, but they were broken into fragments not more than six inches in length and many splinters lay beside the little trunk. At another place among the splinters of fossilized wood were pieces of fossil studded with attractive quartz-like, lightly tinted purple crystals that were up to a half-inch in diameter.

I found one poorly preserved fossil gastropod, similar to those common at Snow Hill Island. We also found other fossils that we thought were corals and sponges but were unable to positively identify. We left this rich little area and headed into the valley westward, crossed an eight-foot wide stream that flowed freely along the valley's bed, and climbed a long snow slope to another morainic deposit at an altitude of 400 feet. Here, we found many fossilized fragments of plant remains that seemed to have leached out of the sandstone. There were also many spherical nodules, up to about six inches in diameter and composed of a hard, dark grey, fine-grained rock that we could not recognize. In many instances, the nodules were neatly fractured into two pieces of equal size. Their cores contained some well-worn fossilized organic material that stood out in well-marked relief to a depth of half an inch, with dirt and sand filling many of these open-cored hemispheres. I broke one of these into two parts and was surprised to find that the fossil portion was filamentous. Perhaps most astonishing to the uninitiated was the fossil's green colour. Searching about until I found a complete nodule, I broke it open and found the same green colour—though the fossil was quite unrecognizable to us.

By this time, we could not carry back all that we had collected, so we selected about fifty pounds of samples and started back to the camp by a slightly different route. We slid down a steep, sandy slope and dug into it without finding any stones or fossils. This led us to conclude that the surface weathering of the slope face had caused the sand to be carried away by the high winds, and left a concentrated accumulation of stones and fossils upon its surface.

There was little of interest on our return trip to the camp and we travelled at a considerably higher elevation than our outgoing route. As we descended the slope below the cliffy headland, we enjoyed a good view to the northwest and saw no sign of the two islands that Nordenskjöld called Herrström and Red Islands. We concluded that they were considerably misplaced from the positions on his map and were, as we had for some time suspected, the two that we had named Long Island and Monument Island during our earlier journey.

There was plenty to do in the evening as Lamb and I annotated and wrapped up the several-hundred scientific specimens that we had gathered over the course of the day. We packed them in snow in two large tin dog-pemmican boxes. They would remain at the campsite until a later date. The wind from the southwest began to blow an hour before midnight, but when we arose on the morning of 22 November it was a warm, cloudy day that was almost dead calm. Breaking camp, our two teams ran down the gentle slope onto the sea ice and started southward into Sidney Herbert Sound, paralleling the tracks along the shoreline Russell and I had made the day before. A couple of hours of travelling brought us opposite the yellow brown hillsides where we made our fortunate find the day before. The valley cut deeply into this side of the island and rose steeply up in the distance almost to the ice cap lodged above it: the outer fringe of Mount Haddington's mantle.

About a mile beyond this valley we passed close to a well-stratified outcrop of mudstone and clay. I skied over to it and looked at the lower slopes. In less than five minutes, I came away with three good ammonite casts, some yellow quartz-like crystals, and small fragments of wood that I found after breaking open a nodule. Curiously enough, the fossilized wood was brown and seemed to possess no more strength than one would expect from a piece of dried wood. The beds from which these pieces came extended about a mile to the south. Nearby sat a little shelf of snow, a feature that was rare along this shore. We decided then and there that Lamb and I would return to this point for a few days to more fully investigate the area.

After travelling six miles over a surface of glare ice, with few interruptions, we ate lunch on a gravelly shore from which low hills rose gradually up toward the escarpment to the west. We found a few fossil shells along with some wood and coral, but not enough to entice us to remain. We started out over a snow surface that had a fairly firm crust but lacked the strength to support one's weight "barefoot," as Davies called it when one wore neither skis nor snowshoes. The sledge did not sink, so the change in surface did not delay the dogs, and there were still odd patches of bare ice where they made really good time. We approached a headland to the south of where we ate lunch just as a strong southwesterly wind blew up. It was not cold, however, and the sun came out to shine and spread its cheering influence.

Rounding the point toward the west, we encountered a large, seven-mile-deep body of water that we named Glacier Bay.[5] As we struck a more westerly course, a large, broad valley opened to our view in the northwest. The massive face of the escarpment towered on either side of the valley. We continued on our course, headed for the end of the bay, but the wind increased and great grey clouds came up from the southwest. With the wind blowing about force 7, we turned inshore to camp at half past five. We ran onshore but could not find sufficiently deep snow upon which to set the tent, so we returned to the sea ice where we found two-foot-deep soft and sugary snow that had obviously been much deeper at an earlier date (perhaps like that which we had encountered in the Erebus and Terror Gulf in September). Even in the high wind, the warmth of the sun made setting up camp a pleasant task. We had travelled about ten miles that day.

The sun shone thinly through the morning haze of 23 November, with the temperature just below freezing. A massive formation of dark rock rose up deep in Glacier Bay that, similar to Corry Island, was capped with ice and had a small glacier ribboning down its face. To the south of this mountainous mass, three small, steep glaciers streamed down from Mount Haddington's ice cap. A broad glacier spilled down onto the sea from an ice face along the southeast shore, to the east of a long cliff of brown rock adjacent to this corner of the bay. Still farther to the east, the land rose up past a series of hills to the huge brown mound-like mass of the Naze. In the distance beyond, we could make out the outlines of the rocky, island-like eminences near Vega Island, the details of which had been enshrouded from our view during the driving blizzard that we had encountered on our hungry homeward march in September.

Our party once again split up. Near our camp on Ross Island, the valley to the northwest that we had seen the previous day stretched forth enticingly. Russell set off on skis to inspect it with the prospect of viewing Graham Land across the Crown Prince Gustav from the eminence of its summit. Lamb and I set forth to examine a series of low snow-free hills that rose up from a flat foreshore a mile or two inland. We climbed a gentle slope for several hundred yards and found ourselves standing upon the edge of a long, gravelly spit that

---

5. Editors' note: Today, known as Croft Bay. The bay is actually a different size and shape than Taylor's description and map recount.

stretched out about a mile from the mainland to enclose a lagoon-like embay-ment. It was almost circular in shape, ice-covered, and about a mile and a half across. We separated at this point; Lamb crossed the west end of the bay head-ing northward while I followed the spit westward in search of fossils. The spit rose to a summit of 100 feet and had the appearance of a raised beach, for the stones were all rounded, well-worn, and were generally a dark colour with little sand on the surface. Toward the west, a series of low hillocks, separated by rivu-lets of clear water, cut into it. I found little in the way of fossils, but returned with some dried white alga for Lamb, which he accepted as evidence that this part of Glacier Bay might have been open in relatively recent years.

I returned to camp about noon, just as Russell returned from the north. He had been unsuccessful in his mission to reach the summit, which was far-ther off than it had appeared. This deception of distances was an unfortunate feature of our experience in this area throughout the winter, and had caused us to revaluate our plans on several occasions. Davies had been patiently mend-ing the boat tarpaulin, and Lamb returned a little later. After losing the sun and eating lunch, we moved off just before 2:00 p.m., following the shore in a general southwesterly direction.

The land approached our course in a broad, low foreshore for about a mile and then swept away in a receding curve, backed by another series of low, black hills whose summit was a great, jagged, flat-topped peak. To the north of the broad, black formation at the head of the bay sat an outcrop of reddish rock different in appearance from its surroundings. I climbed up several hundred feet, over a huge pile of sharp-edged, large blocks of a moraine to examine it. It proved to be the same sort of basalt tuff that we saw frequently in these areas. In this particular case, the tuff largely predominated the rock's content.

We passed by a long low point that jutted out from the black mountain as we made our way across the end of the bay. Beyond this point, the bay indented deeply into the glacial face of the island for another mile, the narrow glaciers at the head of this indentation frequently roaring down many hundreds of feet in colossal icefalls, even as we passed. We did not enter this fjord-like feature but cut across its mouth toward the southerly shore of Glacier Bay, then headed for the east end of the long, brown cliff that lined this part of the shore. There were a few seals about, and Russell and Davies dispatched one for our use that night while Lamb and I continued our survey of the island.

We had travelled nearly all day over glare ice interspersed with small patches of snow, for the surface of the sea was almost devoid of other ice inclusions. The dogs made easy work of this good surface, and I could not keep ahead of them. Skis and snowshoes were useless in this scenario and our sealskin boots made walking difficult. Consequently, the dogs had to stop frequently to allow me to keep in advance of the sledge.

As we approached the end of the brown cliff, I attempted to get inshore for a rock sample. The shore ice was badly broken up for the last fifty yards and, after going through large tide cracks into deep water a couple of times and wading through the water flooding the shoreline, I turned back without it. Time and again we had noticed that these dark, northward-facing cliff surfaces seemed to absorb the sun's heat so readily that the sea ice along the base invariably flooded.

East of the brown cliff, an old glacier measuring half a mile across (that was much shattered by internal pressure) descended gently to the sea, its snout protruding several hundred feet into the sea ice to terminate in low ice cliffs thirty to forty feet high. Along its foot, pools of green saltwater flooded the surface of the sea. Many jagged lumps of ice, doubtless calved off the glacier, littered below its face.

Russell's stores were visible below a high dark cliff, dumped on the sea ice at the base of the outcrop half a mile east of the glacier. He had left Davies on the ice to butcher a seal in the middle of the lake, ventured to the camp, unloaded the sledge, and then returned to Davies with the dogs to haul the meat to camp. There was little snow on the glare ice along the coast, but the camp sat on one of the largest snow patches in the area. It was difficult to set up camp where snow was scarce, and we had to collect it from some distance around the tent before we had enough to weigh down its apron. It was 8:30 p.m. when Lamb and I stopped the sledge, and we had set up the two tents by the time Russell and Davies returned with the meat. Davies had cut the entire seal, less the blubber, into fifteen pieces weighing about fifteen to twenty pounds each: one for each dog and one for the men. Whether two of the dogs were given smaller portions than the others, I do not know, but Colonel and Hobbs ate all of their portions before morning. After consuming a heavy meal of tender seal steak, we turned in at 11:00 p.m. with no wind and plenty of daylight to see by.

The sun's heat was intense as it shone thinly through the low clouds the following morning, 24 November. We had specimens to wrap up and diaries to write, so we did not get off to an early start. Russell gathered some of the rock from the base of the cliff before we got away at 11:00 a.m., passing a seal by a tide crack within a half mile of our camping site. I went ashore a little farther on, as our course paralleled it, and climbed up to a gravel beach thirty feet above the sea to see agglomerate hills that rose beyond. Two small streams ran down from the hills into the sea, the beds of which were covered with a leathery-looking pink-coloured alga. The beach impounded a small pond of open water that extended a couple hundred feet in diameter. Descending again onto the glare ice of the sea, we more or less followed the shore of Ross Island by threading a course through hummocky pieces of ice, and then changed course to a more northerly direction toward the south end of the Naze that now loomed ahead of us. We followed this new course for half a mile until we saw a narrow bay at the base of the brown cliffs that indented so deeply into the land that it might have been the entrance to a fjord. Accordingly, we altered course again, this time to the southeast, and pulled up onto a beachy shore for lunch. A fresh easterly wind sprang up and it became decidedly cool.[6]

For several days prior to this my feet had been strangely sore. They were very stiff and painful first thing in the morning, and I hobbled along for a couple of hours using a ski stick for support. It was rather puzzling, for we had endured no cold weather, but I presume it was a legacy of the frostbite I suffered on the previous trip.

Once more we headed northward for the Naze passing close inshore below the uniformly brown cliffs that rose to 500 or 600 feet for two or three miles. The ice along this part of the coast was particularly rotten. Deep snow had once lain over it, but most of it had melted away and the remainder was dirty from an accumulation of rock dust. The melting snow from the land had poured over this to form a false crust of ice through which our feet occasionally plunged into the six to twelve inches of water that lay on top of the sea ice.

By this time it began to snow lightly, which cut our visibility down to the immediate coast. There was almost no snow along the land. At the end of the massive rock pile that formed the Naze, the cliffs merged into a low foreshore, above which the brown hills rose up, decorated with the most grotesque forms of geological architecture standing in relief. Our course gently turned to the

---

6.   Author's note: While walking over the snow-covered beach that filled the broad flat valley, I was surprised to find a little stream that was about ten feet across and a foot deep, running full bore at a rate of several feet per second. It was apparently fed by a glacier that filled the upper end of the valley. Lamb found the decaying carcass of a dead seal on a mud flat a quarter of a mile inland.

east as we progressed another couple of miles and ran alongside a high green-ish-grey hill that presented a steep cliff face to the north. A small valley rose up toward a trough of snow that separated this hill from a similar but shorter counterpart, after which the land dropped to a low, flat plateau about fifty feet above the sea. I found a poor camping spot along the fifty-foot mud bank that formed the shoreline of this plateau. While I waited for the dog teams to make the last couple hundred yards to shore, I picked a dozen or so fossils, including gastropods, the spine of a sea urchin, and a variety of shells, out of the bank.

Despite the scarcity of snow, we set up the tents, and water seeped into a couple of holes that we chopped into the dirty ice along the shore. I gave Layther a brief call on the transmitter, for I had still not succeeded at getting the receiving set to function. A heavy snow fell, rapidly covering the fossiliferous plain above us with its white tarpaulin. It was, as Lamb called it, a "dull, depressing day."[7]

---

7.   Editors' note: Taylor is quoting from Lamb, "Operation 'Tabarin' (Base A) Official Diary," 24 November 1945, BAS, ADG/1A/1944/B.

CHAPTER NINETEEN

East Ross Island

ON THE MORNING OF 25 NOVEMBER WE LAY ENCAMPED at a point that could not have been far from where the Swedish South Polar Expedition's vessel *Antarctic* sailed into the mouth of Sidney Herbert Sound and ran aground in early November 1902. Under these circumstances, we were not anxious to head blindly into a snowstorm along the east coast of Ross Island until we examined the sea ice conditions. Consequently, we spent the day laid up. The snowstorm continued and we did not climb up a hill behind the tent to look eastward over the sea from an elevation of 250 feet until the 26th. When we did, we were gratified that there was ice in Erebus and Terror Gulf fast for as far as we could see. Toward the southeast, past a low snow point of Ross Island, Cockburn Island stood out clearly. There was no sign of open water anywhere, so we laid plans to continue our journey.

On our way back to camp on the 26th, we made a quick search of the little plateau for fossils. We found few because, despite considerable melting, snow still covered much of the ground. This wide plateau connected the northerly tip of the Naze to a high, rocky hill that had all the appearance of an island to the north. On this flat were a series of small, open ponds and on the south side of the largest pool we found a deposit of shells that were barely ossified, as though they had recently risen from the sea (despite being twenty or thirty feet above it). We added to our collection good specimens of fossil wood, bivalve shells and casts, as well as gastropods. Lamb discovered sections of a huge ammonite; its short sections were about three inches in diameter and its ribbing and iridescent colouring were still distinctly visible. From our experience, the richest deposits of these fossils lay within twenty or thirty feet of the sea and the hunting seemed best along the face of the mud bank of the northwest shore above our camp.

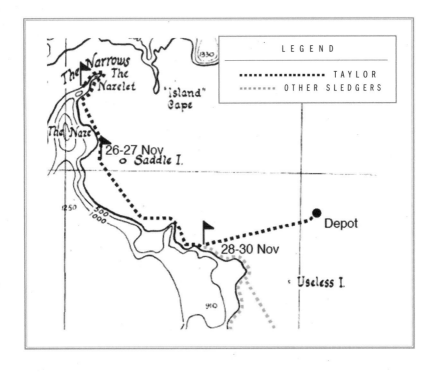

Map 15. The second sledging journey, 26–30 November 1945.

The poor visibility prevented us from seeing Vega Island, but we were satisfied with the ice conditions and decided to move. Because we would return to the same point, we packed ten days of supplies and left behind some food, dog pemmican, and instruments. It was nearly 3:00 p.m. when we set out into the heavy snowfall. The dogs made good time with the light loads. As we passed to the west of the rocky hill north of our previous camp, Russell named it the "Nazelet," and Lamb thought he saw another outcrop of the columnar basalt that he had previously found on Sheppard Island. Here we had the best view to date of a typical geological section of this part of the country: brown tuff on the upper part of the slope overlying a broad hand of basaltic material, and a grey-green sedimentary deposit of loose material at the base. We did not stop to examine it since we intended to return to do some collecting at a later date, and because we did not want to weigh down our sledges with rock specimens as we approached a deep snow area.

Figure 54. Dagger Peak, 6 December 1945.

We turned sharply eastward around the tip of the Nazelet, which rose in a steep slope to a rocky eminence. Proceeding southward past its east side, we saw a solitary, sharp hilltop that a little valley separated from the tip of the Nazelet. We called this summit "Dagger Peak." Toward the east, these hills tapered off into a long low spit. We kept close inshore over rough and rotten ice that our feet occasionally penetrated until they hit the harder surface below. The large number of bergy bits and hummocky ice indicated the presence of shallow water for some distance offshore, and we surmised that the *Antarctic* may have gone ashore near this spot more than forty years before.

At a place where we stopped, I examined part of a raised beach that paralleled the shore about twenty feet above the sea and 100 feet inland. Its lower part was composed of very fine sand, and a horizontal band of dried, bleached, white algae separated this section from the pebbled beach. There were also shells along this level that seemed similar to the ones I had found earlier in the morning near the pond beside our last camp. Their species, Lamb remarked, were of quite recent origin. Nordenskjöld's old maps show the Nazelet as an island well separated from the larger Naze to the south.[1] These two features are now joined by the large, flat, beach-like area where we found these modern shells, but it seems probable that the sea covered it four decades before. The shortest route that Nordenskjöld could have taken when he returned with Andersson from Cape Well Met to Snow Hill Island would have brought him very close to both these features, so it is most unlikely that Duus would have mistaken this flat to be sea ice. This conclusion, when coupled with the shells we found, strongly suggests that an elevation took place at this point within the last forty-two years.

We continued south and crossed a water run that had eroded a course about four feet deep and three feet wide into the sea ice. One of the dogs fell into this running water and had to be extricated. The pup bitch, Rebecca (by this time known as Becky), refused the jump and had to be thrown across. Not long after, we passed below the hill where we had stood earlier in the morning to view the sea ice. The broad beach curved westward, passing a small morainic islet, and ran into the brown rock cliffs that formed the shore along this sector of the coast. A few miles farther south, we stopped to examine another raised beach, which presented a six-foot eroded vertical face on the seaward side. The face was mostly composed of rock dust that may have been an aeolian deposit from the Naze above it. A foot below the surface of this laminated face, an even seam measuring about a foot thick contained shells similar to those we had found earlier in the day at two places on the Naze.

The red-cliffed shore continued for another mile, turning sharply inland toward a deep valley that extended inland for some distance and which consisted of a high formation of black rock on the south side. Once past the seaward outcrop of this rock, the character of the coast changed completely from the bare, almost snow-free rocks that we had encountered into a heavily glaciated coast that descended to the sea in steep slopes shredded with crevices.

To the left of our course lay a peculiar saddle-backed island to which we appended the obvious name "Saddle Island."[2] It had two high summits with steep, black scree slopes descending on all sides. Under these slopes lay horizontal stratified rock. We did not deviate our course toward the island, as it was another point that we intended to visit upon our return north.

We instead headed for a distant series of high, black cliffs and wove through a small series of hummocky bergs when Russell spotted a seal about a quarter

---

1. Editors' note: See Introduction.

2. Editors' note: Today known as Humps Island.

of a mile to starboard of our course. We camped near it, and the dogs had "a good feed," as Davies called it; he thought as much of their stomachs as he did of his own. Much to our surprise, the thick, fresh snow had hardly impeded our progress that day because there was a hard bottom to it with a good crust. Visibility to the north had been poor. To the south, however, we could clearly see Cockburn Island; there was blue sky to the east, and cascades of stratus clouds enveloped the cliffs of Ross Island beside us. The temperature was 19°F.

The next day the snow continued to fall heavily, obscuring our landmarks and carpeting the surface of the sea ice to a depth of nine inches. We spent the day plotting survey notes, unsuccessfully trying to repair the radio, and butchering another seal. In addition, Davies devoted more time to repairing the tarpaulin. Russell tried to fish through a crack beside a grounded iceberg but was surprised to encounter another layer of ice four feet below the eighteen-inch-thick surface layer. Unsurprisingly, he caught no fish.

There was no wind on 28 November and visibility was good, though the sky was overcast. Before we left the camp at 10:30 a.m., Davies buried all of the remaining dog food beneath a seal pelt in case we needed it on our return journey. The dogs moved along at a good speed despite the deep snow. The sun came out for a time and made the atmosphere hot and sultry. The snow softened and tended to ball up on our skis and snowshoes.

At 1:30 p.m., we were below black cliffs of the same basalt tuff that we had found elsewhere. The shore swung sharply eastward, and we altered course to suit. To the south, a small glacial shelf terminated in calving ice cliffs of undulating heights up to fifty feet. Except for one small and narrow glacier, this glacial shelf was fed entirely by calvings from the ice cap of the cliffs that encircled it. These frequent and thunderous deposits dropped from 400 to 800 feet above the shelf. The small tongue of ice formed by the shelf was forced out into the sea ice, forming a ring of pressure ice around the snout.

As we crossed this ridge, the dogs displayed hesitancy. Davies, Russell, and I in turn broke through into knee-deep water and filled our mukluks. Davies went the deepest of the three of us and experienced some difficulty extricating himself because the skis that he wore snubbed themselves on the underside of the ice. There was a lead at this point about eight feet across, and after having such difficulty getting the first sledge across the pressure ice, the second one swung wide and followed around it while the first sledge returned without difficulty.

During the first crossing of this lead, Shaggy slipped his trace and got loose. He was well named, for his thick coat hid his collar and harness, and he had a playful nature. A loose dog like Shaggy distracted the others from their work and added to our difficulties. Four seals lay within the ridge of pressure and Shaggy developed a lively game with two of them, racing around them and barking as the two seals rolled about to face him, snapping their jaws with ineffective clicks. We caught Shaggy as we got out onto the good ice again and, with a guilty but unsubdued look, he retook his place with the team.

Upon reaching Bullnose Point, which had snow petrels nesting near its 500-foot flat summit, we continued eastward toward the next point a few miles distant across a slight embayment. It began to snow, the wind changed to the south, and the temperature dropped almost immediately. The surface had steadily deteriorated all day, and our progress became slower and slower as the dogs waded belly-deep in the snow, with little footing on which to pull. Our boots were full of water and became so uncomfortably cold that I stopped to empty mine and wring out my socks.

In passing along this coast, we intended to try to locate the dump of stores we had abandoned on the Erebus and Terror Gulf in September (see Chapter 16). The dump's position was plotted on our chart, and our shoreline course passed closest to the east end of Vega Island at a bearing of 8° Magnetic. We had meant to continue down the coast that day and camp when we had such a bearing, but the falling snow obliterated our view of Cape Gordon. Consequently, when we rounded the next point and Russell said that he saw a seal, we decided to camp. The seal turned out to be a rock half-submerged in the snow, but the raw biting wind convinced us to camp anyhow at 7:30 p.m. The sun shone, and there was blue sky to the north, but the weather looked unsettled.

Half an hour after midnight, the sounds of great activity among the dogs awakened us. Looking out of the tent we saw that two of the pups from Russell's team, Rube and Rachel, had broken loose from their chains and were leading the other dogs on a merry chase that made the other animals vociferously envious. We hoped they might hole up somewhere and settle down, as the far end of our tethering line was particularly poorly anchored at this camp. Half an hour later, however, the ice axe that fixed the line withdrew from the crack in the sea ice, and Lamb and I got up to disentangle the mess. Russell tied up the two pups and gave us a hand, untangling the ball of wire, chains, ropes, and dogs. Lamb got a box of dog pemmican from the other sledge as an additional anchor for our tethering line. Before returning to bed, we took advantage of the improved visibility and I discovered that our bearing on Cape Gordon was the 8° we had wanted. Our stores should have lay dead offshore from our camp. We turned in again at 2:00 a.m.

After the disturbance of the night before, we slept in until nearly 8:00 in the morning. We found a clear, sunny day awaiting us that was ideal for searching on the sea ice for our stores. Water had underlain the deep snow when we crossed the Erebus and Terror Gulf in September with the temperature at −40°F. We consequently did not consider the sea ice to be of any great thickness. We were, moreover, about to sledge over a gulf that the *Antarctic* had sailed across forty years before. The prevailing southwest wind was offshore; we knew it could arise quickly and with little warning. For these reasons, we arranged our stores so that we would have sufficient equipment with us to live on a floe for a few weeks should we suffer the misfortune of being cast adrift through a storm. We took one tent, two bedrolls, one cooking outfit, three-quarters of our supply of paraffin, the remains of a box of rations, the radio, and all of our fish lines, guns, and ammunition. I measured off a bearing from the relative plot of our position and that of the stores dump, and we started off on 44° Magnetic, travelling toward the supposed position of our objective at 10:30 a.m.

Lamb went ahead on skis and the two teams followed with their light loads in his tracks. The surface was rather sticky but fairly firm; it was about three feet, six inches with slush in the bottom foot, and did not support one's weight without skis or snowshoes. The atmospheric temperature was a little below freezing. We went ahead for about two hours, checking bearings against the landmarks at every opportunity, and using the same points Russell had used to fix the site of the dump the previous September. A haze began to close in from the north, and we soon lost sight of Cape Gordon, just as we had all but attained our required bearing to it. Ross Island also began to fade from sight and Cape Gage was only faintly visible. It appeared as though Fate conspired against us when retrieving our stores; it enticed us out onto the sea ice just in time to hide all from our view.

Though we were now close to our estimated position about five miles offshore, I was no longer hopeful of success. On our left, a string of small bergs paralleled our course and appeared somewhat like those that had been near the dump. I searched the area as we passed by and spotted something dark on the surface. I reached for the glasses but it proved to be a seal or a black stone. At any rate, it was not our stores and my hope struck a new low. There seemed little point in going farther to search in vain through limited foggy visibility of less than a quarter of a mile.

Five minutes later another dark object to our left caught my eye. Thinking that the area was alive with seals, I took another look through the glasses. This time it did not look like a seal, but it was about a quarter of a mile away. Though one side of it seemed to have a slant more than a little like the leg of the tripod, I could not be certain. At my direction, Lamb cynically changed course toward it, and as we approached it became evident that we had found the dump with almost unbelievable ease.

A foot to eighteen inches of snow had fallen since we had visited the same point eighty-six days before. Four and a half feet down, a foot of slush sat over the sea ice. Little of the dump protruded above the snow. After Lamb took a photograph, we excavated it. The Big Boys sledge took most of the dump's stores; we piled the balance on our sledge and began our return to camp at 2:30 p.m. The dogs pulled well over the trail that we had made in coming out, and we were able to ride the loaded sledge almost all of the five miles back to camp. Even before we found the camp, the fog closed in so that all of the shore was completely invisible to us. Except for the hissing noise made by the sledge runners, the place was as silent as the grave. We made it back to camp by 5:00 p.m. The day's work gave us all a tremendous feeling of satisfaction. It was as though we had finished a job that we had been forced to leave uncompleted in September. Since we carried a few bottles of Mr. Bagley's celebrated beverage, left by the Argentines in 1903 on Seymour Island, we had a drink.

Amongst our acquisitions was the radio set we had carried so futilely on the first trip. It was exactly the same model as the sea-immersed one we carried on this journey, so I coupled the receiver of the former with the transmitter of the latter (for the sending apparatus of the former was supposed to be inoperative, and the receiver of the latter definitely did not work). Like many other marriages, this one was not a success: Layther boomed in on the new receiver, but his failure to reply to my signals indicated that he was not receiving us. Accordingly, I switched the receivers back and tried the September set as a unit. Much to my surprise, it worked perfectly, with nearly fifty percent more power than the other set had ever had. We made immediate contact at 7:30 p.m., and Layther passed us the news that the bitch, Pretty, had produced six pups at Hope Bay up to the late afternoon.

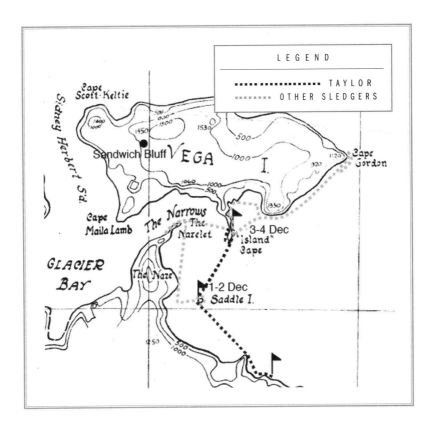

Map 16. The second sledging journey, 1–4 December 1945.

At this period we were forced to begin to turn night into day, a procedure that we continued until the end of this journey. The snow reflected a blinding light from the sun's rapidly increasing altitude. We wore snow goggles continuously to combat this problem but the sun did more than that. It also threw down heat that caused the snow to lose its strength, forcing us to labour along on a soft surface and make very poor travelling time. We still had crisp frosts at night, however, when the melted snow crust froze quite hard. Except for the decreased light, this latter circumstance created excellent travelling conditions, so we began to travel on this night surface.

On the morning of 30 November, Lamb and Russell left the camp at 3:30. My ailing feet prevented my accompanying them. They took the Odds and Sods along, and set out to extend our survey down to Cape Gage, the most easterly point on Ross Island where Nordensjöld's large-scale survey had ended. On their way, the group passed below another raised beach containing fossils. Just north of Cape Gage they crossed a wide bay, finding at the head of it active ice cliffs fed by glaciers that extended a long way inland. Lamb remarks that "At one place, there was a freshwater pond in a hollow, thinly iced over and with snow up to its edge, and in going out to get some water for drinking I inadvertently walked out onto snow-covered ice, and suddenly went in up to the middle when the ice gave way under my weight. I scrambled out quickly, and my windproof clothing fortunately prevented most of the water from soaking through; nevertheless, I had to keep moving briskly for an hour or so before I became dry again."

Lamb and Russell continued until they reached the cliffs of Cape Gage which, as Lamb wrote, "are almost vertical, with a talus slope at their base. . . . I made a small collection of lichens and a moss from the slope below the cliffs. We followed the high headland of Cape Gage round for about four miles before coming to the end of it; we had from here a good view of Cockburn, Seymour, and Snow Hill Islands, and it was 1400hrs. before we reached the end of the cape and started on our return journey."[3] The dogs pulled well on the homeward journey, despite a sticky surface, and one man was able to ride at all times. The tired pair of men returned to our camp after seventeen hours on the trail.

Meanwhile, Davies and I re-sorted our stores. We had a surplus, and made up a depot to leave things of little intrinsic value with which we could afford to dispense. In addition, we left a tin of paraffin that may someday be useful to someone travelling through this "Horrible and Terrible Gulf," as Davies referred to it. The depot lies atop a forty-foot knoll, below an old laminar ice face.

Not having caught sight of Lamb and Russell from a nearby hill that I had examined in the late afternoon, we became anxious on their account and prepared to follow their tracks if they did not return by 7:30 p.m. The sledge was half loaded and we had started to take down the tent when I caught sight of their figures half a mile away. We turned on both Primuses and had hot food and drinks ready for them within a few moments. The dogs were all but exhausted,

---

3.   Editors' note: Taylor's manuscript paraphrased this content from Lamb, but readers will appreciate Lamb's matter-of-fact account of this important point in the second sledge journey's progress.

Map 17. The second sledging journey, 5–11 December 1945.

and were barely able to pull the nearly empty sledge. Widgeon, a rather useless article, had been left behind when the team departed in the early morning and howled and moaned all day until his companions returned.

December came with another dull day, but we decided not to move until nightfall. Since the good radio set worked, calling up Layther at scheduled times was just like making a phone call. I had talked to Farrington at Deception Island for a short time, and we later learned that Donnachie picked our signals up at

Hope Bay very well and regularly once we were approximately fifty miles away. We spent the rest of the day trying to bank some sleep, but met little success.[4]

A light snowfall began to fill the air as we left camp at 8:15 that night. With the temperature just below freezing, a good crust formed on the snow and the teams pulled the sledges with little effort. We headed for the west end of Saddle Island, which we hoped to survey at about midnight before continuing on to the Naze where we had left our stores a week before. The snow began to fall more heavily, however, and we lost sight of land. Consequently, we travelled the last mile or so on a compass bearing. Forced to camp when we reached the island at 11:00 p.m., we drank a cup of cocoa before turning in at midnight while it was still quite light.

At noon the next day, Russell and Davies set out to survey the island while the weather was still dull and the temperature remained around freezing. Lamb and I started up toward the two summits to make collections. On the south side, the island flattens out to a little plateau with a surface largely composed of round, worn pebbles, no snow, and a great deal of sticky, ankle-deep mud. We found gastropod and ammonite fossils scattered almost everywhere on the lower slopes beneath the summits. Of the two summits, Lamb used an aneroid to determine that the westerly one is slightly higher at 615 feet. Skuas, terns, and gulls swam in a small pond a couple of hundred yards across on the southeast part of the island. The shore sloped down in steep mud banks. There was much disturbed ice close inshore and two-foot-deep pools of freshwater filled the hollows.

In the evening, Davies and Russell left us with the Big Boys to pick up some seal meat for dog food that we had left near Saddle Island on 26 November. From this point, they headed back to the Naze to leave the specimens, as well as some other things, and pick up the remaining ration boxes.[5] They planned to meet us the following morning at the island-like cape on the south side of Vega Island, where we had camped on 5 September during our first journey (see Chapter 16). Lamb and I broke camp an hour later and made a course for the same spot. It was a dull night, but visibility at sea level was good and the surface over the deep snow of this "bog" was firm and hard. We made the six miles in

---

4. Editors' note: A slightly longer version of this sentence is in Taylor, "Operation Tabarin Second Sledge Journey," 1 December 1945, Taylor fonds, UMA, MSS 108 Box 6 File 1.

5. Editors' note: The details of this sentence are augmented using Lamb, "Operation 'Tabarin' (Base A) Official Diary," 2 December 1945, BAS, AD6/1A/1944/B.

little over an hour, and set up our tent at the same spot that we had occupied once before. In the poor light of the late evening there seemed little to observe, for the passing scenery was flat and colourless. We heard the dogs barking as the other team arrived at 2:00 in the morning on 3 December.

I rose at 8:30 a.m. to assume the radio to talk with Layther and discovered that we had lost a bag containing our microphone. A heavy snowfall, however, reduced visibility to less than a mile, so we again spent the day catching up on sleep. That evening, Davies and I retraced the Odds and Sods' trail from the night before. The freshly fallen snow obscured our tracks, but after two and a half hours of difficult searching, we retrieved the bag. We returned to the camp at midnight, passing some seals to the south of our cape.[6]

Lamb and Russell left with the other team to start surveying the south shore of Vega Island to the east. A broad bay indented itself into Vega Island to the east of our camp. It was well-fed by glaciers from the north and the east, and the flat, white back of Vega rose well above all else. They passed a muddy beach two miles from camp where they found one gastropod and ammonite fossil. Then they crossed the bay toward the high headland at its easterly entrance and, after completing their survey as far as intended for the night, they returned to camp half an hour past midnight on 4 December. Davies and I, meanwhile, headed south and retrieved our radio kit bag. We went to bed just after midnight. The light snow continued to fall all day, and we slept fitfully.[7]

The two dog teams left the camp at 6:30 in the evening on 4 December. Lamb and Russell departed with the Odds and Sods to complete their survey to Cape Gordon at the east end of Vega Island, while Davies and I took the other team and headed to our camp at the south end of the cape in search of one of the seals that we had passed the day before. We crossed westward over the low spit, which seemed like another raised beach about twenty feet above the sea. On the old maps, this feature appeared as a channel separating the high headland to the south from Vega Island. Unlike the Naze, however, it is unlikely that this formation arose in the interval since the Swedish explorers sailed. They made their observations of it from the ship's deck and could have easily

---

6. Editors' note: We have added content from Taylor, "Operation Tabarin Second Sledge Journey," 3 December 1945, Taylor fonds, UMA, MSS 108 Box 6 File 1, to this paragraph.

7. Author's note: At 9:00 an on 4 December, I made contact with Layther, and we heard that our lead bitch Dainty had borne four dogs and five bitches: she was an excellent puller herself, so that the pups should prove useful another year.

mistaken this feature as we did when first we saw it, for we were within a mile of it before we could correct the mistaken assumption that a channel existed.

The visibility conditions that we experienced since leaving Cape Lachman on 22 November had been very poor indeed (see Chapter 18). Clouds usually covered the entire sky at an elevation below 1,000 feet, which obscured all the high land and made our survey work extremely difficult. We had been unable to see Mount Haddington for more than a few moments throughout the entire fortnight, and the sun seldom broke through at all. Photography was an uninspiring task, yielding poor results. On this occasion, however, the sun broke through over Sidney Herbert Sound and I took a few worthwhile photographs.

We followed the west side of the cape for a mile and a half, its rugged side rising to the sharp crest of the ridge of weathering brown agglomerate 500 or 600 feet above the sea. The black forms of the two seals we had seen the night before still lay off the tip of the cape. I stopped the dogs some distance off and anchored the sledge, but they were considerably agitated at the sight of Davies butchering the seal. It was only with difficulty that I restrained them from approaching it. We loaded the meat onto the sledge and returned to camp down the east side of the narrow cape where the base of the ridge broadened out into a shelf fifty feet above sea level and melting snows ran in rivulets that eroded deep clefts in the cliff-like walls. Back at camp by 10:30 p.m., we crept into our sleeping bags at midnight.

We were aroused at 4:00 a.m. by our dogs welcoming back the other team. The eight-mile coastline that Lamb and Russell had traced over the previous day consisted largely of medium-sized worn and inactive ice cliffs, with no embayments along its length. From Cape Gordon, they had viewed the northeastern part of the Trinity Peninsula, Sphinx, Uruguay, Irizar,[8] and Paulet Islands. They had also climbed up the precipitous slopes at the base of the cliffs where Lamb gathered a snow petrel's egg at an elevation of 150 feet. From this vantage point, no open water was visible. They returned to our camp without incident, having noticed a total of nine seals along that section of the coast.

After keeping a 9:00 p.m. radio schedule, I returned to bed and it was noon before we got up on 5 December. Lamb and I spent most of the afternoon examining the rocks in the vicinity. We broke camp at 8:30 in the evening and

---

8. Editors' note: The claim that they saw Uruguay and Irizar Islands seems a bit unlikely as these islands are small (compared to their surrounding islands) and are hundreds of kilometres away. Taylor transcribed this claim from Lamb's journal.

headed westward again as a cold, fresh breeze blew up from the northeast. It was a fairly clear evening and the sun shone through the clouds in many places. Cockburn Island and the north end of Seymour Island stood out with remarkable clarity thirty miles away.

We turned northward into an ill-defined bay and ran below a long, straight, flat-topped, and snow-capped formation of rock. It had exposed, vertical cliffs for several hundred feet near its top but was largely hidden by the scree slopes and hills that banked its base. Below obvious formations of basalt and agglomerate lay a greenish-grey exposure of a friable structure resembling the previous sedimentary deposits that we had encountered. The shore was half a mile distant, however, and I hesitated to interrupt the excellent progress the dogs were making over the hard, flat surface, for they were actually running with their loads with all hands riding but the trail-maker. It looked like an interesting spot, and might well repay a visit by someone else in the vicinity at a later date.

The shore bent sharply westward as we approached the laminar ice cliffs that filled the end of the embayment, and we ran along below the roughened slopes of Vega Island. The latter were decorated with *nunataks*, scree slopes, and high, rocky, ice-capped bluffs; the glacial cover of the island, with its many crevasses, flowed between these features. We camped on the sea ice just beyond the foot of a long moraine that stretched up into the interior of the island prior to midnight and checked our chronometer with the BBC pips.

It was broad daylight at midnight, but we wanted an astronomic fix near this area so we set up the instruments. The sky was clear, visibility was perfect, and the temperature was about 10°F. To the northeast, we picked up Sirius, and got another unidentifiable star in the southeast quadrant, but we could not find anything in the other two quadrants. We made an unsatisfactory fix with a bearing on Cockburn Island. The sun came over our horizon at 1:50 a.m. as we turned in to sleep.

We left the camp standing and departed with empty sledges to pick up the remaining stores we had left at the Naze ten days before.[9] The day was dull with a temperature well above freezing, and the surface of the snow became wet and sticky. Lamb and I dropped off at the Nazelet and intended to spend a short

---

9. Author's note: At 9:00 in the morning of 6 December, I went on the air to Layther at Port Lockroy. Our contacts had not been successful for a few of the previous mornings. His signals had been weak and at the time we attributed this deficiency to our location, but we subsequently believed that we might have had better results on a frequency other than the 6.3 m/c's we utilized.

time collecting before walking to the old campsite and meeting up with the others at the stores dump. When we went into the little valley that separates Dagger Peak from the summit of the Nazelet, we found such a rich bed of fossils that we got no farther.

Many fragments of long, sharp, tooth-like fossils that would have been about eight inches in a complete specimen were strewn all over the surface. They were an uncommon find and Lamb thought that they might be shark's teeth. We found many beautifully preserved specimens of ammonites and gastropods, pieces of fossil wood, as well as a variety of shells and their casts. One of our most striking finds was nautiloids that were as large as a small football. Some of these were complete while others were fractured into two hemispheres that displayed their interior "workings."

The sedimentary deposit that held our find was about 300 feet thick. Aside from the fossils that could be readily found on the surface, the muddy slopes also contained many hard nodules that frequently laid bare fossils when they were broken open. We also found casts of ammonites and shells higher up Dagger Peak in a formation of hard, red rock that we had not previously encountered and which we could not identify. We did not have time to examine the south side of this hill.

The Nazelet, a formation of rock about 400 feet high that tails off into the flats toward the Naze, is a mile long and half as wide. I took a panoramic photograph from its summit, though the light conditions were far from good. We could have spent a week at the place but Russell and Davies were returning with the stores, so we loaded our weighty collection onto the sledges. We left two fifty-pound boxes of dog pemmican that we did not need at the time above a small promontory on the northwest side of Dagger Peak, about fifty feet above the sea. The snow had, by this time, hardened and we were back at camp by 10:00 in the evening.

We then ate a hot meal, broke camp, and got away by half past one in the morning. In the calm, clear weather, the mercury dropped to 5°F—the lowest temperature we experienced on this journey. The dogs pulled well on the hard surface. The sun rose at 2:00 a.m. just as a heavy ground fog enveloped us. We were travelling along much the same course that we had blindly tried to keep during a furious blizzard in September. Heavy snow lay over the hills along the shore, and though we should have run over to investigate them, the temptation to keep going while we were making such good progress proved overwhelming.

Off the point of Cape Maila Lamb[10] at the southwestern tip of Vega Island, the ridges of hummocky ice still lay as they had three months before but the snow between them was deeper. The brown hills continued to fringe the west coast of Vega Island, but they receded from the shore and gave way to a large moraine as we moved north. To the north of the moraine, the island was almost completely glaciated, with smooth, rounded sweeps of white that were unbroken by crevasses. Outcrops of rock were only visible on the steep cliffs above the shore.

The sea ice became rougher as we approached the great, black rock that overlooked the place where we had butchered our dog Mutt in September. We turned west across Sidney Herbert Sound over a smooth, hard surface, arrived at the site where I had found the sedimentary outcrop on 22 November,[11] and set up camp at about 6:00 in the morning. At 9:00 I spoke to Layther for a few moments, and then we slept for five hours.

There was a great deal of work to be done preparing the hundreds of specimens we had collected for shipment back to Sheppard Island. We did not have enough packing materials to wrap each one individually, so we imbedded a large proportion of them in snow before packing them into four pemmican boxes. Layther had nothing for us at 6:30 p.m., and Russell and Davies left just before midnight to pick up the boxes we had left at Cape Lachman, and then to return with another three weeks' supplies from Sheppard Island after surveying part of Vega Island en route.[12]

It may seem strange that we spent so much time keeping radio schedules twice a day on our journey, but we were all anxious to learn as soon as possible about whatever arrangements were being made for our removal back to civilization. None of us relished the thought of a ship coming down to take the others away while we remained 100 miles or so distant from the base. Therefore, at each camp we removed the walkie-talkie from its canvas sack, hooked up the batteries, threaded the aerial through the tent ventilator, and suspended the other end from a ski. Occasionally, personal messages got through to us; I even received a message within a day of its original transmission from central Canada.

---

10. Editors' note: Today, this is known as Cape Lamb.

11. Editors' note: Taylor's manuscript incorrectly states that they reached the outcrop on 23 November.

12. Editors' note: The details of this sentence are augmented using Taylor, "Operation Tabarin Second Sledge Journey," 7 December 1945, Taylor fonds, UMA, MSS 108 Box 6 File 1.

On 8 December, the weather was again dull and the temperature high. To the south of our camp, I spent a disappointing morning examining the slopes of the hillside that had caused us to choose this spot for our camp but found nothing of great interest. Across the summit of the hill, I descended into a small valley and located a bed of fifteen-foot-thick conglomerate that contained clusters of fossil bivalve shells and a few gastropods and belemnites. The latter long, narrow, pencil-like things were difficult to extract in one piece from the comparatively hard rock. I also found shells with a fluted surface, but they also proved difficult to collect because they shattered at the slightest impact. Across the valley, which was marked by a snow-bridged stream, there was a similar bed that was about forty feet thick. Its shells were more diverse and much better preserved. It contained ammonites, and I also found a clear fragment of the shark teeth that Lamb had referred to at the Nazelet. The latter's fluted surface was exceptionally well defined.

In my mind, I related these beds to those discovered by Andersson high on Cockburn Island, but Lamb came along a few minutes later and dispelled this false impression. For almost an hour I split open piece after piece of rock in an effort to break out an intact belemnite, but each of them broke transversely. At last, I got one that was only attached by the thin end to a sizeable lump of rock. When I returned it to camp with the collection, I carefully carried this particular specimen in my hand. While crossing the snow-filled valley, however, my foot slipped deeply into a small crevasse and my hands involuntarily swung into the air. After walking a further 100 yards, I noticed that the belemnite had detached and was lost. There was no purpose in carrying the lump of rock farther and I arrived back at camp by 5:00 p.m. We took the survey camera up onto a hill to the south of the fossil beds two hours later and photographed the west end of Vega Island from a height of 400 feet. In descending, we found another small shell bed at 300 feet, but did not take the time to collect anything.

Davies and Russell returned to the camp from Sheppard Island at 4:30 in the morning on Sunday 9 December, and turned in for a sleep. Lamb and I walked north of the camp toward the place where Russell and I had made our earlier collection, and returned to the camp around the same time with nothing to show for our day's effort except an identifiable leaf from the deposit of plant remains that we had previously examined. We prepared to move at midnight, but Russell awakened us to report heavy snowfall and to advise against moving during such poor conditions. Tired as we were, he had no trouble in convincing us of this point, and we rolled over and went back to sleep. The snow continued throughout the next day, when a howling southwest wind also began to blow.

On 11 December, Russell, Davies, and I went back to the beds of shells that I had found a few days previously. We dug out another boxful of fossils including several good belemnites, ammonites, shells, and numerous gastropods. Davies also found what appeared to be a small tooth as well as something that looked like it had been a part of a deciduous leaf. We returned to camp for a couple more hours of sleep. After the sun had shone all day, the sky became overcast at 6:00 in the evening.

We left our campsite with the clouds showing signs of breaking to the north at 10:00 that night. The temperature was a little below freezing and we encountered a sticky surface for the first hour, but a cool breeze from the north seemed to freeze it within a few moments. From then on, the sledges slid along easily. We reached Cape Lachman about midnight as a dozen gulls wheeled screechingly over us. We left two boxes full of recently collected specimens that we would pick up on our return.[13]

---

13. Author's note: The gulls had their nests on a shelving moraine to the north of the Cape. Davies tested an egg, but it had been laid too long before to be appetizing.

CHAPTER TWENTY

West Ross Island

IT WAS JUST PAST MIDNIGHT ON 12 DECEMBER when we left Cape Lachman to begin examining the west side of Ross Island. It was daylight but dull. The sky to the north had cleared, but a low cloud swept toward us from the east and completely filled the Crown Prince Gustav Channel. We watched it envelop Corry Island as we ran beneath the black-brown agglomerate cliffs of Cape Lachman that rise steeply for several hundred feet above the sea along the island's northwest side. The shore swept into a shallow bay to the south, where there were many bergy bits and pressure ridges. The snow surface that we travelled over was so hard that the heavily loaded sledges scarcely left a track.

Low, snow-free hills surmounted the shores of this bay and led into a high valley that indented itself deeply into the island. The great square headland that overlooked Cape Lachman formed the east wall of the valley. On the other side, a massive cape of red rock jutted out, its high summit enshrouded in cloud. Banded into the cape's face was a greenish-grey outcrop of rock that was strange to us. As we rounded this prominence, the sun came up and illuminated the Graham Land coast in a rosy light. It first touched the mountain summits, and then spread over the land until all of the snowfields were pastel pink.

The shore took us into another bay full of small bergs and bergy bits. One of these had a large cave through it and many crystal-clear icicles that glistened with an iridescent light in the morning sunshine. We also found grey-green rock near the shore that Lamb believed to be glauconite, a type of rock that also exists on Cockburn Island. Later in the day, I found further specimens of rock containing well-marked casts of ammonites and shells.

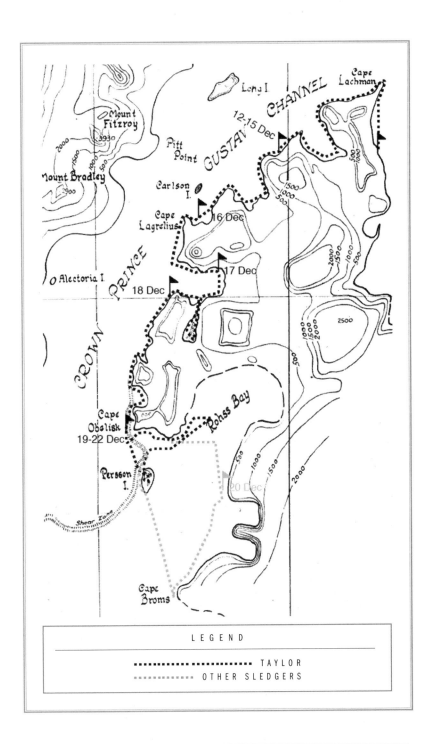

Map 18. The second sledging journey, 12–22 December 1945.

Deep in the bay there was a broad beach, toward which the fast-frozen ice was unbroken by tide cracks for half a mile. From the beach, stretching off to the southeast, was a valley that we thought was the one that Russell had once walked up from its south end. We followed the flat beachland southward and found along the southwest shore of the embayment a long morainic foreland, beyond which lay a broad valley more than half a mile across at the base, running inland for several miles toward the south while maintaining this width. All these hills were almost completely snow-free, and there were many pools of water ashore and on the sea ice.

We travelled offshore because the sea ice along this sector of the coast was rough, with many old and comparatively large bergs littering its surface. Our party spent the morning vainly searching for signs of Nordenskjöld's Red and Herrström Islands, and our failure to locate them seemed to confirm our inference that he had incorrectly charted the two islands that we called Monument[1] and Long Islands on the opposite shore of the channel. After making nearly twenty miles since leaving our fossil camp on Sidney Herbert Sound the night before, we pulled in toward the foot of a valley and camped at 8:00 a.m. An hour later, I talked to Layther, informed him of our position, and learned that he had no news for us. Then we ate a meal and turned in just as the weather closed in about us so that neither the mainland nor any of the islands were visible by 10:30 that morning.

Later that evening, it began to snow heavily and the poor visibility prevented our departure. The ensuing storm raged for the next two days. On 13 December, our dog team pulled the ice axe that anchored their tethering line out of the ice. There was an unusually bad mess to untangle as the dogs huddled round the little tent for protection from the wind. The storm repeatedly knocked down our twenty-five-foot, rubber-coated, solid-copper wire aerial, and on each occasion that we left our tent to re-erect it, a roaring blanket of snow carried by the wind reduced visibility to less than 100 yards.

We were glad to leave this camp at 2:00 in the morning on Sunday 16 December. A little drift snow still drove from the southwest in the dull daybreak, but it was not enough to bother us and subsided within a few hours. A typical rocky cape towered up into the mists ahead of us; the long slope of scree and debris along the base seemingly supported its high black face. As we entered another square-shaped bay, we saw the ice face of an old but inactive glacier at

---

1. Editors' note: Known today as Red Island.

its head, with rounded and weather-worn protuberances all along its termination. The glacier stretched up toward the high land beyond it, and cliffed walls banked the two sides of the bay. A thin, lateral moraine wove across the north side of the glacier's surface, and below the south end of the cliffs three seals lay on the sea ice. Davies and Russell stopped to kill one for dog food while Lamb and I continued the survey. We rounded the southerly entrance to the bay marked by the usual high, rocky cape. Terns and snow petrels nested in its heights. Five more seals lay half a mile offshore as we approached Carlson Island's brown- and yellow-banded mass on our starboard bow. The new snow blown onto the sea by the recent winds became very sticky, and we experienced great difficulty starting the sledge.

We recognized that we were about to enter yet another indentation into the shoreline. It was well-filled with small bergs, and many seals were scattered about on the surface of the sea. This bay had two shallow arms, each fringed with low hills. The south shore extended westward along a low, black cliff with an overhanging tip that formed Cape Lagrelius. We headed into the bay for a couple of miles before making camp off the shoreline's dividing point, beside a grounded bergy piece of ice around which seven seals clustered. Davies butchered one of them and gave the dogs another of his "good feeds." Fifteen minutes after stopping the sledge, I spoke to Layther on the 9:00 p.m. schedule. Once again, he had no word about a ship to take us home. That morning, the weather seemed inclined to settle down. The wind completely subsided, and the sun shone thinly through the clouds. Parts of the Graham Land coast came into view. In the afternoon, the sky cleared and the sun came out. I counted fifteen more seals off of Cape Lagrelius as five ghastly "stinkers" took possession of the remains of the seal Davies had killed, tugging and tearing at the meat as they gorged themselves.

At 3:00 the next morning we were on the move again. We observed a glorious sunrise in which the clouds between us and the mountains of the coast took on the loveliest shades of purple and pink. It was a pretty scene; yet the topographic details of the coast were too obscured to make a survey photograph worthwhile. Consequently, I had to postpone recording the landscape that I had so desired to capture from about that point. I hoped to find improved conditions on the journey back northward.

We made good time as we crossed over the south arm of the embayment and passed below Cape Lagrelius. Compared to the massive headlands that we had passed when coming down this coast, Cape Lagrelius was disappointingly insignificant. It is less than 200 feet tall and stretches out like a tongue from the base of the high hills and escarpment that form its backdrop. Within a quarter of a mile of the tip, gentle snow slopes ascend the cliffs from the sea on both sides of the cape. Nevertheless, it is *the* point from which to get a comprehensive view of this part of the east coast of Graham Land; one can see from Cape Longing to Tabarin Island, intercepted in only one place by the bulky mass of Carlson Island two miles distant.

As we passed the cape, a dozen seals still lay scattered about some hummocky bits of ice beneath the overhanging cliff. One or two large bergs were stranded inshore, beyond which we caught a glimpse of Cape Obelisk. For three miles we passed below some brown, rocky cliffs, under 200 feet high and surmounted by a massive snow-free hill that was similar to the Naze in its general appearance. When we approached another high headland, low clouds swept down the slopes of the coastal glacier of the mainland across the channel and limited our visibility. Seals lay scattered about the ice, and a Wilson's petrel flew by as we entered yet another bay of James Ross Island—this one larger than any of the others we had seen. As we turned toward the east, the high scree slopes that embanked the entrance to the bay gave way to receding morainic hills. It began to snow heavily and limited our visibility to something under a quarter of a mile, so we made camp at 7:00 in the morning in four-foot-thick snow. Behind the camp was a high, steep-faced morainic deposit composed of interspersed layers of stones and several feet of dirty ice. The warming effect of the rising sun caused its face to actively disintegrate before our eyes. The sky cleared a little by the time we had set up the camp, and we found ourselves along the north shore of the head of the bay, which was formed of ice cliffs fed by at least two broad glaciers. The southerly shore of the bay was cut by a broad valley with high hills on either side that extended south for a considerable distance.

We packed up at about midnight on 18 December, but a light snowfall threatened our visibility and led us to pause before taking the tents down. We did not start off until 2:30 a.m., when we headed southward across the end of the bay. Here an undulating ice cliff extended for a couple of miles. It was old and well striated, yet the clusters of fresh ice embedded along the base still constituted signs of activity. We followed westward along the south shore below a high hill with loose rock slopes before turning south into the valley that we had seen from the last camp.

Figure 55. "Hidden Lake" on Ross Island, 18 December 1945.

Figure 56. Camp at "Cape Obelisk," 19 December 1945.

Near the entrance to the valley, I found several pieces of fossil wood among the sharp, angular fragments of limestone and sandstone that composed the shore. From a slight eminence, Russell reported a snow route through the valley to some ice cliffs in the distance and we decided to follow it. Our course wound sinuously along the base of the valley, and we passed several pools of dammed water while ascending its gentle gradient. After following this course for about a mile past colourful outcrops of rocks (while flanked on both sides by the high, ice-capped escarpment of Ross Island), we came at last to the end of the valley. We were surprised to find ourselves standing on the shores of a freshwater lake— surely a rarity in these parts. It was seventy feet above the sea, two miles in length, about a mile across at the far end, and defined by low, forty-foot ice cliffs to the south. The lake was frozen, but there were many places near the shore that were flooded with the water that poured down from the adjacent hills. Scree-faced hills rose up toward the escarpment on both sides of the lake, which we named "Hidden Lake." We found fossil specimens along the slopes to the west before continuing northward back to the exit to the lake (which appeared to have no other outlet) and descending it to the sea.

By 9:00 a.m., the sun was blazing down, and the snow surface of the sea ice began to soften. Lamb and I spent an unsuccessful hour collecting in a small bay with a shelving foreshore that rose up toward the high hills around the base of an isolated tabular section of the escarpment. We then rounded the southerly entrance to the bay where we had spent the day and found a dozen seals below the cape, lying within a 100-yard radius close inshore. We pitched camp in the midst of them at 1:00 p.m. and, after Davies killed one of the animals for dog food, slept for the balance of the day.

We received an important piece of news from Layther at 6:30 that evening. The *William Scoresby* would pay a visit to Hope Bay in early January. We expected to be back at Eagle House before that date, so this news did not alter our plans. In the interim, we would complete our survey of Ross Island down as far as Cape Bröms (north of which Nordenskjöld had not made his survey in much detail).

The weather had cleared by this time, so Russell and I dashed off with the survey camera and theodolite for a mile and a half until we could see both Cape Obelisk and Cape Lagrelius. Unfortunately, by the time we arrived at this point a thin layer of cirrostratus clouds had curtained the sun, and the light was diffused when we took the picture. We read a round of angles and left the instruments there before returning to camp at 9:00 p.m. for a few more hours of sleep.

Figure 57. A view of the Sjögren glacier system from Cape Bröms, 21 December 1945.

At 3:15 on the morning of 19 December we again headed southward. The seals that had surrounded our camp the previous day were gone, presumably having re-entered the water in search of food. The sky was clear before the sun rose, but a high haze began to form so that light conditions were no better than they had been the previous night. We picked up our instruments and then followed a course for three miles below the usual scree-buttressed cliffs. This route took us over a thin, flexible ice surface and our sledges occasionally broke through it, falling into the foot of water that overlay the permanent ice. The slush ice was caused by runoff from the cliffs, and extended for more than half a mile offshore.

We turned into another small bay fed by a wide glacier. The central third of its ice face was smothered in an extensive moraine. A series of low-rounded, snow-free hills rose up from its southerly shore to the usual ice-capped tabular escarpment. This one had particularly precipitous cliffs of over 1,200 feet in elevation, and snow petrels whiled about its summits. Seven seals lay scattered over the ice off the northwestern tip of the cliff, and we wove a course between them. After following the westerly face southward for a couple of miles, the great square cliffs turned eastward into yet another bay with a large moraine at its head and an actively calving ice cap on the black escarpment high above it.

A couple of miles toward the south sat the peculiarly columnated rock formation known as Cape Obelisk. It had an impregnable look that was similar to some Moorish castle, for great cylindrical bastions rose to its upper heights. It was a reddish agglomerate and connected to the main escarpment of the island by a much lower spiny ridge of rock. In the middle of this ridge, a solitary stout pillar of rock rose like a stony sentinel to form Obelisk Point. We had spotted this feature from across the channel in August but now, as we advanced from the north, the Obelisk seemed to have a twin-pointed tip. As we moved west of it, however, the spike assumed a more symmetrical appearance.

Approaching Cape Obelisk, we encountered a zone of heavy pressure ice that we penetrated with some difficulty by selecting a course that crossed the ridge at a right angle, and followed higher ice to avoid the deep pools of green water covering much of the surface. We counted sixteen seals within a quarter of a mile of our course through this rough ice. After crossing over the worst of it, we swung south and then southwest, following the outer edge of a disturbed zone of ice that was twisted and contorted into the most fantastic forms and bounded by a huge, smooth fold in the surface that rose about fifty feet above sea level. We saw no open fracture along the summit of this ridge, and from it we had a good view of the extensive roughened area that stretched for miles eastward toward the east side of Röhss Bay, where the ice was also crushed and broken into unbelievable forms. This pressure zone extended southward toward Persson Island, constituting the northward continuation of the southerly shear zone of the shelf ice that extended from the Sjögren system of glaciers, seven miles to the west. We followed this marginal ridge for several miles, vainly attempting to find a course across the rough ice that would take us inshore. It appeared impenetrable, however, so we finally camped on the seaward side of the ridge due south of Cape Obelisk, beside a seal that Davies again butchered for the dogs. Though the sun did not shine, it became very hot and humid as we camped just after midday. After 6:00 in the evening, I contacted Layther for a few unsatisfactory moments: the wind had dropped, the temperature was 36°F, and it seemed intensely hot. At 7:00 p.m., we saw a "sun dog" on the south side only, because the northerly side was obliterated by a haze.

We were up at midnight on the morning of 20 December to make plans for the day. Russell and Lamb would proceed to the east side of Röhss Bay and continue the survey southward along the Ross Island coast as far as Cape Bröms before returning to our campsite. Their trip, we estimated, would take two days. Davies and I would leave our tent standing, accompany the other two as far as the entrance to the bay, inspect it, and then proceed to Persson Island within the same period. After rearranging the loads, we left camp at 4:00 in the morning and negotiated the first six-foot-wide open-pressure ridge without difficulty. The surface upon which we travelled was hard and fast, and we made good progress for the first hour as we traversed the curving shore to the south of Cape Obelisk. A series of morainic hills spread out below the jagged ridge that contained the Obelisk, and gave way to a broad snowfield fed by a glacier on the summit of the escarpment. We approached the toe of a moraine that crept out from beneath the glacier along the shore at sea level and encountered a series of crevices in the ice surface. As we passed over these, the snow bridge gave way and one of the dogs plunged about eight feet down into the gaping hole. Fortunately, the harness was a tight fit, and the dog hung by the harness and trace, swinging like a pendulum and whining piteously until we hauled him back up above the surface.

Our two teams separated at 6:30 a.m., not far past the point where this incident occurred. Davies and I turned northward to investigate the large bay spread out before us. We followed the low, brown hills that rose below the cliffs of the escarpment for about a mile. There were no tide cracks along what we thought should have been the shore, and the surface began to undulate considerably. We turned eastward for another mile and passed a long ice face of some antiquity with several deep chasms in front of it. The barometer indicated that we had climbed sixty feet since parting with the other sledge, so we concluded that we were on glacial ice and that there was little point in attempting to trace so indefinable a shoreline. We therefore headed southward toward Persson Island. I could tell by the depression that Davies made as he broke a trail for the dogs that we were going downhill, and we continued to do so for a considerable time after crossing the tracks that Lamb and Russell had made earlier in the day as they moved eastward.

Layther had requested that I contact him at 9:00 that morning, so we stopped the sledge, dug the walkie-talkie out of our load, set the radio up on the sledge, and strung the aerial out to a ski. I called for nearly half an hour but did not receive a response. By this time, the sun blazed down upon us through a high haze and a hot and strong wind blew from the north. These forces drove the thermometer well above 40°F, and melted the snow surface that our sledge roved over with decreasing speed.

At 11:00 a.m., we were very surprised to pass an Adelie penguin headed from Cape Obelisk to Cape Bröms. It was tobogganing along on its silvery white breast, making about a mile an hour, and diverted its course onto our tracks to catch up with us. Needless to say, the dogs were mutually anxious to arrange the meeting, but we succeeded in preventing it. Assuming that the bird had come down the west coast of Ross Island, it must have travelled more than sixty miles from the nearest open water.

As we approached Persson Island, we again encountered the heavily disturbed zone of ice that surrounds it. Just to the east of the island, a huge mound of ice that rises about 100 feet above the surrounding sea ice is visible for miles. I went ahead at this point and we negotiated the roughened area that extended for more than half a mile offshore in this direction. The rocky summit of the island was clothed with long talus slopes, and the island seemed to taper off toward the south into a long, black cliff of considerably lower elevation.

We landed at the north end of the island on a moraine composed of yellow clay that created a snow-filled moat, about thirty feet deep, around the island. Running down the steep sides into this moat, we followed it around to the west shore of the island where a continuous pool of deep green water lay. By keeping inshore and above the water, we were able to follow the west shore south until stopping the dogs at the foot of a high, bare valley that we thought we could ascend to the summit of the island. Because we expected to be away for some time, we stretched out the tethering line that we had brought from the camp for this purpose, and chained the dogs to it. Toward the south, the moat where the dogs were tethered deepened until the sides were sixty feet high and had a steep-faced ice wall to the west. It probably had been formed by the dual action of the pressure from the distant glaciers to the west and the erosive power of the sun and wind along the high, dark cliffs that stood above it on this southern part of the island. From the tops of these cliffs, streams of water flowed in volume; the high wind caught and blew this moisture hundreds of feet from the cliffs in such a manner that one momentarily thought that a jet of steam was blowing off the island.

Several moraines composed entirely of igneous rocks were scattered over the sea ice at the base of the island's hills. These schists and granites were so obviously different from anything else on the island that they had in all likelihood been transported there from the mountains of the Graham Land coast, and were caught at Persson Island from the long, sweeping curve of this glacial transport. The moraines lay within fifty feet of the island, and their matrix appeared to coarsen as one followed their line southward.

We gathered up the survey camera and began to climb a less well-defined valley that lay slightly to the north of the one under which we had stopped. Snow lay in its shallow hollow, and it rose steeply toward the summit. We climbed about 300 feet without noticing any rocks of particular interest. The slopes were composed of loose and fragmented pieces of the usual basalt and disintegrating tuff, but at that elevation we began to find fragments of laminar shale and soon encountered fossil shells whose surface was characterized by broad, concentric flukes. The shells were remarkably uniform in size: about 2.5 inches in diameter. We did not halt to collect many of them, for we had more climbing to do.

When we reached the summit of the brown hillside, we looked down from an altitude of 400 feet upon a broad valley, 100 feet below us to the south, which bisected the island. After absorbing the remarkable view over the extremely roughened area of ice that extended westward toward the Sjögren Glaciers, we crossed the valley. The sea ice was bent and buckled into the most tormented of shapes; the broad ice moat grew to 150 feet across and fifty feet deep as it continued to border the shore to the south.

The south end of the island, that incidentally is only about two miles in length and less than a mile across, is largely fringed by sheer 300-foot-high black cliffs. Between these cliffs, the land rises in uniform slopes to an elevation of 500 feet. The strong, hot wind still blew from the north with a velocity of forty miles an hour. With the legs of the tripod each anchored in a small cairn of stones, and with the head of the tripod weighted down by another heavy block of stone suspended from it, I set up the survey camera and exposed a film on the coast of Graham Land. I had particularly wanted to get this photograph, and chose to take it from the southerly summit rather than the northerly one, for the Sjögren Glaciers open out so much more from this aspect.[2]

We turned back northward, re-crossed the valley, and climbed the muddy slopes to the northern (and real) 700-foot summit of Persson Island. From this point we had an excellent view of the roughened areas of ice that completely

---

2. Author's note: I have not seen any of the photographs taken during this journey as I write, but light conditions were poor on account of the diffusion and I imagine that this photograph was marked with rippling waves because the wind whistled through the tripod and shook it screamingly.

surround the island, which apparently acts as a buffer to the coalescence of two glacial forces: the larger one from Graham Land and the lesser one originating from Röhss Bay. This creates minor forces for some distance around the island, which are manifested by the ridges and high mounds of ice that abound in the area. It is difficult to traverse this sector of sea ice by dog team, particularly if travelling with heavily laden sledges. Nordenskjöld commented on the rough ice he had found when passing this way, and our own experience led us to conclude that the best passage southward over the area of shelf ice at this point in the channel lies toward—but not adjacent to—the western shore.

After returning to the point where we had left our equipment near the outcrops of fossiliferous rock, we made a further examination of the area. Lacking a geological hammer (which we had forgotten when leaving camp that morning), we had to content ourselves with picking up weathered specimens. Casts and moulds of the shells were abundant; the shells themselves had apparently disintegrated. All except one of the finds were the same varieties that I have previously described. Davies and I also found traces of fossil wood and plant remains. We returned down the sodden hillside to the place along the shore where we had left the dogs tethered, sinking knee-deep into the muck along the lower slopes.

Davies climbed onto the sea ice to prospect a way out of the huge trough in which we stood, for the horizon from west to north was completely lost from view. While he was doing this, I skied along to the north end of the island to fulfill my plans to gather some botanical specimens for Lamb at a point that Davies and I had passed that morning.

At 7:30 on the evening of 20 December we started from Persson Island for our camp, climbing quickly up the long, icy slope that lifted us out of the island's moat. We followed a tortuous route through a series of pressure ridges. At many places along our course, we encountered erratic boulders and small moraines, all of which were of a volcanic nature and many highly metamorphosed. The hot, north wind had blown continuously the whole day, and though the sun was hidden from view, snow and ice melted everywhere. We crossed several pressure ridges, some of which had gaping crevasses toward their summits that were two and three feet across and seemed to extend down for a considerable distance. While travelling the last mile to the camp, we waded through a foot of slush ice that, as often as not, plunged the body of the sledge under water. It was heavy pulling for the tiring dogs. We reached camp at 10:00 p.m. after an interesting day and eighteen hours on the trail.

When we had left the tent in the morning, we had weighted down the tent apron, as usual, by piling two feet of snow around it. When we returned, not a spot of the snow remained. The warmth of the north wind had melted it, and the five wooden tent pegs had also melted out of place, so that the entire outer parts of the tent flapped in the breeze. The tent was only held in place by the rigidity of its frame and the weight of the articles that we had left within it. Under these circumstances, we were grateful that we had not lost the tent and a good part of its contents in the high wind. We set out the guy ropes and banked another two feet of snow around the tent before retiring at 11:00 p.m. It was quite light, but still cloudy and warm, though the wind seemed to be subsiding.

The north wind continued to blow gently all night long, and it was still dull and 40°F the next morning. All the new snow had again melted off the tent's apron. To judge from the relative positions of various articles lying about our camp, the hard-packed, windblown snow on the surface of the sea had melted at least nine inches in less than thirty hours. I received no reply from Layther when I tried to contact him, and spent the ensuing hours writing up my journal, packaging the films, and annotating and packing the specimens that we had collected the day before. Davies, in the meantime, went about a quarter of a mile offshore to an open pressure crack to try his hand at fishing. The water's surface was about three feet below, and he found no bottom with ten fathoms of line. He also found no fish.

The wind dropped until it became dead-calm and, with a wet snow falling, we heard the other team approaching after 3:00 in the afternoon. Davies went out to lead them back to camp at 4:30 p.m. They had been on the trail since midnight, and the dogs were exhausted from the heavy pulling they had encountered in the softening snow and rough ice. In marked contrast to the snow-free slopes that we had seen along the northerly part of the island, the part of Ross Island that they had examined was heavily glaciated. They had crossed Röhss Bay, followed the coast southward past a couple of large glaciers that descended from the island's ice cap, and ventured across a rifted area near five seals basking in the warmth of the hot sun at the foot of a heavily creviced glacier. They camped a mile and a half further on at 10:00 a.m. on 20 December. They awoke at 8:30 that evening to find, as we had, that almost all the snow about the flaps of the tent had melted. After skiing a quarter of a mile from their

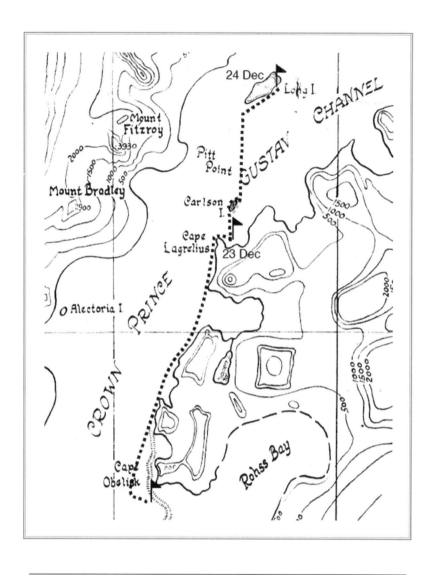

Map 19. The second sledging journey, 22–24 December 1945.

camp to a rocky headland, they found "cascades of snowmelt[ed] water gushing over the raised ice foot, like streams flowing over the basin of a fountain," to quote Lamb's diary. "We had some difficulty in threading our way between the pools of open water and scrambling over the wide cracks separating us from the shore." Leaving their camp at about 10:30 p.m., they "headed . . . across Röhss

Bay toward Cape Bröms, a long straight track of ten miles, and eventually got there at 0500 hours. Cape Bröms consists of reddish-brown cliffs about 300 feet high, mostly of agglomerate. . . . The ice for some distance out round the foot of the cliffs was very chaotic, with upheaved masses, and wide deep rifts and cracks." After stopping to eat a quick lunch, they had started back toward our camp near Cape Obelisk, arriving there an hour after midday. "The sun was shining hotly through a thin layer of cloud," Lamb wrote,

> and we could feel the intense radiation burning one's face strongly.
> The ice between Persson Island and Ross Island is thrown up into
> undulations 70 to 80 feet high, and near the shore of Persson Island
> there are a number of deep crevasse-like cracks up to a yard wide,
> obviously subject to considerable movement, for continuous groan-
> ing and grunting sounds were emitted from their depths. . . . When
> we came to the first of the long pressure ridges running out from
> Persson Island, Russell tried in several places without success to find
> a route through, and we had to follow the ridge along for about two
> miles, occasionally having to negotiate cracks, up to a yard wide.[3]

On the evening of 21 December, Layther informed us that he had been unable to hear us for two days. This period, incidentally, coincided with the duration of our hot north wind, though we could not say whether there was any direct connection between the wind and the poor reception conditions. He had no further news for us about our ship.

Snow continued to fall sporadically and left a soft surface in the high tempera-ture, but the surface started to harden in the evening when the mercury dropped and a southern breeze blew up. By 2:00 the next morning, the surface was hard frozen. Since Russell and Lamb had suffered such an arduous journey the day be-fore, I let them rest. Russell and I spent the day plotting our survey notes, for we had fallen a little behind, while Lamb dried and labelled the lichens he had recently collected. Davies repacked our supplies so that we would start out with seven days in hand. We planned to create an emergency depot with balance of supplies some-where on the return route for anyone who might require them the following year.

Breaking camp after midnight on Sunday 23 December, we hit the trail at 2:45 a.m. The newly drifted snow was fairly well packed on the surface and the

---

3.   Editors' note: Taylor is quoting from Lamb, "Operation 'Tabarin' (Base A) Official Diary," 21 December 1945, BAS, ADG/1A/1944/B.

temperature was below freezing, so the dogs made a couple of miles an hour—despite our laborious struggles to extricate the sledge from the slush when it broke through the snow crust every now and then. We rounded Cape Obelisk, headed northward, and travelled about five miles before emerging from the pressure ice. The mountaintops of Graham Land were completely enshrouded in cloud, but visibility was excellent at sea level.

As we passed several miles clear of the headland to the north of Cape Obelisk, Russell and Davies struck inshore with their stronger team to deposit the small depot of surplus supplies. The stores were packaged in a tin box, and there was enough to sustain ten men for about ten days. Actually, the man pemmican slightly exceeded this ration, and there was also a two-gallon tin of paraffin. (The box was set on an exposure of rock fifty feet above the sea and 100 yards inshore at the north end of the headland that comprised the southerly lip of the second bay north of Cape Obelisk.)

Meanwhile, Lamb and I continued northward with our team and twice swung westward for half a mile to avoid the flooded area of the sea surface. Conditions seemed to improve a little until 9:00 a.m., when the sun came out and the snow suddenly became soft and sticky. The wind blew incessantly from the south. As we swung inland again across the mouth of the largest bay, water poured down in streams from the mile-distant cliffs along the shore. When the sledge broke through the thin ice crust it was sometimes all but submerged in the floodwater. It was all we could do to keep it going.

Half a dozen seals lay off the northern entrance to the bay into which Hidden Lake emptied, and another herd of thirty seals lay off Cape Lagrelius. As we turned eastward into the bay where we had camped on 16 December near Carlson Island, we could see approximately thirty-five seals beside the small grounded berg near our campsite.

The old site where we erected our tent was merely a sludgy patch of snow on a thin ice crust that overlay another nine inches of water. Within fifty feet of the tent, six-inch-deep puddles broke the surface. We piled more of the saturated snow about the apron. At first, we had difficulty discerning which pelt covered the meat that Davies had left for our return, for it was just another mound of blubber among the other live seals that surrounded the cache. We had to move a couple of the beasts with snowballs to get at the dog food. The Weddells did not take the slightest interest in our activities, and we dragged the lumps of meat along an aisle of them that was ten to fifteen feet wide. The heat had undoubtedly caused some putrefaction, but the dogs nevertheless seemed to enjoy the meat.

It had been a tiring day's travel. Lamb was particularly affected, for he suffered from an upset stomach. In addition, his face was burned by the sun and wind; his lips were especially swollen and almost raw. We had travelled nineteen miles over the soft surface, and I had counted over 100 seals in the course of our day's march. The other team arrived two hours after us, with a twenty-mile-an-hour south wind blowing in brilliant sunshine that drove the temperature well above freezing. Clouds still hung over the mountains of Graham Land and prevented me from taking the survey photograph of the coast that I particularly wanted.

By midnight, the wind moderated but returned in its usual southwesterly quarter. The sky was overcast and the temperature was close to freezing. Our travelling surface, which was one of the first things we assessed each morning, was not hard but would support our sledges. The sixty-odd seals that had been beside our camp and at Cape Lagrelius had all disappeared, and none reappeared when we left the camp at 3:00 in the morning on 24 December. We struck a course for the south side of Carlson Island a couple of miles distant. The two teams separated as we approached this mile-long island, whose great brown cliffs rise more than 1,000 feet above the surface. We took the western side of Carlson Island, and found for some length the same long scree slopes created by the friation of the rock near the summit of the island. Three "stinkers" squatted predaciously along a tide crack as though waiting for their breakfast to appear. High above us, snow petrels circled about the brown cliff tops. Wilson's petrels fluttered over the dozens of seals that littered the ice. We crossed through several pools of surface water before meeting the other sledge and continuing on a northwesterly course that was tangential to the south end of Long Island six miles distant. At several points we crossed penguin tracks that were always headed south.

The sea surface between Carlson and Long Islands was very rough, but its roughness was not caused altogether by pressure ice. Many small icebergs and bergy bits of ice studded the sea surface. Drifting snow rippled the surface around these obstructions and formed drifts several feet thick that often dipped steeply downward as we crossed the line of their formation. We continued to pass seals until they suddenly ceased to appear three miles off Carlson Island. Once again, I counted more than a hundred in the course of the day's travel. The fact that their occurrence on the sea ice preponderates as one

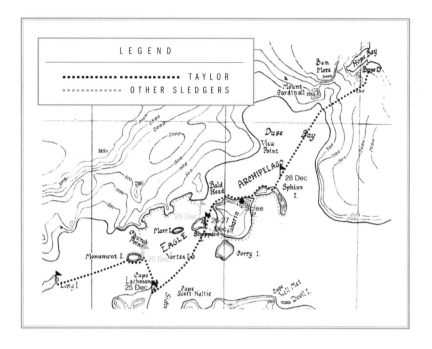

Map 20. The second sledging journey, 25–29 December 1945.

approaches Ross Island in this area leads one to consider if they do not occur in numbers in the area between Carlson Island and Cape Lagrelius, even in the depth of winter.

It is interesting to note that nearly all of the islands in this channel have steep, near-vertical cliffs along their east sides, and talus slopes to their west. Vortex and Carlson Islands are almost identical, and are even composed of the same shade of red-brown agglomerate. Marr, Corry, Sphinx, Tabarin, and Monument Islands are similar, though they are generally composed of darker rocks. This sweeping geological statement, however, only partially applies to Sheppard Island, and does not apply at all to Persson or Long Islands because the latter have a distinctly different type of rock on their mainland.

We turned northward along the east shore of Long Island. The sea ice was disturbed toward the south end of the island where, on more than one occasion, the sledges slipped into open tide cracks that contained brown, discoloured water in many places. It seemed as though a shallow shelf extended out from the southwest part of the island where much of this ice sat aground at low tide. The island is largely formed of loose, scree-covered hills that are 200 to 300 feet high at the south end and gradually rise toward the north. Snow filled the valleys along the east side, where a broad foreshore generally lay. At one or two places, aged ice cliffs formed a shore of no great height.

A curious Adelie penguin approached our team from the north and, before we could prevent its approach, the dogs lunged powerfully forward once they caught sight of it. The bird was dead before it could utter a squawk. Shortly afterward, at 9:00 in the morning, we made camp near the north end of the island where I still hoped to take my survey photograph. We had by this time concluded that the place we called Long Island must be the one that Nordenskjöld had incorrectly mapped as Herrström Island. We turned in before noon and were very tired, having travelled through deep, soft snow for the last few hours of the day.

At about midnight on the morning of 25 December we packed up and got under way by 2:00 a.m. It was the same dull and dreary sort of weather we had endured for almost the entire trip: low cloud, poor visibility, and a light southwest wind. The north end of Long Island was clear when we passed by, its steep face to the north flattening into an irresolute summit about 700 feet high. We hit out on a course calculated to take us to Monument Island. It was nine miles distant and indiscernible through the fog that closed in about us. An extensive field of small bergs forced us to take a tortuous and winding course. The temperature was near-freezing and, even before we started out, the surface was exceedingly sticky and tended to ball up on skis and runners when we stopped for even a moment. In addition, the dogs were lethargic and apathetic. Perhaps it was from eating "high" seal meat the previous day, or from overwork, or due to the heavy hauling surface. Whatever the cause, some of them acted just as they had toward the end of our previous journey, walking along with slack traces.

Considerable friction had been apparent among the Big Boys for several days. The malevolent, malcontent Popeye was successfully challenging the leader's supremacy. On this day, Captain was in such bad shape that he did not even wear a trace. The other dogs anxiously watched these daily battles with great interest but seldom took sides. Davies was not above giving Popeye a surreptitious poke or a violent squeeze where it proved most painful when Popeye was busily engaged with a mouthful of Captain. Popeye then rushed off howling at what he took to be an unfair and puzzling advantage that Captain had apparently taken in unexpectedly tackling these tender parts.

We plodded along through the field of ice in near silence as a snowstorm enveloped us, travelling blind for a while in an eerie blue-white light produced by the ghostly outlines of the fantastically shaped icebergs. At times, our course brought us up against one of these big bergs, and we frequently diverted from a straight course to blindly weave our way around the obstacles. It was one of my weirdest experiences during the two years that I spent in the south. We saw no seals but passed a solitary Adelie that, like all of those we saw since leaving Hope Bay, was headed south. Approaching Monument Island at 7:00 a.m., the weather cleared, though its upper heights were still obscured in mists.

At this point, we split up again to survey Monument Island. It is nearly two miles long, half as wide, and generally runs in an east-west direction. The island's agglomerate cliffs rise out of the sea for probably 800 feet and overhang the water in places, and are surmounted by a scree slope. Pieces of rock from these slopes frequently dropped into the sea with a terrific roar. Russell and Davies took the northern part while Lamb and I followed along the south shore. A new thin crust of ice had formed over the flooded sea ice that allowed Lamb and me to easily traverse the area. Our route took us along the base of a fine scree slope, out of which stretched a pedestal of rock stretching up a couple of hundred feet like a totem pole. Then we came to a line of sheer cliffs, and followed them around the east end of the island until we met Russell again on the northeast side at 9:00 p.m.[4]

Davies had stopped along the south side of the island to work on a seal and he and Russell intended to camp alongside it. They planned to continue to survey the north shore of Crown Prince Gustav Channel from Church Point to Bald Head and meet us at Sheppard Island, so we transferred the sledge meter to their team so that they could determine their course and distance travelled. Lamb and I then parted from Russell and headed for Cape Lachman four miles to the south, where we planned to pick up the boxes of fossils that we had left there on 11 December. Soon after clearing Monument Island, we passed through a broad belt of hummocky ice and, in their tired conditions, the dogs stopped on every little hill. By this time, the wooden runners of our sledge, which had been more than

4. Editors' note: This paragraph amalgamates two paragraphs from Taylor's draft, and also incorporates additional details from Taylor, "Operation Tabarin Second Sledge Journey," 25 December 1945, Taylor fonds, UMA, MSS 108 Box 6 File 1.

an inch and a half thick, were so worn that barely enough wood remained to hold the structure that supported the handlebars. There were many penguin tracks heading toward the southwest and the northeast, and the impression in the snow created by the flippers of several penguins that had followed each other along the same breast track reminded one of marks left by a tracked vehicle.

The surface flattened out after a mile and we made better time. As we approached the cape, the seals began to multiply. I counted more than 120 on this day, and all but eight of them were within a two-mile radius of Cape Lachman. Penguin tracks also abounded in this area and crisscrossed each other in all directions. A northbound convoy of six birds approached us at a good speed, but one stopped to inspect the dogs and the reduced convoy continued its passage. Another belt of rough ice slowed our progress over the final mile to Cape Lachman, where we arrived at noon on 25 December.

Two years before, we had spent Christmas Day basking in the Mediterranean sun at Gibraltar. The next year, we sat at a heavily laden festive table prepared by Berry at Port Lockroy. On this Christmas Day, I shot some brown skuas, the bird known as the eagle of the Antarctic. I gave most of them to the dogs but we saved one, and Lamb served it up for our Christmas dinner. It was a cheerless meal on a damp, dull day that both of us will long remember. The dogs preferred their pemmican to the birds, but we dressed our bird with a little pemmican and it was not too unsavoury.

After the meal, we carried our two boxes of fossils to the sledge. I also set up the aerial and exchanged Christmas greetings with the bases through Layther. Then we turned in for some sleep. The dogs were restless in the evening and made a good deal of noise. Only when we arose at 12:30 a.m. did we discover the skeletal remains of the two penguins that had caused the disturbance.

Lamb walked over to the foot of Cape Lachman's cliffs while I packed up the camp, and we did not get away until after 4:00 a.m. The dogs pulled well as we struck off for Vortex Island over a smooth-crusted surface on another dull day, and I was able to ride the sledge part of the way. I had been riding it with some frequency since being bothered with my feet a month previously, and they seemed to have improved a little, as they were not quite so painful in the mornings as they once had been.

We passed several penguins tobogganing on this part of the trip, including some headed southward to Sidney Herbert Sound. One bird came too close and our dog Sydney, who had become quite expert at nipping them at the nape

Figure 58. Repacking samples and equipment at Sheppard Island on 26 December 1945 prior to returning to Hope Bay. Ivan Lamb quipped that the display reminded him of the Caledonian Market in London.

of the neck, nabbed it as quick as a flash. The penguin tracks became thicker as we approached Vortex Island. Skirting close inshore to the west of the island, we halted below the rookery at 7:00 a.m. While I made a pace and compass traverse of the island, Lamb killed a dozen penguins for dog food and cut off some of the breasts for ourselves.

We left Vortex Island at 9:00 a.m., and the sun came out an hour later to make the surface soft and sticky. Nonetheless, we arrived at our old campsite on Sheppard Island before 11:00 a.m. After setting up the camp we watched the dogs eat their pemmican, and then gave each one a penguin which they tackled with gusto. After that, we lay down to sleep in the hot sun.

After sleeping most of the afternoon, I talked to Layther in the evening who passed on the rather cryptically worded message from Flett at Hope Bay that "you would be well advised to speed up your return." Lamb and I spent some time conjecturing just what Flett's message might signify, for there were certain security restrictions that prevented open discussion of operational plans on the air.

The conditions promised a good night for travelling: it was freezing and we had our first clear evening sky in weeks. At 10:00 p.m., Russell and Davies arrived from their camp a couple of miles away on the north side of Sheppard Island where they had stopped for a seal. We talked over the plans, and decided that we had to spend the next day repacking the geological specimens that we had packed in tins full of snow because they were now half full of water. We would have liked to have known if the ship was near enough to prevent Davies from making another trip to Sheppard Island, for if it was not close we were inclined to leave a part of the collection behind. If there was any doubt on this point, however, we would try to take it all despite the heavy weight that it would add to our loads. Accordingly, I talked to Layther first thing on the morning of 27 December. He held a direct C.W. link with Donnachie at Hope Bay which permitted us to hold an interrupted conversation. During our transmissions, Flett initially recommended leaving a portion of the load at the bay. When he also mentioned that Hope Bay had not received official news about the ship's arrival, however, we decided that it was best to attempt taking all of the collections with us.

At 10:30 a.m. we were all busily engaged sorting and repacking. Fortunately, the day was calm. We transferred the fragile fossils into wooden boxes, using an old sleeping bag for packaging between the layers. When this job was complete, we packed the collection into ten boxes that collectively weighed over a quarter of a ton. In addition, we intended to take with us the survey camera (which I still hoped to use en route), one theodolite, and both radios. One of the latter would be left at the Duse Bay camp for Marshall's subsequent use, and the damaged one would go back to Donnachie. With all our odds and ends spread over tarpaulins, Lamb remarked that it reminded him of the Caledonian Market. We then packed the boxes and equipment and separated them into a dump largely consisting of food, another dump that Davies would return to retrieve in a few days, and loaded another two piles onto the sledges (each of which weighed about 800 pounds with the extra loads). By 3:00 p.m. the job was finished and we turned in.

By 10:30 that night, we had eaten, packed up, and left Sheppard Island. Davies, Lamb, and I accompanied the two dog teams while Russell proceeded on skis to make a pace and compass traverse of the east side of Tabarin and the south side of Sphinx Islands. With the two heavily loaded sledges containing all our collections and results, we rounded the northwest tip of Tabarin Island and passed below Horn Peak at midnight.

There is little of interest to describe along the north side of Tabarin Island, except that Lamb took a colour movie of a pretty scene overlooking a pool of water at the base of a small berg. Two seals lay near it, and beyond, the sun painted Ben More with its golden glow.

A light coating of fresh snow overlay a hard, smooth surface; it was one of the best we travelled upon, and we were grateful for it given our heavy loads. While crossing the channel between Tabarin and Sphinx Islands we caught sight for a few moments of Russell collecting on the hillside to the east of Scree Peak. Following along the north shore of Sphinx Island, we entered the bay at the head of which lay the same col that we had crossed over in August. At this point, Lamb and I left the sledges and went ashore. Toward the north side of the col, I found a stream running six to eight feet wide. It was quite shallow and I estimated that it delivered at least 100 gallons a minute, even at the early hour of 4:30 in the morning. The stream was the source for a small lake that was about half a mile in diameter to the east of the col. The bed of the stream was deep pink, the result of a coating of fresh water alga, and I took a sample that Lamb was pleased to receive.

We continued eastward around a brown hill that drooped off into an ice tongue. Below the high agglomerate cliffs that form the east coast of this peculiarly shaped island, we met Russell at 6:15 in the morning on 28 December just as a part of its crest gave way and thundered into the sea. The surface was still excellent, and the dogs pulled well despite the brilliant sunshine, so we decided to continue for the tent in the northeast arm of Duse Bay to shorten our march that evening. We passed to the south of a tabular berg that was half a mile in length and 100 feet high, before camping on the open sea ice at 8:30 a.m. We had made nearly seventeen miles since leaving Sheppard Island. The surface of the sea around our camp was smooth and flat and hardly broken by any ice inclusions at all. Although the travelling conditions were still good when we camped, the heat from the blazing sun was intense and the dogs had begun to feel its effect. They had done a good day's work. Russell plotted our position by a resection, and found that we still had seven to eight miles to go before we would reach the Duse Bay tent. Despite the sunshine, clouds clung to the hoar-frosted mountains at altitudes between 1,000 and 3,000 feet and photographic conditions were not good enough to expose one of our precious films with the big camera.

At 10:00 a.m. I asked Layther to have Flett arrange to have four men at the Duse Bay tent camp at 2:00 a.m. on 29 December. We turned in an hour later, just as a fresh, cooling breeze began to blow from the north. It increased in intensity toward mid-afternoon, by which time the sun had melted the crust on the snow, and the powder beneath had the consistency of loose rice. We could not have moved at this time had we wanted to, for the snow would never have supported the sledges. By evening, the wind increased to forty miles an hour and increasingly drifted the snow. Yet visibility to the north was good up to Summit Pass. Later, the wind velocity decreased a little, and we left the camp at eleven o'clock that night, as a glorious sunset silhouetted Sphinx Island against a sky shot blood-red. The surface was frozen hard, and we made good time, travelling four miles by midnight.

In October, 1903, Andersson, Duus, and Grunden reported seeing hundreds of seals in the Duse Bay area in groups of up to twenty. We had by this time crossed Duse Bay six times in August, September, November, and December, and never saw anything comparable to these numbers. On this last trip, we saw about twenty, which was probably the greatest number we saw on any of our crossings. One of three things may explain this discrepancy: the number of seals may have drastically reduced since 1903; seals in such numbers may have moved farther south toward the Cape Lagrelius area; or they only exist in such numbers in Duse Bay in October, the only month between August and January that we did not cross the bay.

We travelled toward the bay camp at the foot of the glacier for another hour and a half after midnight on the morning of 29 December. The day was destined to be the last for our trip. Our progress was rather slow for the last half mile because we followed a winding course through a hummocky ice field laced with crevices a couple of feet across, and around numerous pools of blue-green water. At 1:30 a.m. we drew up to the base of the glacier, only to find that the tent left by James and Russell in September had blown down and was badly torn. Its contents, consisting of ration boxes, still lay *in situ* in a pit about three feet deep, which indicated the snowfall that had accumulated since that time.

We erected Davies and Russell's tent, since it was the larger of the two, against the rising force of the wind that again blew at nearly forty miles an hour. We had just got it up when we saw the four figures from Hope Bay cresting the glacier. Matheson, Marshall, Blyth, and Back arrived just before 2:00 a.m. The eight of us somehow managed to crowd into the little tent and shared a tot of "rum and Bagley's," a hot drink, and some buns and pastry that Berry had sent over for us.

We repacked the loads, leaving behind the tents, bedrolls, utensils, and ration boxes, taking little more than the collections we had made in the previous couple of months with us. The area at the foot of the glacier had been subject to some pressure and movement since we had last been there, and several respectable crevasses had opened up. Considerable traffic moved over these gaps until we finished repacking the sledges.

Davies and Russell started up the hill first with the assistance of Marshall and Matheson. Blyth and Back helped our team, and we all struggled arduously to climb the steep gradient against a wind that all but took the breath away and was strong enough to blow one backward on occasion. The dogs could haul the load up the hill much more quickly than we could move, so we were of little assistance to them once we got them up the steep initial slope.

As we approached Summit Pass, still three-quarters of a mile distant, we lost Russell and Davies's track in the poor lighting after we entered a dense cloud. Having by this time completely lost sight of the other sledge, it became extremely difficult to find the lost track. We stumbled slowly forward against the rising force of the wind and reached the pass. From this point on, we travelled entirely by compass bearing. Our progress up to the pass was so slow that it was 8:30 a.m. when we left it. Striking blindly forward on our compass bearing, we were confronted by the ghostly outlines of the lower slopes of Pyramid Peak. We diverted our course slightly toward the east and I had raced off about half a mile when we found the tracks of the other sledge. As if to add insult to injury, nature, in a last wild display of her power at the conclusion of our trip, unloosed the floodgates and soaked us all in a cold, driving rain. We lost the train again after travelling less than a mile, but we eventually discerned Nobby Nunatak ahead of our compass course.

At this point, Back undertook to guide us downhill toward the base, for he had made the trip up to this *nunatak* on many previous occasions while making sea ice observations. We followed him down through the mist and fetched up on the brink of a moraine above Boeckella Lake, half a mile north of the moraine we had aimed at near the brow of the glacial slope. Visibility had been under 100 yards, but we passed the cloud's base and could see Seal Point, Hope Bay, and the steel-grey waters of Antarctic Sound. We followed around the brow of the hill until we at last stood on the brink of the hill above the base. Here we released half of the dogs and the other four tore down the hillside after them as we rode the sledge down, swinging and lunging about as dogs, brakes, and gravity took control in turn. We arrived back at Eagle House at 11:00 a.m. on 29 December, after an absence of fifty-one days.

After tying up the dogs with the willing help of other members of the base, we unloaded the sledges and entered the house to get cleaned up and to change into dry clothes. We were all struck by the changes that Ashton's typical industry brought to the messroom. Bookshelves, cabinets, a phonograph table, a first aid box, and a settee had all appeared.

All told, we had travelled about 500 miles on this second sledging journey. It had not been the least sensational. We had set out to examine the coastline of Ross Island from Cape Gage to Cape Bröms, all of the other islands in the area, as well as a small portion of the mainland coast that we had not previously surveyed. We had also intended to attempt to retrieve the dump of stores that we had left on the sea ice of Erebus and Terror Gulf the previous September. Our two teams accomplished all of these things during a spell of particularly depressing weather in which, above all, the photographic results suffered heavily. We returned with good botanical specimens and geological collections that were rich in fossils; a good survey of the shoreline and something of its topography; meteorological results; and additional information on the glaciers and wildlife of the region. We also left small depots that may be of use to someone in difficulty. Complete harmony had permeated every day's work. This made it one of the most pleasant journeys that one could well experience. More equable and cooperative companions one could not have found.

CHAPTER TWENTY-ONE

North Toward Home

THE FIRST THING WE WANTED TO KNOW UPON RETURNING to base was any news regarding a ship. No official news had been received, but rumours that a ship was nearing Port Stanley still circulated. In fact, the signal from Flett that had startled us in the field had been on the basis of this report. Port Stanley had also recently requested weekly ice reports from all of the bases, and we considered this to be another hopeful omen. It seemed probable that definite news on the subject of a relief ship was imminent and, with this in mind, we made our plans. I also directly requested the governor of the Falkand Islands arrange for me to be informed of any projected ship movements with the following message:

> We have at all times attempted to keep the Discovery
> Committee informed of the progress . . . and the complete
> ignorance in which the Colonial Office is keeping us
> concerning the now imminent plans for our relief and of next
> season's work is incomprehensible to us. This has made the
> intelligent planning of the field work unnecessarily difficult, not
> to say hazardous, and has had a definite deleterious effect upon
> morale, especially at the smaller bases. Russell still does not
> know whether he is to remain here another year or not. On our
> behalf, could you please make representations to the Colonial

Office requesting this information, for which we would be extremely obliged.[1]

Our stores at Sheppard Island had been so well sorted that we did not need to return for anything before our departure from Antarctica. Since Russell planned to remain with the operation for a second year, however, the stores were of some consequence to him. Several members of the base were also anxious to participate in a sledge trip, however brief it might be, so we arranged for Davies to return to Sheppard Island with the two teams accompanied by Back, Marshall, and Matheson. Back's departure as doctor was countenanced by arranging for the medical office at Port Stanley to be "on call" to any of the bases if the need arose.

This party left Hope Bay on the morning of 3 January and returned to Eagle House early on the morning of 8 January. Their party took the same walkie-talkie radio that we had used on the previous journey (with new batteries). Despite this provision, we had no radio contact with them throughout the trip, the set having been in Marshall's charge. They had a good trip, but the extensive presence of thaw pools over the sea ice, lightly covered with fresh ice that was barely thick enough to support the sledges, made parts of the journey arduous. They had left the base in the morning but, like us, were soon forced to only travel at night when the temperatures were consistently close to freezing.

Early January brought some fine weather for a change. When these conditions were coupled with the air of anticipation that pervaded Eagle House, the days slipped by swiftly. We worked hastily to complete the reports and pack up our personal gear. The same air of activity was doubtless prevalent at the other two bases. For example, reducing the mass of notes we took on our previous trip provided plenty of work for Russell, Lamb, and myself. Russell accepted the task of plotting the survey notes and added the new information to the chart that I had begun from the notes of the first trip. This job had to be hurriedly completed if we were to leave him a copy of the chart before our departure.[2]

---

1.   Editors' note: Taylor did not include this message in his draft of *Two Years Below the Horn*. It appears in Taylor, "Official Journal," 30 December 1946, Taylor fonds, UMA, MSS 108 Box 5 File 1.

2.   Author's note: During the winter, we had spread a network of triangulation points over the Hope Bay area, and James used this net during our absence as a control on which to hang some plane table details. He conducted the survey without the supervision of Russell or myself, but produced a rough map by the time we returned.

Russell also had to prepare a glaciological report and a copy of his diary. (Unfortunately, time did not allow him to finish the latter project before our ship arrived.) Meanwhile, packing up the many hundreds of geological specimens that we had brought back on our trip kept Flett and Ashton going at top speed. While we had been away, the two of them had amassed an extensive collection of plant fossils from Hope Bay. The specimens had been collected by many members of the base, and much of the collection also still required packing.

Few Antarctic parties received first word of their relief in the same manner as us. On 4 January, I had been informed of the arrival of Commander E.W. Bingham at Port Stanley, and was advised that he would take charge of Operation Tabarin to facilitate the changeover. Yet no one told us when our relief would arrive. On the afternoon of Sunday 6 January, we sat round the messroom listening to the broadcasting station at Port Stanley, as was our custom. At 4:00 p.m. every Sunday, the station broadcast a program largely designed for people in the outlying parts of the Falkland Islands. The program had occasionally transmitted news that was of interest to the bases. During the newscast that day, we heard that the *Fitzroy* would sail for the South Shetlands on 9 January. We also learned about the arrival of a motor vessel at Port Stanley that was on its way to the Dependencies, but were so surprised that no one caught its name. The next day, the galley wireless learned that this latter vessel was named the *Trepassey*, and that Captain Sheppard was her master. The news was very cheering to us all and everyone bubbled over with good spirits and optimism. We finally knew that we could depend on leaving Hope Bay that spring.

On 7 January we received word to prepare to be relieved within ten days. This information astonished the sledgers when they read it on our notice board after returning at 6:00 the following morning. Signals came thick and fast for the next few days, inquiring about our dogs and the dog food situation, and advising all except Russell, Reece, and White of their imminent passage northward. Reece would probably move to another station, but the other two would remain at the same bases that they currently occupied. We also received last-minute requests from Port Stanley for the capture of a few live penguins to return to the British Museum.[3]

---

3. Author's note: On 9 January, we learned that the *Scoresby* had sailed directly for Hope Bay from Port Stanley to evacuate returning personnel direct to Port Lockroy, where we might expect to contact the *Fitzroy*. At this time, Hope Bay was quite free of ice; Antarctic Sound contained only a small amount of brash ice, though some light pack ice was discernible ten miles to the north.

Everyone was feverishly busy packing up and completing the last of the reports. By this time, the specimen boxes alone amounted to seventy boxes, and we had about three tons of stores including our luggage to load. Not the least busy of us all was Russell, who would soon accept charge of the base's articles, as well as copies of our charts and reports, cypher books, and all the paraphernalia that went with the appointment of postmaster. On the evening of the 11th, we learned that the *William Scoresby* was supposed to arrive at 8:00 the next morning and that we were to "arrange [for] a rapid departure."

We were all packed up and ready to move the following morning, but by 6:00 the wind and poor visibility made it obvious that the ship was unlikely to reach us. The drift snow stopped by 10:00 a.m., but the wind continued to blow a force 6, with the temperature just below freezing. The messroom was cluttered up with boxes as we fidgeted the hours away. A constant stream of people found it necessary to have a look out the front door to see if they could sight the ship. By noon, the weather cleared up considerably and we could see well beyond Sheppard Point, off which a sizeable iceberg lay. But the drift occasionally restarted and reduced visibility to about 100 yards. Thus the afternoon dragged past, and no ship appeared. By evening, we began to suspect that the *Scoresby* had encountered ice, and this was confirmed when we received a signal at 3:00 a.m. stating that she was proceeding to Deception Island.

The next morning, Bingham ordered the *Scoresby* to make another attempt to reach Hope Bay immediately and asked us for a further ice report on conditions in Antarctic Sound. The conditions were unchanged from the previous day, but we took the opportunity to suggest a passage close in toward the Graham Land coast—an obvious conclusion derived from our year's observations. The high wind continued to blow from the southwest at Hope Bay, but the drift snow that it carried changed to fog in the afternoon.

At 3:00 in the morning of 14 January, I was aroused from my bunk by the sound of a voice shouting, "Anybody here; don't you want to be relieved?" Rubbing the sleep from my eyes, I found Marchesi and the new doctor standing in the middle of the messroom. The *Scoresby* wheeled about the entrance to Hope Bay without dropping her anchor. Dressing quickly, we hurried round to finish up the last-minute packing, for the arrival of the ship took us by surprise.

The southwest wind still blew freshly as the ship's longboat was loaded at the little rocky point below the base and slid away to begin the long pull off to the ship circling about a mile offshore. It took all hands to move our stores and

luggage down to the loading point along the shore. The new doctor, James Andrew, would remain with Russell at Hope Bay, and David James was also granted
permission to stay until the next ship and meet us in Port Stanley later. (This latter arrangement, however, did not mature, and it was the last we saw of him.) It required three boatloads to transport all our men and materials out to the ship, but
it was all accomplished by 7:00 a.m. After goodbye handshakes with James and
Russell, and a farewell pat to a few of our four-legged friends, the last boatload
made its way over the heavy swells and was transferred to the ship. The *Scoresby*
sailed for Deception Island a few moments later, rounded Sheppard Point, and
passed below Mount Bransfield. The ship wallowed in a heavy sea as the wind
increased a little. After we sailed thirty or forty miles from Hope Bay, we passed
to the south of an extensive field of pack ice. However, a five-mile-wide channel
to the Graham Land mainland, containing virtually no ice, remained open.

The weather moderated a few hours after we left Hope Bay, with the wind
blowing lightly from the northeast as the swell subsided. The sun came out
shortly afterward, and with only a few scattered icebergs about, we had a good
passage across Bransfield Straits where there was less ice than on any passage of
Hope Bay since the *Fitzroy*'s visit in 1944.

The most important avocation for all Tabarin personnel was scanning the
mail that Berry had immediately begun to sort upon going aboard. The ship's
wardroom was a shambles, as one bag after another was emptied onto the table
and distributed. There were dozens of letters for each of us, and over 100 for
some; many dated back more than a year. Reading this mail made the ship's passage go quickly, and we found ourselves sailing through Neptune's Bellows just
after 7:00 in the evening. When we entered Whaler's Bay, we got our first view
of Captain Sheppard's new vessel, the *Trepassey*. The *Scoresby* sailed across her
bow, and tied up to the oil barge. The barge was piled high with coal and other
stores, and along its decks we quickly picked out former *Eagle* crew members
Bob Whitten, "Sparks," and Captain Sheppard. They were down on the deck
among us before the lines were on the ship and there was a great ceremony of
handshaking all round. I also was introduced to Surgeon Commander Edward
W. Bingham for the first time, and renewed acquaintances with Captains Roberts and Pitt. Reece was there too, and I had a few words with him before going
aboard the *Fitzroy* with Bingham to recount our activities over the past year.

The failure of the *Scoresby* to reach Hope Bay directly, as planned, resulted
in a revision of the plans. Following our scheduled departure from Hope Bay,

Figure 59. The *Trepassey*, n.d.

the *Trepassey* was to have called there with the incoming members of the base while the *Fitzroy* returned us to Port Stanley via Port Lockroy. In the revised proposal, all of the people being evacuated would board the *Fitzroy* for Port Lockroy while the other two vessels sailed for Hope Bay. The *Fitzroy* would contact them later at the South Orkneys before continuing to the Falklands.

Toward evening, we congregated on the 300-ton *Trepassey*. Her black wooden hull contrasted with the whiteness of her trim superstructure. For a while we listened to Captain Sheppard recount the exploits that followed the *Eagle*'s hurried departure from Hope Bay, and looked through his photographic album entitled "The Voyage of the Eagle" with great interest. The pictorial records showed the damage that his ship had suffered following her collision with the two icebergs, and also documented the patches fitted to her bows at sea and Port Stanley. A lot of water had flowed under the bridge since that St Patrick's Day, and we enjoyed exchanging stories in the clean and cozy cabin of the *Eagle*'s successor. Our only disappointment (and I understand that it was theirs as well) was that the *Trepassey* had not brought us away from Hope Bay. We gave

Captain Sheppard a copy of our sounding survey that, I am told, subsequently enabled Sheppard to use the anchorage that Matheson had located in Hut Cove.

While we had been away from Hope Bay in November, Reece had sent reports of Bonner's steadily deteriorating health to Back. We met Bonner for the first time at Deception Island. He was emaciated and as thin as a proverbial rake, but he still smiled at the prospect of finally returning to his home in the Falklands. It was difficult to converse with him without feeling some measure of responsibility for his condition, but he began to eat with better appetite as soon as he came aboard the ship, and brightened up considerably on the voyage northward.

The morning of 15 January began another fine day, and we sailed south from Deception Island at 9:00 a.m., bound for Port Lockroy. Reading and rereading our mail occupied most of us for the day, but visibility was exceptional so many took their cameras on deck. There was almost no ice about, and the channels were by far the clearest that we saw on any of our passages as we slipped through the Neumayer Channel and into the ice-cliffed anchorage of Port Lockroy. It was 11:45 p.m. when we moved into the harbour, and the entire population of Goudier Islet came on a dinghy to meet us. They came aboard before the ship slowed to a stop, and the sounds of chattering resumed as people tried to exchange a year's experiences in the first few moments of the conversation.

16 January was another beautiful day, and the *Fitzroy*'s crew began discharging the base's cargo early. By noon it was all unloaded and Lockley's specimens, including the precious seal, were transferred aboard. In the afternoon, the crew bunkered the ship while we went ashore to inspect the house that we had built nearly two years previously. Lockley had looked after it well, for it was as clean and tidy as the day we left it. The day drew to a close with beautiful sunset that was typical for Port Lockroy in January.

At four o'clock the next morning, the *Fitzroy* sailed out of Port Lockroy, leaving behind the new officers-in-charge and his men. We enjoyed the scenery along these magnificent channels for the last time on our passage northward. Our ship did not call at Deception Island, but skirted to the north of Graham Land's coast and swung on a northeasterly course toward the South Orkneys. A great variety of birds wheeled about, including several species that we had not known at our shore bases. Whales broke water on both sides of the ship at various times, and were especially numerous just north of Hoseason Island, where a couple of dozen surfaced. Some were "killers," though most were of a larger species. The sea was almost ice-free, though toward afternoon we passed through a scattering of small bergs to the south of Deception. The conditions were not the same elsewhere. The same day our ship received a report from the *Trepassey* stating that it had encountered light pack ice forty miles north of Hope Bay. Later in the day, we received another signal explaining that the ice had thickened and forced the ships to turn about and travel to the base by skirting to the west of the ice field.

On the morning of the 18th, we were busy eating the ship's fresh food at a rate that continued to astonish the stewards when we were informed that the *Trepassey* and *Scoresby* had joined us at 3:00 a.m. The *Trepassey* led the little fleet through a field of light pack ice that extended for two miles before we again sailed into open water. She sailed prettily ahead of us, but seemed to roll rather heavily in the very light swell. The *Trepassey* continued to lead the convoy as we passed to the north of Gibbs, Aspland, O'Brien, Clarence, and Elephant Islands, before proceeding on a course for the South Orkneys. Great numbers of birds continued to follow the ship all day long, with Cape Pigeons by far the most numerous. We also saw Antarctic and Wilson's petrels in roughly equal numbers, as well as what we believed to be two black-winged albatrosses sitting on the water.

At 6:00 the next morning, we had the unusual experience of falling in with another ship—a whale catcher called the *Suderoy Seven*. The *Trepassey* went alongside her to inquire about the ice conditions ahead, for we were following the fringe of a field of open pack ice toward the south. As the *Trepassey* passed us to starboard, a megaphoned message informed us that there was no serious ice ahead, and that the *Trepassey* could continue to skirt to the north of the pack. The *Suderoy Seven* then headed southward through the field at considerable speed without hesitation. The ice in this field had a much fresher appearance than any we had previously encountered. At 7:00 that evening, Back informed me that we had broken away from the other two vessels after receiving a signal from Port Stanley instructing us to head to the capital independently. We expected to arrive on 22 January.

The *Fitzroy* encountered dull weather for the next two days and, except for learning that the other two vessels had reached the South Orkneys and that the cargo for a new base on Laurie Island was being discharged at Cape Geddes, nothing of interest occurred. Toward evening, fog closed in about the ship, and we were still in it as we approached the Falklands on the morning of 22 January. The fog cleared at about 10:30 a.m. and we immediately sighted land. The

Figure 60. Main Street, Port Stanley, n.d.

sun came out when we approached the white lighthouse at Pembroke Point at noon, and within a few moments we entered Port William, with Port Stanley but a few miles distant.

Quite a crowd collected on the quay to welcome the ship, and she was barely tied up before the executive engineer and the governor's aide-de-camp came aboard with an efficiently organized billeting system for us all. We were dispatched in groups of twos and threes to various private homes and hotels while Lieutenant Colonel Mayne and myself were invited to Government House as guests of the governor, Sir Alan W. Cardinall. Colonel Mayne had played a prominent role in preparing for our relief in London, and he would probably have been Commander Bingham's right-hand man if an old back injury had not prevented him from remaining in the south.

The *Fitzroy*'s commitment to visit the "coast" (as the southern tip of South America was known locally) prevented her from sailing to Montevideo for several weeks. This delay in our departure gave us plenty of time to complete almost all of our reports and draw better copies of some of our maps and charts.

All of the boxes of specimens sent to Port Stanley from Port Lockroy and Deception Island in 1944 were also collected and, in some cases, repacked. Executive Engineer Lieutenant Colonel Woodgate gave us every assistance with these tasks, and even placed a small drafting office at our disposal.

Considering that we had been "out of this world" for so long, the members of our expedition behaved surprising well at Port Stanley. The odd individual imbibed "one over the eight" but this seldom happened, and I do not know of any occasion when unpleasantness resulted. We enjoyed the three weeks in Port Stanley's occasional summer sunshine and fresh sea winds. Brief though our stay there was, I feel that I speak for all of us when I say that we left behind many personal friends and that we felt greatly indebted for the warm and spontaneous hospitality that confronted us at every turn. We were all present at a dinner that His Excellency held in honour of the expedition's members at Government House on 29 January. Two nights later, the people of Port Stanley threw a dance at the gymnasium in our honour. The Falkland Islands have long been renowned for such hospitality, and the pleasurable reception that we received in Montevideo on our southward voyage was the only experience that compared with the cordiality of Port Stanley.

Shortly after our arrival at Port Stanley, we learned that the name of our organization had been altered from "Operation Tabarin" to the "Falkland Islands Dependencies Survey." We also heard varying rumours up and down Port Stanley's long and straight main street regarding our homeward voyage. One day they said that we might have to spend a month at Montevideo awaiting a ship heading to England. This prospect did not produce crocodile tears, let alone any real ones. Another day, the *Highland Monarch* (the ship which had brought us to Port Stanley) was mentioned, for at that moment she was at Buenos Aires with the HMS *Ajax* picking up the *Graf Spee* prisoners. Another persistent rumour contended that we would return to England on the *Ajax*.

Despite our pleasant visit at Port Stanley, none of the party was sorry to board the *Fitzroy* and begin our long journey home on 11 February. We left Back behind, whom the governor had enlisted to take the place of an ill medical officer.[4] Our own five-day passage over the "roaring forties" was, like our previous voyage, stormy, but the *Fitzroy* approached Montevideo on a fine, sunny morning on 16 February. In the course of our passage, we exchanged messages of gratitude and good wishes with His Excellency the governor and

---

4.   Editors' note: Back consequently arrived in England about three months later.

Commander Bingham, whose parties had by that time installed themselves in our old bases. We passed a lightship and some coastal vessels before catching sight of our first landmark: the crazily tilted and rusted *Graf Spee*. The *Fitzroy* berthed in the harbour a little after 10:00 in the morning.

An ambulance waited to take Bonner off to the hospital. He had been at Port Stanley's facility throughout our visit, and it had been decided to send him away for treatment. His wife accompanied him and most of us saw him for the last time as the attendants carried him off the ship on a stretcher. Lamb, who arranged to stop over at Montevideo months later, wrote to tell us of Bonner's death in the British hospital on 2 March 1946.

We had five hours at the capital of Uruguay and, despite our attempts to make arrangements by signal in advance, we spent two of these hours waiting for currency. Although it was Saturday afternoon, arrangements were made to keep a store open for an extra hour so that we could buy a few articles of clothing and gifts to take home. After spending all of our money under high-pressure purchasing conditions, we were back at the docks by 3:30 in the afternoon.

As it turned out, there was an element of truth in the rumours that we had heard at Port Stanley. All service personnel boarded the HMS *Ajax* while all of our party's civilians took the *Highland Monarch*. While stationed in Antarctica, we had often remembered our pleasant visit in Uruguay and anticipated the pleasures that our homeward visit might promise, but we had not reckoned on the two ships that stood some miles offshore. We nevertheless boarded a tug with all of our gear and soon bobbed over a rolling swell toward them. Lockley, Marshall, Smith, Lieutenant Colonel Mayne (who was also accompanying us back to England), and I boarded the cruiser at sea, while all of the others subsequently rode across to the *Highland Monarch*.

Captain Cuthbert welcomed us aboard the *Ajax* and gave us the best that his ship had to offer. The luckless Smith, who was pressed into service as cook with little delay, was the only exception. The homeward voyage passed quickly. The *Ajax*'s officers made our passage interesting by arranging inspections and demonstrations for us in various parts of the cruiser. We also enjoyed the fresh food loaded onto the wardroom table.

At Freetown, Sierra Leone, the civilian personnel from the *Highland Monarch* transferred to the *Ajax*. After calling at Lisbon in Portugal and Bilboa in Spain to pick up additional prisoners of war (POWs), the *Ajax* broke off and allowed some destroyers to take over escort duties for the *Highland Monarch* during the hours of darkness. It steamed on toward Hamburg while we sailed up the English Channel and docked at Chatham at 4:00 in the afternoon of Saturday 9 March 1946.

It is probably true to say that no government-sponsored expedition to the Antarctic ever set forth from its country of origin as unostentatiously as "Operation Tabarin" had in 1943 because our entire mission was shrouded in secrecy. The quietness of our return, however, exceeded that of our departure. A knot of people stood alongshore on that dreary afternoon, but they had come to meet friends and relatives from the *Ajax*'s crew. Half an hour after the cruiser docked, a handful of government officials arrived, including J.M. Wordie of the Scott Polar Research Institute. We struggled to procure money for our party at that particular time of the English week, but the *Ajax*'s paymaster, Commander Bennett, obliged us by cashing a personal cheque of mine. With these funds in hand, I doled out sufficient money for each man to last through a rather lean weekend. The lack of prearranged reservations made locating hotel rooms difficult, and three of our group spent their first night back in England stretched out with their luggage in one of London's derelict air raid shelters. I was fortunate in deciding to remain aboard the deserted *Ajax* for the night.

Given the attention we gave to our records and reports, I did not anticipate a lengthy delay before returning to Canada. I took with me many memories of pleasant days and friendships in the south. It was a great privilege to have known many members of Operation Tabarin. Scattered as they already are in places such as Sweden, South America, the Pacific Islands, and Newfoundland, my thoughts often return to the clean atmosphere where we discovered our interdependence in the far south. Each man's reaction to events revealed his character to all who looked. Our isolation caused us to focus on each other like a very piercing light. Under such conditions, ostentation and self-advertisement could rarely remain concealed. There were, however, a few of our group who withstood such minute attention. I cannot mention their names here, but I know that some of our number would join me in doffing their caps to these men. Meeting them made it all worthwhile, and the memories of associating with them will long remain with me. Perhaps someday we will meet again.

Taylor and His Manuscript

ANDREW TAYLOR TRIED TO CLOSE *TWO YEARS BELOW THE HORN* on a positive note by calling attention to his "many memories of pleasant days and friendships" in its final paragraph. The penultimate paragraph, however, betrayed this effort. His frustrations with the Discovery Committee, which Chippie Ashton had pejoratively dubbed the "Block and Tackle Brigade,"[1] began in late 1945 and solidified after his return to England. The Canadian Army also refused to officially recognize Taylor's command of Operation Tabarin by backdating his promotion to major to late 1944 or early 1945—a decision that left him tailing behind other officers for further promotion. These experiences embittered Taylor and coloured his sense of where he did—and should—fit in polar history. Ultimately, Taylor's failure to find a willing publisher for his memoir of the Antarctic mission prevented his accomplishments from being better known and recognized. He lamented that British and Canadian officials ignored his contributions to Antarctic exploration and research. Only in the early 1990s, at the twilight of his life, did a series of Canadian institutions, including the federal government, recognize Taylor's Antarctic achievements.

In articulating his frustration with the Discovery Committee's handling of Operation Tabarin's return to the United Kingdom in 1945, Taylor failed to mention that the wives and families of Flett and Smith, as well as a friend of Mayne, were at the dock when the *Ajax* docked at Chatham. No officials, however, initially greeted the Antarctic party. Half an hour passed before a small group arrived including James Wordie, Dr. Brian Roberts, and Dr. Neil Mackintosh. They briefed the returning men on how to respond to press inquiries[2] and then distributed letters to everyone except the scientists. These letters welcomed their recipients home before explaining that they would be terminated once their leave was complete. These officials had also misunderstood Taylor's repeated requests for a £10-per-person advance, and subsequently did not bring the money that the men needed for room and board. Since it was a Saturday, the banks were closed, and Taylor only managed to acquire £30 after prevailing upon the *Ajax*'s paymaster to cash a personal cheque. Moreover, the Discovery Committee had not arranged any accommodations or transportation for the expedition's amassed specimens, reports, and returning personnel and it fell upon the ship's executive officer to make arrangements for the latter. The individuals who had homes near London departed by 9:00 p.m. Davies, Donnachie, and Matheson, however, lived further away and left the ship hoping to find accommodations ashore. They ultimately failed, and spent their first night in Britain sleeping in a deserted air raid shelter.[3] To ensure the safety of Tabarin's reports and specimens, Taylor spent the night aboard "the same place [that] I had spent the preceding three weeks and a few days—in my cabin aboard the *Ajax*."[4]

In his landmark study of Britain in Antarctica, Sir Vivian Ernest Fuchs speculated that the Discovery Committee's apparent indifference to the arrival of Operation Tabarin's personnel and specimens owed to the persistence of wartime secrecy.[5] Historian Stephen Haddelsey, however, discounts this possibility. The "apparently cavalier treatment of the personnel of Operation Tabarin did not result from an ongoing need for secrecy" because "the existence of the expedition had been public knowledge since April 1944." Instead, he attributes the Discovery Committee's neglect and "official indifference" to the expeditioners' return to the postwar context.[6] With hundreds of thousands of returning veterans from across the globe, "the reappearance of a handful of Antarctic veterans failed to attract much attention in official circles."[7] Privately, Fuchs, a geologist and explorer who eventually became the director of the British Antarctic Survey from 1958 to 1973, offered another explanation to Taylor. In 1954, Fuchs tried to assuage the latter's grudge by suggesting that "at the time there was no organization to deal with the material returned to this country" and this could have given the false impression that the "authorities were disinterested and unappreciative of the very considerable field work accomplished."[8]

The lack of organization that Fuchs described persisted for many years. During the war, the Admiralty officially but reluctantly ran Operation Tabarin, insisting that the Colonial Office fund and oversee all practical aspects of the operation. The navy exercised direct command only over the expedition's ships and their crews. As the exigencies of the war receded, the Admiralty's association was no longer necessary. In July 1945, Operation Tabarin was "civilianized" and, since the Falkland Islands would continue to provide the closest administrative support, the operation was renamed the "Falkland Islands Dependencies Survey" (FIDS).[9] The new organization, however, remained a "haphazard and disjointed administration."[10] As John Dudeney and David Walton explain,

> Organisationally, the UK end of FIDS was now run from the Mediterranean Office of the CO, essentially by one principal grade officer (J. Barton), whilst the cost was met from the colonial and Middle Eastern services vote from the end of the 1945–1946 season. Barton was advised and assisted by an informal committee comprising of Mackintosh and Wordie with Roberts acting as its secretary. Meanwhile operational command rested with the field leader (by then Surgeon Commander Bingham), under the direction of the governor. Organisationally this was hardly optimum. Difficulties quickly arose through poor communication amongst the various groups with a finger in the pie. Barton and the informal committee members pressed for reform, particularly for the Discovery committee and FIDS to be merged, and, although the organisational deficiencies were well recognised within the CO, reform was slow to come. The FIDS committee was formalised in June 1946, but stability was only achieved by the establishment in May 1948 of the FIDS scientific committee by the CO with a membership approved by the Secretary of State and Wordie as the first chairman.[11]

With the obscurity that still clouded Operation Tabarin's activities, the return of millions of armed-forces personnel, and the organizational growing pains that continued to plague Britain's Antarctic activities during the immediate postwar period, it is not surprising that the Colonial Office was not adequately prepared for the return of Taylor and the other Antarctic veterans.

Regardless of what caused the cold reception at Chatham, Taylor later noted that it personally "forecast the 'shape of things to come.'"[12] Before returning home, Taylor had to finish several incomplete or un-typed reports. Although he subsequently had few interactions with Wordie and wrote positively about Mackintosh, Taylor worked extensively with Roberts. At first, Taylor and Roberts (who was the youngest and most active of the three) got along fairly well. Taylor, the consummate philatelist, exchanged postage stamps with Roberts after visiting the latter's home for dinner.[13] Roberts also lobbied the Canadian military to promote Taylor to the rank of major for his service in Antarctica (discussed below). Yet the two men soon developed what Taylor subsequently described as a strong and mutual "antipathy."[14] Roberts, for example, took nearly a month to find Taylor a desk in London where he could complete his operation reports. By the time he found one, Taylor, who was eager to return to his family in Canada and was tired of the delays, had already set up a study with all of the necessary supplies and draft reports at the home of friends in Sussex. "I blew my top," Taylor reported in his Tabarin diary, when he received Roberts's instructions to relocate to London. The Canadian took the matter up with Mackintosh, who eventually supported Taylor's preference to remain in Sussex.[15] During another meeting at the end of April, Taylor presented Roberts with a draft article concerning Tabarin for the press and the latter "tore my newspaper account to bits." Taylor responded that he was "losing interest in the entire project very swiftly" and complained that his business and familial obligations necessitated returning to Canada by June. According to Taylor's account of the encounter, Roberts replied that he was "unaccustomed to dealing with people having any personal interests," but offered to consider Taylor's timeline if he justified it in writing.[16] Although Taylor did leave in June, he internalized his confrontations with Roberts.[17]

Despite these frustrations with the British, Taylor considered the Canadian military's failure to recognize his Antarctic command to be "the most humiliating experience of all."[18] Before departing Britain for Antarctica, Taylor's superiors had assured him that his "prolonged secondment" would not harm his chances for promotion.[19] Marr had outranked him, and Bingham outranked him by two promotions. Four of Tabarin's personnel, moreover, had shared Taylor's rank for the year he commanded the expedition. When Taylor returned to London in 1946, however, he was told that Canada Military Headquarters had not received any notification of his command from the Colonial Office. To make matters worse, a routine order had just been issued barring retroactive promotions exceeding thirty days. After a few weeks of lobbying, Taylor prevailed upon the Colonial Office to write to Canada's Military Headquarters on his behalf. The ensuing letter described Taylor's increased responsibilities within Operation Tabarin, as well as the simple fact that his predecessor's and replacement's ranks both exceeded Taylor's captaincy. It also reiterated Taylor's belief that "his secondment to this work in the Antarctic has prejudiced his promotion in his unit," recognized that Operation Tabarin was a secret operation, and requested that corrective action be taken if Taylor had suffered unjustly. The letter did not, however, explicitly recommend a retroactive promotion to 8 December 1944 as Taylor had requested.[20] A few weeks later, the Canadian Army promoted Taylor to major effective to 1 April 1946.

The Canadian Army initially added insult to injury by refusing to pay Taylor fully for the ninety-five days of leave that he accumulated while seconded to Operation Tabarin in Antarctica. Instead, Canadian Military Headquarters only agreed to give him thirty days paid leave. Taylor demanded that he receive the remaining sixty-five days. Roberts accordingly wrote to J. Barton of the Colonial Office on Taylor's behalf recommending that the treasury grant the request and make it commensurate with a major's pay.[21] The consequent inquiry by the Colonial Office, in addition to Taylor's continued lobbying, proved to be sufficient: the Canadian Army eventually recognized that Taylor had been "completely divorced from the outside world" and granted him the additional sixty-five days leave.[22]

By early June, Taylor had completed his Tabarin work. He spent his last few days in England on leave visiting friends, packing, and writing personal letters to friends (as well as letters of recommendation for Davies and Ashton). He boarded the *Lady Rodney* on 11 June and sailed for Halifax. Unlike his trip on the *Highland Monarch*, the *Lady Rodney* was crowded with nearly 500 returning veterans. When he reached Canada on 21 June 1946, he caught a train to Ottawa where he had orders to meet with Colonel Henry Lloyd (Jerry) Meuser, the chief engineer at Army Headquarters. After Taylor reached Canada's capital, Meuser entertained him for the next two days at his home and toured him through his office. All the while, the senior engineer encouraged Taylor to remain in the Army and take up a position in research and development.[23] After completing this business visit, Taylor continued home by train and reunited with his family on 26 June 1946.[24]

Taylor grew increasingly aware of the need to publish his own account of Operation Tabarin if he wanted his contributions to be recognized. In July 1946, Wordie published an article in the *Polar Record* detailing Tabarin's main accomplishments. Although the article focussed on events and paid comparatively little attention to personnel and leadership, Taylor's predecessor and replacement received limited praise, while Taylor faced passive or negative analysis. When commenting that it was "unfortunately" necessary for Taylor to replace Marr, for example, Wordie added that it was Taylor's first time in Antarctica while Marr was an Antarctic "veteran" whose first voyage had been with Shackleton on the *Quest* in 1921. "No one," he continued, "even among the ship's officers, has had such intimate knowledge of the waterways of the South Orkneys and of the South Shetlands and Bransfield Strait."[25] Ashton complained in a letter to Taylor that the article also suggested that the war's completion "made it possible to release suitable men" for Antarctic service.[26] The slight may have been unintentional, however, as Wordie later wrote to Taylor expressing how "impressed" he was by "the good work done by your party," regretting Taylor's delayed departure from England, and encouraging Taylor to "write something up" after returning to Canada.[27]

Additional competing voices also loomed large. The United States mounted its massive Operation Highjump from 1946 to 1947. The unprecedented scale of this operation, which included thirteen ships (including an aircraft carrier), thirty-three aircraft, and nearly 5,000 men, led Taylor to worry that the publication of competing Antarctic adventure narratives would overshadow the work of Tabarin.[28] Back in England, Chippie Ashton also worried about Taylor's prospects as an author. The former Antarctic carpenter continued to work at the FIDS and was well aware of other Tabarin publicity. In the fall of 1946, he warned Taylor that James was undertaking his own book project, and over the following year he regularly provided updates on James's progress, urging Taylor to finish *Two Years Below the Horn* before his rival beat him to the punch.[29]

Ashton also noted that the British press eagerly printed Antarctic content—unlike the Canadian situation. Despite the importance that Operation Tabarin's recruiters had attributed to Taylor's "cold weather" surveying experience in Manitoba, few Canadians took note of their countryman's work in establishing the first permanent presence on the Antarctic mainland. Aside from a 1946 interview with Taylor that was published in the Toronto *Star Weekly*, the Canadian press did not promote his achievements.[30] Indeed, Taylor complained that even the *Star Weekly* story provided a "rather warped account" of his interview where he had emphasized the contributions of each Tabarin member.[31]

After spending his first months back in Canada recuperating with his family, Taylor devoted himself to "chasing up" job offers.[32] He received several after exploring teaching positions at four universities and crisscrossing Manitoba to meet with old business connections. He also considered the Army's offer to remain on active service. "I am not greatly enthused at spending the rest of my life in the army [*sic*]," he told Ashton. In the end, however, Taylor eventually elected to remain in military service.[33] High housing prices in Ottawa, however, made a move to Canada's capital city extremely challenging and forced his family to spend several weeks in a hotel before moving into their new home on Besserer Street on 23 December.[34]

All of this activity made it impossible for Taylor to begin writing his account of Operation Tabarin. He was unable to assemble all of the necessary "papers, documents and books of reference" in Ottawa until January 1947[35] when, with his home base finally established, he launched a crash-writing program. By 3 February he had completed drafts of the first 120 pages and urgently wrote to the Canadian Department of National Defence and the British Colonial Office asking them to "expeditiously" vet his manuscript for security concerns.[36] Both departments responded quickly and cleared his work.[37] On 19 February he submitted a further 120 pages and once again received prompt and assenting replies.[38] Two weeks later, however, the Army sent Taylor to Fort Churchill's cold weather research program as a technical observer. The month-long posting prevented him from completing the manuscript,[39] but despite the "terrible grind" Taylor persevered by writing whenever possible after attending to his daily duties.[40] By the time he returned to Ottawa in the second-last week of March, he bragged to Ashton that the manuscript was "three-quarters finished."[41] In late April, despite the birth of his daughter Adelle and moving the family to a new home deeper in suburban Ottawa, Taylor completed his manuscript and secured final permissions from the Canadian military and imperial authorities to seek a publisher.[42]

Taylor contacted a series of international publishing houses in late May and early June 1947 including Simon & Schuster Inc., Alfred Knopf, G.P. Putnam's Sons, Harcourt Brace & Co., and W.W. Norton & Co. to solicit interest in his manuscript. In his cover letters, Taylor contended that no exploration account concerning the Antarctic had been published for a decade and that "popular interest in that remote part of the world is rapidly approaching a peak." This suggested that his volume had "more than average chance of success." He admitted that his writing was "mediocre" and acknowledged that the text required "some editing," but he was confident that the revisions would be limited to omitting "repetitive and redundant material." Time constraints, he pleaded, prevented him from attending to this task himself.[43] The responses were prompt and positive, with each press requesting copies of the manuscript.[44]

Over the next few weeks, however, each publisher read and rejected Taylor's draft. The explanations ranged from form statements that the submission did not fit the press's "publication plans"[45] to personalized responses that attempted to soften the blow. The editor-in-chief for G.P. Putnam's Sons, for example, generously noted that the text's style was "easy going and straightforward" before demurring that it was "too specialized" to attract a strong response from "general reader[s]."[46] Two other delicate but brief responses suggested pursuing other presses.[47]

Before Taylor could react, however, military duties once again pulled him away from his authorial work. In the first week of July, the Defence Research Board (DRB) sent Taylor to join a team of Canadian observers on an American/Canadian weather station reconnaissance venture dubbed U.S. Naval Task Force 68.[48] On 13 July, he departed Ottawa for Boston where he subsequently joined other Canadian observers aboard the task force of two American icebreakers and a freighter. The task force visited Greenland before heading to a series of sites in the Canadian Arctic archipelago including Dundas Harbour, Resolute Bay, Slidre Bay, Radstock Bay, and Pond Inlet. As a DRB observer, Taylor watched the unloading of stores, observed the siting and construction of the Resolute and Eureka weather stations, and sought out information about American icebreaker designs. He also collected specimens of botanical, geological, paleontological, and archaeological interest. Throughout the voyage, he maintained regular contact with the task force's leadership, including the United States Weather Bureau's J. Glenn Dyer and Charles Hubbard, as well as the first officer-in-charge of the weather station at Resolute, John Cleghorn.[49]

Taylor's Antarctic experiences afforded him a discerning perspective during this voyage. He told Eric Back that "the polar land in the north is altogether different from that which we found in Grahamland [*sic*]."[50] Such bi-polar juxtapositions proved useful. He noted, for example, the "great thickness and hardness" of Arctic ice compared to its southern counterpart.[51] Yet he admitted that there was "considerable resemblance" between the Antarctic mainland and certain sections of the Arctic, such as the coasts of Greenland and Baffin Island. "Much of the northwestern Arctic," he continued in a letter to Back, "reminded me of Deception Island and the small ones in Crown Prince Gustav Channel which you saw. There are a few cliffs, but the land is barren."[52] Lichens, he noted, abounded in numbers that were akin to Deception Island or even the Falkland Islands.[53] The Canadian Department of Mines and Resources also recognized the value of Taylor's Antarctic experience. According to Deputy Minister Hugh Keenleyside, Taylor's "training as a Dominion Land Surveyor, his considerable field experience in Canada, and the time spent in the Antarctic a few years ago" made him "especially well qualified to carry out" the studies being conducted by his department as well as the Department of National Defence.[54] Antarctic experience also provided valuable "common" ground for Taylor and the American naval crews who had just returned from Operation Highjump. Consequently, Taylor got on well with the Americans and found them "very easy to talk to."[55]

Upon returning to Canada, Taylor wrote observation reports "almost continuously" until the spring of 1948.[56] These documents covered a host of subjects including engineering, ice conditions, mapping, archaeology, physiography, tides, and currents.[57] In the midst of these activities, Taylor continued to search for a publisher for his Tabarin manuscript. First, he changed his mind about the first letter of interest that he had received in March 1947 from Herbert and Joseph Limited publishers in London, which had indicated their desire for a manuscript on the history of the British Empire in Antarctica.[58] At the time, Taylor had replied that his manuscript was not the generalist work that they sought and was "a rather detailed account of the one little and relatively unimportant expedition with which I happened to be connected." He offered to help with the composition of a general history of British exploration in Antarctica, but otherwise let the matter drop.[59] In mid-January 1948, however, Taylor reconnected with the publisher and blamed his lack of correspondence on his prolonged work in the Canadian Arctic and in Greenland.[60] In turn, the publisher acknowledged receipt of Taylor's draft and promised to examine it, but did not send a response for six months.[61] "We have been hoping for some time that despite many production and labour difficulties we might be able to give you a favourable reply," the rejection letter confessed, "but this, unfortunately, we are unable to do."[62] Taylor was crushed, but persisted in his efforts to find a way to get his work into print.[63]

Frustrated by repeated rejections, Taylor even hired a publishing agent. Howard Moorepark, however, was not optimistic about the prospects for Taylor's manuscript. "This is not a very good year for books like this," he warned. Book sales had fallen steeply and costs had increased, but Moorepark promised to "do his best."[64] Over the next six months he contacted Appletons, Oxford, Coward McCann, Dutton, Harpers, Whittlesey House, Viking, and Odyssey Presses—to no avail.[65] By January 1948, Taylor terminated his relationship with Moorepark and continued to solicit publishers on his own.[66]

Early that year, Taylor solicited the support of Trevor Lloyd, the chief of the Geographic Bureau in the Canadian Department of Mines and Resources, who in turn consulted the famous Arctic explorer Vilhjalmur Stefansson.[67] The latter subsequently recommended Taylor to the University of Oklahoma Press.[68] Editor Savoie Lottinville promised to send Taylor's draft to his readers "immediately,"[69] but Taylor's frustration mounted as winter approached. When Taylor inquired about his manuscript's status in December, Lottinville replied that the manuscript had "definite possibilities" but explained that the readers commissioned by the press were "not yet unanimous on it." He promised a decision by mid-January 1949.[70] When March came and went without a response, Taylor again sought an update.[71] This time he received a rejection letter pronouncing the manuscript to be "entirely publishable" and its contents appropriate for publication by a scholarly press. Finances, Lottinville claimed, were the obstacle in this case. The "tightness" of the university press's budget, combined with declining sales, rendered it unable to publish the manuscript. He encouraged Taylor to try contacting other presses or return to the University of Oklahoma Press in seven or eight months if he was still in need of a publisher. Ultimately, further exchanges between them did not result in the book appearing in print.[72]

Part of Taylor's inability to find a publisher for *Two Years Below the Horn* reflected shifts in polar scientific culture that had led him away from the sort of heroic account that publishing houses generally sought. Although there was an abiding public interest in tales of polar adventures, his manuscript focussed on professionalism, surveying, and scientific observations. As we noted in the introduction, wartime technological transportation and communication advancements led field scientists to believe that they could overcome polar environments and undertake systematic studies. Imperial powers previously relied on exploration and cartography to claim territory, but states increasingly relied on conducting science and contributing to international environmental knowledge to justify their postwar influence in Antarctica. Taylor's writing was an early example of this genre but he was not the only Canadian to suffer for emphasizing professionalism and detail over hazards. Other Canadians who subsequently worked in Antarctica and published accounts emphasizing competence over hazards similarly "failed to capture the public imagination like previous expeditions to polar frontiers," as historian Peder Roberts observes.[73]

The fact that David James successfully published his more sensational account of his involvement in Operation Tabarin is further evidence of continued appetite for traditional explorer narratives. James's discussion of the first sledging team's slow progress in poor snow conditions in early September 1945, for example, is a brooding account that emphasizes his worries about running out of food, fuel, or energy before the four men and their dog teams reached the depot at Vortex Island.[74] Taylor's account of the latter stages of the first sledging journey, by contrast, is much more optimistic and matter-of-fact. Indeed, Taylor's description of this short period is one of the few occasions when he emphasizes his leadership. Yet his discussion emphasized professionalism and risk management rather than worry. Thus, while Taylor acknowledged the exhaustingly slow pace and the shortage of supplies and the dog teams' withering condition, he also offered detailed observations of his surroundings, described his team's careful rationing of food and fuel with little fanfare, and discounted James's concerns (see Chapter 15). James's decision to provide his readers with an account emphasizing introspection, worry, and the sense of beating hard odds, however, proved more attractive to publishing houses than Taylor's attempts to dispel poor assessments of his leadership and professionalism.

Despite Taylor's failure to secure a publisher for his Antarctic manuscript, he received one significant honour in the immediate postwar period. The U.K. Antarctic Place-Names Committee, whose membership included Wordie and Roberts, determined the names of geographic features in the British sector. In 1948, it honoured Taylor by naming a mountain near Hope Bay (which Operation Tabarin's personnel named "Ben More") after him. No records of the committee's deliberations concerning Mount Taylor survive, but Taylor interpreted the honour as yet another slight. Russell, who assumed command for Hope Bay in 1946, had named the entire peninsula south of Hope Bay "Taylor Peninsula" during his postwar sledging work,[75] but the committee rejected this suggestion. It named the peninsula after Operation Tabarin, and instead gave Taylor's name to the 1,000-metre mountain that Taylor subsequently described as a "relatively unimportant feature at the head of Hope Bay."[76]

For its part, the Canadian Army encouraged Taylor to pursue graduate studies in geography. Toward this end, he attended McGill's University Summer

School at Stanstead, Quebec, in 1948 and completed courses on polar themes, practical geography, geography of cold lands, climatology, and the scientific analysis of scenery. Despite achieving straight As in these courses, the bulk of his academic background had focussed on engineering rather than geography.[77] Consequently, a half-dozen Canadian and American universities rejected his applications to their graduate programs because he lacked the pre-requisite two years of undergraduate courses in the discipline. After meeting with Trevor Lloyd and "bemoaning" his rejection, the geographer arranged for Taylor to meet with Dr. Pierre Dagenais at L'Université de Montréal.[78] Dagenais, in turn, secured Taylor's admittance. Therefore, the following year, at the age of forty-two, Taylor began graduate studies in a new discipline—and in a second language. "I had little or no knowledge of the French language," he later confessed, "and sat through the first few classes listening to what to me was pure Greek."[79] It did not take him long, however, to work out a solution:

> First, I produced what must be the worst French into English translations ever made of two textbooks required for the geography course which immediately extended my vocabulary. Then, I borrowed French notes kept by several of my fellow students who appeared most interested in the lectures, and translated them into English. From that point, I wrote my own notes and read English texts extensively. And the most redeeming factor of all—I was permitted to write my exams in English.[80]

In the end, Taylor finished his coursework with "an average just under 90%" and had taken so many classes that he accidentally qualified for both the MA and PhD programs.[81] Taylor submitted his MA thesis on the geography of the Queen Elizabeth Islands in 1950, and it was subsequently published by the Geographical Branch of the Department of Mines and Surveys.[82]

Throughout his postwar service, the Canadian Army also committed Taylor to various polar projects. For example, it repeatedly seconded Taylor to the U.S. Corps of Engineers' Research and Development Laboratories at Fort Belvoir, Virginia, where he worked "for months at a time" on cold-weather training manuals, including "Land Navigation by Dead Reckoning" (1949) and "Arctic Construction"—a guide that proved extremely valuable to planners during the construction of the Distant Early Warning (DEW) Line. During these years, Taylor also developed a strong interest in constructing snow roads and runways, and he joined the Snow, Ice and Permafrost Research Establishment's (SIPRE) Sub-Committee of the Building Research Division at the National Research Council of Canada.[83] Taylor and his research team subsequently developed a series of experiments to better understand how to improve snow's density and hardness. These results led them to break with the conventional use of rollers to compact snow; instead, they employed a modified rotary tiller that mixed the snow before packing it down. This alternative process allowed the snow's own thermal differentials to transform each flake into a more ice-like substance. In 1952, Taylor and his team organized a demonstration of their ideas at Kapuskasing, Ontario, which involved landing a loaded and wheeled (as opposed to ski-equipped) DC-3 aircraft on a snow-compacted runway prepared during the preceding twenty-four hours. Although the Canadian Army never adopted the "snow-compacting thermo vibratory machine" that Taylor developed, the Russians and the Americans used the technology to build Arctic and Antarctic airstrips.[84]

None of these research and professional development activities, however, earned Taylor a military promotion. He blamed his lack of upward mobility on the Army's refusal to backdate his promotion to major to December 1944 or February 1945. He believed that this unwillingness to recognize his lengthy command experience from Operation Tabarin, coupled with his lack of combat experience in Western Europe, limited his seniority and allowed competing officers to secure advancement instead.[85] Taylor repeatedly brought this concern to the attention of his senior officers, but to no avail. The final straw came when the Army offered Taylor a staff appointment at the Royal Military College in Kingston but refused to promote him to Lieutenant Colonel. After twelve years in the Army, the frustrated major gave the Army advanced informal notice of his intention to leave the military, and actually submitted his resignation in September 1952, two years short of pension eligibility. He subsequently estimated that this decision cost him over $200,000 in pension payments.[86]

The timing of Taylor's resignation owed to various factors. First and foremost, he was overqualified for his assignments and thus found himself disillusioned. His wife's health was also failing, and this made his frequent trips to the United States extremely difficult.[87] Accordingly, Taylor had been cultivating other career options for several months. In May 1952, he submitted a proposal for a contract to produce a multi-volume study concerning the physical geography of the northern islands of the Canadian Arctic archipelago to the U.S. Office of Naval Research (and later to the American Geographical Society). The

Figure 61. Andrew Taylor receiving the Polar Medal, 8 June 1954.

proposal noted the dearth of geographical knowledge about the region, and suggested combining centuries-old published and archival records by Arctic explorers with the tens of thousands of tri-metrigon aerial photographs (recently captured by the RCAF and the U.S. air force during their systematic surveys of the Canadian north during the immediate postwar period) to produce a systematic study.[88] Taylor received unofficial notification that the American Geographical Society had decided to fund his thirty-month program of work in mid-October, and he began this new job immediately.[89]

The following year, the British government paid Taylor a prestigious honour. Participation in Operation Tabarin made Taylor eligible for the Polar Medal, which recognized polar service on behalf of the empire.[90] Up to this point, only a few Canadians (most notably the RCMP officers of the *St. Roch* who transited the Northwest Passage in both directions between 1940 and 1944) had received the award.[91] In July 1953, the London *Gazette* announced that the

Crown would grant Polar Medals to several dozen former members of the FIDS and Operation Tabarin.[92] Haddelsey points out that the long period between the end of service and the granting of the medals was not unusual; the British government struggled to overcome a backlog of Second World War decorations until the 1960s.[93] Although Taylor's retrospective account about the medal is somewhat confused, it is clear that he did not receive official notice of his award following the *Gazette*'s publication. Instead, he learned about the honour at a chance meeting on Sparks Street in Ottawa with Geoffrey Hattersley-Smith from the Defence Research Board, who had seen a reprinting of the *Gazette*'s list in the London *Times*.[94] By December, Sir Vivian Fuchs, who had recently begun corresponding with Taylor, tried to soften the blow. Taylor's Polar Medal, he insisted, was "well earned," and he urged Taylor to contact the Admiralty Honours and Awards Branch of Queen Anne's Mansions "at any time" if he wanted to receive the award directly from the Queen.[95] The following year, an increasingly furious Taylor received clippings from British friends and relatives describing the February investiture ceremony hosted by the Queen at Buckingham Palace. Even then he received no official word of his medal. The Crown appeared to be adopting, in the words of Trevor Lloyd, a "come and get it" attitude.[96] Taylor had neither the time nor the finances to take up Fuchs's suggestion, and in the end he was "reduced to requesting" that his investiture take place in Canada.[97]

In May 1954, Taylor finally received an invitation from Governor General Vincent Massey to an investiture ceremony at Rideau Hall on 8 June. Initially, Taylor considered telling the Canadian government to "stuff it up their butts, but cooler heads prevailed" and he proceeded to the ceremony. Afterward, he remained bitter. Although he later recognized that the Canadian state had failed to act on the *Gazette*'s notification, he continued to direct his anger at the imperial government, convinced that the "indignity" he suffered had been "quite deliberate" and inspired by his "colonial" status.[98] He also told Hattersley-Smith that the "Block and Tackle Brigade" intentionally failed to notify the Canadian government of the award.[99] In a letter to Fuchs composed thirty-two years later, Taylor expressed his continued embitterment. Men "who had never been more than a couple of miles from the galley stove in the entire two year period we spent there" had received their awards from the Queen at Buckingham Palace while Taylor, Tabarin's commander and a member of the expedition's surveying journeys, had to lobby for months before he received his medal.[100] "There is no country in the world that can bestow an honor [*sic*] or decoration more ceremoniously than can Britain," he lamented, "[but] there is also no country in the world that can bestow an honor [*sic*] more shabbily than can Britain."[101]

The Canadian press failed to appreciate Taylor's achievement. Most newspapers that covered the awards ceremony either missed or understated Taylor's importance to Operation Tabarin. Both the Ottawa *Journal* and *Citizen,* for example, printed articles focussing on the plethora of decorations awarded to soldiers for service and heroism during the Korean War. When the articles discussed the investiture of Taylor's medal, they overlooked his operational command in Antarctica and simply informed readers that he "took part in the Falkland Islands dependencies [*sic*] survey in 1944–45."[102] Even the local paper for the Winnipeg suburb of Elmwood, where Taylor's parents resided, mentioned in passing that Taylor was "a member"—not the commander—of the Antarctic expedition.[103] Only the *Winnipeg Free Press* acknowledged that Taylor had led Operation Tabarin from 1944 to 1945—but even it failed to elaborate on the significance of his achievements.[104]

Taylor's attention, by this point, was fixated northward rather than southward. In early 1955, while he was in the midst of his Canadian Arctic Archipelago contract, a massive defence construction project took form that required his expertise. Acute concerns about Soviet nuclear capabilities and American abilities to detect bombers overflying the Arctic to attack the North American heartland led the United States to push for the construction of a radar network along the Arctic coastline. Canada consented to the Distant Early Warning (DEW) Line project in November 1954 and, three months later, the Defence Research Board asked Taylor if he would help to lead the team that would determine the sites and layouts for the Canadian stations. In March 1955, he signed a contract with the engineering firm Knappen-Tippets-Abbett-McCarthy (KTAM), as well as an oath of secrecy, flew to Churchill, Manitoba, and took up his role as the assistant engineer and senior Canadian assigned to the work. For the next three months, Taylor and his team of two dozen engineers and draftsmen worked twelve- to fourteen-hour days, six days a week.[105] By May of the following year, Taylor had also finished writing the draft of his Canadian Arctic Archipelago research, and then spent a month proofreading and collecting images for the publication. His study was eventually published as the twelve-volume *Physical Geography of the Queen Elizabeth Islands.*[106] From an early stage in the project, Taylor had recognized that the project's research could also be reused as the basis for a doctorate, which he successfully defended at Montreal in 1957.[107]

These additional professional activities and academic achievements did not lead to a career of military contract work. Taylor formed his own Arctic geography and engineering consulting firm in 1955, but it was not active until he finished his KTAM contract and began to actively seek further DEW Line–related work. In 1957, he secured a contract from the Defence Research Board to inspect DEW and Mid-Canada Line stations, interview station personnel as well as design engineers, and prepare a report outlining the content and justifying the need for a manual on "Building in the Arctic." He ultimately lost the contract to produce a manual from his work,[108] and his company spent the next decade working on civil engineering projects in Manitoba and the Northwest Territories.

On the side, Taylor dedicated the late 1950s to indexing the Arctic Blue Books—a 6,000-page series of reports and papers submitted to the British Upper and Lower Houses between 1818 and 1878. After consulting the Blue Books extensively during his graduate studies and publishing a short guide to the material in the *Arctic Circular,* Taylor began to compile an index independently in 1957 before securing a $7,000 contract from the Department of Northern Affairs and Natural Resources to finish the work two years later. The process was slow and tedious, and Taylor enlisted the help of his wife and three children to see it through.[109] "When it was completed," Taylor later recalled, "I had produced about 44,000 index cards (at about fifteen cents apiece), involving 250,000 entries. The total number of pages in the 47 *Blue Book Papers* with which I had become involved was about 4,300 pages which means that the indexing of each page involved roughly sixty entries. I was being paid about $1.75 a page; or three cents per entry."[110] Taylor subsequently joked that he should have sued the Canadian government under the Minimum Wage Act, and recognized that he had "badly underestimated" the job's size.[111] (Despite multiple attempts by Taylor, Alan Cooke, and the Toronto Public Library to publish the index, it remained on a single set of index cards for decades.)[112]

After Taylor retired in 1970 and opened an antiquarian bookshop in Winnipeg, broader interest in Operation Tabarin—and his manuscript *Two Years Below the Horn*—began to resurge. The British Antarctic Survey (BAS) still held the copy that Taylor had sent to the Colonial Office in 1947 and, in 1974, Fuchs sought the Canadian's permission to "quote short extracts" in exchange for a "general acknowledgment" of Taylor's work.[113] Taylor allowed Fuchs to quote from the manuscript and his journal, but required him to cite each section. "It has always been my intention," Taylor explained, "to revise the book" and submit it for publication.[114] When Fuchs published the official history of the BAS (*Of Ice and Men*) in 1983, the chapter concerning Operation Tabarin was sympathetic to Taylor's frustrations with the Colonial Office, but only drew occasionally from Taylor's reports and journal.[115]

The appearance of Fuchs's book led Taylor to once again contemplate Operation Tabarin. His friend, former BAS archivist and editor of the *Polar Record* Alan Cooke, encouraged him to revisit publishing *Two Years Below the Horn* and Taylor made some initial moves in this direction.[116] Taylor's personal copy of the manuscript had faded, so he re-initiated contact with the BAS (the FID's successor). Cooke used his connections to inquire whether Taylor could reclaim his 1947 duplicate or, cognizant that archives do not readily relinquish their holdings, whether the BAS would copy Taylor's manuscript.[117] The BAS agreed to the latter, but notified Taylor that it would charge him $30 to do so.[118] This fee became a new bone of contention for Taylor. He paid the sum, but complained that "it seems rather indecent of the powers that be to confiscate my copy as they have done."[119] Veteran BAS explorer Charles Swithinbank agreed that this seemed unfair but pleaded that "we live under government rules which do not always allow for sensible solutions to problems of this kind."[120] Taylor responded by sending the BAS the missing page to their copy, expressing his distrust of "civil servants," and threatening to write to Prime Minister Margaret Thatcher about the matter unless the BAS returned the 1947 copy to Taylor in exchange for the duplicate.[121]

Fortunately, cooler heads prevailed. BAS archivist Joan Smith arranged to refund Taylor's money and assured him that he retained the copyright to his work.[122] Rather than seek a publisher as he had attempted early after the war, Taylor elected to retype a clean copy of the entire manuscript in 1985 and to distribute seven privately printed copies of the unaltered manuscript amongst his family members.[123] Two years later, he returned to Britain to hold a reunion dinner with Operation Tabarin's remaining personnel and meet with BAS archivist Joanna Rae for an interview. Although the Tabarin gathering was ruined by a cyclone, Taylor enjoyed his interview with Rae and the two continued to correspond regularly thereafter.[124] By the end of 1987, he was "very glad that you—Joanna—are there at BAS, so that you will attend to subsequent references to Operation Tabarin to make certain that the long continuing campaign of

Figure 62. Taylor (left) receiving the Northern Science Award from Tom Siddon (right), 1992.

belittlement and denigration of our work and results comes to a complete stop, as I am now certain it will."[125] Taylor and Fuchs also maintained a healthy correspondence during the early 1990s.[126] For example, Taylor sent Fuchs money to purchase three copies of the latter's book, asking him to sign them for his children.[127] Fuchs obliged, inscribing each with the handwritten note, "In appreciation of all your father did for British Antarctic work."[128]

Despite these friendships, Taylor would not forget past—or what he perceived to be ongoing—indiscretions. In June 1993, the BAS held a celebration honouring the fiftieth anniversary of Operation Tabarin. This time, Taylor received an invitation promising that the event would "promote due recognition of the expedition and those who served on it," but the letter addressed Taylor as "a member of Operation Tabarin."[129] The invitation's failure to recognize that Taylor was, to use his own words, "the oldest living commander of BAS expeditions" still stung the begrudged veteran.[130] Initially, Taylor concluded that "the policy of studied belittlement continues," but he subsequently recognized that the inconsiderate salutation was likely an "inadvertent" mistake by a new generation of polar administrators.[131] Nonetheless, he still mourned the lack of "public recognition" for his leadership and he did not attend the festivities.[132]

Canada, however, showed a greater propensity to recognize Taylor's polar accomplishments in the last two decades of the twentieth century. In April 1986, Taylor received a letter from the Governor General informing him that he had been recommended to become an Officer of the Order of Canada.[133] Taylor found this to be a "wonderful surprise for an old man."[134] The full citation read as follows: "Geographer, historian, author and polar scholar, he was a pioneer in the development of the science of arctic engineering under permafrost conditions while serving as senior Canadian engineer during the establishment of the DEW Line."[135] Notably, the citation neglected to mention Taylor's Antarctic contributions,[136] and he grumbled that it was "restricted to a description of my accomplishments in and for Canada"[137] rather than his significant contribution to the British Commonwealth and to polar science more generally.

Taylor's investiture into the Order of Canada, coupled with the completion of the international Convention of the Regulation of Antarctic Mineral Resource Activities in 1988 and Alan Cooke's decision to publish an article describing Taylor as an "unsung hero," led the Tabarin veteran to take more decisive action to promote his Antarctic service. In 1988, he wrote to Prime Minister Brian Mulroney, Minister of Veterans Affairs George Hees, and Minister of External Affairs Joe Clark about his wartime leadership role and the Canadian government's failure to recognize the operation's significance.[138] According to Taylor, the only answer came from Hees, who acknowledged Taylor's letter without responding to its substance. The exasperated Manitoban wrote that "despite the staffs of hundreds that both the PM and the MEA had, not one person possessed the acuity to discern that I had written them about an historic incident in Canada's history—the first command of an expedition by a Canadian in Antarctica."[139]

Taylor continued to receive honours in the 1990s, satiating his longstanding quest for recognition. The University of Manitoba recognized Taylor's contributions with the Vilhjalmur Stefansson Award for excellence in Canadian Northern Studies in 1990, citing his "long and distinguished career as a polar researcher" in both the Arctic and Antarctic,[140] and with an honorary doctorate of science the following year. During the convocation ceremony, the university's vice-president and provost James Gardner touted Taylor's many polar accomplishments since graduating from the program's civil engineering program sixty years before. He noted Taylor's responsibility for commanding the Antarctic expedition, his team's addition of "more than forty names to the map of Antarctica," and his postwar contributions to Arctic research.[141] Taylor considered this honour to be "one of the highlights of my life."[142]

The Canadian government also recognized Taylor's Antarctic accomplishments when it presented him with the 1992 Northern Science Award for "significant contributions to the advancement of knowledge and understanding of the Canadian North."[143] Taylor gratefully accepted the award which included a cash prize of $5,000 and the Centenary Medal (commemorating the first International Polar Year). "For one whose pension has averaged less than $500 a month for the past twenty years," he wrote in his acceptance letter, "the promise of the gift you are appending to the Centenary Medal is overwhelming."[144] On 26 November, Taylor received the award from Minister of Indian and Northern Affairs Tom Siddon in the West Block of Parliament. The accompanying speech from the minister acknowledged that Taylor's contributions extended "beyond Canadian borders" to "all polar regions."[145]

It should come as no surprise that the Canadians emphasized Taylor's Arctic contributions in the early 1990s, given that the Arctic state was spearheading initiatives to promote northern circumpolar scientific collaboration and cooperation.[146] The important acknowledgment of Taylor's contributions as a *polar* expert, whose work transcended both poles, however, was a significant addition for a country whose polar gaze typically focussed northward. In earlier heroic eras, explorers such as Robert Falcon Scott, Ernest Shackleton, and Roald Amundsen moved between both poles.[147] This also held true for Taylor, albeit in a "modern" era. In the case of the Canadian, he leveraged his scientific, engineering, and logistics experiences to advance his career in Antarctica and the High Arctic, making substantive contributions to Canadian, American, and British polar knowledge.

Taylor spent his final year comforted that the Canadian government had, at last, recognized his polar accomplishments. His frustration with the British government, however, continued until he died in October 1993 at age eighty-five. "For all the honours that he had received from his fellow countrymen, Taylor told me that his proudest achievement was his less-recognized work on Operation Tabarin, especially as its commander at Hope Bay," noted Gwion "Taff" Davies,

Tabarin's invaluable "handyman," in his obituary of Taylor. Davies and his wife had visited Taylor at his home in Winnipeg in 1990. "We were amazed at the amount of [Taylor's] literary work cramming the bookshelves, and the wide scope of his interests," Davies recalled. Taylor had spent the last decades of his life preparing detailed accounts of other Canadian history topics which, like *Two Years Below the Horn*, went unpublished.[148] Nonetheless, they elucidate how embodied knowledge from Manitoban winters shaped his personality, his conduct of operations, and his approach to leadership in the southernmost reaches of the planet. "We spent much of the week reading as much of it as we could manage," Davies recalled, "especially the best account of Operation Tabarin that I had yet seen."[149]

After the war, Taylor and his friends believed that his memoir had to appear in print before rival publications on Operation Tabarin and other expeditions of the immediate postwar period relegated Taylor's leadership during the expedition to obscurity. In recent decades, historians and literary scholars have revealed how polar explorers used print media to generate public interest and build support through shameless self-promotion, with book sales critical to an explorer's reputation and future prospects.[150] Those explorers who failed to publish their memoirs faded from public view or left their reputations to the literary whims of their contemporaries and subsequent historians. Because Taylor failed to secure a publisher for his manuscript, he lamented that his polar contributions went overlooked for much of his life. Indeed, publications written by others that referred to Tabarin often downplayed his roles or questioned his leadership. After Taylor's death, however, those who had served under his command remembered a professional who had proven an effective leader and colleague. Davies, who had travelled with Taylor on two sledging trips, painted a positive portrait of Taylor as a man with "stolid endurance of the cold," a leader who was "easy-going and good company, with a roguish sense of humour"—yet a person who "could also be very firm when the need arose," commanded respect, and whose word carried. Beneath his "big, hefty, . . . hard-bitten hide," Davies explained, Taylor was a "brave and kind-hearted man, . . . a staunch and hardy companion in trying times."[151] Although Taylor never claimed such credit for himself in his writings, the publication of his memoir about his *Two Years Below the Horn* ensures that his recollections of Operation Tabarin are available to a wide audience, and that his unique contributions to Antarctic science and history are better appreciated.

Notes

EDITORS' NOTE

1. Taylor to Simon and Schuster, 26 May 1947, Taylor fonds, UMA, MSS 108 Box 15 File 1.

2. Taylor to Fuchs, 27 October 1974, Taylor fonds, UMA, MSS 108 Box 43 File 16.

3. Taylor's private journal is preserved in Taylor fonds, UMA, MSS 108 Box 3 File 11.

INTRODUCTION

1   Taylor, notes, 14 August 1988, Andrew Taylor fonds, University of Manitoba Archives (UMA), MSS 108 Box 2 File 9.

2   Douglas Liversidge, "World's Loneliest Address," *Star Weekly* [Toronto], 10 August 1946, Taylor fonds, UMA, MSS 108 Box 9 File 33.

3   Although the American Antarctic Service Expedition (1939 to 1941) had similar intentions, rival nations and the war in Europe led the United States to withdraw all personnel from the bases after overwintering for two years.

4   Sir Vivian Fuchs, *Of Ice and Men: The Story of the British Antarctic Survey, 1943–1973* (Oswestry, UK: Anthony Nelson, 1982), 53. See also Stephen Haddelsey, *Operation Tabarin: Britain's Secret Wartime Expedition to Antarctica, 1944–1946* (Stroud, UK: History Press, 2014), 200–6. During the next fifteen years, subsequent British expeditions travelled farther by dog-sledge but benefited from aircraft, snow vehicles, and improved communications equipment unavailable to the members of Tabarin. These latter expeditions also experienced setbacks, including several deaths.

5   For descriptions of British activities in Antarctica from 1946 to the International Geophysical Year, consult Fuchs, *Of Ice and Men*; Sir Vivian Fuchs and Sir Edmund Hillary, *The Crossing of Antarctica: The Commonwealth Trans-Antarctic Expedition, 1955–58* (London: Cassell, 1958); David Day, *Antarctica: A Biography* (Oxford: Oxford University Press, 2013); and Klaus Dodds, *Pink Ice: Britain and the South Atlantic Empire* (London: IB Tauris, 2002).

6   David James, *That Frozen Land: The Story of a Year in the Antarctic* (Toronto: Falcon Press, 1949); Fuchs, *Of Ice and Men*; and Dean Beeby, *In a Crystal Land: Canadian Explorers in Antarctica* (Toronto: University of Toronto Press, 1994).

7   Haddelsey, *Operation Tabarin*, 161–4, 168, 224–5, 227.

8   In recent decades, the analysis of nineteenth-century exploration and adventure texts has blossomed into a considerable field. Interested readers should consult Janice Cavell, *Tracing the Connected Narrative: Arctic Exploration in British Print Culture, 1818–1860* (Toronto: University of Toronto Press, 2008); T.D. MacLulich, "Canadian Exploration as Literature," *Canadian Literature* 81 (Summer 1979): 72–85; and I.S. MacLaren, "Exploration / Travel Literature and the Evolution of the Author," *International Journal of Canadian Studies* 5 (Spring 1992): 39–68.

9   Marionne Cronin, "Polar Horizons: Images of the Arctic in Accounts of Amundsen's Polar Aviation Expeditions," *Scientia Canadensis* 33, no. 2 (2010): 99–120; Beau Riffenburgh, *The Myth of the Explorer: The Press, Sensationalism, and*

Geographical Discovery (New York: Belhaven Press, 1993).

10 Bruce Hevly, "The Heroic Science of Glacier Motion," *Osiris* 11 (1996): 68.

11 Suzanne Zeller and Christopher Jacob Ries, "Wild Men In and Out of Science: Finding a Place in the Disciplinary Borderlands of Arctic Canada and Greenland," *Journal of Historical Geography* 44 (2014): 31–43; Tina Adcock, "Toward an Early Twentieth Century Culture of Northern Canadian Exploration," in *North by Degree: New Perspectives on Arctic Exploration*, ed. Susan A. Kaplan and Robert McCracken Peck (Philadelphia: American Philosophical Society, 2013), 110–41.

12 Trevor J. Barnes and Matthew Farish, "Between Regions: Science, Militarism, and American Geography from World War to Cold War," *Annals of the Association of American Geographers* 96, no. 4 (2006): 807–26; Matthew Farish, *Contours of America's Cold War* (Minneapolis: University of Minnesota Press, 2010).

13 Stephen Bocking, "A Disciplined Geography Aviation, Science, and the Cold War in Northern Canada, 1945–1960," *Technology and Culture* 50, no. 2 (April 2009): 265–90; Richard Powell, "'The Rigours of an Arctic Experiment': The Precarious Authority of Field Practices in the Canadian High Arctic, 1958–1970," *Environment and Planning A* 39 (2007): 1794–1811; G.E. Fogg, *A History of Antarctic Science* (Cambridge: Cambridge University Press, 1992), 3; Michael Bravo and Sverker Sörlin, eds., preface to *Narrating the Arctic: A Cultural History of Nordic Scientific Practices* (Canton, MA: Science History, 2002), vii.

14 "The Antarctic Treaty," article IX(2); Fogg, *A History of Antarctic Science*;

Dodds, *Pink Ice*; Klaus Dodds, *The Antarctic: A Very Short Introduction* (Oxford: Oxford University Press, 2012); Adrian John Howkins, "Frozen Empires: A History of the Antarctic Sovereignty Dispute Between Britain, Argentina, and Chile, 1939–1959" (unpublished PhD dissertation, University of Texas at Austin, 2008); Peder Roberts, *The European Antarctic: Science and Strategy in Scandinavia and the British Empire* (New York: Palgrave Macmillan, 2011).

15 Taylor to Olive and Chippie, 26 October 1947, Taylor fonds, UMA, MSS 108 Box 42 File 3.

16 See, for example, Peter Kikkert, "Grasping for the Ends of the Earth: Framing and Contesting Polar Sovereignty, 1900–1955" (unpublished PhD diss., Western University, 2016).

17 Taylor to Sir Vivian Fuchs, 6 August 1986, Taylor fonds, UMA, MSS 108 Box 43 File 16.

18 "Personal autobiographical sketch 1907–c1961," Taylor fonds, UMA, MSS 108 Box 1 File 7.

19 Taylor, "Crumpled Hat," 4–15, Taylor fonds, UMA, MSS 108 Box 52 File 9.

20 Ibid., 18–23. He recalled that "I had discovered that I was no great shakes as a shoe salesman, a pot and pan packer, a heavy hardware stock boy, a notions stock boy, nor as a farmer."

21 Taylor, "Speech: Centenary Award," 26 November 1992, Taylor fonds, UMA, MSS 108 Box 2 File 14.

22 "Vital Statistics" and "III Professional Experience," Taylor fonds, UMA, MSS 108 Box 1 File 5.

23 "III Professional Experience."

24 "Personal Taylor's Resume/ Autobiography w/ List of Important

Dates," Taylor fonds, UMA, MSS 108 Box 1 File 17.

25   "Vital Statistics." Taylor became an associate member of the Engineering Institute of Canada in 1936, and received his designation as a professional engineer in Manitoba in 1944.

26   "III Professional Experience."

27   Alan Cooke, "An Unsung Hero: Dr. Andrew Taylor," 3, Taylor fonds, MSS 108 Box 1 File 19.

28   Taylor, "Crumpled Hat," 30, 77. The marriage date was provided by the Taylor family, and contradicts his claim that he was married on the day that the war broke out.

29   Taylor, "Crumpled Hat," 30; "III Professional Experience"; military correspondence on Taylor fonds, UMA, MSS 108 Box 16 File 24.

30   Taylor, "Resume: September—1943," Taylor family, Letterbook 1943.

31   Ibid.

32   See Beeby, *In a Crystal Land*, 7–10, *passim*.

33   Taylor, "Crumpled Hat," 78.

34   Major F.J. Fleury to Office-in-charge (O.i/c) Records, 29 September 1943, Taylor fonds, UMA, MSS 108 Box 16 File 25. The Canadian Army continued to pay his salary and dependents' allowance for the duration of the war.

35   Taylor, "Resume: October—1943," Taylor family, Letterbook 1943.

36   Janice Cavell, "The Second Frontier: The North in English-Canadian Historical Writing," *Canadian Historical Review* 83 no. 3 (September 2002): 371. See also Janice Cavell, "The True Northwest Passage: Explorers in Anglo-Canadian Nationalist Narratives," *Northern Review* 32 (Spring 2010): 5–34.

37   As Maria Pia Casarini notes, defining the limits of the Antarctic and Antarctica has been a subject of longstanding debate. "It is now officially accepted that the term ['Antarctica'] refers to the continent itself and the off-lying islands, while the term 'Antarctic' indicates the area south of the Antarctic Convergence, a belt around the continent at about 56°–58°S where the cold Antarctic surface water, flowing northwards, sinks beneath the warmer sub-Antarctic water" (Casarini, "Activities in Antarctica Before the Conclusion of the Antarctic Treaty," in *International Law for Antarctica*, 2nd ed., ed. Francesco Francioni and Tullio Scovazzi [The Hague: Kluwer Law, 1996], 628).

38   Fogg, *History of Antarctic Science*, 8–15.

39   Hugh Robert Mill, *The Siege of the South Pole: The Story of Antarctic Exploration* (London: A. Rivers, 1905), 96.

40   Day, *Antarctica*, 10–12.

41   Casarini, "Activities in Antarctica," 637.

42   On this theme, see Hugh Wallace, *The Navy, the Company, and Richard King: British Exploration in the Canadian Arctic, 1829–1860* (Montreal: McGill-Queen's University Press, 1980), 5.

43   A.G.E. Jones, "Captain William Smith and the Discovery of New South Shetland," *Geographical Journal* 141, no. 3 (1975): 445–61. A Russian expedition under Captain Gottlieb von Bellingshausen circumnavigated the Antarctic in 1820 and 1821, investigated the South Shetlands and South Sandwich Islands, and discovered Peter I and Alexander Island (although he mistook the latter for part of the continent) (Day, *Antarctica*, 20–3, 32–6). While he

gave Russian names to islands and geographical features, Bellingshausen did not land on or try to claim territory for his country. Thanks to Peter Kikkert for sharing this information.

44 Philip Mitterling, *America in the Antarctic to 1840* (Urbana: University of Illinois Press, 1959), 31–5; Edouard Stackpole, *The Voyage of the "Huron" and the "Huntress": The American Sealers and the Discovery of the Continent of Antarctica* (Mystic, CT: Maine Historical Association, 1955), 51–2; Kenneth J. Bertrand, *Americans in Antarctica, 1775–1948* (New York: American Geographical Society, 1971).

45 Susan Barr, *Norway's Polar Territories* (Oslo: Aschehoug, 1987), 63.

46 Casarini, "Activities in Antarctica," 634.

47 Howkins, "Frozen Empires," 9.

48 Chris Turney, *1912: The Year the World Discovered Antarctica* (Berkeley, CA: Counterpoint, 2012), 19–21. In *Two Years Below the Horn*, Taylor describes John Franklin's voyage with Joseph D. Hooker to Cockburn Island in 1843, where they made a series of important botanical collections. See Sir Joseph Dalton Hooker, *Botany of the Antarctic Voyage of H.M. Discovery Ships, Erebus and Terror: Under the Command of Captain Sir J.C. Ross, 1839–43* (London: Reeve Brothers, 1847), 535.

49 Sanjay Chaturvedi, *The Polar Regions: A Political Geography* (London: Wiley, 1996), 62.

50 Howkins, "Frozen Empires," 9. On sealing in this era, see E.W. Hunter Christie, *The Antarctic Problem* (London: George Allen and Unwin, 1951), 143–58, and R.K. Headland, *Chronological List of Antarctic Expeditions and Related Historical Events* (Cambridge: Cambridge University Press, 1989).

51 John R. Dudeney and David W.H. Walton, "From *Scotia* to 'Operation Tabarin': Developing British Policy for Antarctica," *Polar Record* 48, no. 247 (2012): 342.

52 Peter J. Beck, "British Antarctic Policy in the Early 20th Century," *Polar Record* 21, no. 134 (May 1983): 476.

53 Dodds, *The Antarctic*, 28.

54 Turney, *1912*, 27.

55 Carsten Borchgrevink, *First on the Antarctic Continent* (London: George Newnes, 1901) and T.H. Baughman, *Before the Heroes Came: Antarctica in the 1890s* (Lincoln: University of Nebraska Press, 1994), 90–113.

56 On Evans, see Beeby, *In a Crystal Land*, 11–30.

57 Dianne Preston, *A First Rate Tragedy: Captain Scott's Antarctic Expeditions* (London: Constable, 1997), 57–9.

58 Day, *Antarctica*, 115; Adrien de Gerlache, *Quinze mois dans l'Antarctique* (Brussels: Ch. Bulens, 1902); Geir O. Kløver, ed., *Antarctic Pioneers: The Voyage of the Belgica, 1897–99* (Oslo: Fram Museum, 2010).

59 Otto Nordenskjöld and Johan Gunnar Andersson, *Antarctica or Two Years Amongst the Ice of the South Pole* (Toronto: McClelland and Stewart, 1977); Andrew Taylor, "Echoes of the Swedish South Polar Expedition of 1902–03," *Revue canadienne de géographie* 4 (1950): 47–62; and Fuchs, *Of Ice and Men*, 13–16.

60 Casarini, "Activities in Antarctica," 645–6; Mill, *Siege of the South Pole*, 135–9; Fuchs, *Of Ice and Men*, 6–7; Henri Queffélec, *Le Grand départ, Charcot et le "Pourquoi pas ?"* (Paris: Presses de la cité, 1977); Marthe Emmanuel, *J-B Charcot, le polar gentleman* (Paris: Alsatia, 1945). On

the other side of the continent, Erich von Drygalski led the first German expedition to the Antarctic from 1901 to 1903, which focussed on science yet discovered a section of coastline in eastern Antarctica they called Kaiser Wilhelm II Land (Day, *Antarctica*, 116–18).

61 On Bruce, see P. Speak, *William Speirs Bruce: Polar Explorer and Scottish Nationalist* (Edinburgh: National Museums of Scotland, 2003).

62 Dudeney and Walton, "From *Scotia* to 'Operation Tabarin,'" 343. Bruce returned to Laurie Island with three Argentinian scientists, sailed into the Weddell Sea, discovered Coats Land (named after his patron) in 1904, and his oceanographic work established the underwater link between South America and the Antarctic Peninsula (Casarini, "Activities in Antarctica," 645).

63 Dudeney and Walton, "From *Scotia* to 'Operation Tabarin,'" 344–5. The claim reflected Britain's focus on the sub-Antarctic islands, but the inclusion of Graham Land demonstrated its increased economic interest in the region (Beck, "British Antarctic Policy," 476–7). On whaling in this era, see J.N. Tonnessen and Arne Odd Johnsen, *The History of Modern Whaling* (Berkeley: University of California Press, 1982). On the history of Britain's sovereignty over the Falkland Islands, see Barry M. Gough, *The Falkland Islands/ Malvinas: The Contest for Empire in the South Atlantic* (Atlantic Highlands, NJ: Athlone Press, 1992). In 1917, Britain modified the definition of the Falkland Islands Dependencies to include "all islands and territories whatsoever between the 20th degree of West longitude and the 50th degree of West longitude which are situated south of the 50th parallel of South latitude; and all

islands and territories whatsoever between the 50th degree of West longitude and the 80th degree of West longitude which are situated south of the 58th parallel of South latitude" (W.M. Bush, *Antarctica and International Law: A Collection of Inter-State and National Documents* [London: Ocean Publications, 1988], 3:265).

64 Howkins, "Frozen Empires," 9.

65 See Dodds, *Pink Ice.*

66 Kikkert, "Grasping for the Ends of the Earth."

67 See, for example, Paul Simpson-Hausley, *Antarctica: Exploration, Perception and Metaphor* (London: Routledge, 1992); Max Jones, *The Last Great Quest: Captain Scott's Antarctic Sacrifice* (Oxford: Oxford University Press, 2003); Francis Spufford, *I May Be Some Time: Ice and the English Imagination* (London: St. Martin's Press, 1996); David Crane, *Scott of the Antarctic: A Life of Courage, and Tragedy in the Extreme South* (London: Harper Collins, 2005); and Richard McElrea and David Harrowfield, *Polar Castaways: The Ross Sea Party of Sir Ernest Shackleton, 1914–1917* (Montreal: McGill-Queen's University Press, 2004).

68 Ernest Shackleton, *The Heart of the Antarctic: Being the Story of the British Antarctic Expedition 1907–1989*, vol. 1 (London: William Heinemann, 1909), 348, and Roland Huntford, *Shackleton* (London: Hodder and Stoughton, 1985), 272.

69 For further inofrmation on Mitchell, see Beeby, *In a Crystal Land*, 31–44.

70 On Wright, see Beeby, *In a Crystal Land*, 45–76.

71 Casarini, "Activities in Antarctica," 647–50.

72 Peter J. Beck, *The International Politics of Antarctica* (London: Croom Helm, 1986), 26.

73 Fuchs, *Of Ice and Men*, 19. After the war, advances in hydrogenation made whale oil a viable source for margarine production, thus augmenting interest in whaling (Casarini, "Activities in Antarctica," 653).

74 Beck, "British Antarctic Policy," 477–80; D. Graham Burnett, *The Sounding of the Whale: Science & Cetaceans in the Twentieth Century* (Chicago: University of Chicago Press, 2012).

75 Howkins, "Frozen Empires," 16.

76 Christie, *Antarctic Problem*, 206–19; Fogg, *History of Antarctic Science*, *passim*; Casarini, "Activities in Antarctica," 655–6; Fuchs, *Of Ice and Men*, 19.

77 Howkins, "Frozen Empires," 17. On the British Graham Land Expedition of 1934 to 1937, see J.R. Rymill, *Southern Lights* (Malvern, UK: Knell Press, 1986 [1939]); Christie, *Antarctic Problem*, 225–32; Beck, *International Politics of Antarctica*, 28–9; and G.C.L. Bertram, "Antarctica Sixty Years Ago," *Polar Record* 32, no. 181 (1996): 101–83.

78 Roberts, chapter 3 of *European Antarctic*.

79 Beck, *International Politics of Antarctica*, 27–8. On Norway's claims, see Bush, *Antarctica and International Law*, 3:113–14, 131–5.

80 Beeby, *In a Crystal Land*, 8. On contributions by Canadians Alward Cheesman, Frank "Taffy" Davies, Alan Innes-Taylor, and Herbert Hollick-Kenyon, see G. Hattersley-Smith, "Some Canadians in the Antarctic," *Polar Record* 39, no. 4 (December 1986): 369; and Beeby, *In a Crystal Land*, 165–176.

81 Beck, *International Politics of Antarctica*, 30.

82 Howkins, "Polar Empires," 42.

83 On Norway's interests as a whaling nation and its claim to Queen Maud Land (east of the Weddell Sea) to pre-empt a possible claim by Nazi Germany, see Stephen Martin, *A History of Antarctica* (Kenthurst, Australia: Rosenberg, 2013), 189–90.

84 Howkins, "Polar Empires," 41, 46–9.

85 Ibid., 42–74. On Argentina's moves toward asserting sovereignty in Antarctica, see also Bush, *Antarctica and International Law*, vols. 1 and 2 (London: Oceana Publications, 1982), 1:579–87, 594–5, 599–600, and 2:310–11, 323–4.

86 Howkins, "Polar Empires," 51; Dudeney and Walton, "From *Scotia* to 'Operation Tabarin,'" 347–8. Hitler's Germany had mounted the German Antarctic Expedition from 1938 to 1939 and claimed the territory of Neu-Schwabenland (previously claimed by Norway) in early 1939, prompting Norway to formally annex the Antarctic area (Dronning Maud Land) between the British and Australian boundaries. See Colin Summerhayes and Peter Beeching, "Hitler's Antarctic Base: The Myth and the Reality," *Polar Record* 43, no. 224 (2007): 1–21; Bush, *Antarctica and International Law*, 3:2–3, 140, 149, and 154; and Casarini, "Activities in Antarctica," 663–4. On German raider activities in the southern ocean in 1940 and 1941, see J.D.M. Blyth, "German Raiders in the Antarctic during the Second World War," *Polar Record* 6, no. 43 (January 1952): 399–403.

87 Dudeney and Walton, "From *Scotia* to 'Operation Tabarin,'" 348. For a detailed discussion of internal British debates, see pages 349–50.

88 See Galen Perras, "Anglo-Canadian Imperial Relations: The Case of the Garrisoning of the Falkland Islands

89 Howkins, "Polar Empires," 76–8, 86–92. On the mission of *Carnarvon Castle*, see Dudeney and Walton, "From *Scotia* to 'Operation Tabarin,'" 350–1.

90 Howkins, "Polar Empires," 91–2. Although funded out of the Admiralty budget, British officials anticipated that the costs of the operation would be offset by revenues earned from philatelists (stamp collectors) who would purchase special Falkland Islands Dependencies stamps issued during the operation. Ironically, the issuing of these stamps undermined the secrecy of the operation (Dudeney and Walton, "From *Scotia* to 'Operation Tabarin,'" 351, 352–3).

91 Dudeney and Walton, "From *Scotia* to 'Operation Tabarin,'" 351.

92 Ibid., 352.

93 Howkins, "Polar Empires," 93–4.

94 "Draft Ubique article—Operation Tabarin—Dr Andrew Taylor," Taylor fonds, UMA, MSS 108 Box 9 File 42.

95 The purchase of second-hand ships was a common practice for polar expeditions during the interwar period (Fogg, *History of Antarctic Science*, 134).

96 James, *That Frozen Land*, 156–60.

AFTERWORD

1 Taylor, "Dr Cooke and the Block and Tackle Brigade," 13 July 1990, Taylor fonds, UMA, MSS 108 Box 10 File 37.

2 For a copy of these instructions, see "Note for Returning Members of Operation Tabarin," n.d., UMA, MSS 108 Box 8 File 54.

3 Taylor, "Operation Tabarin: Official Journal, 1944–6," 5–7 and 9 March

1946, Taylor fonds, UMA, MSS 108 Box 5 File 1; Taylor "Chatham – Arrival," 20 May 1950, Taylor fonds, UMA, MSS 108 Box 10 File 33.

4 Taylor, "Dr Cooke and the Block and Tackle Brigade."

5 Fuchs, *Of Ice and Men*, 54.

6 Haddelsey, *Operation Tabarin*, 215.

7 Ibid., 230.

8 Fuchs to Taylor, 12 January 1954, Taylor fonds, UMA, MSS 108 Box 43 File 16.

9 Dudeney and Walton, "From *Scotia* to 'Operation Tabarin,'" 355.

10 Fuchs, *Of Ice and Men*, 56.

11 Dudeney and Walton, "From *Scotia* to 'Operation Tabarin,'" 355.

12 Taylor, "Dr Cooke and the Block and Tackle Brigade."

13 Taylor, "Operation Tabarin: Official Journal, 1944–6," 18 March 1946.

14 Taylor, "Dr Cooke and the Block and Tackle Brigade."

15 Taylor, "Operation Tabarin: Official Journal, 1944–6," 18 and 24 April 1946.

16 Ibid., 30 April 1946.

17 In subsequent decades, Taylor struggled to understand why he received command of Operation Tabarin only to encounter such difficulties when he returned home. Taylor's May 1990 written account of subsequent meetings with Dr. Alan Cooke, who got to know Roberts while working as a curator at the Scott Polar Research Institute and editing the *Polar Record*, described Roberts as "a born egoist, and a small man at heart. You would have had to be very foolish indeed not to comprehend that he would not allow anyone else, no matter who they were, to usurp that position. He would do everything necessary to prevent such a thing happening. And the least one he would want to have gaining a good

reputation from *Operation Tabarin* was a Colonial, as he evidently considered you to be" (emphasis in original, Taylor, "Dr Cooke and the Block and Tackle Brigade"). Taylor's account of Cooke's comments is probably reliable because the latter's favourable opinion of Taylor is well established [see Alan Cooke, "Dr. Andrew Taylor, OC," *Arcana Poli* 1, no. 1 (July 1988): 16–18]. Taylor internalized Cooke's assessment and concluded that his treatment caused him to lose faith in "British fair play and justice" (see Taylor, "Dr Cooke and the Block and Tackle Brigade").

18 Taylor, "Release," June 1993, Taylor fonds, UMA, MSS 108 Box 11 File 14.

19 Taylor, "Polar Medal," 12 August 1988, Taylor fonds, UMA, MSS 108 Box 2 File 9; Taylor, "Draft Ubique article – Operation Tabarin," 1993, Taylor fonds, UMA, MSS 108 Box 9 File 42.

20 Juxon Barton to Hunt, 8 April 1946, UMA, MSS 108 Box 8 File 54; Taylor, "Operation Tabarin: Official Journal, 1944–6," 23 March 1946.

21 Roberts to Barton, 17 April 1946, UMA, MSS 108 Box 8 File 54.

22 Abbott to District Office Commanding, 26 June 1946, Taylor fonds, UMA, MSS 108 Box 16 File 27. See also Murchie to Secretary (DND), 10 May 1946, Taylor fonds, UMA, MSS 108 Box 16 File 27.

23 Taylor, "Operation Tabarin: Official Journal, 1944–6," 2, 11–12, 21, 23–24 June 1946; Taylor, note, 13 July 1990, Taylor fonds, UMA, MSS 108 Box 10 File 37.

24 Taylor, "Operation Tabarin: Official Journal, 1944–6," 26 June 1946.

25 J.M .Wordie, "The Falkland Islands Dependencies Survey, 1943–1946," *Polar Record* 4, no. 32 (1946): 376. Taylor read Wordie's article and was not impressed by it (see Taylor, "Polar Medal").

26 Wordie, "The Falkland Islands Dependencies Survey," 380; Ashton to Taylor, 30 May 1947, Taylor fonds, UMA, MSS 108 Box 42 File 3. Wordie, it appears, subsequently spoke positively about Taylor's work in the Antarctic (Unidentified to Taylor, 23 August 1947, Taylor fonds, UMA, MSS 108 Box 16 File 21).

27 Wordie to Taylor, 5 July 1946, Taylor fonds, UMA, MSS 108 Box 45 File 19.

28 Taylor to Doucet, 3 February 1947, Taylor fonds, UMA, MSS 108 Box 15 File 1; Casarini, "Activities in Antarctica," 668.

29 Chippie to Taylor, 22 October 1946, Taylor fonds, UMA, MSS 108 Box 42 file 2; Ashton to Taylor, 13 February 1947, Taylor fonds, UMA, MSS 108 Box 42 file 3; and Ashton to Taylor, 14 April 1947, 30 May 1947, 3 June 1947, Taylor fonds, UMA, MSS 108 Box 42 file 3.

30 Douglas Liversidge, "World's Loneliest Address," *Star Weekly* [Toronto], 10 August 1946, Taylor fonds, UMA, MSS 108 Box 9 File 33.

31 Taylor to Chippie, 8 September 1946, and Taylor to Taff, 29 September 1946, Taylor fonds, UMA, MSS 108 Box 43 File 2.

32 Taylor to Chippie, 27 September 1946, Taylor fonds, UMA MSS 108 Box 42 File 2.

33 Taylor to Chippie, 8 September 1946, and Taylor to Chippie, 27 September 1946, Taylor fonds, UMA MSS 108 Box 42 File 2.

34 Taylor to Chippie, 3 January 1947, Taylor fonds, UMA MSS 108 Box 42 File 3.

35 Taylor to Doucet, 3 February 1947, Taylor fonds, UMA, MSS 108 Box 15 File 1.

36 Ibid.

37 Doucet to Taylor, "Memorandum," 8 February 1947; "Canadian Pacific Telegraphs," n.d.; and "Army Message,"

n.d., Taylor fonds, UMA, MSS 108 Box 15 File 1.

38   Taylor to Doucet, 19 February 1947, and "Canadian Pacific Telegraphs," 22 March 1947, Taylor fonds, UMA, MSS 108 Box 15 File 1.

39   Taylor to Chippie, 18 February 1947, Taylor fonds, UMA, MSS 108 Box 42 File 3.

40   Taylor to Chippie, 31 March 1947, Taylor fonds, UMA, MSS 108 Box 42 File 3.

41   Ibid. See also Taylor to Schonfield, 27 March 1947, Taylor fonds, UMA, MSS 108 Box 42 File 3.

42   Taylor to Doc, 7 July 1947, Taylor fonds, UMA, MSS 108 Box 42 File 4; Taylor to Doucet, 15 April 1947; Colonel to Taylor, "Two Years in the Antarctic," 17 April 1947 and 22 April 1947; Taylor to Doucet, 21 April 1947; "Canadian Pacific Telegraphs," n.d., Taylor fonds, UMA, MSS 108 Box 15 File 1.

43   Taylor to Simon & Schuster, 26 May 1947; Taylor to Knopf, 3 June 1947; Taylor to G.P. Putnam's Sons, 3 June 1947; Taylor to Harcourt Brace & Co., 3 June 1947; Taylor to W.W. Norton & Co., 3 June 1947, Taylor fonds, UMA, MSS 108 Box 15 File 1.

44   Singer to Taylor, 3 June 1947; Lowell to Taylor, 6 June 1947; Brockway to Taylor, 9 June 1947; Caplor to Taylor, n.d.; Newsom to Taylor, 11 June 1948, Taylor fonds, UMA, MSS 108 Box 15 File 1.

45   Knopf to Taylor, 18 June 1947, Taylor fonds, UMA, MSS 108 Box 15 File 1.

46   Rawson to Taylor, 17 July 1947, Taylor fonds, UMA, MSS 108 Box 15 File 1.

47   Newsom to Taylor, 15 July 1947; Dailey to Taylor, 29 July 1947, Taylor fonds, UMA, MSS 108 Box 15 File 1.

48   Taylor to Doc, 7 July 1947, Taylor fonds, UMA, MSS 108 Box 42 File 4; Davies to Commander US Naval Task Force 68, 11 July 1947, Taylor fonds, UMA, MSS 108 Box 16 File 21.

49   Taylor, "Personal Diary of Major Andrew Taylor, RCE Covering Operations of U.S. Navy Task Force 68 Through the Queen Elizabeth Islands N.W.T. Canada," 1947, Taylor fonds, UMA, MSS 108 Box 15 File 14; "Vital Statistics," Taylor fonds, UMA, MSS 108 Box 1 File 5.

50   Taylor to Doc, 2 April 1948, Taylor fonds, UMA, MSS 108 Box 42 File 4.

51   Taylor, "Personal Diary . . . Covering Operations of U.S. Navy Task Force 68," 21 August 1947.

52   Taylor to Doc, 2 April 1948.

53   Taylor, "Personal Diary . . . Covering Operations of U.S. Navy Task Force 68," 24 July 1947; and Taylor to Doc, 2 April 1948.

54   Keenleyside to Mills, 14 January 1948, Taylor fonds, UMA, MSS 108 Box 16 File 21.

55   Taylor to Taff, 18 July 1947, Taylor fonds, UMA, MSS 108 Box 43 File 2.

56   Taylor to Doc, 2 April 1948.

57   "Vital Statistics."

58   Schonfield to Taylor, 6 March 1947, Taylor fonds, UMA, MSS 108 Box 15 File 1.

59   Taylor to Schonfield, 27 March 1947, Taylor fonds, UMA, MSS 108 Box 15 File 1. The firm was with MacMillians Press. Aside from a passing mention in Taylor to Moorepark, 12 November 1947, Taylor fonds, UMA, MSS 108 Box 15 File 1, no documentation concerning his dealings with this company survives.

60   Taylor to Schonfield, 13 January 1948, Taylor fonds, UMA, MSS 108 Box 15 File 2.

61   Clark to Taylor, 24 February 1948, Taylor fonds, UMA, MSS 108 Box 15 File 2.

62   Clark to Taylor, 4 June 1948, Taylor fonds, UMA, MSS 108 Box 15 File 2.

63 Taylor's reply to Herbert and Joseph Limited confessed that "the earlier letters which I had had from your firm perhaps allowed my hopes to soar unwarrantably" (Taylor to Clark, 24 August 1948, Taylor fonds, UMA, MSS 108 Box 15 File 2).

64 Moorepark to Taylor, 5 August 1947, Taylor fonds, UMA, MSS 108 Box 15 File 1.

65 Moorepark to Taylor, 8 September 1947, and Moorepark to Taylor, 14 November 1947, Taylor fonds, UMA, MSS 108 Box 15 File 1.

66 Taylor to Moorepark, 13 January 1948, Taylor fonds, UMA, MSS 108 Box 15 File 2.

67 Lloyd to Stefansson, 29 January 1948, and Stefansson to Lloyd, 30 January 1948, Taylor fonds, UMA, MSS 108 Box 15 File 2.

68 Lottinville to Taylor, 2 August 1948, and Taylor to Lottinville, 24 August 1948, Taylor fonds, UMA, MSS 108 Box 15 File 2.

69 Lottinville to Taylor, 1 September 1948, Taylor fonds, UMA, MSS 108 Box 15 File 2.

70 Lottinville to Taylor, 30 December 1948, and Taylor to Lottinville, 10 December 1948, Taylor fonds, UMA, MSS 108 Box 15 File 2.

71 Taylor to Lottinville, 31 March 1949, Taylor fonds, UMA, MSS 108 Box 15 File 2.

72 Lottinville to Taylor, 19 April 1949, Taylor fonds, UMA, MSS 108 Box 15 File 2. Taylor replied that the press's long possession of his draft had made him too optimistic. His letter went on to "assume" that Lottinville's "flattering comments" were "sincere" and suggested two strategies to secure the press's support. First, he suggested eliminating "some of the drier and more descriptive parts of the material" until it was three-quarters of its current length. He hoped that this measure would reduce the book's cost and increase its "saleability." Alternatively, Taylor offered to raise additional funds if Lottinville clarified the amount that the University of Oklahoma press required "to guarantee" the publication of his manuscript (Taylor to Lottinville, 23 April 1949, Taylor fonds, UMA, MSS 108 Box 15 File 2). In reply, Lottinville politely acknowledged that he could try to provide a financial estimate, but suggested that Taylor could "beat that figure by dealing either a general house or with a press closer at hand," such as the University of Toronto Press (Lottinville to Taylor, 3 May 1948, Taylor fonds, UMA, MSS 108 Box 15 File 2). Taylor had already solicited the University of Toronto Press to no avail (Burns to Taylor, 27 July 1948, Taylor fonds, UMA, MSS 108 Box 15 File 2). Although Taylor persisted with his attempts to secure an estimate, they did not result in his manuscript's publication.

73 Roberts, *The European Antarctic*, 137. Roberts analyzes this trend by tracing the writings of several scientists who participated in the Norwegian-British-Swedish Expedition (1949–1952), including its chief geologist, a Canadian named Fred Roots. Like Taylor, Roots contextualized the expedition "as a continuation of the heroic expeditions of Nansen, Amundsen, Scott, Shackleton, and Nordenskjöld" but then "focused on comparatively mundane routine rather than on hazardous travel" since he interpreted the latter as a sign of "incompetence." The expedition's book adopted a similar focus and sold fewer copies than expected. See also John Giaever, *The White Desert: The Official Account of the Norwegian-British-Swedish Antarctic Expedition* (New York: Greenwood Press, 1954) for another similar publication.

74 James, *That Frozen Land*, 152–60. James's diary (4 September 1945, BAS, ADG/1D/1945/K1) expressed much

75 Russell to Taylor, 15 March 1947, Taylor fonds, UMA, MSS 108 Box 44 File 22.

76 Taylor's notes contain several references to a photograph of the mountain from Ellery L. Anderson's *Expedition South*. See Taylor to Smith, "Operation Tabarin (1943–6) Antarctic Place Names," 4 December 1989, Taylor fonds, UMA, MSS 108 Box 45 File 2; and Taylor to Hattersley-Smith, 17 February 1987, Taylor fonds, UMA, MSS 108 Box 43 File 21.

77 Kimble, "Geography Summer School, 1948," Taylor fonds, UMA, MSS 108 Box 16 File 29.

78 Taylor to Lloyd, 1 January 1951, Taylor fonds, UMA, MSS 108 Box 44 File 12.

79 Taylor, "Arctic Blue Books Online: 'Blue Books and Rat Tails': The History of the Arctic Blue Books Index," *University of Manitoba Archives and Special Collections*, https://www.umanitoba.ca/libraries/units/archives/collections/subject/arcticstudies/arcticbb/rattails.shtml (accessed 11 June 2015).

80 Taylor, "Arctic Blue Books Online."

81 Taylor to Lloyd, 1 January 1951.

82 Taylor, "Crumpled Hat," 33–34, Taylor fonds, UMA, MSS 108 Box 52 File 9.

83 Ibid., and Cooke, "Dr. Andrew Taylor," 18.

84 Martin Zeilig, "Bitter cold etched in memory," *Winnipeg Free Press*, 10 July 1990; Taylor, "Snow Compaction," 16 June 1948, Taylor fonds, UMA, MSS 108 Box 19 File 16; Cooke, "Dr. Andrew Taylor," 17–18; Major Andrew Taylor, *SIPRE Report No 13: Snow Compaction* (Wilmette, IL: Snow, Ice and Permafrost Research Establishment, U.S. Army Corps of Engineers, 1953).

85 Taylor, "Awards," 28 December 1991, Taylor fonds, UMA, MSS 108 Box 2 File 13. In later years, Taylor repeatedly claimed that he accumulated "17 months" of command experience while serving in Operation Tabarin. He appears to have calculated it by counting from his assumption of command at Port Lockroy in December 1944, to the termination of his Tabarin duties in June 1946 (Taylor, untitled, n.d., Taylor fonds, UMA, MSS 108 Box 2 File 9).

86 Taylor, "Polar Medal," and Taylor, notes, 14 August 1988, Taylor fonds, UMA, MSS 108 Box 2 File 9.

87 Taylor to Director of Engineer Development, 19 September 1952, Taylor fonds, UMA, MSS 108 Box 17 File 1.

88 Taylor, "Physical Geography of the Northern Islands Region of the Canadian Arctic Archipelago," 19 May 1952, Taylor fonds, UMA, MSS 108 Box 26 File 18. On these photographic operations, see Peter Kikkert, "The Polaris Incident: 'Going to the Mat' with the Americans," *Journal of Military and Strategic Studies* 11, no. 3 (Spring 2009): 1–29.

89 George to Andy, 14 October 1952, Taylor fonds, UMA, MSS 108 Box 26 File 18.

90 For more on the Polar Medal, consult Neville W. Poulsom, *British Polar Exploration and Research: A Historical and Medallic Record with Biographies, 1818–1999* (London: Savannah Publications, 2000).

91 Neville W. Poulsom, *The White Ribbon: A Medallic Record of British Polar Expeditions* (London: B.A. Seaby, 1987), 80–2, 180. On the *St. Roch* and its historic voyages, see James P. Delagdo, *Arctic Workhorse: The RCMP Schooner St. Roch* (Victoria: Touch Wood Editions, 2003).

92 "Third Supplement," *London Gazette* [UK], 17 July 1953, 3925–3926. Marr's name was not included, but he had already received the Bronze medal in 1934 and additional clasp in 1941. Marr did not receive the silver medal until 1954. See *London Gazette,* 1 May 1934, 2788; "Fifth Supplement," 3 October 1941, 5785; and "Third Supplement," 26 November 1954, 6790.

93 Haddelsey, *Operation Tabarin*, 230. This author dismisses Taylor's frustration with the mistakes and delay that preceded the Canadian's investiture.

94 Taylor's most extensive account of these events confuses the public notice awards in 1953 with their actual investiture at Buckingham Palace in 1954. Indeed, Taylor partially admits this confusion when discussing John Blyth's medal (Taylor, "Polar Medal." See also G. Hattersley-Smith to Cooke, 28 September 1988, Taylor fonds, UMA, MSS 108 Box 42 File 23).

95 Fuchs to Taylor, 2 December 1953, Taylor fonds, UMA, MSS 108 Box 43 File 16.

96 Lloyd to Taylor, 11 May 1954, Taylor fonds, UMA, MSS 108 Box 2 File 8.

97 J.F. Delaute to Taylor, 7 May 1954, Taylor fonds, UMA, MSS 108 Box 2 File 8.

98 Taylor, "Polar Medal."

99 Taylor to Hattersley-Smith, 8 October 1988, Taylor fonds, UMA, MSS 108 Box 42 File 21. Hattersley-Smith did not disagree with Taylor's rage or sense of entitlement (G. Hattersley-Smith to Taylor, 26 October 1988, Taylor fonds, UMA, MSS 108 Box 42 File 21).

100 Taylor to Fuchs, 6 August 1986, Taylor fonds, UMA, MSS 108 Box 43 File 16.

101 Taylor, "Polar Medal."

102 "Governor General Decorates 26 at Rideau Hall Investiture," *Ottawa Journal,* 9 June 1954; "Ottawans Among 26 Decorated at Government House Investiture," *Ottawa Citizen,* 9 June 1954.

103 "Former Local Man Receives Polar Medal from Governor-General," n.d., Taylor fonds, UMA, MSS 108 Box 2 File 8.

104 "Ex-City Man Awarded U.K. Polar Medal," *Winnipeg Free Press,* 17 July 1954.

105 "Employment Agreement," 1 March 1955, Taylor fonds, UMA, MSS 108 Box 38 File 1; "Oath of Secrecy," 19 February 1955, Taylor fonds, UMA, MSS 108 Box 38 File 1; Taylor to Bakst, "Consultant's Proposal," 1956, Taylor fonds, UMA, MSS 108 Box 38 File 8; Lymburner to all personnel, 5 March 1955, Taylor fonds, UMA, MSS 108 Box 38 File 7; and Taylor, "DEW Line," 25 July 1984, Taylor fonds, UMA, MSS 108 Box 44 File 12. Some of these documents claim that Taylor initially agreed to work for a four- or even six-month period, but his contract specified a minimum three-month term.

106 Taylor to O'Reilly, 2 September 1956, Taylor fonds, UMA, MSS 108 Box 38 File 8.

107 Taylor to Kimble, 29 October 1952, Taylor fonds, UMA, MSS 108 Box 26 File 18.

108 For more on Taylor's defence contract pursuits, consult Taylor fonds, UMA, MSS 108 Box 38 Files 8, 9, 19–21.

109 Taylor, "Arctic Blue Books Online"; W.W. Koolage, "Arctic Blue Books Online: Introduction and Acknowledgements," *University of Manitoba Archives and Special Collections,* https://www.umanitoba.ca/libraries/units/archives/collections/subject/arcticstudies/arcticbb/intro.shtml (accessed 11 June 2015).

110 Taylor, "Arctic Blue Books Online."

111 Taylor, "Crumpled Hat," 37.

112 Taylor "Arctic Blue Books Online."

113 Fuchs to Taylor, 8 October 1974, Taylor fonds, UMA, MSS 108 Box 43 File 16.

114 Taylor to Fuchs, 27 October 1974, Taylor fonds, UMA, MSS 108 Box 43 File 16.

115 Fuchs, *Of Ice and Men*, 22–54.

116 Cooke to Taylor, 23 March 1984, Taylor fonds, UMA, MSS 108 Box 42 File 18.

117 Cooke to Swithinbank, 17 May 1984, Taylor fonds, UMA, MSS 108 Box 42 File 10.

118 Swithinbank to Taylor, 8 August 1984, Taylor fonds, UMA, MSS 108 Box 42 File 10.

119 Taylor to Swithinbank, 23 August 1984, Taylor fonds, UMA, MSS 108 Box 42 File 10.

120 Swithinbank to Taylor, 26 September 1984, Taylor fonds, UMA, MSS 108 Box 42 File 10.

121 Taylor to Swithinbank, 24 May 1985, Taylor fonds, UMA, MSS 108 Box 14 File 2. Swithinbank responded to Taylor's threat by explaining that the BAS archivist lacked the "authority" to release the document into Taylor's care and questioned why Taylor required the 1947 copy when a typist could work just as well from a duplicate. He ended his letter by suggesting that Taylor could "try Mrs. Thatcher, but I would not hold out much hope" (Swithinbank to Taylor, 13 June 1985, Taylor fonds, UMA, MSS 108 Box 14 File 2).

122 Smith to Taylor, 23 July 1985, Taylor fonds, UMA, MSS 108 Box 14 File 2.

123 Taylor, "Below the Horn: Antarctica, 1944–46," 19 April 1985, Taylor fonds, UMA, MSS 108 Box 14 File 2.

124 Taylor to Rae, 25 November 1987, Taylor fonds, UMA, MSS 108 Box 14 File 2.

125 Taylor to Rae, 4 December 1987, Taylor fonds, UMA, MSS 108 Box 14 File 2.

126 For this correspondence, consult Taylor fonds, UMA, MSS 108 Box 43 File 16.

127 Taylor to Fuchs, 20 March 1990, Taylor fonds, UMA, MSS 108 Box 43 File 16.

128 Robert Taylor to Daniel Heidt, email, 21 May 2015.

129 Drewry to Taylor, 16 February 1993, Taylor fonds, UMA, MSS 108 Box 42 File 11.

130 Taylor, "Draft Ubique article."

131 Taylor, "A Brief Personal History of Operation Tabarin (1943–1946)," 1993, Taylor fonds, UMA, MSS 108 Box 11 file 14.

132 Taylor, "Draft Ubique article." As it turned out, distance prevented any of the Tabarin veterans residing outside of the United Kingdom from attending (Rae to Taylor, 24 June 1993, Taylor fonds, UMA, MSS 108 Box 42 File 11).

133 Nantel to Taylor, 22 April 1986, Taylor fonds, UMA, MSS 108 Box 2 File 10. Fuchs authored one of the letters supporting Taylor's nomination (Taylor to Fuchs, 6 August 1986, Taylor fonds, UMA, MSS 108 Box 43 File 16).

134 Taylor, "Polar Medal."

135 "Resumé Addenda," n.d., Taylor fonds, UMA, MSS 108 Box 2 file 11.

136 Darcy DeMarsico to Daniel Heidt, email, 9 June 2015.

137 Taylor, "Polar Medal."

138 Taylor to Cooke, 26 May 1988, Taylor fonds, UMA, MSS 108 Box 42 File 23.

139 Taylor, notes, n.d., Taylor fonds, UMA, MSS 108 Box 2 File 9.

140 W.W. Koolage, prepared text for Vilhjalmur Stefansson Award, 20

November 1990, Taylor fonds, UMA, MSS 108 Box 2 file 11. W.O. Pruitt Jr. and W.W. (Skip) Koolage, who had taken up the project of digitizing Taylor's Blue Book index, put his name forward. The digitization project, completed in 1998, can be accessed at https://www.umanitoba. ca/libraries/units/archives/ collections/subject/arcticstudies/ arcticbb/.

141 A. Naimark, 24 October 1991, Taylor fonds, UMA, MSS 108 Box 2 File 12.

142 Taylor, "Crumpled Hat," 43.

143 "Communiqué: Northern Science Award Winner Announced," 26 November 1992, Taylor fonds, UMA, MSS 108 Box 2 File 14; Siddon to Taylor, 14 August 1992, Taylor fonds, UMA, MSS 108 Box 2 File 15.

144 Taylor to Siddon, 21 August 1992, Taylor fonds, UMA, MSS 108 Box 2 File 15.

145 "Communiqué: Northern Science Award Winner Announced." Ironically, Taylor's acceptance speech did not even mention his Arctic and Antarctic activities. Instead, the speech honoured the generosity of the late Alex and Kathleen Campbell who had loaned him the money to resume his engineering studies at the University of Manitoba sixty-five years before. The British *Polar Record* noted the award and its brief note, provided by Hatterlsey-Smith, equally emphasized Taylor's Arctic and Antarctic accomplishments ("In Brief," *Polar Record* 29, no. 168 (January 1993): 76).

146 See, for example, John English, *Ice and Water: Politics, Peoples and the Arctic Council* (Toronto: Penguin Canada, 2013).

147 Peter Kikkert's recent work on bi-polar diplomacy demonstrates the continuation of polar dialogue into the Cold War. See his "Grasping for the Ends of the Earth: Framing and Contesting Polar Sovereignty, 1900–1955" (PhD diss., Western University, 2015).

148 Copies are held at UMA.

149 Obituary of Taylor by Gwion Davies, *Polar Record* 30, no. 173 (1994): 154. On Davies, see his obituary in *The Telegraph* [London], 2 July 2005.

150 See, for example, Marionne Cronin, "Polar Horizons: Images of the Arctic in Accounts of Amundsen's Polar Aviation Expeditions," *Scientia Canadensis* 33, no. 2 (2010): 99–120; Janice Cavell, *Tracing the Connected Narrative Arctic Exploration in British Print Culture, 1818–1860* (Toronto: University of Toronto Press, 2008); T.D. MacLulich, "Canadian Exploration as Literature," *Canadian Literature* 81 (Summer 1979): 72–85; I.S. MacLaren, "Exploration/Travel Literature and the Evolution of the Author," *International Journal of Canadian Studies* 5 (Spring 1992): 39–68; I.S. MacLaren, "From Exploration to Publication: The Evolution of a 19th-Century Arctic Narrative," *Arctic* 47, no. 1 (March 1994): 45–53; and Beau Riffenburgh, *The Myth of the Explorer: The Press, Sensationalism, and Geographical Discovery* (New York: Belhaven Press, 1993).

151 Obituary of Taylor by Davies.

Bibliography

ARCHIVAL MATERIAL

British Antarctic Survey, Cambridge, United Kingdom
Acc No. 1986/58/1 G12/2/3– E.H. Back Diary
AD6/16/1986/1.1 – Oral History Interview with V.A.J.B. Marchesi
AD6/16/1986/4.1 – Oral History Interview with E.H. Back
AD6/16/1987/2.1 – Oral History Interview with Andrew Taylor
AD6/24/1/3.1 – Oral History Interview with Gwion Davies
AD6/24/1/5 – Oral History Interview with J.E.B.F. Farrington
ADG/1A/1944/A – First Report on Work of Operation Tabarin
ADG/1A/1944/B – Operation Tabarin (Base A) Official Diary by "
    I. Mackenzie Lamb
ADG/1A/1944/K – Narrative of Survey Journey on Wiencke Island
ADG/1B/1944/A – Base "B" Deception Island, Report, 1944
ADG/1D/1945/C – Interim Report on the Establishment of Base D at Hope
    Bay, Graham Land
ADG/1S/32 – "Three Years in Antarctica" by John Blyth
ADG/1S/46(2) – "Release" by Andrew Taylor
Operation Tabarin photograph collection

National Archives, Kew, United Kingdom
Admiralty Records
Colonial Office Records
Meteorological Office Records
Royal Mint Records

University of Manitoba Archives
MSS 108 Andrew Taylor fonds
PC 110 Andrew Taylor Photograph collection
MC 1 Andrew Taylor map collection

Scott Polar Research Institute, United Kingdom
Brian Roberts collection
James Mann Wordie collection
Other government reports and unpublished graduate research concerning
    Operation Tabarin

PUBLISHED MATERIAL

Newspapers

"Ex-City Man Awarded U.K. Polar Medal." *Winnipeg Free Press*, 17 July 1954.

Goldstein, Tom. "Former Falklands official recalls life on frozen islands." *Winnipeg Free Press*, 28 April 1982.

"Governor General Decorates 26 at Rideau Hall Investiture." *Ottawa Journal*, 9 June 1954.

"Gwion Davies." *The Telegraph* [London], 2 July 2005.

Liversidge, Douglas. "World's Loneliest Address." *Star Weekly* [Toronto], 10 August 1946.

London Gazette [UK], 1 May 1934, 3 October 1941, 17 July 1953, 26 November 1954.

"Ottawans Among 26 Decorated at Government House Investiture." *Ottawa Citizen*, 9 June 1954.

Zeilig, Martin. "Bitter cold etched in memory." *Winnipeg Free Press*, 10 July 1990.

Books and Articles

Adams, Peter. "The Arctic Council, Antarctica and Northern Studies in Canada." *Arctic* 53, no. 3 (September 2000): 334–40.

Adcock, Tina. "Toward an Early Twentieth Century Culture of Northern Canadian Exploration." In *North by Degree: New Perspectives on Arctic Exploration,* edited by Susan A. Kaplan and Robert McCracken Peck, 110–41. Philadelphia: American Philosophical Society, 2013.

"Andrew Taylor." In *Canada From Afar: The Daily Telegraph Book of Canadian Obituaries*, 122–4. Toronto: Dundurn Press, 1996.

Barczewski, Stephanie. *Antarctic Destinies: Scott, Shackleton, and the Changing Face of Heroism*. London: Hambledon Press, 2008.

Barnes, Trevor J., and Matthew Farish. "Between Regions: Science, Militarism, and American Geography from World War to Cold War." *Annals of the Association of American Geographers* 96, no. 4 (2006): 807–26.

Barr, Susan. *Norway's Polar Territories*. Oslo: Aschehoug, 1987.

Baughman, T.H. *Before the Heroes Came: Antarctica in the 1890s*. Lincoln: University of Nebraska Press, 1994.

Beck, Peter J. "Britain and Antarctica: The Historical Perspective." *FRAM: The Journal of Polar Studies* 1, no. 1 (Winter 1984): 66–83.

———. "British Antarctic Policy in the Early 20th Century." *Polar Record* 21, no. 134 (1983): 475–83.

———. *Canada as a Bi-Polar Power: Canada's Antarctic Dimension*. Thunder Bay: Lakehead University, 1990.

———. "Identifying National Interests in Antarctica: the Case of Canada."
Polar Record 32, no. 183 (1996): 335–46.

———. *The International Politics of Antarctica.* London: Croom Helm, 1986.

———. "Securing the Dominant 'Place in the Wan Antarctic Sun' For
the British Empire: The Policy of Extending British Control Over
Antarctica." *Australian Journal of Politics and History* 29, no. 3 (1983):
448–61.

———. "Through Arctic Eyes: Canada and Antarctica, 1945–62." *Arctic* 48, no.
2 (June 1995): 136–46.

Beeby, Dean. *In a Crystal Land: Canadian Explorers in Antarctica.* Toronto:
University of Toronto Press, 1994.

Belanger, Dian Olson. *Deep Freeze: The United States, the International
Geophysical Year, and the Origins of Antarctica's Age of Science.* Boulder:
University Press of Colorado, 2006.

Bertram, G.C.L. "Antarctica Sixty Years Ago." *Polar Record* 32, no. 181
(1996): 101–83.

Bertrand, Kenneth J. *Americans in Antarctica, 1775–1948.* New York:
American Geographical Society, 1971.

Blyth, J.D.M. "German Raiders in the Antarctic during the Second World
War." *Polar Record* 6, no. 43 (January 1952): 399–403.

Bocking, Stephen. "A Disciplined Geography Aviation, Science, and the Cold
War in Northern Canada, 1945–1960." *Technology and Culture* 50, no. 2
(April 2009): 265–90.

Borchgrevink, Carsten. *First on the Antarctic Continent.* London: George
Newnes, 1901.

Bravo, Michael, and Sverker Sörlin, eds. *Narrating the Arctic: A Cultural
History of Nordic Scientific Practices.* Canton, MA: Science History
Publications, 2002.

British Antarctic Survey Bulletin 30 (March 1993). Special issue on Operation
Tabarin.

Broadbent, Noel D., and Lisle Rose. "Historical Archaeology and the Byrd
Legacy: The United States Antarctic Service Expedition, 1939–1941."
Virginia Magazine of History and Biography 110, no. 2 (2002): 237–58.

Buckner, Phillip, ed. *Canada and the End of Empire.* Vancouver: UBC Press,
2004.

Buckner, Phillip, and Douglas Francis, eds. *Rediscovering the British World.*
Calgary: University of Calgary Press, 2005.

Burkett, Dave. "Port Lockroy: Most Popular Place in Antarctica." *Polar Times*
(Spring-Summer 1999): 19.

Burnett, Graham D. *The Sounding of the Whale: Science & Cetaceans in the
Twentieth Century.* Chicago: University of Chicago Press, 2012.

Bush, W.M. *Antarctica and International Law*, vol. 1. London: Oceana Publications, 1982.

———. *A Collection of Inter-State and National Documents*, vol. 3 of *Antarctica and International Law*. London: Ocean Publications, 1988.

Carroll, Alan. "Victor Aloysius Jean-Baptiste Marchesi." *Polar Record* 43, no. 226 (2007): 287–8.

Casarini, Maria Pia. "Activities in Antarctica Before the Conclusion of the Antarctic Treaty." In *International Law for Antarctica*. 2nd ed., edited by Francesco Francioni and Tullio Scovazzi, 627–81. The Hague: Kluwer Law, 1996.

Cavell, Janice. "Comparing Mythologies: Twentieth-Century Canadian Constructions of Sir John Franklin." In *Canadas of the Mind: The Making and Unmaking of Canadian Nationalisms in the Twentieth Century*, edited by Norman Hilllmer and Adam Chapnick, 15–45. Montreal: McGill-Queen's University Press, 2007.

———. "The Second Frontier: The North in English-Canadian Historical Writing." *Canadian Historical Review* 83, no.3 (September 2002): 364–89.

———. *Tracing the Connected Narrative Arctic Exploration in British Print Culture, 1818–1860*. Toronto: University of Toronto Press, 2008.

———. "The True Northwest Passage: Explorers in Anglo-Canadian Nationalist Narratives." *Northern Review* 32 (Spring 2010): 5–34.

Chaturvedi, Sanjay. *The Polar Regions: A Political Geography*. London: Wiley, 1996.

Christie, E.W. Hunter. *The Antarctic Problem: An Historical and Political Study*. London: George Allen and Unwin, 1951.

Coates, Ken, Whitney Lackenbauer, William Morrison, and Greg Poelzer. *Arctic Front: Defending Canada's Interests in the Far North*. Toronto: Thomas Allen, 2008.

Collis, Christy. "The Voyage of the Episteme: Narrating the North." *Essays on Canadian Writing* 59 (Fall 1996): 26–45.

Cooke, Alan. "Dr. Andrew Taylor, OC." *Arcana Poli* 1, no. 1 (July 1988) 16–18.

Crane, David. *Scott of the Antarctic: A Life of Courage, and Tragedy in the Extreme South*. London: HarperCollins, 2005.

Cronin, Marionne. "Polar Horizons: Images of the Arctic in Accounts of Amundsen's Polar Aviation Expeditions." *Scientia Canadensis* 33, no. 2 (2010): 99–120.

———. "Technological Heroes: Images of the Arctic in the Age of Polar Aviation." In *Northscapes: History, Technology and the Making of Northern Environments*, edited by Dolly Jøgsen and Sverker Sörlin, 57-81. Toronto: UBC Press, 2013.

Davies, Gwion. "Andrew Taylor." *Polar Record* 30, no. 173 (1994): 153–4.

Day, David. *Antarctica: A Biography.* Oxford: Oxford University Press, 2013.

de Gerlache, Adrien. *Quinze mois dans l'Antarctique.* Brussels: Ch. Bulens, 1902.

Dodds, Klaus. *The Antarctic: A Very Short Introduction.* Oxford: Oxford University Press, 2012.

———. "The End of a Polar Empire? The Falkland Islands Dependencies and Commonwealth Reactions to British Polar Policy, 1945–61." *Journal of Imperial and Commonwealth History* 24, no. 3 (1996): 391–421.

———. *Pink Ice: Britain and the South Atlantic Empire.* London: I.B. Tauris, 2002.

Dudeney, John R., and David W.H. Walton. "From *Scotia* to 'Operation Tabarin': Developing policy for Antarctica." *Polar Record* 48, no. 247 (2012): 342–60.

Emmanuel, Marthe. *J-B Charcot, le polar gentleman.* Paris: Alsatia, 1945.

English, John. *Ice and Water: Politics, Peoples and the Arctic Council.* Toronto: Penguin Canada, 2013.

Farish, Matthew. *Contours of America's Cold War.* Minneapolis: University of Minnesota Press, 2010.

Farish, Matthew, and P. Whitney Lackenbauer. "High Modernism in the Arctic: Planning Frobisher Bay and Inuvik." *Journal of Historical Geography* 35 (2009): 517–44.

Fogg, G.E. *A History of Antarctic Science.* Cambridge: Cambridge University Press, 1992.

Foote, Yolanda. "Marr, James William Slesser (1902–1965)." *Oxford Dictionary of National Biography.* Oxford: Oxford University Press, 2004.

Fuchs, Vivian. *Of Ice and Men: The Story of the British Antarctic Survey, 1943–1973.* Oswestry, UK: Anthony Nelson, 1982.

Fuchs, Vivian, and Edmund Hillary. *The Crossing of Antarctica: The Commonwealth Trans-Antarctic Expedition, 1955-58.* London: Cassell, 1958.

Giaever, John. *The White Desert: The Official Account of the Norwegian-British-Swedish Antarctic Expedition.* New York: Greenwood Press, 1954.

Gough, Barry M. *The Falkland Islands/Malvinas: The Contest for Empire in the South Atlantic.* London: Athlone Press, 1992.

Grace, Sherrill E. "Re-Inventing Franklin." *Canadian Review of Comparative Literature* (September 1995): 707–25.

Grant, Shelagh. *Polar Imperative.* Vancouver: Douglas and McIntyre, 2010.

———. *Sovereignty or Security? Government Policy in the Canadian North, 1936–1950.* Vancouver: UBC Press, 1988.

Griffiths, Tom. *Slicing the Silence: Voyaging to Antarctica.* Cambridge: Harvard University Press, 2007.

Haddelsey, Stephen, with Alan Carroll. *Operation Tabarin: Britain's Secret Wartime Expedition to Antarctica, 1944–1946*. Stroud, UK: History Press, 2014.

Hall, H.R. "The 'Open Door' into Antarctica: An Explanation of the Hughes Doctrine." *Polar Record* 25, no. 153 (1989): 137–40.

Hamilton, C.I. "Naval Hagiography and the Victorian Hero." *Historical Journal* 23, no. 2 (June 1980): 381–98.

Hattersley-Smith, G. "Some Canadians in the Antarctic." *Arctic* 39, no. 4 (December 1986): 368–9.

———. "Walter George Richards." *Polar Record* 39, no. 210 (2003): 269–72.

Headland, Robert. *Chronological List of Antarctic Expeditions and Related Historical Events*. Cambridge: Cambridge University Press, 1989.

Heron, David Winston. "Antarctic Claims." *Foreign Affairs* 32, no. 4 (July 1954): 661–7.

Hevly, Bruce. "The Heroic Science of Glacier Motion." *Osiris* 11 (1996): 66–86.

Hill, Jen. *White Horizon: The Arctic in the Nineteenth-Century British Imagination*. Albany: State University of New York Press, 2008.

Hodgson, Maurice. "The Exploration Journal as Literature." *The Beaver* 298 (Winter 1967): 4–12.

Hooker, Sir Joseph Dalton. *Botany of the Antarctic Voyage of H. M. Discovery Ships, Erebus and Terror: Under the Command of Captain Sir J.C. Ross, 1839–43*. London: Reeve Brothers, 1847.

Howkins, Adrian. "Frozen Empires: A History of the Antarctic Sovereignty Dispute Between Britain, Argentina, and Chile, 1939–1959." PhD diss., University of Texas at Austin, 2008.

———. "Icy Relations: The Emergence of South American Antarctica during the Second World War." *Polar Record* 42, no. 221 (2006): 153–65.

———. "Political Methodology: Weather, Climate and the Contest for Antarctic Sovereignty, 1939–1959." *History of Meteorology* 4 (2008): 27–40.

Huntford, Roland. *Shackleton*. London: Hodder and Stoughton, 1985.

James, David. *That Frozen Land: The Story of a Year in the Antarctic*. Toronto: The Falcon Press, 1949.

Jones, A.G.E. "Captain William Smith and the Discovery of New South Shetland." *Geographical Journal* 141, no. 3 (1975): 445–61.

Jones, Max. *The Last Great Quest: Captain Scott's Antarctic Sacrifice*. Oxford: Oxford University Press, 2003.

Jordan, Gerald, and Nicholas Rogers. "Admirals as Heroes: Patriotism and Liberty in Hanoverian England." *Journal of British Studies* 28, no. 3 (July 1989): 201–24.

Jorgenson, Dolly, and Sverker Sörlin, eds. *Northscapes: History, Technology, and the Making of Northern Environments.* Vancouver: UBC Press, 2013.

Kerry, A.J., and W.A. McDill. *The History of the Canadian Corps of Engineers: II, 1936–1946.* Ottawa: Military Engineers Association of Canada, 1966.

Kikkert, Peter. "Grasping for the Ends of the Earth: The Commonwealth and Polar Sovereignty." Ph.D. dissertation, Western University, 2015. Available at http://ir.lib.uwo.ca/etd/3406.

Livingstone, David N. *Putting Science in Its Place: Geographies of Scientific Knowledge.* Chicago: University of Chicago Press, 2003.

McElrea, Richard, and David Harrowfield. *Polar Castaways: The Ross Sea Party of Sir Ernest Shackleton, 1914–1917.* Montreal: McGill-Queen's University Press, 2004.

MacLaren, I.S. "Exploration/Travel Literature and the Evolution of the Author." *International Journal of Canadian Studies* 5 (Spring 1992): 39–68.

———. "From Exploration to Publication: The Evolution of a 19th-Century Arctic Narrative." *Arctic* 47, no. 1 (March 1994): 45–53.

MacLulich, T.D. "Canadian Exploration as Literature." *Canadian Literature* 81 (Summer 1979): 72–85.

Martin, Stephen. *A History of Antarctica.* Kenthurst, Australia: Rosenberg Publishing, 2013.

Mill, Hugh Robert. *The Siege of the South Pole: The Story of Antarctic Exploration.* London: A. Rivers, 1905.

Mitterling, Philip. *America in the Antarctic to 1840.* Urbana: University of Illinois Press, 1959.

Moore, Jason Kendall. "Tethered to an Iceberg: United States Policy toward the Antarctic, 1939–49." *Polar Record* 35 (1999): 125–34.

Nasht, Simon. *The Last Explorer: Hubert Wilkins, Hero of the Great Age of Polar Exploration.* New York: Arcade Publishing, 2005.

Naylor, Simon, and James R. Ryan, eds. *New Spaces of Exploration: Geographies of Discovery in the Twentieth Century.* London: I.B. Tauris, 2010.

Nordenskjöld, Otto and Johan Gunnar Andersson. *Antarctica or Two Years Amongst the Ice of the South Pole.* Toronto: McClelland and Stewart, 1977.

Perras, Galen Roger. "Anglo-Canadian Imperial Relations: The Case of the Garrisoning of the Falkland Islands in 1942." *War & Society* 14, no. 1 (1996): 73–97.

Poulsom, Neville W. *British Polar Exploration and Research: A Historical and Medallic Record with Biographies, 1818–1999.* London: Savannah Publications, 2000.

———. *The White Ribbon: A Medallic Record of British Polar Expeditions.* London: B.A. Seaby, 1987.

Powell, Richard C. "'The Rigors of an Arctic Experiment': The Precarious Authority of Field Practices in the Canadian High Arctic, 1958–1970." *Environment and Planning A* 39 (2007): 1794–811.

Pratt, Mary Louise. *Imperial Eyes: Travel Writing and Transculturation.* New York: Routledge, 1992.

Preston, Dianne. *A First Rate Tragedy: Captain Scott's Antarctic Expeditions.* London: Constable, 1997.

Queffélec, Henri. *Le grand départ, Charcot et le "pourquoi pas?"* Paris: Presses de la cité, 1977.

Riffenburgh, Beau. *The Myth of the Explorer: The Press, Sensationalism, and Geographical Discovery.* New York: Belhaven Press, 1993.

Roberts, Peder. *The European Antarctic: Science and Strategy in Scandinavia and the British Empire.* New York: Palgrave Macmillan, 2011.

Rymill, J.R. *Southern Lights.* Malvern: Knell Press, 1986 [1939].

Shackleton, Ernest. *The Heart of the Antarctic: Being the Story of the British Antarctic Expedition 1907-1909*, vol. 1. London: William Heinemann, 1909.

Simpson-Hausley, Paul. *Antarctica: Exploration, Perception and Metaphor.* London: Routledge, 1992.

Speak, P. *William Speirs Bruce: Polar Explorer and Scottish Nationalist.* Edinburgh: National Museums of Scotland, 2003.

Spufford, Francis. *I May Be Some Time: Ice and the English Imagination.* London: Faber and Faber, 1996.

Squires, Harold. *S.S. Eagle: The Secret Mission, 1944–1945.* St. John's: Jesperson Press, 1992.

Stackpole, Edouard. *The Voyage of the "Huron" and the "Huntress": The American Sealers and the Discovery of the Continent of Antarctica.* Mystic, CT: Maine Historical Association, 1955.

Stewart, Gordon, T. "Tenzing's Two Wrist-Watches: The Conquest of Everest and Late Imperial Culture in Britain, 1921–1953." *Past & Present* 149 (November 1995): 170–97.

Summerhayes, Colin, and Peter Beeching. "Hitler's Antarctic Base: The Myth and the Reality." *Polar Record* 43, no. 224 (2007): 1–21.

Taylor, Andrew. "Dr. Ivan Mackenzie Lamb." *Polar Record* 26, no. 159 (1990): 343.

——. "Echoes of the Swedish South Polar Expedition of 1902-3." *Revue Canadienne de Géographie* 4, no. 1–2 (January–April 1950): 47–62.

——. "Eric Hatfield Back." *Polar Record* 26, no. 169 (1993): 169–70.

——. "The Physiography of the Queen Elizabeth Islands," 5 vols. PhD diss., University of Montreal, 1956.

———. "Our Polar Islands – The Queen Elizabeths." *Canadian Geographical Journal* 52, no. 6 (1956): 232–51.

———. *Snow Compaction*. Wilmette, IL: US Corps of Engineers Snow, Ice & Permafrost Research Establishment (SIPRE), 1953.

Tønnessen, J. N., and Arne Odd Johnsen. *The History of Modern Whaling*. Berkeley: University of California Press, 1982.

Turney, Chris. *1912: The Year the World Discovered Antarctica*. Berkeley: Counterpoint, 2012.

Wallace, Hugh. *The Navy, the Company, and Richard King: British Exploration in the Canadian Arctic, 1829–1860*. Montreal: McGill-Queen's University Press, 1980.

Warkentin, Germaine. *Canadian Exploration Literature*. 2nd ed. Toronto: Dundurn Press, 2006.

Wordie, J.M. "The Falkland Islands Dependencies Survey, 1943–1946." *Polar Record* 4, no. 32 (1946): 372–84.

Zeller, Suzanne, and Christopher Jacob Ries. "Wild Men In and Out of Science: Finding a Place in the Disciplinary Borderlands of Arctic Canada and Greenland." *Journal of Historical Geography* 44 (2014): 31–43.

Websites

"Arctic Blue Books Online." University of Manitoba Archives and Special Collections. https://www.umanitoba.ca/libraries/units/archives/collections/subject/arcticstudies/arcticbb/.

I n d e x